HEALTHY FOODS

Healthy Foods

George D. Pamplona-Roger

Doctor of Medicine and Surgery (University of Granada, Spain)
Board-certified general and digestive surgeon
Specialist in Health Education (UNED University, Spain)
Master of Public Health (Loma Linda University, California, USA)

Disclaimer

It is the wish of the author and the publisher that the contents of this work be of value in orienting and informing our readers concerning the nutritional, preventive, curative and culinary value of foods. Although the recommendations and information given are appropriate in most cases, they are of a general nature and cannot take into account the specific circumstances of individual situations. The information given in this book is not intended to take the place of professional medical care either in diagnosing or treating medical conditions. Do not attempt self-diagnosis or self-treatment without consulting a qualified medical professional. Some foods and products may cause allergic reactions in sensitive persons. Neither the publisher nor the author can assume responsibility for problems arising from the inappropriate use of foods or recipes by readers.

Collection: **New Lifestyle**
Title: **Healthy Foods**
Original title in Spanish edition: *Salud por los alimentos*

Author: George D. Pamplona-Roger
Illustration credits: See page 375
Design and project development: Editorial Safeliz team

Translation: Holmes-Calleja Translations

Pradillo, 6 · Pol. Ind. La Mina
E-28770 · Colmenar Viejo, Madrid, Spain
Tel.: [+34] 91 845 98 77 · Fax: [+34] 91 845 98 65
admin@safeliz.com · www.safeliz.com

Distributed in USA and Canada by
Review and Herald® Publishing Association
55 W. Oak Ridge Drive, Hagerstown, Maryland 21740, USA
tel. [+1] 301-393-3000
email: hhes@rhpa.org

ISBN: 978-84-7208-147-5
Legal Deposit: V-3781-2007

PRINTED IN THE UNITED STATES OF AMERICA

FOREWORD

Whether based on belief or science, certain foods have been credited with healing powers. More than two thousand years ago, the precursor of modern medicine, Hippocrates, coined the aphorism "May your food be your medicine, and may your medicine be your food." The play on words, by this wise Greek demonstrates that our daily food, more than merely sustaining us, may contain curative properties. Although, postulated through the course of medical history, scientific evidence has only recently established the fact that some nutrients in our diet are agents that cause or cure certain diseases.

It was first demonstrated in studies with laboratory animals and later on humans that the lack of certain foods in the diet caused deficiency diseases, such as rickets, and that the inclusion of other foods cured patients with those diseases. Fortunately, deficiency diseases are not a problem for most of the population. However, many do suffer from illnesses and diseases referred to as "diseases of civilization."

Recent years have brought profound changes in the lifestyle of the industrialized world whereas dietary habits, uses and preferences are concerned. Many follow a diet characterized by excessive caloric consumption and frequent nutritional imbalances. The consumption of animal-derived food products continues to increase, with its accompanying increase in saturated fats and cholesterol. The tendency to eat highly refined or processed products reduces the intake of vitamins, certain minerals and other beneficial substances such as fiber contained in foods in their most natural state.

In recent years, nutritional investigation has concentrated on the effect diet has on the prevention and treatment of circulatory disease, diabetes, cancer and obesity, since these are currently the most frequent. Population and clinical studies have demonstrated, for example, that the abundant use of fruits and vegetables prevents the initiation of certain cancers. The eating of whole grain cereals and oil-bearing nuts reduces excess levels of cholesterol in the blood and the risk of myocardial infarction. On the other hand, the consumption of a great deal of meat increases the risk of cardiovascular disease and some types of cancer. Thus we see that the choice, frequency and quantity of the foods that we eat very directly affects our health.

Foods of vegetable origin, rich in fiber, minerals and vitamins, also bring substances to the diet that, although not well understood nor classified as nutrients, display potent anticarcinogenic and curative effects on a variety of diseases and illnesses. These substances, known as phytochemicals, are currently the subject of intense study and represent the new frontier in nutritional investigation. Phytochemical elements are only found in foods of vegetable origin and possess important health and healing properties.

HEALTHY FOODS provides clear and usable information concerning the composition, nutritional and therapeutic properties of foods. Thus, the reader is led to a prudent selection of the products that form his diet. With this work by Dr. George D. Pamplona-Roger, Editorial Safeliz continues its noteworthy efforts to publish books and materials for an intelligent public interested in maintaining and improving their health by giving preference to natural elements.

DR. JOAN SABATÉ
Professor and Chair of the Department of Nutrition, School of Public Health, Loma Linda University (California, USA).

GENERAL PLAN

OF THE WORK

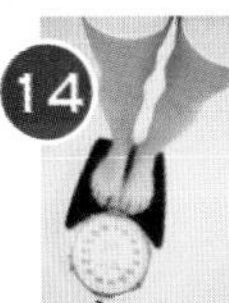

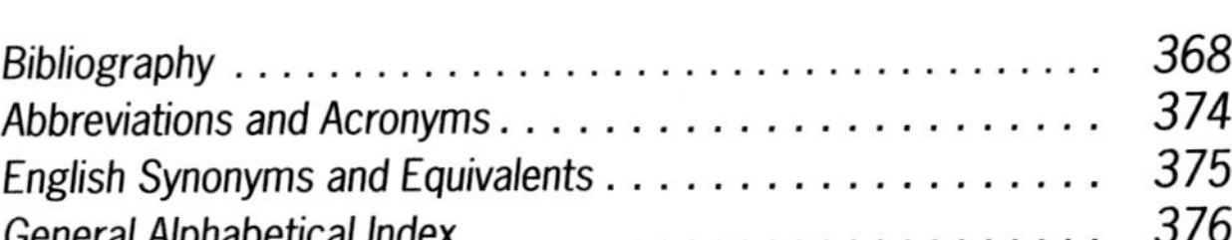

Index of Diseases

Foods Index

See also the General Alphabetical Index, page 376.

Explanation of pages

Icon indicating level of acidity or alkalinity of a food
(See p. 14).

Icon for the botanical portion of the plant used as food
(See p. 14).

Chapter number and title

Icons for other medical indications
(See p. 15).

Scientific name
Is the scientific denomination of the plant species that produces the food. The different plant species within a chapter are arranged alphabetically by their Latin scientific name.

Common name
Is the most widely used for the food described.

Subtitle
Highlights the primary characteristics of the food.

Graph of food composition
(See p. 13).

Lactuca sativa L.

3 - Foods for the Nervous System

Lettuce

Calms the nerves and satisfies the stomach

LETTUCE
Composition
per 100 g of raw edible portion

Energy	16.0 kcal = 67.0 kj
Protein	1.62 g
Carbohydrates	0.670 g
Fiber	1.70 g
Vitamin A	260 µg RE
Vitamin B_1	0.100 mg
Vitamin B_2	0.100 mg
Niacin	0.700 mg NE
Vitamin B_6	0.047 mg
Folate	136 µg
Vitamin B_{12}	—
Vitamin C	24.0 mg
Vitamin E	0.440 mg α-TE
Calcium	36.0 mg
Phosphorus	45.0 mg
Magnesium	6.00 mg
Iron	1.10 mg
Potassium	290 mg
Zinc	0.250 mg
Total Fat	*0.200 g*
Saturated Fat	*0.026 g*
Cholesterol	—
Sodium	*8.00 mg*

1% 2% 4% 10% 20% 40% 100%

% Daily Value (based on a 2,000 calorie diet)
provided by 100 g of this food

Scientific synonym: *Lactuca virosa* L.
Synonyms: *Celtuce, Cos, Garden lettuce, [Green] romaine lettuce.*
French: *Laitue;* ***Spanish:*** *Lechuga.*
Description: *Leaves of the lettuce plant 'Lactuca sativa', of the botanical family Compositae. There are varieties with straight leaves and others with curly ones, and their color varies from green to purple red.*

THE ANCIENT Romans ate lettuce at night as a sleep aid after overeating at supper. Today the stressed inhabitants of modern cities can benefit from this effect of lettuce ***not*** *after*, but ***rather in place*** of a big supper.

PROPERTIES AND INDICATIONS: Lettuce is one of the foods *richest* in **water** (94.9%). However, the relatively high level of ***proteins*** (1.62%) that it provides is surprising. This is only slightly less than the potato (2.07%).

54

Icon for the primary medical indication for the food or nutrient
(See p. 15).

Photograph of the food described

Synonyms and description
Scientific and common synonyms and botanical description of the species that produces the food.

Primary text

Preparation and use
This box includes both dietetic and culinary advice leading to improved utilization of the healing properties of the food.

Preparation and Use

❶ **Raw:** Sunflower seeds are best eaten raw after they have been spread on a flat surface and dried for a few days.
❷ **Toasted:** These are very flavorful, but if they are toasted for a long period their nutritional value suffers.
❸ **Ground to a paste:** Once shelled, the seeds are ground to a homogenous paste, which is excellent for children, the elderly, and those with deteriorated teeth.

Araucaria

The Chilean araucaria (*Pinus araucana* L. = *Araucaria araucana* K. Koch), also known as Chilean pine, reaches a height of 60 meters. It provides excellent nuts that form the staple food for the Araucanian people, who are known for their legendary strength and endurance.

Description of similar species
This type of box describes botanical species with properties similar to those of the food or nutrient described.

Description of the graphs

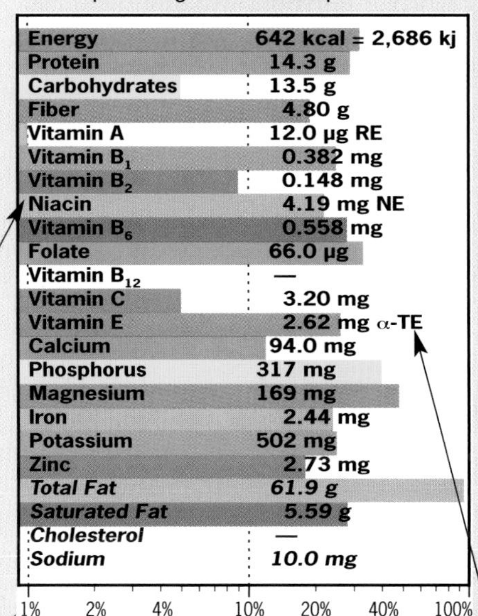

Graph of food composition indicating the **absolute** and **relative quantities** of **energy** and **nutrients contained.** Each is represented by a color.

The scale used for the length of the **bars** is **logarithmic;** therefore the length of the bars is not directly proportional to the nutritional content.

The **numbers** indicate the **absolute energy content** and the mass of each **nutrient** found in 100 grams of a food. This information is provided by the United States Department of Agriculture.[1]

Criteria used in to establish precision of measurement:

- Values less than 1: **3 decimal places**
- Values equal to or greater than 1, but less than 10: **2 decimal places**
- Values equal to or greater than 10 but less than 100: **1 decimal place**
- Values above 100: **no decimal place**

Bar length shows the "% Daily Value" of each food. It indicates the **relative quantity** of a nutrient for an adult male, found in 100 grams of each food.

Nevertheless the **logarithmic scale** for some foods may reach **500%** since some nutrients are present in very high concentrations.

The **length** of the **bars** matches the "**% Daily value**" of each nutrient and food component labeled in food products. The "% Daily Value" shows how a food fits into the overall daily diet.

The length of the bars matching the "**% Daily value**" have always been calculated for a male adult taking a 2,000 calorie diet.

Four bottom bars: Their length show the "**% Daily value**" of food components for which there are no RDAs **(total fat, saturated fat, cholesterol** and **sodium)** provided by 100 grams of the analyzed food. Names and figures of these four food components are displayed in italics.

1. U.S. Department of Agriculture, Agricultural Research Service. USDA Nutrient Database for Standard Reference, Release 11, Nutrient Data Laboratory. Internet: http://www.nal.usda.gov/fnic/foodcomp

Acidifying or alkalizing effect

Acidifying food: This is a food that, when metabolized in the body, produces acidification (**lowers the pH**) of the blood and other body fluids (see p. 272). **Cured cheese, meat, fish,** and **eggs** are the most acidifying foods.

Alkalizing food: This is a food that, when metabolized in the body, produces alkalization (**increases the pH**) of the blood and other body fluids (see p. 272). Fruit, together with vegetables are the most alkalizing foods. Because of this they protect against the acidification that is naturally produced within the body and aggravated by the consumption of foods of animal origin (see p. 273).

Edible part of the plant

Icons used

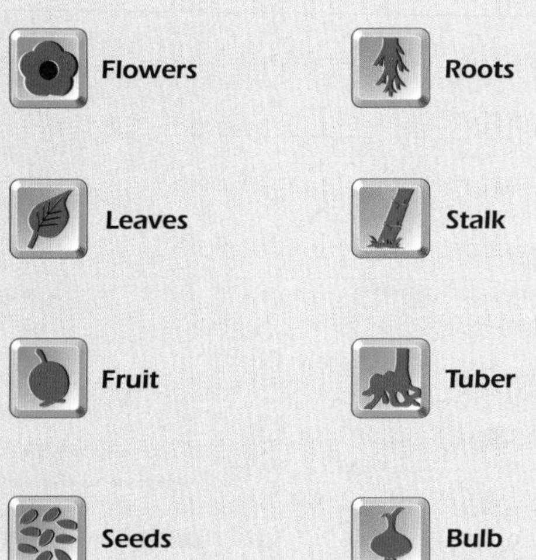

Meaning of icons used in this work for medical indications

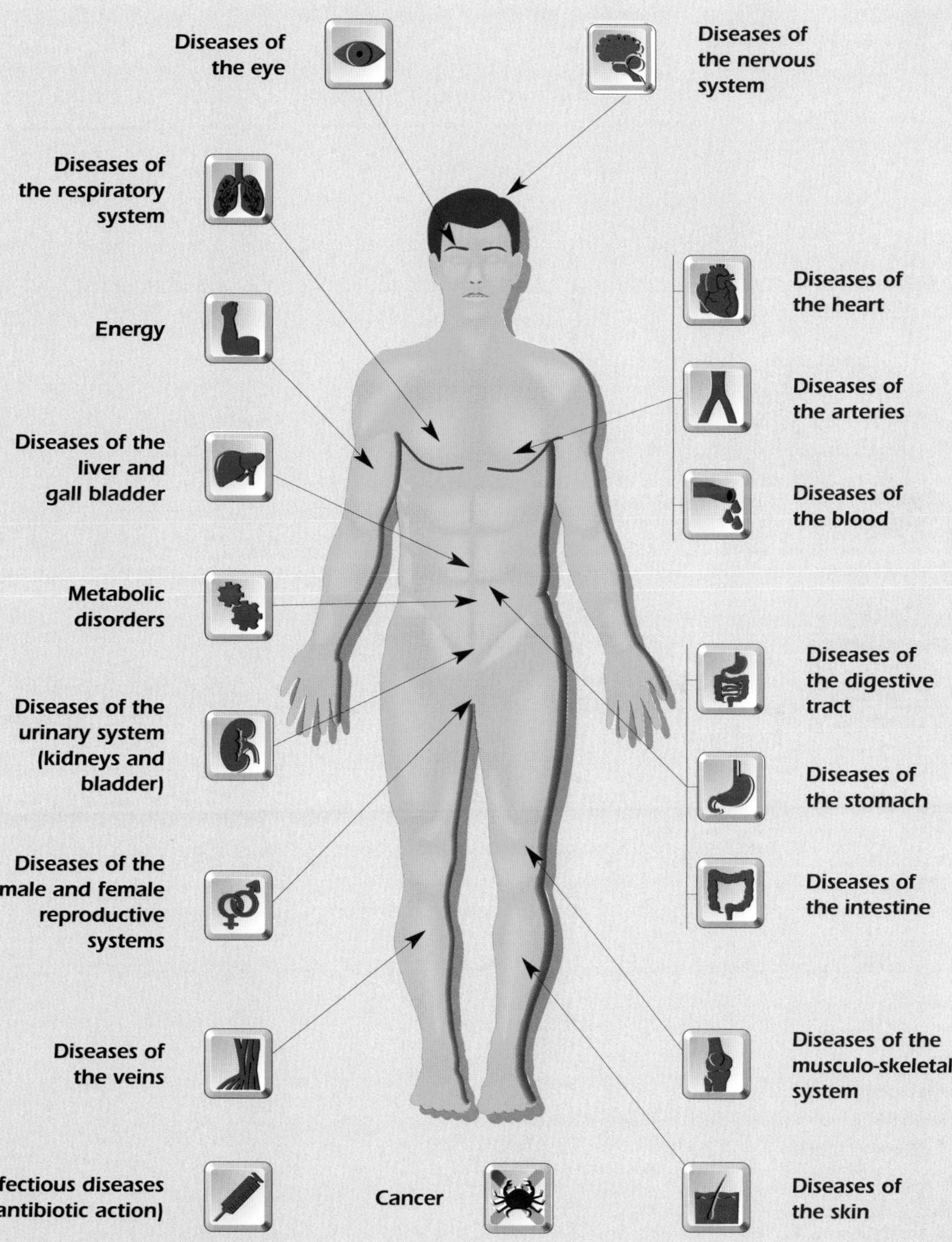

Recommended Daily Allowances (RDAs)
According to the National Academy of Sciences

Age		Proteins[1]	Vitamin A	Vitamin D[8]	Vitamin E	Vitamin K[8]	Vitamin C	Vitamin B_1	Vitamin B_2	Niacin	Vitamina B_6
		g m/f[2]	µg RE[3] m/f	µg[4] m/f	mg α–TE[5] m/f	µg m/f	mg m/f	mg m/f	mg m/f	mg NE[6] m/f	mg m/f
0.0 - 0.5	Year	13	375	7.5	3	5	30	0.3	0.4	5	0.3
0.5 - 1.0	Year	14	375	10	4	10	35	0.4	0.5	6	0.6
1 - 3	years	16	400	10	6	15	40	0.7	0.8	9	1.0
4 - 6	years	24	500	10	7	20	45	0.9	1.1	12	1.1
7 - 10	years	28	700	10	7	30	45	1.0	1.2	13	1.4
11 - 14	years	45/46	1,000/800	10/10	10/8	45/45	50/50	1.3/1.1	1.5/1.3	17/15	1.7/1.4
15 - 18	years	59/44	1,000/800	10/10	10/8	65/55	60/60	1.5/1.1	1.8/1.3	20/15	2.0/1.5
20 - 24	years	58/46	1,000/800	10/10	10/8	70/60	60/60	1.5/1.1	1,7/1,3	19/15	2.0/1.6
25 - 50	years[7]	63/50	1,000/800	5/5	10/8	80/65	60/60	1.5/1.1	1.7/1.3	19/15	2.0/1.6
51+	years	63/50	1,000/800	5/5	10/8	80/65	60/60	1.2/1.0	1.4/1.2	15/13	2.0/1.6
Pregnant women		60	800	10	10	65	70	1.5	1.6	17	2.2
Lactating mothers											
1st 6 Months		65	1,300	10	12	65	95	1.6	1.8	20	2.1
2nd 6 Months		62	1,200	10	11	65	90	1.6	1.7	20	2.1

Daily fiber and potassium needs

	Children	Adults
Fiber	Amount calculated by multiplying the child's age by one gram for children between the ages of 5 and 10	Between 20 and 35 grams (average 25g; about 0.9 ounces)
Potassium	From 500 to 2,000 mg	2,000 mg

Acceptable Daily Intake (ADI)
of certain food components

Certain food components are harmful to health when ingested in excess. For this reason an ADI (Acceptable Daily Intake) has been established for each, which should not be exceeded in a healthful diet.

In the graphs of the composition of each food, these components are shown in italics (see p. 13).

	ADI
Total fat	An amount that represents less than 30% of total caloric intake (approximately 65 g or 2.3 oz for a 2,000 calorie diet).
Saturated fat	An amount that represents less than 10% of total caloric intake (approximately 20 g or 0.7 oz for a 2,000 calorie diet).
Cholesterol	Maximum: 300 mg
Sodium	Maximum: 2,400 mg, which is equivalent to 6 grams (1/5 oz) of common table salt.

# of Nutrients
of the United States *

Age		Folates[9]	Vitamin B_{12}	Calcium	Phosphorus	Magnesium	Iron	Zinc	Iodine[8]	Selenium[8]
		μg m/f	μg m/f	mg m/f	mg m/f	mg m/f	mg m/f	mg m/f	μg m/f	μg m/f
0.0 - 0.5	Year	25	0.3	400	300	40	6	5	40	10
0.5 - 1.0	Year	35	0.5	600	500	60	10	5	50	15
1 - 3	years	50	0.7	800	800	80	10	10	70	20
4 - 6	years	75	1.0	800	800	120	10	10	90	20
7 - 10	years	100	1.4	800	800	170	10	10	120	30
11 - 14	years	150/150	2.0/2.0	1,200/1,200	1,200/1,200	270/280	12/15	15/12	150/150	40/45
14 - 18	years	200/180	2.0/2.0	1,200/1,200	1,200/1,200	400/300	12/15	15/12	150/150	50/50
19 - 24	years	200/180	2.0/2.0	1,200/1,200	1,200/1,200	350/280	10/15	15/12	150/150	70/55
25 - 50	years	200/180	2.0/2.0	800/800	800/800	350/280	10/15	15/12	150/150	70/55
51+	years	200/180	2.0/2.0	800/800	800/800	350/280	10/10	15/12	150/150	70/55
Pregnant women		400	2.2	1,200	1,200	320	30	15	175	65
Lactating mothers										
1st 6 Months		280	2.6	1,200	1,200	355	15	19	200	75
2nd 6 Months		260	2.6	1,200	1,200	340	15	16	200	75

* National Academy of Sciences. Recommended Dietary Allowances. Washington, National Academy Press, 10th ed.
The concept of RDA is described in Vol. 1, p. 384.

1. These amounts of proteins are calculated using the average weight of inhabitants of the United States for each age group. However, protein demand can also be calculated based on total caloric intake. In this case proteins necessary for an adult must provide the 10% of total caloric intake (see Vol. 1, p. 386). The amounts derived in this manner are generally lower than those indicated in the National Academy of Sciences table.
   For example, a male between the ages of 25 and 50 years of age should ingest 63 g of proteins according to the table. But if his lifestyle is sedentary and he eats a 2,000-calorie daily diet, 50 g of protein is sufficient (10% of 2,000 kcal is 200 kcal in the form of proteins, which is obtained from 50 g. Each gram of protein provides 4 kcal).
2. m/f = male/female.
3. 1 μg RE (1 microgram of retinol equivalent) = 3.33 IU of vitamin A (see Vol. 1, p. 389).
4. 1 μg of vitamin D = 40 IU.
5. 1 mg α-TE (1 milligram of alpha- tocopherol equivalent) = 1.5 IU of vitamin E.
6. The mg NE (milligrams of niacin equivalent) measure the preformed niacin found in foods in addition to that formed in the body from the amino acid tryptophan, which is found in the proteins in foods (60 mg of tryptophan transforms to 1 mg of niacin; see Vol. 1, p. 392).
7. RDA (Recommended Dietary Allowance) for males between 25 and 50 years of age, is that used in this work as a base used to calculate the percentage of RDA provided by 100 grams of each food. This percentage is represented graphically by a horizontal bar on the graphs and tables showing the composition of each food (see Vol. 1, p. 16).
8. Vitamins D and K, iodine, and selenium are shown in this table. However, the are not included in graphs and tables showing the composition of foods for two reasons:
   - There is no reliable data concerning their content in many of the foods described in this Encyclopedia of Foods.
   - Their content in foods varies a great deal according to the composition of the soil where the foods were grown.
9. In 1998 the National Academy of Sciences (USA) decided to significantly increase the RDA for folates:
   - Adults: 400 μg (instead of 200 μg).
   - Pregnant women: 600 μg (instead of 400 μg).
   - Lactating mothers: 500 μg (instead of 280 μg).

1

Foods for Humans

SUMMARY | PAGE

HUMAN BEINGS can eat just about anything as food, from mammary secretions (milk) to mineral crystals (common salt), including fruits, flowers, seeds, stalks, leaves, roots, seaweed, fungus, eggs of fish and birds or the dead bodies of various animals.

All of these, processed to a greater or lesser degree, provide thousands of different foods to the market.

Does the fact that we can eat this whole variety of foods mean that ***all*** *of them are equally* ***fit*** *for human consumption?* ***Is there*** *an* ***ideal diet*** *for humans that, in addition to being nourishing,* ***maintains*** *health and* ***prevents*** *disease?*

Chance or intelligent plan

The engineer has finished his work. The shining engine he has built is sitting on the test bench ready to be started for the first time.

"Here is the type of fuel that must be used in this engine", says the engineer to his assistants,

With the exception of mother's milk during infancy, no food by itself provides all of the nutrients needed by humans. Therefore, knowing how to select foods and appropriately combine them is of vital importance.

"No other will give optimal results. And don't forget the oil. It must be exactly of this type!"

Only the one who has planned and built an engine can knowledgeably prescribe the type of fuel and lubricant the mechanism needs.

Specifically recommended foods

And is it not this way with humans? If human presence on planet Earth is just a random and unexpected consequence of evolutionary chance, then there should not be any particularly ideal foods. Man would have simply adapted to whatever foods were available, and whatever those might have been, they would have provided good health and wellbeing.

However, if humans were created by a superior Intelligence according to a specific plan and for a particular purpose, there should be, as well, foods specially created to maintain optimal physiological performance. Many believers find answers to these questions in the first chapters of Genesis, where it says that plants that bear seeds, **grains**, and, in a broader sense, **legumes, fruit** from trees[1] and **vegetables** that were added later,[2] constitute the ideal **diet** for the human species.

Adaptation, Yes, but Not by Eliminating Necessary Foods.

Humans possess great capacity to adapt physiologically to many different types of foods. In spite of this, nutrition science has demonstrated that there are certain foods that ***cannot be eliminated,*** such as **fruit** and **fresh vegetables.** Not just any diet can produce good health. No matter how well we adapt to certain foods that are not ideal, such as those of animal origin, we continue to need vegetables, which are the most healthful and suitable. For example, Alaskan Eskimos have adapted to a diet rich in fish but they suffer a number of chronic diseases due to low consumption of fruit and vegetables.[3]

Vegetable foods, source of health and healing powers

There has been a rapidly increasing number of scientific discoveries in recent years related to foods of vegetable origin. As methods of chemical analysis have become more precise, it is being proved that fruits, grains, legumes and vegetables contain, in addition to nutrients found in all foods, two types of compounds that are not found in foods of animal origin:

Healing foods

Plant-based foods, like medicinal plants, contain substances that produce pharmacological effects similar to any other medication, but with these **advantages:**

- They **prevent** and **correct the tendency** toward disease, in addition to having curative properties.
- *Generally speaking, they have* **no side effects.**

- antioxidants (certain vitamins and minerals), and
- phytochemicals with curative properties.

Many scientists are inquisitive about the origin and significance of these beneficial substances found only in vegetables. Why do humans need them for their health? Why do they continue to need them after centuries or millennia of adaptation to a carnivorous diet, such as the traditional diet of the Eskimos? Why is there an ideal diet for the health of humans?

Two options ...

There are those that believe that humans found plants and vegetable foods possessing healing powers by mere chance. These vegetables, according to this reasoning, evolved the capacity to synthesize precisely those nutritional and healing substances that would be needed by humans long before humans existed.[4]

But we may also consider, with no less validity, a rational alternative: that a superior Being created Man and Woman and provided them with an ideal "fuel": vegetable foods.[5]

Without a doubt many things have happened since then. Therefore in the present state of nature and humanity, **foods of animal origin** can become **necessary** *in some cases;* although ***never*** **indispensable.** This notwithstanding, the basis of human nutrition as well as the most important source of health-producing materials continue to be fruit, grains, seeds, and vegetables. The exception, of course, is the first phase of life (lactation).

... and the same conclusion

In either of these cases, no matter what one may believe about origins, numerous scientific studies demonstrate that vegetable foods prepared simply provide the ***best*** **'fuel'** for our "engine." They supply the energy necessary to function and the substances to slow the "wear and tear" of the years and helps prevent "breakdown."

And do not forget to provide the ***best*** **oil** for this "engine!"

Foods and health

Our health depends on the sum total of the many **"small" decisions** that we take each day, in other words, our **lifestyle.**

Generally speaking, the decisions we make that ***most affect*** our health have to do with the foods we eat. There are so many options

Mango

Broccoli

Corn

Fruits, grains and legumes, as well as vegetables, are particularly rich in antioxidants and accompanying substances known as phytochemical elements, that act as true natural pharmaceuticals.

available that we must continually decide which foods to select and how they are best prepared.

Information + Correct Choices = Health

The more complete the information we have concerning available foods, the easier it is to make the best choices for health.[6]

Harmful foods, beneficial foods

Humans need food throughout their lives. While all foods provide nutrients and energy, some can cause disorders and diseases; while others bring health and healing. Therefore, there are potentially harmful foods, and, of course, beneficial foods.

Throughout the pages that follow the reader will come to understand that all foods are not of equal value.

Knowing foods well

It is vital to understand foods well in order to select those that maintain our health, which is so threatened today, and those that treat various diseases. This new book of the *New Lifestyle* series, HEALTHY FOODS, is designed to provide that understanding.

Sources of foods

Humans can adapt to eating almost anything, whether mineral, vegetable or animal. But simply because something can be eaten it does not mean that this may be done without risking good health.

From the mineral kingdom

Water and **salt** are two foods (in the broad sense of the word), of mineral origin. Unlike any other food, the water and salt we eat do not originate with any living thing.

From the animal kingdom

Certain secretions, eggs, and meat of various aquatic and land animals can be used for food. However, ***not all*** of them are **beneficial.**

From the vegetable kingdom

These foods are the ***healthiest*** and have the ***most* healing properties.** Various types of vegetables can be used as food:

- **Seaweed:** These are eaten whole, whether they are microscopic single-cell (such as Spirulina) or multicellular such as the rest of the seaweed.
- **Higher plants:** Customarily, these foods are a part of the plant: fruit, seed, bulb, root, etc.
- **Fungi:** Although they are grouped with foods of vegetable origin, fungi belong to an independent kingdom with its own characteristics.

The healing power

Diuretics

Celery: increases urine production, aids kidney function and reduces edema.

Other diuretic foods: eggplant, melon, watermelon, leeks, and asparagus.

Celery

Artichoke

Hepatic tonic

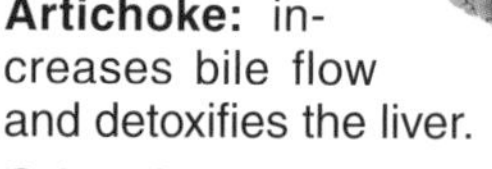

Artichoke: increases bile flow and detoxifies the liver.

Other foods that act as hepatic tonics: loquats, cardoom.

Persimmon

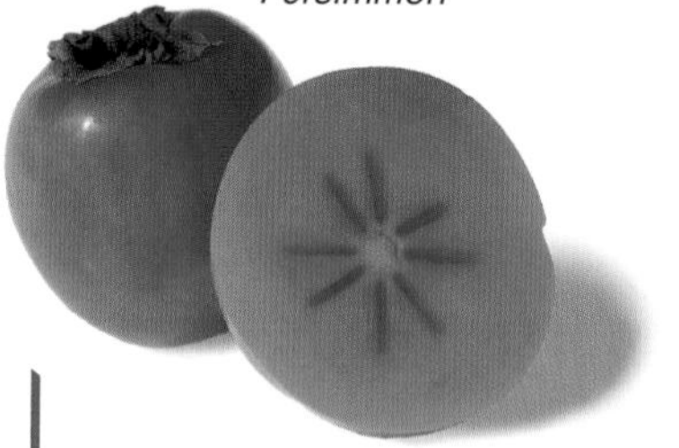

Astringents

Persimmon: Contains tannins that dry the intestinal mucosa and mucilage that softens it.

Other astringent foods: quince, apple, caimito, pomegranate, and loquat.

Coconut

Mineral restorers

Coconut: very rich in magnesium, calcium and phosphorous.

Other mineral restoring foods: almonds, alfalfa, cabbage, oranges, turnip greens.

Cranberry

Urinary antiseptics

Cranberry: Counters the effects of cystitis and other urinary infections without activating bacterial resistance.

# of vegetables

Avocado

Hypolipidemic

Avocado: antianemic, protects the digestive lining and acts as a tonic in addition to lowering blood cholesterol and triglyceride levels.

Other hypolipidemic foods: beans, English walnuts, sunflower seeds, yams.

Oranges

Antioxidants

Oranges: contain four potent antioxidants: vitamin C, beta-carotene (provitamin A), flavonoids and folic acid. They help avoid arteriosclerosis and thrombosis.

Other antioxidant foods: strawberries, citrus fruits, and nuts.

Pineapple

Digestives

Pineapple: aids digestion.

Other digestive foods: papaya, zucchini, potatoes, and okra.

Anticarcinogens

Broccoli: Its phytochemicals retard or stop the growth of cancerous cells.

Other anticarcinogenic foods: Cauliflower, cabbage, oranges, lemons, plums, grapes, tomatoes.

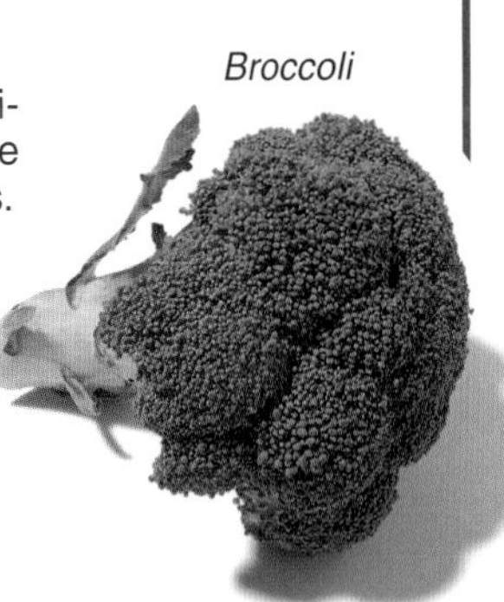
Broccoli

Laxatives

Plums: stimulate intestinal function.

Other laxative foods: eggplant, chard, and whole grain cereals.

Plums

Antianemics

Pistachios: Contain as much or more iron as lentils, in addition to copper and other trace elements that serve to promote blood production.

Other antianemic foods: red beets, apricots, passion fruit, spinach, and lamb's lettuce.

Pistachios

Exotic fruits:

Fruits considered exotic in countries where they are not produced are just a healthful and nutritious as any other fruit. They do not possess any special properties not found in more common fruits, as was once thought. However eating them gives a special pleasure that enriches the food experience. This chart displays some of the more attractive.

Litchi

This fruit of a tree from China is noted for its ***high vitamin C* content**, which is greater than that of oranges or lemons. They enhance the **immune system** (see p. 352).

Tamarillo

Also called **tree tomato,** because of its appearance, which is similar to the tomato. They are native to South America. They are eaten fresh and have a slightly acid taste.

Mangosteen

These are native of Thailand, where they are considered a true delicacy. Its bittersweet taste is reminiscent of plums.

Tamarind

The slightly acid pulp of this legume-like fruit is an effective **laxative.**

delights of paradise

Rambutan

This native of Malaysia has a pulp similar to the litchi, with a flavor similar to almonds.

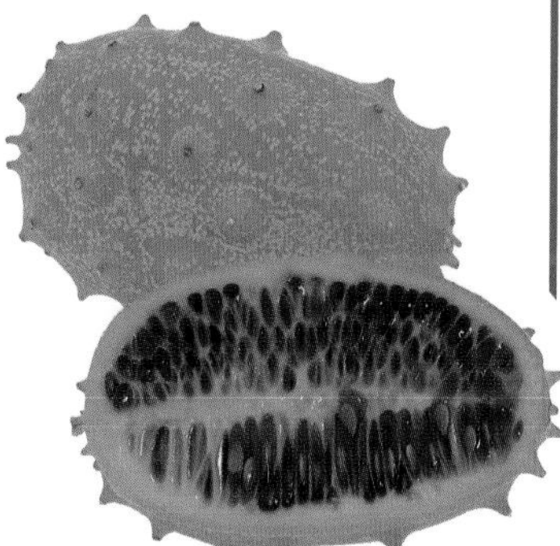

Winter cherry

Originating in East Asia and China, these are now grown in Colombia. It is like a cherry with a pleasantly tart flavor.

Kiwano

This native of Africa is, in reality, a wild cucumber, very aromatic and flavorful. The spines on its rind are fleshy and its pulp, gelatinous. It has **digestive** and **laxative** properties.

Night-blooming cereus

This fruit is covered with spines, like the cactus that it is. Its pulp, however, is very sweet and aromatic.

Foods for the Eyes

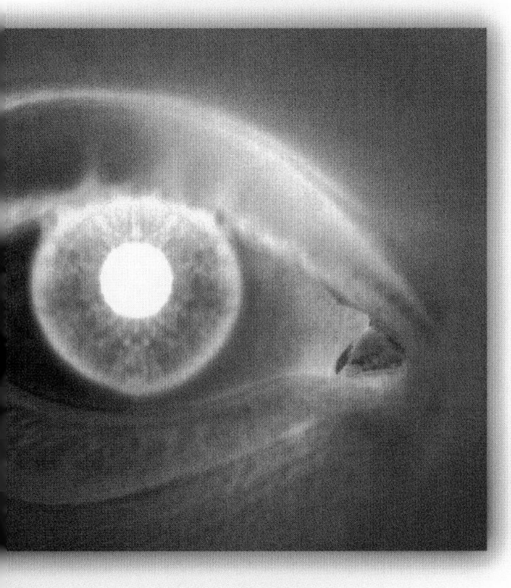

An Amazing Organ ...

Because of its incredibly high precision and performance, the eye is one of the most amazing of organs in the body.

All of the muscles of the eye are in constant movement to carry out three simultaneous functions necessary for vision:

- exploration of the **field of vision,**
- opening and closing of the **pupil** according to the light available (diaphragm),
- modification of the curve of the **lens** of the eye according to distance of the viewed object, thus bringing it into sharp focus.

At the same time it is performing all of these tasks, the eye continuously sends information to the brain through the **optic nerve.** It is calculated that while awake, the million or so nerve cells that form the retina send information to the brain at a rate equivalent to 100 Mb per second.[1] Today only the fastest computer networks can match this transmission speed.

... That needs very little

To carry out all of these complex functions, the eye only needs a *small amount* of **oxygen** and a few other substances found in foods, such as these:

- ***Vitamin A:*** This is necessary for the formation of rhodopsin, the light-sensitive pigment found in the cells of the retina. It is also necessary for maintaining the **conjunctiva** (the anterior membrane of the eye) moist and in good condition.
- ***Carotenoids:*** These are natural dyes found in plant-based foods. They act as **antioxidants** and help prevent macular degeneration of the **retina.**
- ***Vitamins C and E:*** these are also antioxidants found almost exclusively in fruits, vegetables, nuts, and grain germ. Their ***lack*** *leads to* **cataracts** and **vision** *loss.*

Plant-based foods, particularly those mentioned in this chapter, provide the nutrients that the eyes need in order to function properly.

Orange

The orange is rich in carotenoids, vitamin C, and other antioxidants that protect the retina. Additionally, it contains flavonoids whose action protects the capillaries and improves blood flow to the retina.

CONJUNCTIVITIS

Causes

This may have a variety of causes, such as an infection by various types of germs or smoke irritation.

Diet

A diet *lacking* in *vitamins A* and *B predisposes* to dryness of the conjunctiva and *fosters* or *aggravates* conjunctivitis.

Increase

APRICOT
VITAMIN A
VITAMINS B

Apricot

MACULAR DEGENERATION OF THE RETINA

Definition

This is the most important cause of blindness in persons over the age of 65. The macula, which is only 2 mm across, is the most sensitive area of the retina, in which the most visual acuity is concentrated.

Causes

Its deterioration is fostered by:

- ***Prolonged* exposure** to ***intense* light.**
- **Free radicals** produced by the body or from tobacco smoke or other pollutants.
- The *lack* of **antioxidants** capable of *neutralizing* **free radicals.**

Diet

The substances that have been shown to be *most* effective in the prevention of macular degeneration are *carotenoids* (vegetable pigments), particularly *zeaxanthin* and *lutein*, which are found in spinach and cabbage.[2] Beta-carotene found in carrots is not as effective.

Increase

SPINACH
CABBAGE
ORANGE
ZINC
ANTIOXIDANTS

Cabbage

Like spinach, cabbage is also rich in carotenoids that protect the retina.

VISUAL ACUITY, LOSS OF

Definition

This can have many causes, among them, cataracts (see previous page) and cerebral lesions or tumors. But the most common cause is the retinal dysfunction occasioned by diabetes or arteriosclerosis (narrowing of the arteries).

Diet

Antioxidant deficiency due to a diet lacking in fruits, vegetables, oil-bearing nuts, and seeds can contribute to the deterioration of the retina and foster the loss of visual acuity.

Increase

CARROT
SPINACH
APRICOT
SQUASH
BLUEBERRY
BLACKBERRY

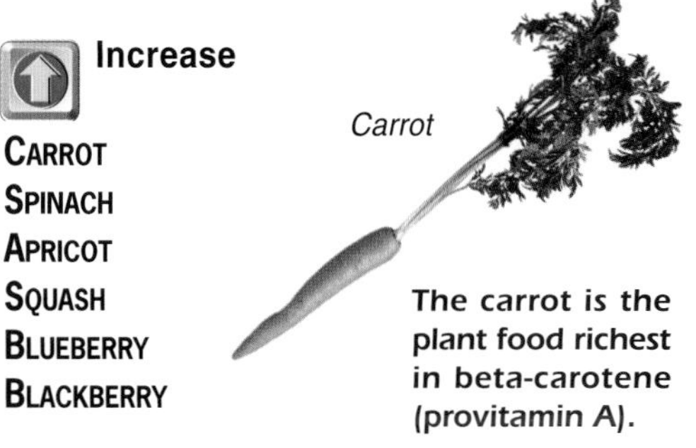

Carrot

The carrot is the plant food richest in beta-carotene (provitamin A).

GLAUCOMA

Definition

This is due to an increase in the pressure of the liquid within the eye. This causes atrophy of the retina and the optic nerve with serious vision repercussions.

Heath Counsels

Although closed-angle glaucoma, which is the *most common* form of this disease, is due to an *anatomical alteration* of the eye, the type of diet *can influence* intraocular pressure, *improving* or *aggravating* glaucoma.

Increase

VITAMIN B1
VITAMIN A
ORANGE

Reduce or eliminate

TRANS-FATTY ACIDS
COFFEE
PROTEINS

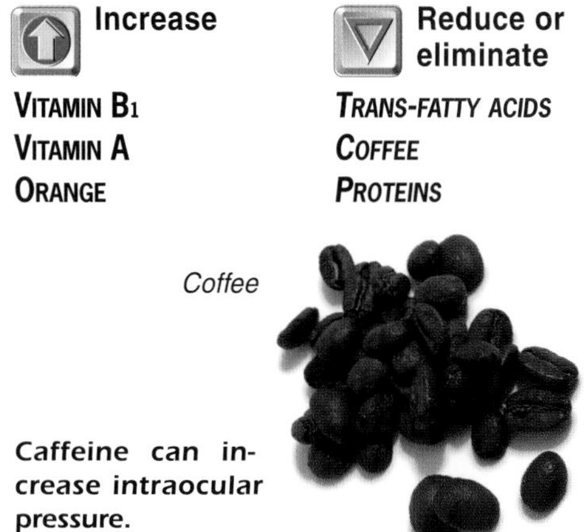

Coffee

Caffeine can increase intraocular pressure.

CATARACTS

Definition

A cataract is the opaqueness of the lens. Until some years ago it was thought that this was a consequence of the aging process and that little or nothing could be done to prevent it.

Diet

Today it is known that there is a rather close relationship between diet and the formation of cataracts. Abundant use of foods containing Provitamin A and antioxidant vitamins C and E, such as vegetables, fruits and seeds can prevent the formation of cataracts in old age.

Heath Counsel

Diabetes, the use of certain medications and exposure to ultraviolet and x-ray radiation also favor the formation of cataracts.

Increase

SQUASH
ANTIOXIDANTS
VITAMIN C
VITAMIN E

Reduce or eliminate

DAIRY PRODUCTS
TOTAL FAT
BUTTER
SALT

Butter

According to research, butter is the food that increases the most the risk of suffering from cataracts when it is consumed regularly.[3]

NIGHT BLINDNESS

This is a slowing or complete lack of the ability to adapt to seeing in the dark. It constitutes one of the first symptoms of a *vitamin A* deficiency.

Increase

CARROT
APRICOT
MANGO

Mango

Mango is one of the richest fresh fruits in provitamin A.

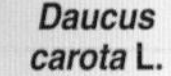

Carrot

A true medicinal food

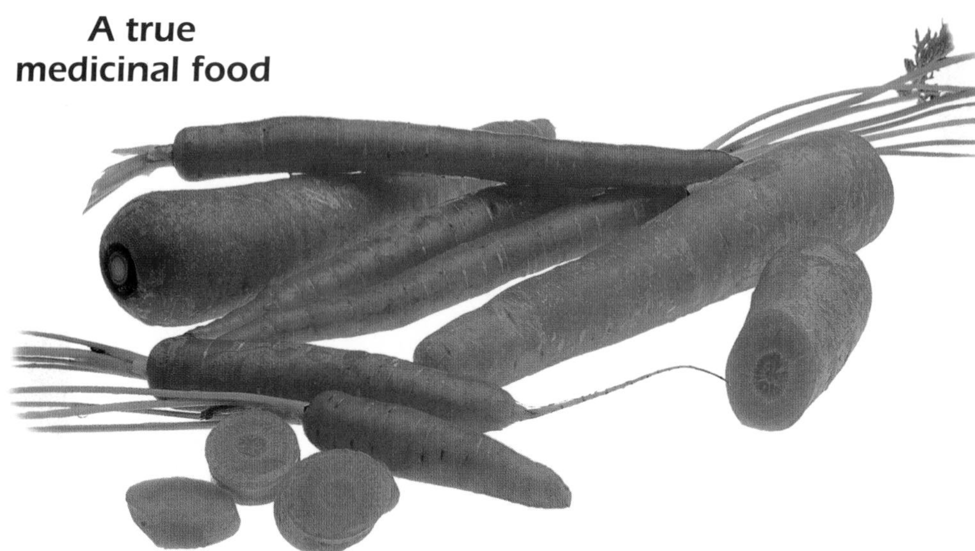

French: *Carotte;* ***Spanish:*** *Zanahoria.*

Description: *Root of the carrot plant ('Daucus carota' L.), a herb of the family Umbelliferae that reaches up to one meter in height. It is usually orange in color, although there are varieties purple or yellow.*

CARROT
Composition
per 100 g of raw edible portion

Energy	43.0 kcal = 181 kj
Protein	1.03 g
Carbohydrates	7.14 g
Fiber	3.00 g
Vitamin A	2,813 µg RE
Vitamin B_1	0.097 mg
Vitamin B_2	0.059 mg
Niacin	1.11 mg NE
Vitamin B_6	0.147 mg
Folate	14.0 µg
Vitamin B_{12}	—
Vitamin C	9.30 mg
Vitamin E	0.460 mg α-TE
Calcium	27.0 mg
Phosphorus	44.0 mg
Magnesium	15.0 mg
Iron	0.500 mg
Potassium	323 mg
Zinc	0.200 mg
Total Fat	*0.190 g*
Saturated Fat	*0.030 g*
Cholesterol	—
Sodium	*35.0 mg*

1% 2% 4% 10% 20% 40% 100% 200% 500%

% Daily Value (based on a 2,000 calorie diet)
provided by 100 g of this food

CARROTS, together with alfalfa greens, are the food richest in provitamin A, which makes them a true dietary medicine. In the *Encyclopedia of Medicinal Plants* (see p. 133) its medicinal properties are explained in greater detail.

PROPERTIES AND INDICATIONS: carrots contain a small but significant amount of proteins (1.03%), approximately half of that of the potato. Fats are almost completely absent (0.19%), and carbohydrates make up 7.14% of their weight. They are a rather good source of B group vitamins, as well as vitamins C and E. All minerals and trace elements are present, including iron (0.5 mg/100 g).

Three substances stand out in the composition of carrots:

✓ ***Carotenoids,*** among the most notable of which is ***beta-carotene,*** which the body *transforms* into ***vitamin A.*** Carotenoids are essential for the proper functioning of the **retina**, particularly for **night vision** or in low light situations. They also help maintain the **skin** and **mucosa** in good condition.

✓ ***Vegetable fiber:*** Carrots contain about 3%, most of which is in the form of pectin. This helps regulate the transit of stool and soothes the intestinal mucosa.

✓ ***Essential oil:*** This is active against intestinal parasites.

Carrots are *very useful* in **diseases of the retina** and **of the eyes in general, skin disorders, gastritis, excess of gastric acid, colitis,** and in the *prevention* of **cancer** (see p. 361).

One hundred grams of carrots (about one medium sized carrot) provide enough beta-carotene for the body to produce almost three times the vitamin A needed daily by an adult.

Preparation and use

❶ **Raw:** In salads, whole or grated and dressed with lemon juice. Carrots strengthen children's teeth.

❷ **Cooked:** Carrots combine well with potatoes and other vegetables. They are sweeter when cooked. They maintain their beta-carotene content after cooking.

❸ **Juice:** Carrot juice makes a refreshing, delicious, and nutritious beverage. It combines very well with apple juice or lemon juice.

Apricot

Gives sparkle and beauty to the eyes

Synonym: *Apricock.*

French: *Abricot;* ***Spanish:*** *Albaricoque, damasco.*

Description: *Fruit of the apricot tree ('Prunus armeniaca' L.) from the botanical family Rosaceae. The tree may reach a height of ten meters.*

APRICOT
Composition
per 100 g of raw edible portion

Energy	48.0 kcal = 201 kj
Protein	1.40 g
Carbohydrates	8.72 g
Fiber	2.40 g
Vitamin A	261 µg RE
Vitamin B_1	0.030 mg
Vitamin B_2	0.040 mg
Niacin	0.850 mg NE
Vitamin B_6	0.054 mg
Folate	8.60 µg
Vitamin B_{12}	—
Vitamin C	10.0 mg
Vitamin E	0.890 mg α-TE
Calcium	14.0 mg
Phosphorus	19.0 mg
Magnesium	8.00 mg
Iron	0.540 mg
Potassium	296 mg
Zinc	0.260 mg
Total Fat	*0.390 g*
Saturated Fat	*0.027 g*
Cholesterol	—
Sodium	*1.00 mg*

1% 2% 4% 10% 20% 40% 100%

% Daily Value (based on a 2,000 calorie diet)
provided by 100 g of this food

THE APRICOT TREE is famous for being one of the most traveled trees known. Its origin is in the north of China, where it is still found wild.

It was taken to Greece by Alexander the Great on the return from his conquests in India. From Greece it passed to Rome, from where its cultivation spread throughout the Mediterranean region. In the 18th century it was taken to North America, where it acclimated to California and states along the Mississippi River. And its long journey does not end here. American astronauts took it to the moon on one of their space journeys.

PROPERTIES AND INDICATIONS: The fact that the apricot has a low calorie content (about 48 kcal /100 g) makes it an excellent part of **weight-loss diets.** It has an **alkalizing** effect because of its richness in alkaline mineral salts. It is particularly noted for its *low **sodium content** and* its *high levels of **potassium.*** It contains various trace elements of great physiological importance, such as manganese, fluorine, cobalt, and boron. It is rich in sugars (***fructose*** and ***glucose***).

Dried apricots are an important source of ***protein*** (up to 5%). They also are an important source of ***iron,*** one of their principal minerals.

However, the most important component of apricots, whether fresh or dried, is beta-carotene or ***provitamin A.*** This component provides most of its therapeutic value, which are the following:

- **Diseases of the eye:** Consumption of apricots maintains vision in good condition and gives the sparkle and beauty to the eyes that are characteristic of good health. This is not due exclusively to the action of provitamin A, but also to the combined action of other vitamins and minerals that accompany it.

Apricots are recommended in cases of **conjunctival dryness, chronic irritation** or **itching** of the conjunctiva, **loss of visual acuity** due to retinal atrophy, and **night blindness.**

The *best results* are obtained by following an **apricot treatment** regime **[❹]**.

- **Anemia** (due to lack of iron): The iron content of fresh apricots is not significant, whereas it is in the dried fruit **[❷]**.

The amounts of provitamin A and iron found in apricots are actually quite small compared to the large doses that pharmaceutical preparations may contain. In spite of this, the results obtained from regular consumption of this fruit are superior to those to be expected from their content of ***iron*** and ***provitamin A.***

- **Disorders of the skin and mucosa,** due to their content of provitamin A. Apricots increase resistance to infections. They are recommended for chronic **pharyngitis, sinusitis,** and **eczema.**

- **Nervous disorders:** Dr. ***Valnet*** points out the apricot's properties of maintaining equilibrium within the nervous system and recommends it in cases **of asthenia, depression, nervousness,** and **lack of appetite.** These effects are attributed to the apricot's richness in **trace elements.**

Preparation and use

❶ **Fresh** and ripe.

❷ **Dried.**

❸ **Preserves:** compotes and marmalade.

❹ **Apricot treatment:** This is carried out over the course of 15 days by eating 1/2 kilo (one pound) of ripe apricots a day, preferably as the only dish at supper. They may be eaten with toasted bread.

Besides being delicious, dried apricots are a good source of provitamin A because of their richness in beta-carotene.

Spinach

In addition to providing strength to muscles, it protects the retina

French: *Épinard;* ***Spanish:*** *Espinaca.*

Description: *Spinach ('Spinacia oleracea' L.) is a herbaceous plant of the botanical family Chenopodiaceae.*

SPINACH Composition
per 100 g of raw edible portion

Energy	22.0 kcal = 94.0 kj
Protein	2.86 g
Carbohydrates	0.800 g
Fiber	2.70 g
Vitamin A	672 µg RE
Vitamin B_1	0.078 mg
Vitamin B_2	0.189 mg
Niacin	1.37 mg NE
Vitamin B_6	0.195 mg
Folate	194 µg
Vitamin B_{12}	—
Vitamin C	28.1 mg
Vitamin E	1.89 mg α-TE
Calcium	99.0 mg
Phosphorus	49.0 mg
Magnesium	79.0 mg
Iron	2.71 mg
Potassium	558 mg
Zinc	0.530 mg
Total Fat	*0.350 g*
Saturated Fat	*0.056 g*
Cholesterol	—
Sodium	*79.0 mg*

1% 2% 4% 10% 20% 40% 100%

% Daily Value (based on a 2,000 calorie diet)
provided by 100 g of this food

POPEYE, the famous cartoon sailor, owed his great strength to eating spinach. Today, both clinical and laboratory investigations confirm that Popeye was correct in eating so much spinach for strength. Besides, new diet therapy applications have been discovered for this excellent vegetable, such as its protective properties concerning the retina and vision.

PROPERTIES AND INDICATIONS: Spinach is possibly the *highest nutritious* **green leafy vegetable** known, although it only contains 22 calories per 100 grams. Its protein content is quite high for a green (2.86%), but it contains little carbohydrates (0.8%) and fats (0.35%).

The nutritive power of spinach derives from its richness in vitamins and minerals, as 100 g of spinach provides:

✓ *two thirds* (672 µg RE) of the daily need for ***vitamin A*** (1,000 µg RE),

✓ practically *all* (194 µg) of ***folic acid*** or folates needed daily (200 µg),

✓ *half* of the ***vitamin C*** (28.1 mg) needed daily (60 mg),

✓ *almost one-fourth* (79 mg) of the daily requirement for ***magnesium*** (350 mg),

✓ *more than one-fourth* (2.71 mg) of the daily need for ***iron*** (10 mg).

These are some of its more important applications:

• **Retinal disorders:** A very precise investigation carried out at the Massachusetts Eye and Ear Infirmary and at Harvard University (USA)[4] shows that persons between 55 and 80 years of age who regularly eat spinach present a much lower risk of losing visual acuity due to **macular degeneration.**

Regular consumption of spinach is recommended to all who wish to preserve sight, particularly those over the age of 50.

• **Anemia:** Spinach contains 2.71 mg of iron /100 g, a proportion greater than that found in meat. Although iron from plant sources is more difficult to absorb than that from animal sources, the presence of vitamin C from the spinach itself[5] and from other foods, significantly improves the assimilation of this mineral.

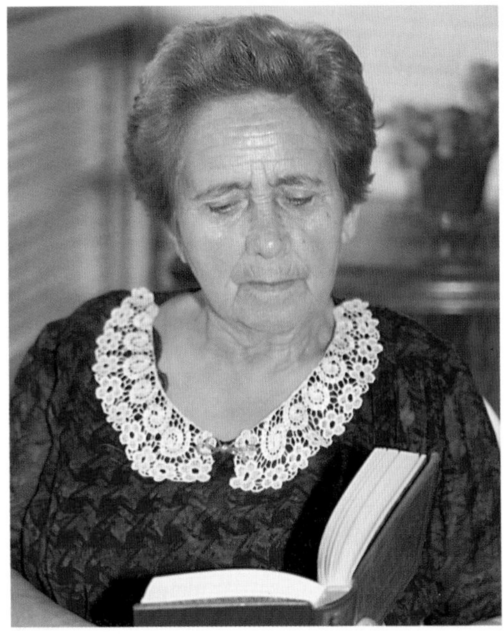

Spinach is very rich in lutein and zeaxanthin, two carotenoids that prevent vision loss because of degeneration of the macula, the most sensitive point of the retina. This disorder is the most common cause of blindness among the elderly.
Spinach is even more effective than carrots in the prevention of senile macular degeneration.

Preparation and use

❶ **Raw:** When spinach is tender, it may be eaten in salads.

❷ **Frozen:** Frozen spinach loses a small portion of its vitamin C, but it has the advantage of being available year-round.

❸ **Cooked:** The ideal method is steaming, which preserves most of its vitamins and minerals.

❹ **Fresh juice:** one-half glass a day sipped before lunch or supper is the recommended dose.

Fresh spinach juice [❹] is an *effective* way to consume it in cases of **anemia.**

• **Elevated cholesterol level:** Experiments with animals[6] have shown that spinach proteins inhibit the absorption of cholesterol and bile acids. Its regular use aids in reducing blood cholesterol level.

• **Pregnancy:** Because of its rich folic acid or folate content, (194 µg/100 g), which prevents certain fetal malformations, in addition to its antianemic action, spinach is an *ideal* green for **pregnant women.**

• **Physical activity and growth:** Because of its rich vitamin and mineral content, spinach is highly recommended for those engaged in **physical activities** such as athletes and **adolescents** during periods of rapid growth.

3

Foods for the Nervous System

THE BRAIN only requires two substances to function: ***oxygen and glucose.*** However, many other nutrients are needed for higher functions such as **thought, memory,** and **self-control.**

B group vitamins are those that ***most* influence** the healthy function of the brain and nervous system. The lack of vitamin B_1, for example, produces irritability and depression, and lack of B_6 produces nervousness and fatigue.

Minerals are directly involved in the activity of the **neurons.** For example, lack of magnesium produces nervousness and anxiety.

Unsaturated fatty acids, such as linolenic acid, which is present in nuts, are necessary for the development of the nervous system and brain in **children.**

On the other hand, *excess* **sugar consumption** and of certain **additives** such as coloring, affect the nervous system and ***alter* behavior.**

NERVOUSNESS

Definition

The nervous system reacts disproportionately to what would be considered normal stimuli when in an excited or irritated state.

Causes

All **drugs** act on the nervous system and *produce* nervousness or *aggravate* it. However, in some cases they may give the *impression* that they provide *momentary* relief, although their negative effect soon ***reappears*** even *more strongly.* Tobacco, alcoholic beverages, coffee, or other stimulant beverages are the most common causes of nervousness and imbalance in the nervous system.

Treatment

In addition to the foods recommended here for nervousness, there are healthy **habits** that *help* ***combat*** it:

- Eat a ***good breakfast*** to avoid **hypoglycemia** (lack of sugar in the blood) that usually manifests itself midmorning, which can produce nervousness and irritability.
- **Eat at regular hours** to avoid **abrupt drops** in blood glucose levels.
- ***Get sufficient* sleep on a *regular basis.***
- **Exercise** regularly, particularly walking or hiking.

Increase

OATS
WHEAT GERM
SUNFLOWER SEEDS
BRAZIL NUT
WALNUT
LETTUCE
AVOCADO
CASHEW
GREEN PEA
PASSION FRUIT
APRICOT
POLLEN

Reduce or eliminate

STIMULANT BEVERAGES
ALCOHOLIC BEVERAGES
WHITE SUGAR

Passion fruit

Even though the sedating action of the passion fruit is much milder than the flowers and leaves of its botanical cousin, the passion flower, it can be quite effective.

HYPERACTIVITY AND AGGRESSIVENESS

Definition

Infantile hyperactivity is an ever-increasing problem in developed countries. Unfortunately so are **aggression** and **violence** among youths and adults as well.

Dietary and other causes

It is becoming more and more evident that diet plays an important role in behavioral disorders.[1] In addition to the products to reduce or eliminate, these are other causes of hyperactivity and aggression:

- **Inadequate breakfast:** Children that do not begin the day with a complete and healthful breakfast suffer from nervousness, fatigue, irritability and even aggressive behavior.[2] The same can be said of adults.
- **Lead contamination:** a study conducted at the University of Pittsburgh (USA) showed that children who have been exposed to lead contamination are at *higher* **risk** of displaying **antisocial behavior, delinquency,** and **aggressiveness.** Meat and fish raised in environments close to industrial areas are usually the foods containing the highest levels of lead contamination.[3]

Increase

WHOLE-GRAIN CEREALS
WHEAT GERM
VITAMIN B_1

Reduce or eliminate

ADDITIVES
WHITE SUGAR
STIMULANT BEVERAGES
ALCOHOL
MEAT
REFINED BAKED GOODS

Sweets

Some artificial coloring such as tartrazine can unleash hyperactive and even aggressive behavior, particularly in children.[4, 5]

INSOMNIA

Food or nutrient

The **type** of **foods** one eats influences the ability to sleep well. ***When*** these are eaten also plays a very important role.

Heavy meals, even those consisting of healthful foods, can disturb sleep. Ideally, both for sleep and digestion, is not to eat **two to three hours** before going to bed.

The only things that those suffering from insomnia should consume before going to bed is a cup of malt beverage or of sedative plants with honey.

Increase

OATS
MALT BEVERAGE
HONEY
CARBOHYDRATES
LETTUCE

Reduce or eliminate

STIMULANT BEVERAGES
CHOCOLATE
SPICES
MEAT
MATURED CHEESES
PROTEINS
SOFT DRINKS

Honey

ANOREXIA NERVOSA

Definition

This is a psychological disorder that is quite prominent among adolescents in which food is refused with the objective of rapid weight loss. It tends to be preceded by low self-esteem, and is accompanied by more or less serious undernourishment or malnutrition.

Food or nutrient

Contributors to its prevention are:

- A **balanced diet from infancy and childhood.**
- Consumption of ***more*** **conventional** dishes such as salads, grains, legumes, potatoes, etcetera, and **fewer** fast foods, sandwiches, chocolate, sweets and ice cream.

See "Bulimia" (p. 43).

Increase

CARBOHYDRATES
LEGUMES
ZINC

Reduce or eliminate

WHITE SUGAR
TOTAL FAT
WHEAT BRAN

DEPRESSION

Food or nutrient

Depressed individuals in general tend to **crave** refined sweets (pastries, candy, chocolate, etc.) that have **very little nutritional value.** They also may have an appetite for saturated fat as found in sausages and other meat products.

All of these foods tend to **worsen** depression, placing the patient in a vicious circle. Special effort is required on the part of the patient and those around him or her to find healthful and attractive foods.

If the desire for sweets is intense, sweet dried fruits, honey, or molasses are a more healthful option since, in addition to sugars, they provide various vitamins and minerals needed specifically to metabolize the sugars.

Whole grains, legumes, nuts, and vegetables prepared simply provide a vitality and energy that more sophisticated dishes cannot equal.

Life style

Antidepressant drugs do not replace the need to follow a healthful diet and abstain from all other types of drugs, including those considered legal since all of them attack the nervous system.

Increase

OATS
WHEAT GERM
CHICKPEA
ALMOND
WALNUT
BRAZIL NUT
CASHEW
PINE NUT
AVOCADO
BREWER'S YEAST
ROYAL JELLY
VITAMINS B_1, B_6 AND C
LECITHIN
FOLATES
POLLEN
IRON

Reduce or eliminate

WHITE SUGAR
SATURATED FAT
STIMULANT BEVERAGES
ALCOHOLIC BEVERAGES

Brazil nut is very rich in vitamin B_1, which is necessary to balance the nervous system.

Brazil nuts

STRESS

Causes

This is produced when the events of life, whether physical or psychological, are greater than the ability to cope.

Psychological stress may be for positive reasons (a new job) or negative (the !oss of a job). In all stress cases the repercussions on the body are very similar.

Effects

While stress can affect all of the organs ad functions of the body, its **effects** tend to be concentrated on:

- The **heart and the cardiovascular system,** which is obliged to work harder.
- The **immune system,** which is weakened in favor of other bodily functions. This reduces resistance to **infections,** and probably to **cancer** as well, and other diseases.

Food or nutrient

Certain **foods** can **help** the body **adapt** to stress, while others **weaken it.**

Increase

PROTEINS
CARBOHYDRATES
WALNUT
ALMOND
PINE NUT
CHICKPEA
WHEAT GERM
B VITAMINS
VITAMIN C

Reduce or eliminate

STIMULANT BEVERAGES
ALCOHOLIC BEVERAGES
WHITE SUGAR

Walnuts

MENTAL FATIGUE

Food or nutrient

Those involved in intense mental activity are in greater need of certain nutrients. The foods that best meet these needs are **whole grains** (oats, in particular) and **oil-bearing nuts** (especially almonds and walnuts).

Increase

OATS
ALMOND
WALNUT
WHEAT GERM

Almonds

HEADACHES AND MIGRAINES

Definition

Headaches are general head pain. **Migraines** are a special type of headache, sharp and throbbing, which occurs suddenly and may be accompanied by nausea, vomiting, and blurred vision.

Causes

The possible causes of headaches are numerous. They may be something unimportant or the first signs of a tumor or a serious brain lesion.

In addition to the described foods, other factors can **unleash** or **aggravate** headaches or migraines:

- **Allergies,**
- **Nervous tension** and **stress,**
- **Menstruation,** particularly during the days preceding it.

Food or nutrient

There are no known foods able to prevent or cure headaches or migraines. But certain foods can **cause** them. **Avoiding** these can be the most effective course of **prevention,**[6] once other potential organic causes such as arterial aneurysms or tumors have been eliminated.

Reduce or eliminate

ALCOHOLIC BEVERAGES
BEER
WINE
CURED CHEESES
CHOCOLATE
SHELLFISH
CURED MEATS
PROTEINS
ADDITIVES
STIMULANT BEVERAGES
WHITE SUGAR
DAIRY PRODUCTS
ICE CREAM
CITRUS FRUITS

Cured cheese

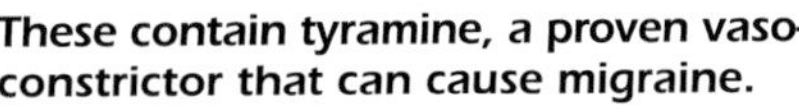

These contain tyramine, a proven vasoconstrictor that can cause migraine.

Anxiety

Definition

This is an undesirable and unjustified emotional state primarily psychosomatic. It initially affects the brain and then the other organs of the body producing **tachycardia, stomach pain, irritable bowel** (alternating constipation-diarrhea), etcetera.

Worsening factors

Anxiety is **exacerbated** by:

- **Unbalanced weight-loss diets,** which produce an inevitable reduction in the intake of the **carbohydrates, vitamins, and minerals,** all of which are necessary for a healthy nervous system.
- Consumption of **alcoholic beverages, stimulants** (such as caffeine), and **tobacco.** Although these may briefly relieve anxiety, it usually reappears with greater intensity after the effect of the substance in question has passed. Since these are **addictive drugs,** they all have a deleterious effect on the nervous system.

Increase

WHEAT GERM
WHOLE GRAINS
BANANA
NUTS
YOGURT
VITAMIN B_6
MAGNESIUM

Reduce or eliminate

STIMULANT BEVERAGES
MEAT
ALCOHOL

Rye

Whole grains provide complex carbohydrates and B vitamins that are necessary to the balance of the nervous system.

Bulimia

Definition

This is the *opposite* of **anorexia** (see p. 43): a ***voracious, uncontrollable* appetite**. Bulimia tends to alternate with anorexia and is one of the most common eating disorders in developed countries.

Food or nutrient

- ***Remove*** all **sweets** and **fatty foods** from the bulimic's diet.
- Replace these with **whole grains, salads,** and other **healthful foods** that can **satisfy** the appetite.

Increase

WHOLE GRAINS
SALADS
FRUIT
FIBER

Reduce or eliminate

WHITE SUGAR
TOTAL FAT

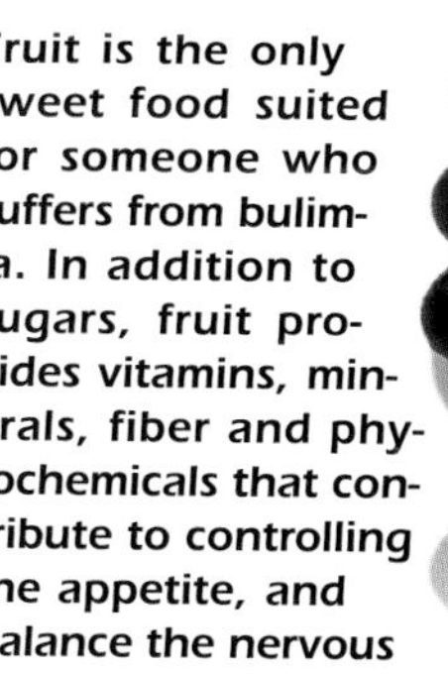

Grape

Fruit is the only sweet food suited for someone who suffers from bulimia. In addition to sugars, fruit provides vitamins, minerals, fiber and phytochemicals that contribute to controlling the appetite, and balance the nervous system.

Neuralgia

Definition

This is a disease of sensitive nerves that produces sharp burning pain along their course. In some cases there is a known cause that irritates the nerve, but not in others.

Food or nutrient

Foods rich in B vitamins can **alleviate** neuralgic pain.

Increase

WHEAT GERM
BREWER'S YEAST
VITAMINS B_1 AND B_{12}

Reduce or eliminate

ALCOHOLIC BEVERAGES

EPILEPSY

Definition

This disease of the central nervous system is manifested by seizures of varying intensity from loss of memory or absentmindedness to serious convulsions with loss of consciousness.

Food or nutrient

Lack of ***B group vitamins*** and certain ***minerals***, **stress, tiredness, fever,** and consumption of **alcoholic beverages** are the factors that most frequently unleash seizures.

Increase

- B VITAMINS
- VITAMIN B_6
- FOLATES
- MAGNESIUM
- MANGANESE

Reduce or eliminate

- ALCOHOL BEVERAGES
- SWEETENERS
- PRIMROSE OIL

Sweeteners

Chemical sweeteners such as aspartame have been linked to the appearance of epileptic crises in sensitive individuals.

MULTIPLE SCLEROSIS

Definition

This disease tends to manifest between 25 and 40 years of age and affects more women than men. It is due to alterations in the myelin sheath that covers the nerves. It displays a variety of symptoms depending on the nerves affected: altered vision or speech, loss of skin sensitivity, and motor disturbances.

Related factors

The course of this disease tends to oscillate with periods of worsening and improvement. Although its cause is not well known, there are **foods** that **make symptoms worse** and others that produce slight improvements. **Tobacco** and **alcoholic beverages** use **aggravate** it markedly.

Increase

- OILS
- SELENIUM
- WHOLE GRAINS
- LEGUMES
- SALADS
- FRUIT

Reduce or eliminate

- SATURATED FAT
- ALCOHOLIC BEVERAGES
- MEAT
- DAIRY PRODUCTS
- WHITE SUGAR

PARKINSON'S DISEASE

Definition

This usually appears after 50 years of age, and it is characterized by three principal symptoms: muscular rigidity, akinesia (loss of power for voluntary movement), and tremor. It is due in part to the fact that the brain does not produce sufficient **dopamine**, a substance that intervenes in the transmission of nerve impulses between the neurons.

Food or nutrient

There is no known food that makes this condition better or worse. However, the consumption of plant-based foods rich in vitamins B, C, and E can contribute to **slowing** the progress of the disease.

Increase

- WHOLE GRAINS
- FRUIT
- VEGETABLES
- OILS
- VITAMIN B_1
- VITAMIN E
- FOLATES
- NIACIN

Reduce or eliminate

- SATURATED FAT
- WHITE SUGAR
- STIMULANT BEVERAGES

Peanuts

Peanuts are a good source of niacin, so they are ideal for Parkinson patients.

DEMENTIA

This is a progressive and generally irreversible loss of mental faculties.

Although there are a variety of causes, studies show how the **regular consumption** of certain foods throughout life, primarily **animal fat** and **meat,** increases the **risk** of dementia.

Alcohol

Alcohol irreversibly deteriorates the neurons, and its regular use is a frequent cause of dementia.

Reduce or eliminate

- ALCOHOLIC BEVERAGES
- SATURATED FAT
- CHOLESTEROL
- MEAT
- FISH

ALZHEIMER'S DISEASE

Definition

This is a type of **progressive dementia** caused by the degeneration of brain cells. It begins with memory loss, followed by mental confusion, apathy, and depression.

Causes

Its cause is unknown, although it has been proven that **ingestion of high levels of aluminum** favors its onset. Aluminum is toxic to nerve cells, and higher levels of this element are found in the brains of Alzheimer's patients than in the healthy population. Mercury may also be implicated in Alzheimer's but this has not been proven.

Prevention

To **prevent** Alzheimer's, in addition to the accompanying dietary advice, it is wise to avoid the following:

- The use of **aluminum cooking utensils,** particularly when cooking acidic foods such as tomatoes, which can release even more aluminum.
- The use of **antacid** medications containing aluminum.
- Drinking **soft drinks** in aluminum **cans.**
- **Tap water** if it has high aluminum content.

Increase

LEAFY GREEN VEGETABLES
BREWER'S YEAST
ANTIOXIDANTS
VITAMIN E
CHOLINE

Reduce or eliminate

ALCOHOLIC BEVERAGES
CURED CHEESES

Watercress

Green leafy vegetables are a good source of silicon. This trace element hinders the absorption of aluminum in the intestine, a mineral considered related to the onset of this disease.

SCHIZOPHRENIA

Definition

This is a hereditary mental disease characterized by changes in personality and hallucinations. Even though it has an inherited component, its cause is unknown. It is possibly due to subtle **changes** in the **chemistry** of the **neurons** in the brain.

Food or nutrient

Diet can contribute to the course of the disease, either **positively** or **negatively.** Lacking more concrete data, these are recommended:

- Eat **abundant** amounts of simply prepared **plant-based foods:** fresh fruits and vegetables, legumes, and nuts.
- **Avoid** all foods or products that can produce allergies.
- **Avoid** situations leading to hypoglycemia (low blood sugar) in which the brain suffers a lack of glucose. Lack of regular meals, poor breakfasts, or a diet lacking in complex carbohydrates are the most frequent dietary causes.

Increase

WHEAT GERM
FRUIT
VEGETABLES
LEGUMES
NUTS

Reduce or eliminate

ALCOHOLIC BEVERAGES
STIMULANT BEVERAGES
ADDITIVES
DAIRY PRODUCTS
GLUTEN

Wheat germ

Wheat germ is one of the best sources of B group vitamins, vitamin E, and minerals that balance the nervous system.

Cashew

Very rich in magnesium

CASHEW NUT
Composition
per 100 g of raw edible portion

Energy	574 kcal = 2,402 kj
Protein	15.3 g
Carbohydrates	29.7 g
Fiber	3.00 g
Vitamin A	—
Vitamin B_1	0.200 mg
Vitamin B_2	0.200 mg
Niacin	5.35 mg NE
Vitamin B_6	0.256 mg
Folate	69.2 µg
Vitamin B_{12}	—
Vitamin C	—
Vitamin E	0.570 mg α-TE
Calcium	45.0 mg
Phosphorus	490 mg
Magnesium	260 mg
Iron	6.00 mg
Potassium	565 mg
Zinc	5.60 mg
Total Fat	*46.4 g*
Saturated Fat	*9.16 g*
Cholesterol	—
Sodium	*16.0 mg*

1% 2% 4% 10% 20% 40% 100%

% Daily Value (based on a 2,000 calorie diet) provided by 100 g of this food

Synonyms: *Cashew apple, Cashew fruit, Cashew nut.*

French: *Anacarde, pomme de cajou;* ***Spanish:*** *Anacardo.*

Description: *This is the seed of the fruit of the cashew tree ('Anacardium occidentale' L.), a tree of the botanical family Anacardiaceae that reaches 9 to 12 meters in height.*

THE CASHEW is one of the most highly prized of nuts. The fact that it is produced in tropical climates only increases its value and attractiveness.

PROPERTIES AND INDICATIONS: Cashews are an oil-bearing nut with a sweet, pleasant taste. They are rich in ***unsaturated fatty acids*** such as oleic and linoleic; in ***vitamins*** such as ***B_1, B_2,*** in ***pantothenic acid;*** and in ***minerals*** such as magnesium (260 mg /100 g), potassium, iron, and phosphorous.

It is noted for its ***magnesium*** content, one of the highest in the vegetable kingdom, surpassed only by sunflower seeds (354 mg /100 g, see p. 110). Meat, milk, and eggs are poor in magnesium, none exceeding 24 mg/100 g.

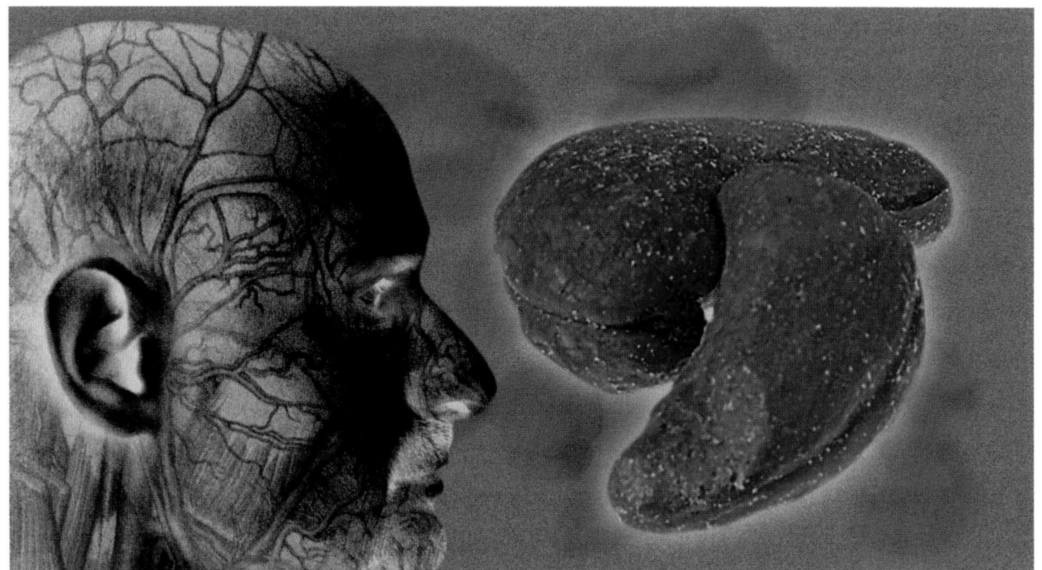

Cashews are rich in group-B vitamins, as well as in magnesium, phosphorus, and zinc. All these nutrients are essential for the proper operation of the nervous system.

MAGNESIUM is involved in a variety of metabolic functions, but particularly the transmission of nerve impulses. Its *lack* produces **nervousness** and **irritability,** and even **cramps** and **spasms.** Since the cashew is very rich in magnesium as well as ***vitamins*** B_1 ***and*** B_2 (superior to almond and walnut, see pp. 58, 74), which are also essential for nervous stability, its use is recommended in cases of:

- **Nervousness, irritability, depression, weakness** and abnormal **tiredness.**
- **Spasms** in hollow organs: the colon (irritable bowel), the uterus (dysmenorrhea), or the coronary arteries (angina pectoris).

Preparation and use

❶ **Roasted nut:** these are eaten with or without salt, much like peanuts or any other nut.

❷ **Fleshy fruit** (the stalk on which the nut grows): This fleshy, somewhat sour stalk is eaten fresh, in compote, marmalade, or juice. The juice must be drunk immediately since it is difficult to preserve.

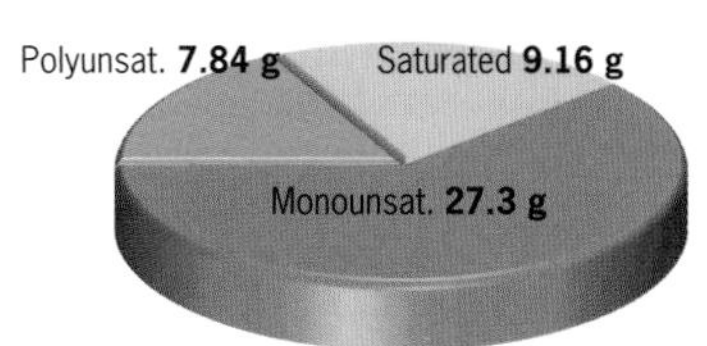

Percentage distribution of **fatty acids**

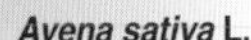

Oats

Balance the nerves and lower cholesterol

Synonyms: *Rolled oats, Steelcut oats.*
French: *Avoine;* ***Spanish:*** *Avena.*

Description: *Fruit of the oat plant ('Avena sativa' L.), an annual herbaceous plant of the botanical family Gramineae. This special fruit is a grain composed of a pericarp or bran and a seed or the grain itself.*

OATS
Composition
per 100 g of raw edible portion

Energy	389 kcal = 1,629 kj
Protein	16.9 g
Carbohydrates	55.7 g
Fiber	10.6 g
Vitamin A	—
Vitamin B_1	0.763 mg
Vitamin B_2	0.139 mg
Niacin	4.86 mg NE
Vitamin B_6	0.119 mg
Folate	56.0 µg
Vitamin B_{12}	—
Vitamin C	—
Vitamin E	0.700 mg α-TE
Calcium	54.0 mg
Phosphorus	523 mg
Magnesium	177 mg
Iron	4.72 mg
Potassium	429 mg
Zinc	3.97 mg
Total Fat	*6.90 g*
Saturated Fat	*1.22 g*
Cholesterol	—
Sodium	*2.00 mg*

1% 2% 4% 10% 20% 40% 100%
% Daily Value (based on a 2,000 calorie diet) provided by 100 g of this food

TRADITIONAL practice in some Central European countries is to have those suffering from nervousness or insomnia sleep on a mattress of oat hay. It is very possible that this custom is not without basis since oats contain an alkaloid that is sedating to the nervous system.

PROPERTIES AND INDICATIONS: Oats are the most ***nutrient-rich*** of any grain. They contain more than twice the fat as wheat (see p. 292), more proteins, and more carbohydrates. They are very rich in ***phosphorous, iron*** (4.72 mg/100 g, which surpasses meat with no more than 3 mg/100 g), and ***vitamin*** B_1.

The *most abundant* nutrient in oats is ***CARBOHYDRATES.*** Due to the particular structure of the oat grain, these carbohydrates are easily assimilated and absorbed slowly. For this reason, oats provide energy for several hours. The following carbohydrates stand out on oat:

✓ ***Starch*** and products of its decomposition: ***dextrin, maltose,*** and ***glucose.*** These are very easily assimilated substances that the body converts quickly into energy.

✓ ***Fructose:*** This is found in a small amount together with other carbohydrates. It has the peculiarity of not requiring insulin to penetrate the cells and be utilized by them. As a result, oats are *highly recommended* for **diabetics.**

✓ ***Mucilage:*** This is a type of carbohydrate with a gelatinous consistency and a propensity to retain water. It constitutes a special type of ***soluble fiber.*** It lubricates and softens the interior of the digestive tract. This makes oats appropriate in cases of **gastritis** and **colitis.**

✓ ***Vegetable fiber:*** This is found particularly in the outer layer of the grain, and it remains in whole-grain flakes. It may also be eaten separately in the form of oat ***bran.*** Its primary component is ***beta-glucan,*** a soluble derivative of cellulose. It has a mild **laxative** effect, but above all, it lowers **cholesterol** levels since it absorbs and removes bile acids from the intestine, a raw material for the manufacture of cholesterol within the body.[7]

Oat ***PROTEINS*** are abundant (16.9%) and easily digested. They contain all of the ***essential amino acids,*** but not in optimal proportions. Oats are relatively poor in ***lysine*** and ***threonine,*** while they have an excess of ***methionine.*** On the other hand, legumes (chickpeas, lentils, or beans) are rich in lysine and threonine, but are deficient in methionine. Because of this, the combination of grains such as **oats** with **legumes** is very beneficial; the proteins of both types of foods complement each other to form a ***complete protein.***

The ***FATS*** found in oats are also of great nutritional value. They are formed of:

✓ ***Fatty acids:*** Unsaturated (80%) including ***linoleic acid,*** and saturated (20%). The predominance of unsaturated fatty acids has a regulating effect on the synthesis of **cholesterol.**

✓ **Avenasterol,** a phytosterol, which is a vegetable substance similar to **cholesterol** and has

Preparation and use

❶ **Flakes:** This is the best way to eat oats and take advantage of all its nutritive properties. They may be prepared boiled in milk or vegetable broth.

❷ **"Porridge" (oatmeal):** This may be prepared in the following manner: place four spoonfuls of oat flakes to soak. The following morning, boil 1/2 liter of water and add the soaked flakes. Cook for 15 minutes over low heat. Serve with honey. Milk may be added as well.

❸ **Flour or cream:** Used for soups and baby foods.

❹ **"Muesli":** Oat flakes are one of the basic ingredients in "muesli" as a breakfast food, along with other grains, almonds, hazelnuts, raisins, etc. "Bircher-muesli" is prepared with these ingredients together with fresh fruit, milk, and a little honey.

❺ **Oat water:** This is prepared by placing two soupspoons of oat grain in one liter of water. This is boiled for five minutes then strained. The resulting liquid may be sweetened with honey. Oat water can be used as a beverage throughout the day.

Oat flakes boiled with milk and served with honey and pieces of apple or banana makes an excellent breakfast for children, youth, athletes, and pregnant or lactating women. After this type of breakfast there is no need for a midmorning snack.

the interesting effect of interfering with the absorption of true cholesterol in the intestine, reducing its level in the blood.

✓ ***Lecithin:*** Oats contain a small amount of this phospholipid that is of great importance to **nervous system** function. Lecithin also contributes to lowering blood **cholesterol** levels.

Even though oats are rich in fat, they should not be avoided by those wishing to reduce cholesterol; quite the contrary.

Because of their enormous nutritional value and easy digestibility, oats constitute a ***staple food*** in the human diet. Like bread, it can be eaten every day since it is well known that grains are the basis of human nutrition.

Oats, because of their therapeutic value, are particularly indicated in situations such as those described below.

• **Nervous system complaints:** Oats provide the most important nutrients for the proper function of the neurons: ***glucose*** (released from starch), **fatty acids, phosphorous, lecithin,** and ***vitamin B1.*** All of these have an invigorating and stabilizing effect, and improve mental performance. Additionally, oats contain small amounts of the nontoxic alkaloid **avenine,** which has a mildly **sedative** effect on the nervous system.

Regular oats consumption in any form, including oat water **[❺]**, is indicated in the following situations: **nervousness, fatigue or mental exhaustion, insomnia,** and **depression.** It is a food that should be included in the diet of **students,** particularly at exam time.

• **Digestive disturbances:** Due to their mucilage content and their ease of digestion, oat flakes (oatmeal) **[❶]** have an emollient effect. Cooked with milk or vegetable broth they are highly recommended for **gastritis,** gastroduodenal **ulcer** or intestinal disorders such as **diverticulosis** (the presence of diverticula in the intestine), or **colitis** caused by microorganisms, toxins, medications, or certain food intolerances.

• **Celiac disease:** This disease is caused by **intolerance to gliadin,** a *protein* found in the **gluten** of wheat and other grains. Its symptoms

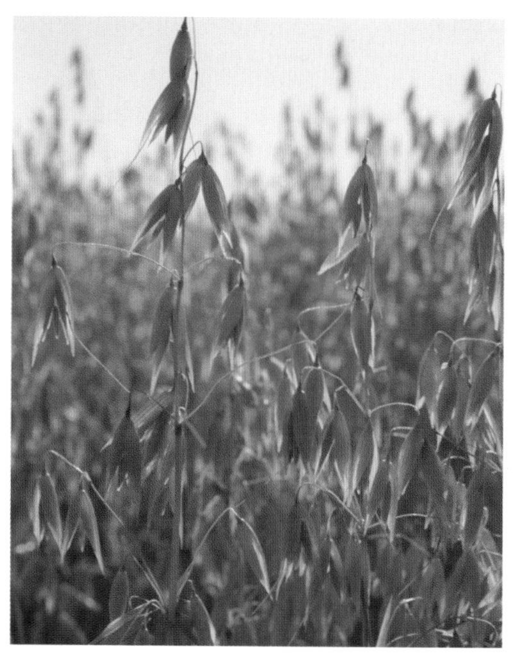

are severe diarrhea and undernourishment. Oats contain very little gliadin and are well tolerated by those suffering from this disease. This has been shown in various scientific studies.[8]

• **Diabetes:** In spite of their high carbohydrate content, oats are ***very well* tolerated** by diabetics, particularly if they are eaten as whole-grain flakes including the bran **(❶)**. This is due to their ***fructose*** content, and above all, to the ***BETA-GLUCAN*** found particularly in oat bran. Beta-glucan is a type of soluble vegetable fiber demonstrated to greatly improve tolerance by diabetics of glucose released from oat starch during digestion, according to a study by the United States Department of Agriculture.[9]

• **Increased cholesterol:** the composition of the fats in oats promotes a lowering of cholesterol. This effect is facilitated by the action of ***beta-glucan,*** a substance found in oat bran. Beta-glucan retains and eliminates the bile salts in the intestine while reducing the absorption of fats, as well.[10, 11] Bile acids are the raw material that the body uses to produce cholesterol. As these are eliminated through the feces, internal cholesterol production is reduced.

This property of oats has been proven in various studies,[12, 13] therefore the consumption of whole-grain oats, including the bran (as in wholemeal oat flakes **(❶)**), is highly recommended for those suffering from high cholesterol.

• **Arteriosclerosis and hypertension:** Regular consumption of oats, at least once a day in any form, provides very good results as a treatment and preventive for these disorders.

Oat water has a stabilizing and invigorating effect on the nervous system. It is highly recommended in cases of nervousness and arterial hypertension.
Its preparation is described in the Preparation and Use box (see p. 49).

Brazil nuts

Rich in vitamin B1

BRAZIL NUT
Composition
per 100 g of raw edible portion

Energy	656 kcal = 2,745 kj
Protein	14.3 g
Carbohydrates	7.40 g
Fiber	5.40 g
Vitamin A	—
Vitamin B1	1.00 mg
Vitamin B2	0.122 mg
Niacin	5.96 mg NE
Vitamin B6	0.251 mg
Folate	4.00 µg
Vitamin B12	—
Vitamin C	0.700 mg
Vitamin E	7.60 mg α-TE
Calcium	176 mg
Phosphorus	600 mg
Magnesium	225 mg
Iron	3.40 mg
Potassium	600 mg
Zinc	4.59 mg
Total Fat	66.2 g
Saturated Fat	16.2 g
Cholesterol	—
Sodium	2.00 mg

1% 2% 4% 10% 20% 40% 100% 200% 500%
% Daily Value (based on a 2,000 calorie diet)
provided by 100 g of this food

Synonyms: *Creamnuts, Paranuts.*

French: *Noix du Brésil;* ***Spanish:*** *Nuez del Brasil, coquito de Brasil, almendra del Amazonas.*

Description: *This is the seed of the tree 'Bertholletia excelsa' Humb., of the botanical family Lecythidaceae, that reaches 40 meters in height.*

THE TREE that produces Brazil nuts stands out among tropical trees because of its majesty and beauty. However, efforts to cultivate them have failed to the point that most of the commercially available nuts are from wild trees in the Amazon basin.

PROPERTIES AND INDICATIONS: Brazil nuts contain more than 66.2% ***fat*** that becomes rancid quite easily. These are composed of up to 25% ***saturated fatty acids.*** Together with the palm and the coconut, this is one of the vegetable ***fats*** richest in this type of fatty acid, and, therefore, are the *least advisable* from a dietary standpoint. They should not be eaten to excess, particularly in cases of elevated **cholesterol.**

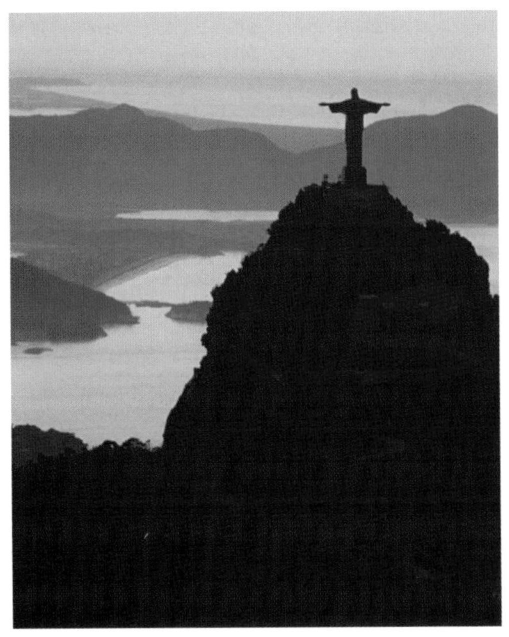

Brazil nuts are rich in ***proteins*** (14.3%) ***vitamin E,*** and ***minerals*** (phosphorous, magnesium, calcium, and iron).

But their most important dietary property is their *high* ***vitamin B1*** *content,* higher than meat, milk, or eggs. Only wheat germ, brewer's yeast, sunflower seeds, and pine nuts contain more vitamin B1 than Brazil nuts.

This makes them appropriate for those suffering from **nervous disorders,** such as irritability, depression, memory loss, and lack of concentration or mental performance.

Those who are following a treatment plan to **stop smoking** should include Brazil nuts in their diet because of the desirable effects of ***vitamin B1*** on the nervous system.

The fruit of this tree is a husk similar to a coconut approximately 16 cm in diameter. When it ripens it opens and reveals 20 to 24 kidney-shaped seeds. These seeds, which measure 3-4 cm, have a woody shell and contain a thick nut known as a Brazil nut.

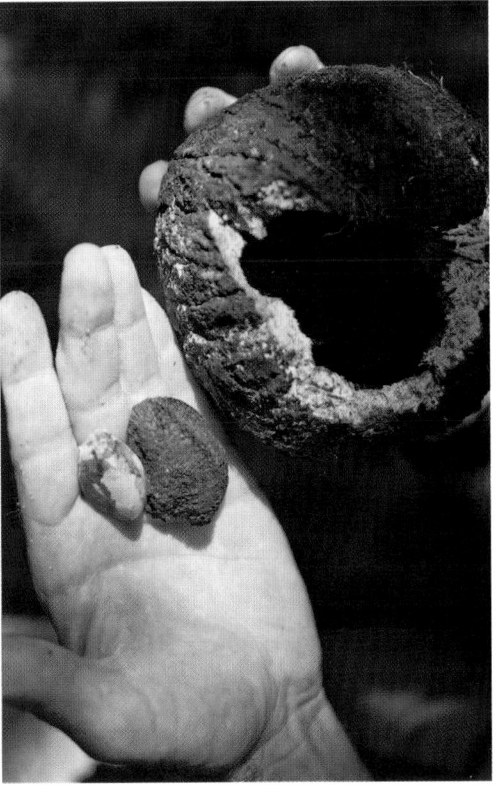

Preparation and use

❶ **Raw:** this is the way Brazil nuts are usually eaten. They must be well chewed, as is the case with all oil-bearing nuts.

❷ **Toasted:** 5 to 10 minutes in the oven is usually sufficient to turn them golden brown and give them a pleasant taste.

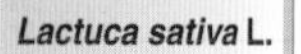

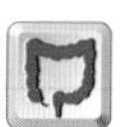

Lettuce

Calms the nerves and satisfies the stomach

Scientific synonym: *Lactuca virosa* L.

Synonyms: *Celtuce, Cos, Garden lettuce, [Green] romaine lettuce.*

French: *Laitue;* ***Spanish:*** *Lechuga.*

Description: *Leaves of the lettuce plant 'Lactuca sativa', of the botanical family Compositae. There are varieties with straight leaves and others with curly ones, and their color varies from green to purple red.*

LETTUCE
Composition
per 100 g of raw edible portion

Energy	16.0 kcal = 67.0 kj
Protein	1.62 g
Carbohydrates	0.670 g
Fiber	1.70 g
Vitamin A	260 µg RE
Vitamin B_1	0.100 mg
Vitamin B_2	0.100 mg
Niacin	0.700 mg NE
Vitamin B_6	0.047 mg
Folate	136 µg
Vitamin B_{12}	—
Vitamin C	24.0 mg
Vitamin E	0.440 mg α-TE
Calcium	36.0 mg
Phosphorus	45.0 mg
Magnesium	6.00 mg
Iron	1.10 mg
Potassium	290 mg
Zinc	0.250 mg
Total Fat	*0.200 g*
Saturated Fat	*0.026 g*
Cholesterol	—
Sodium	*8.00 mg*

1% 2% 4% 10% 20% 40% 100%

% Daily Value (based on a 2,000 calorie diet) provided by 100 g of this food

THE ANCIENT Romans ate lettuce at night as a sleep aid after overeating at supper. Today the stressed inhabitants of modern cities can benefit from this effect of lettuce ***not*** *after*, but ***rather in place*** of a big supper.

PROPERTIES AND INDICATIONS: Lettuce is one of the foods *richest* in **water** (94.9%). However, the relatively high level of ***proteins*** (1.62%) that it provides is surprising. This is only slightly less than the potato (2.07%).

Lettuce is a very poor source of carbohydrates (0.67%) and fat (0.2%), which explains its low energetic contribution. The nutritional and therapeutic value of lettuce is based on the following components:

✓ ***Provitamin A:*** 100 g of lettuce provides 260 µg RE (micrograms of retinol equivalents), which represents a quarter of the daily requirement of this provitamin.

✓ ***B group vitamins:*** Lettuce is quite rich in vitamin B_1 (0.1 mg/100 g) and B_2 (0.1 mg/100 g), and, above all, ***folates*** (135.7 µg/100 g).

✓ ***Vitamin C:*** The concentration of this vitamin in lettuce is 24 mg/100 g, a little less than half that of the orange or lemon.

✓ ***Minerals:*** Lettuce is noted for its potassium (290 mg/100 g) and iron (1.1 mg/100 g) content. It has significant amounts of calcium, phosphorous, and magnesium, as well as the trace elements zinc, copper, and manganese.

✓ ***Vegetable fiber*** (1.7%) that contributes a mild laxative effect.

✓ ***Sedative and sleep-inducing substances,*** the same as found in the latex of wild lettuce[14] (lactucarium), but in much lower proportion. These substances are chemically similar to those from opium, but they are completely lacking in toxicity and addictive properties.

Because of this composition, lettuce has the following properties: sedative, sleep inducing, aperitif, alkalizer, and remineralizer. It is indicated for the following conditions:

- ***Functional disorders of the nervous system,*** such as nervousness, stress or psychological tension, or anxiety. Regular lettuce consumption produces a mild, and sometimes imperceptible sedative effect, while providing necessary B vitamins for nervous system stability.
- **Insomnia:** A large supper consisting of *only lettuce* is *recommended at night* for insomnia.
- **Digestive disorders:** When eaten *before a meal,* lettuce tones the stomach and facilitates digestion.
- **Constipation:** Lettuce facilitates intestinal function because of its excellent digestibility and ***fiber*** content.
- **Obesity:** Lettuce produces a great sense of satiety, but provides few calories. At the same time, it helps relieve nervousness and anxiety regarding food that often accompanies obesity.
- **Diabetes:** Lettuce is *very low* in ***carbohydrates;*** therefore, diabetics can eat it limited only by the appetite.

Having a good dish of lettuce, properly dressed with oil and lemon, eases digestion and helps to induce sleep, besides producing a remarkable sensation of satiety.

Preparation and use

❶ **Raw:** This is best way to enjoy its freshness and pleasant taste. It is dressed with a little oil (preferably olive oil) and a few drops of lemon juice. Green leaves are much more nutritious than the white ones on the inside.

❷ **Cooked:** The toughest leaves can be cooked like any other green.

Pinus Pinea L.  

Pine nuts

A good food for the brain

PINE NUT Composition
per 100 g of raw edible portion

Energy	629 kcal = 2,632 kj
Protein	11.6 g
Carbohydrates	8.60 g
Fiber	10.7 g
Vitamin A	3.00 µg RE
Vitamin B_1	1.24 mg
Vitamin B_2	0.223 mg
Niacin	6.80 mg NE
Vitamin B_6	0.111 mg
Folate	57.8 µg
Vitamin B_{12}	—
Vitamin C	2.00 mg
Vitamin E	—
Calcium	8.00 mg
Phosphorus	35.0 mg
Magnesium	234 mg
Iron	3.06 mg
Potassium	628 mg
Zinc	4.28 mg
Total Fat	*61.0 g*
Saturated Fat	*9.38 g*
Cholesterol	—
Sodium	*72.0 mg*

1% 2% 4% 10% 20% 40% 100%

% Daily Value (based on a 2,000 calorie diet)
provided by 100 g of this food

Synonyms: *Pine kernel, Indian nut, Nut pine, Mexican nut pine.*

French: *Pignon;* ***Spanish:*** *Piñón.*

Description: *The seed of the pine nut tree ('Pinus pinea' L.), of the botanical family Pinaceae. It reaches 30 meters in height, and its leaves or needles tend to be longer than those of other pines.*

PINES are gymnosperm plants; that is, their seeds are naked and not covered by a fruit. Pine cones are not pine fruit, but rather the female inflorescence, which contain the seeds or pine nuts among their woody scales.

PROPERTIES AND INDICATIONS: Pine nuts are delicious, and due to their relative scarcity and high price, their use is generally reserved as a decorative element in baked goods or as an exquisite condiment in fine cuisine.

However, pine nuts possess a *great deal* of ***nutritional*** *value* that many ignore. They contain 61% of ***fats*** composed primarily of ***polyunsaturated fatty acids*** such as ***linoleic*** and ***pinolenic*** acids,[15] which are

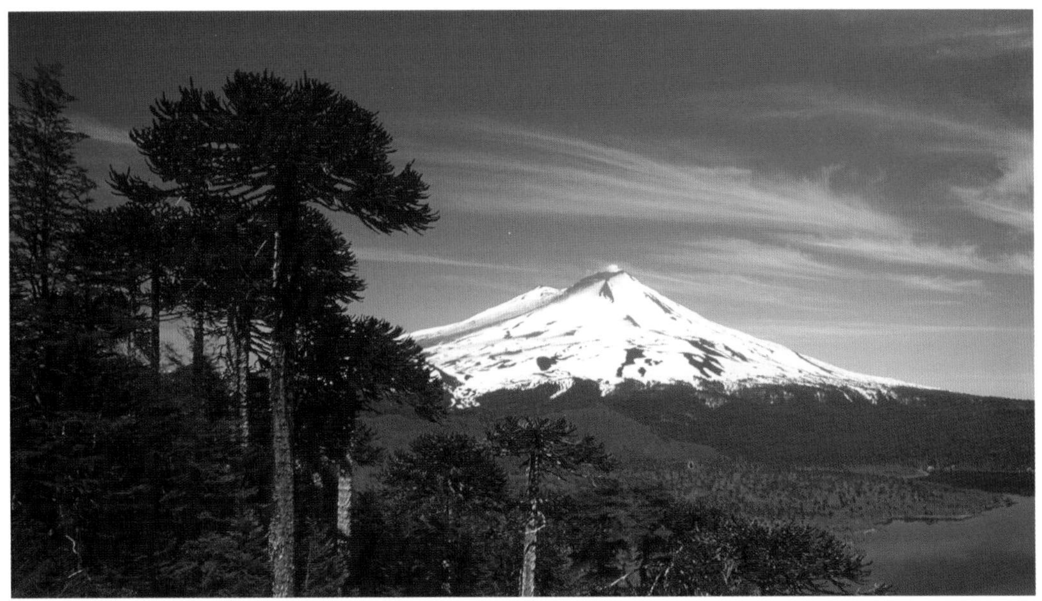

The araucarias that grow in southern Chile provide excellent pine nuts.

very important in the *formation* of **nerve tissue** and the *reduction* of blood **cholesterol.**

They are also rich in high biological quality (*complete*) ***proteins*** (11.6%), as well as ***vitamin B1*** and ***iron*** (3 mg/100 g). Pine nuts stand out because of their vitamin B1 content, surpassed only by sunflower seeds, wheat germ, and brewer's yeast. These are the most important applications of pine nuts:

- **Nervous system disorders,** due to its ***vitamin B1*** content and its ***essential fatty acids***. They are indicated for those suffering from **stress and depression,** as well as for **students.**
- **Anemia** and other weakened bodily conditions, because of their elevated nutritive and mineral content.
- **Cardiac disease and arteriosclerosis,** due to the beneficial action of their fatty acids on the arteries.

Preparation and use

❶ **Raw:** raw pine nuts have a very pleasant flavor. A handful of them may be eaten if well chewed. They must be stored in a well-sealed container because they become rancid easily.

❷ They may be used in a **variety** of culinary preparations, as a **condiment** because of their pleasant flavor and high nutritional value.

Araucaria

The Chilean araucaria (*Pinus araucana* L. = *Araucaria araucana* K. Koch), also known as Chilean pine, reaches a height of 60 meters. It provides excellent nuts that form the staple food for the Araucanian people, who are known for their legendary strength and endurance.

Almond

Invigorates the nervous system and reduces cholesterol

Scientific synonym: *Amygdalus communis* L.

Synonym: *Sweet almond.*

French: Amande; ***Spanish:*** Almendra.

Description: *Dicotyledonous seed (formed of two dicotyledons and germ) of the fruit of the almond tree ('Prunus amygdalus' Batsch.), of the botanical family Rosaceae, which grows to 3 to 6 meters in height.*

ALMOND
Composition
per 100 g of raw edible portion

Energy	589 kcal = 2,465 kj
Protein	20.0 g
Carbohydrates	9.50 g
Fiber	10.9 g
Vitamin A	—
Vitamin B_1	0.211 mg
Vitamin B_2	0.779 mg
Niacin	9.33 mg NE
Vitamin B_6	0.113 mg
Folate	58.7 µg
Vitamin B_{12}	—
Vitamin C	0.600 mg
Vitamin E	24.0 mg α-TE
Calcium	266 mg
Phosphorus	520 mg
Magnesium	296 mg
Iron	3.66 mg
Potassium	732 mg
Zinc	2.92 mg
Total Fat	*52.2 g*
Saturated Fat	*4.95 g*
Cholesterol	*—*
Sodium	*11.0 mg*

1% 2% 4% 10% 20% 40% 100% 200% 500%

% Daily Value (based on a 2,000 calorie diet)
provided by 100 g of this food

WELL INTO the winter, when deciduous trees are displaying their skeletal branches, the almond tree is covered with lovely white and pink blossoms, announcing the coming of spring.

Although almonds are considered a nut, the edible portion is the seed of the fruit and not its mesocarp or fleshy portion as in many other edible fruits. The fleshy portion of the almond fruit is formed by the inedible outer greenish shell.

Almonds form part of the human diet from time immemorial. Its nutritive and culinary properties make almonds a very special food, along with the tree that produces them.

PROPERTIES AND INDICATIONS: Almonds are rich in all primary nutrients:

✓ ***Proteins:*** Almond proteins are easily assimilated and offer the *complete* set of essential **amino acids;** surpassed in quality among plant-based foods only by soy proteins (see p. 254). The percentage of proteins present is very high (13.3%) bearing in mind that this is a vegetable product (meat and fish possess between 15 and 20 g of proteins for each 100 g).

✓ ***Fat:*** More than *half* of the weight of the almond is formed of fat, whose composition is displayed in the pie chart on the left side of the preceding page. These are predominantly monounsaturated (34.1%) and polyunsaturated (11%) fatty acids, among which ***linoleic*** acid stands out. Linoleic acid performs important functions in the nervous system.

✓ ***Carbohydrates:*** Almonds contain less of this nutrient than proteins and fat. Therefore, it is well to combine them with bread or sweet dried fruit such as raisins or figs.

✓ ***Vitamins:*** Almonds are relatively rich in vitamins B_1, B_6 and, above all vitamin E. Its vitamin C content is very low (0.6 mg/100 g).

Dried almonds are easier to chew and digest if they are soaked over night. The next morning they will have become tender, and after removing the skin that covers them, they give the sensation of having been freshly picked from the tree.
It is also easier to peel dried almonds by dipping them in boiling water (blanching). Peeled almonds are easier to digest.

✓ ***Minerals:*** Almonds are among the richest plant-based foods in calcium and phosphorous. They also contain significant amounts of magnesium, potassium, and iron.

Preparation and use

❶ **Raw:** Almonds, freshly picked from the tree and shelled can be eaten just as they are. Fresh almonds are more digestible than dried almonds.

❷ **Dried:** Some time after they have been picked, the moisture content is reduced and they become hard. They can be eaten raw, very well chewed, or lightly toasted. In this case, they lose some of their vitamins, but they are easier to chew and digest.

❸ **Almond milk:** This is usually prepared by adding water to almond cream, a light brown paste prepared industrially of almonds and sugar (preferably fructose). It can also be made at home. It is drunk in place of cow's milk.

❹ **Marzipan:** This is a homogeneous mixture of ground almond and sugar. Toledo, Spain, is world-famous for its exquisite marzipan.

❺ **Turrón (nougat):** This is prepared from almonds and honey. It may be hard or soft, depending on whether the almonds are ground or whole. The turrones made in Alicante, Spain, are famous.

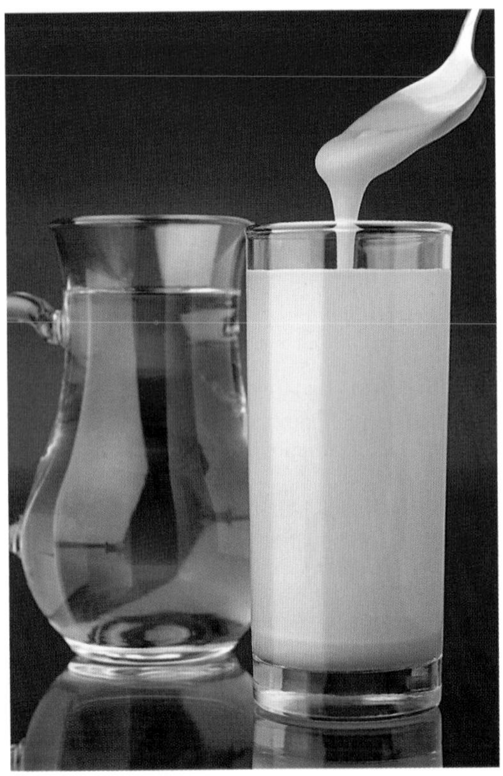

Almond milk is a nutritious and refreshing beverage, highly recommendable for children in periods of growth. It is easily prepared dissolving a couple of spoons of almond cream in a glass of water.

The ***calcium*** content of almonds (247 mg /100 g) is much greater than milk, although, of course, the amount of almonds that are usually eaten is less than that of milk or dairy products.

But it is not only the amount of ***minerals*** that almonds contain, but also how *balanced* their proportion is. Calcium, as well as phosphorous and magnesium in the blood must be in proper balance. Therefore, the closer a food comes to that balance, the better for the body.

It has been demonstrated that a *high* ***phosphorous*** *diet,* such as one that is **meat-based,** *diminishes* the intestinal *absorption* of ***calcium.***[16] Additionally, large quantities of proteins cause calcium loss through the urine.[17]

✓ ***Trace elements:*** As with other nuts, almonds are very rich in zinc, copper, and manganese, trace elements that carry out important corporal functions.

Because of this splendid composition and easy digestion, assuming that they have been *well chewed,* the almond is the *most valued* and *useful* oil-bearing nut, particularly for the following cases:

- **Nervous system disorders,** stress, depression, and mental or physical fatigue: The appropriate balance among calcium, magnesium, and potassium ions, maintain muscle tone and prevents nervous irritability. *Lack* of ***calcium*** in the blood produces **nervousness.**

The almond's proportion of these minerals is very adequate to achieve the function of the nervous system. In addition to its richness in phosphorus and polyunsaturated fatty acids (such as linoleic acid) promotes the production of ***phospholipids,*** essential ingredients of the cellular membranes of the neurons.

Regular **consumption** of almonds strengthens the nerves, tones the muscles, and helps overcome **stress, depression,** and **fatigue. Athletes** and others involved in hard **physical labor** will find in almonds a food that provides a great deal of energy, and which is in addition of being invigorating, and healthful.

- **High cholesterol:** Contrary to what many may believe, a food so rich in fat as the almond not only does not raise cholesterol, but actually lowers it. The same is true of walnuts (see p. 74). This is due to the almond's balanced fatty acids composition, and possibly its richness of vitamin E with its *intense* **antioxidant** *action*.

- **Cardiac disease and arteriosclerosis:** Calcium is directly involved in each heartbeat and in controlling arterial pressure. The almond's richness in calcium, together with its vitamin E content, has a very beneficial effect on cardiovascular health. ***Vitamin E*** is a *power-*

Almond milk

*Almond milk is a **very nutritious** and **delicately flavored** beverage whose richness in proteins and minerals is comparable to **cow's milk.***

Almond milk is particularly suggested in the following cases:

- ***Intolerance** of **cow's milk** generally caused by lactose intolerance (milk sugar).*
- ***Infantile eczema and diarrhea:** Cow's milk is responsible for a large number of cases of infantile allergies manifested by eczema and skin rashes. Dr. Bircher-Benner, a classic of the German school of natural medicine, popularized a treatment based on almond milk for infants and children with cutaneous and atopic allergies, with very good results.*

*In the same manner, **serious infantile diarrhea, intestinal disorders, flatulence,** and other digestive ailments, respond well to almond milk in place of cow's milk.*

- ***Excess blood cholesterol:** Almond milk contains no cholesterol, and is rich in unsaturated fatty acids.*
- ***Infancy and growth periods:** Almond milk is a refreshing beverage, rich in calories and nutrients, much more appropriate for children than most of the soft drinks that they usually drink. It is particularly good for **nervous children** or those with **concentration problems** since its richness in **linoleic acid** and **phosphorous** fosters **mental performance.***
- ***The elderly:** The elderly who have difficulty chewing almonds may drink all the almond milk they wish.*
- ***Lactating mothers:** Almond milk is recommended to lactating mothers because of its effect in increasing milk production.*

ful **antioxidant** that prevents the formation of arteriosclerosis plaque in the arteries.

- **Bone disorders:** Almonds contain high levels of the minerals that form the skeleton (calcium, phosphorous, and magnesium). Additionally, almonds are **alkalizing,** which fosters calcium retention. On the other hand, acidifying foods such as meat, increase calcium loss through the urine.[17] All of this makes almonds an ideal food for those suffering from **osteoporosis** or bone **demineralization.**
- **Diabetes:** because of their small carbohydrate content and the quality of their proteins and fats, diabetics tolerate almonds are very well.
- **Pregnant and lactating women:** Because of their nutritional richness, particularly their content of minerals essential for fetal development, almonds are ideal for pregnant women.

Almonds are proven to **increase milk** secretion in nursing mothers.

4

Foods for the Heart

ATTEMPT to rhythmically open and tightly close your hand once a second. After a few minutes it is possible that you would begin to feel uncomfortable, and it would not be long before you would give up the exercise.

The heart muscle performs a very similar exercise to opening and closing the hand, but it does it *unceasingly,* without stopping, from birth to death, and without tiring, as long as it is maintained in good health.

This capacity of the myocardium, the muscle that forms the heart, to work unceasingly and without rest, is one of the more surprising facts of animal as well as human physiology.

However, in reality the heart **does rest.** It does so in the brief period between beats. During some tenths of a second, the myocardium relaxes and receives blood and nutrients by means of the coronary arteries.

A heart-healthy diet

Eat at least five portions of fresh **fruit** a day.

Eat a minimum of two or three portions of **legumes** a week.

Eat at least one fresh vegetable **salad** a day dressed with olive or seed oil.

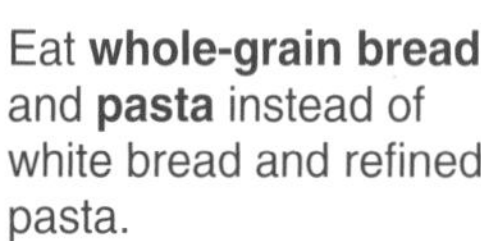

Eat **whole-grain bread** and **pasta** instead of white bread and refined pasta.

Reduce **salt** and **sugar** consumption.

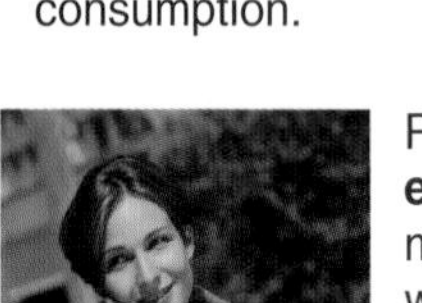

Perform **physical exercise** for at least 40 minutes three times a week.

Avoid **tobacco** and **coffee.**

A diet based on fruits, oil-bearing nuts, vegetables, legumes, and whole grains simply prepared gives the best results for heart attack prevention. **Fruits** and **vegetables** must form the ***base*** of a heart-healthy diet, as numerous studies carried out around the world have demonstrated, particularly the one done at Forvie Site University at Cambridge (UK).[1]

The wine and the heart

Beneficial action on the heart: Various statistical studies show that drinking between ***100 and 200 ml*** (1/2-1 cup) of red wine a day (not white wine) lowers the risk of death from heart attack.[2, 3, 4] This effect *only* seems to involve ***men*** over the ***age of 50.***

These same statistics report that when more than this amount of wine (***200 ml*** or about 1 cup of wine or 20 g of pure alcohol) is ***exceeded,*** the **mortality rate** due to **cardiovascular** disease ***increases,*** and ***many other disorders*** are fostered.[5]

The possible beneficial effect of red wine has been attributed to *Phenolic* ***flavonoids:*** these substances come from the grape and its skin, which give red wine its color.[3] They act to inhibit the oxidation of lipoproteins, and by so doing, prevent cholesterol deposits within the arteries known as **arteriosclerosis.**[6] **Fruit** in general, and **grapes** in *particular,* are the *best* sources of ***flavonoids.***

In other words, whatever small benefit may come from wine is from the grape. Eating **grapes** themselves or drinking **grape juice** is *much more* ***healthful*** for the heart and the entire body.

What should one eat after a heart attack?

After suffering a heart attack a diet rich in fruits and vegetables is highly recommended. Their **antioxidant** action reduces necrosis (cellular death) in the heart muscle.[7]

The **arteriosclerosis** that causes heart attack can also be reversed. An investigation carried out in California (USA) demonstrates that after a year of a heart-healthy diet and lifestyle, as described on this page, there is a 10% reduction of stenosis (narrowing) of coronary arteries.[4]

ANGINA PECTORIS

Definition

This consists of spasms or reversible narrowing of the **coronary arteries.** These arteries are responsible for providing blood flow to the heart muscle, thus allowing it to beat.

Angina pectoris or angor pectoris manifests through intense, oppressive pain on the left side of the thorax, radiating down the left arm. It is generally experienced after some physical effort, intense emotion, or stressful situation.

Contrary to an infarction, angina is ***reversible*** and usually does not leave permanent heart damage.

Diet and risk factors

Diet has a *great* ***influence*** on the condition and function of the **coronary arteries.**

Risk factors for angina are:

- **Arteriosclerosis** (narrowing and hardening) of the coronary arteries. A diet that is *poor* in **plant-based** foods and *rich* in **saturated fats** is one of its primary causes along with **tobacco** and **lack of physical exercise.**
- **Tendency to spasms** or contractions of the smooth (involuntary) muscles, such as those that form the wall of the arteries. A *deficiency* of ***magnesium*** and other nutrients fosters these spasms.

Increase

GRAPES
WALNUT
ONION
WHOLE GRAINS
BARLEY
RYE
POTATO
PEACH
STRAWBERRY
SQUASH
ZUCCHINI
CASHEW
MANGO
NON-ALCOHOLIC WINE

Reduce or eliminate

SATURATED FAT
SODIUM

Onions

Onion prevents arteriosclerosis, improves the fluidity of the blood and improves blood flow through the coronary arteries.

MYOCARDIAL INFARCTION

Definition

This is produced as a consequence of a **complete obstruction** of a **coronary artery** or one of its branches. It produces ***irreversible*** damage to the heart muscle, consisting of necrosis or tissue death in that area of the heart.

Causes

Coronary artery obstruction is produced by a combination of these ***mechanisms:***

- **Arteriosclerosis,** progressive narrowing and hardening of the artery.
- **Thrombosis,** or the formation of a blood clot in the interior of the narrowed artery, closing the blood flow completely.

Diet

Diet is ***very important*** in relation to heart attack for two reasons:

- Certain foods serve a clearly ***preventive*** role, while others ***encourage*** it.
- A correct diet ***after*** a heart attack can ***contribute*** *decisively* to **rehabilitation** and the **prevention** of new crises.

Increase

FRUIT
LEGUMES
VEGETABLES
GRAPE
WALNUT
SOY
CHICKPEA
GARDEN PEA
ARTICHOKE
STRAWBERRY
SQUASH
PEACH
MANGO
MACADAMIA
POTATO
WHEAT BRAN
OLIVE OIL
FISH
ANTIOXIDANTS
VITAMIN A
FLAVONOIDS
COENZYME Q10
FIBER

Reduce or eliminate

MEAT
IRON
SATURATED FAT
CHOLESTEROL
SAUSAGES
HAM
TRANS FATTY ACIDS
MARGARINE
BUTTER
FRIED FOODS
MILK
DAIRY PRODUCTS
ALCOHOLIC BEVERAGES
WHITE SUGAR
SODIUM

Squash

ARRHYTHMIA

Definition

This is an alteration in the heartbeat rhythm, which is usually perceived as a **palpitation.** If this alteration is **serious,** it can reduce the heart's ability to efficiently pump blood throughout the tissues of the body, leading to **heart failure** and in some cases to cardiac arrest.

Causes

Causes of arrhythmia are varied, and at times unknown. However, there are various factors that ***promote*** it:

- **Diet:** certain nutrients help avoid it; others promote it.
- **Food allergies:** These can be cause of arrhythmia due to the toxic substances released as a result of the allergic reaction.
- **Toxins:** Alcoholic beverages, coffee, and tobacco can cause more or less serious arrhythmia.
- **Hormonal factors:** Hyperactive function of the thyroid gland.

Increase

CALCIUM
MAGNESIUM
POTASSIUM
OILS
COENZYME Q_{10}

Reduce or eliminate

STIMULANT BEVERAGES
ALCOHOLIC BEVERAGES
SATURATED FAT

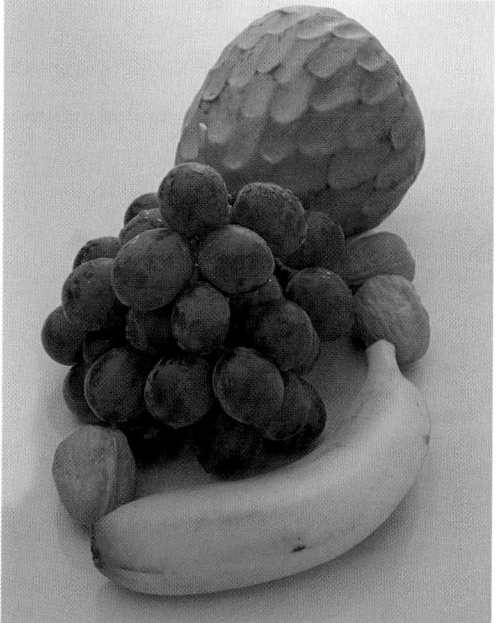

CARDIAC FAILURE

Definition

This disease is a consequence of the inability of the heart to pump the necessary volume of blood.

Causes

Among the **causes** leading to heart failure, some are diet-related:

- **Weakened heart** due to ***lack*** of **nutrients** needed to function properly, such as ***vitamin*** B_1 or certain minerals (***calcium, magnesium,*** and ***potassium,*** particularly).
- **Excess fluids** in the body, generally brought about by excess **sodium** or salt consumption, or poor **kidney** function. This means greater blood volume, requiring more effort by the heart, fatiguing it.

Treatment

Treatment for cardiac failure requires a nourishing and invigorating diet to the heart, in addition to a lower sodium/salt intake. Diuretic foods recommended in cases of low urine volume are also of value.

Increase

WALNUT
CHERIMOYA
GARDEN PEA
BROCCOLI
CHERRY
GRAPEFRUIT
COENZYME Q_{10}

Reduce or eliminate

SODIUM
ALCOHOLIC BEVERAGES
(INCLUDING BEER)

Grapefruit

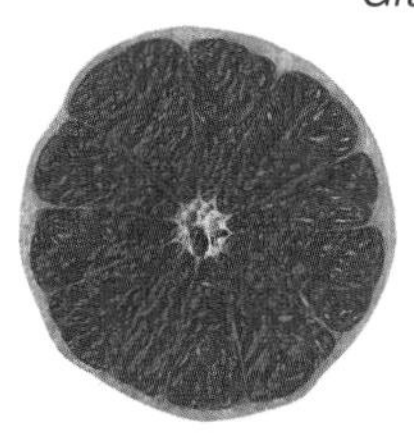

All fruits and fresh greens exert a preventive action on heart ailments. Oleaginous nuts, legumes, and wholemeal grains are also healthy for the heart.
Among all of them, custard apples, grapes, bananas, and walnuts stand out, as presented in this chapter.

Cherimoya

Strengthens the heart

Synonyms: *Custard apple, Anona, Sherbet-fruit.*

French: *Chérimole;* ***Spanish***: *Chirimoya, Anona chirimoya.*

Description: *The cherimoya is the fruit of the Cherimoya tree ('Anona cherimola' Mill.), a tree of the botanical family Annonaceae that reaches a height of 8 meters. The fruit is heart-shaped and can weigh from 100 g to over a kilo. It is covered with a green rind with a scalelike design reminiscent of a reptile. The pulp contains numerous black seeds that are easily removed.*

CHERIMOYA
Composition
per 100 g of raw edible portion

Energy	94.0 kcal = 394 kj
Protein	1.30 g
Carbohydrates	21.6 g
Fiber	2.40 g
Vitamin A	1.00 µg RE
Vitamin B_1	0.100 mg
Vitamin B_2	0.110 mg
Niacin	1.30 mg NE
Vitamin B_6	0.200 mg
Folate	14.0 µg
Vitamin B_{12}	—
Vitamin C	9.00 mg
Vitamin E	—
Calcium	23.0 mg
Phosphorus	40.0 mg
Magnesium	—
Iron	0.500 mg
Potassium	264 mg
Zinc	—
Total Fat	*0.400 g*
Saturated Fat	—
Cholesterol	—
Sodium	*5.00 mg*

1% 2% 4% 10% 20% 40% 100%

% Daily Value (based on a 2,000 calorie diet)
provided by 100 g of this food

IT IS NOT EASY to describe the flavor of the cherimoya to one who has not experienced it. For some it is reminiscent of the strawberry, for others it tastes like pineapple, for still others it is like a pear or a banana.

The cherimoya is typical of the Andean region. Its name is derived from the Quechua word *chirimuya*. Even though it is a tropical fruit, it grows at high elevations. Natives of the Andean Altiplano have a saying that although the cherimoya cannot tolerate snow, it likes to see it in the mountains.

PROPERTIES AND INDICATIONS: The cherimoya stands out for its ***sugar*** content (more than 21%). Among these, fructose and saccharose predominate. Its ***protein*** and ***fat*** content is *very low*.

Among the vitamins present in the cherimoya, those of the ***B group*** are the *most prominent:* B_1 or thiamin, B_2 or riboflavin, B_6 or pyridoxine, and niacin. *No other* **fresh fruit** of equal weight provides as *many* ***B group vitamins*** as the cherimoya.

Where ***minerals*** are concerned, the cherimoya's richness in ***calcium, phosphorous, iron,*** and ***potassium*** is outstanding. Only oranges, loquats, dates, and raspberries have more ***calcium.***

Its ***energy content*** of 94 calories per 100 g is *considerable*, bearing in mind that this is a fresh fruit. Cherimoyas are recommended for all ages, *particularly* for **adolescents. Athletes** and **students** also will gain energy together with the vitamins and minerals appropriate to their activities.

The diet therapeutic applications of cherimoyas are:

- **Heart failure:** the cherimoya provides a significant amount of energy in the form of sugars, together with ***B group vitamins*** that the body needs to take advantage of this energy. The B group vitamins present in the cherimoya act as *catalysts* or facilitators of the combustion of ***carbohydrates,*** and also ***fatty acids,*** which constitute the two most important energy sources for the heart's cells.

The most common causes of **heart failure** or "tired heart" are lesions in the heart valves, arterial hypertension, or narrowing of the coronary arteries. Lack of B group vitamins can also cause or aggravate heart failure.

Additionally, cherimoyas exhibit these benefits: They contain vegetable ***fiber,*** are **diuretic,** *rich* in ***potassium,*** and *very low* in ***sodium*** and ***fat,*** which meets the requisites of a **heart-healthy food.** As if this were not enough, cherimoyas contain a certain amount of ***calcium,*** a necessary mineral to regulate the heartbeat.

- **Stomach ailments:** the cherimoya's creamy, smooth pulp, together with its antacid effect, is beneficial to the stomach. It is highly recommended in cases of **gastritis** and gastroduodenal **ulcer.**

- **Obesity:** In spite of their relatively high carbohydrate content, cherimoyas are quite effective in weight-loss treatments. This is because of their satiating effect. A 300 g cherimoya provides less than 300 calories, but is as filling and satisfying as a plate of food or a sandwich, which may contain more calories and be higher in fat.

In addition to **satisfying** the appetite, cherimoyas are naturally **invigorating** because of their high nutrient content. This allows a reduction in calories without an accompanying feeling of faintness.

From harvest until they reach their optimal ripeness usually takes 5 or 6 days.

Preparation and use

❶ **Fresh:** This is how cherimoyas are normally eaten. In this manner, one enjoys their exquisite flavor and benefits from their therapeutic properties to the fullest extent.

❷ **Shakes:** Cherimoyas combine very well with orange juice or milk. The pulp must be appropriately strained to remove the seeds and create a puree (see p. 71).

The Annonaceae family

The genus "Annona," with more than 120 species, is the most important of this family of Central American tropical fruits. Of these 120 species about 20 are cultivated for their fruit, but only four are of dietary importance. The terms "annon" or "annona" are commonly used to refer to any of the fruits in this family. The composition and properties of these fruits are very similar to the cherimoya. Variations among them are primarily in shape and flavor.

Cherimoyas

Cherimoya (see p. 68)

Annona cherimola Mill.

This is the most economically important of the annonas, and its **medicinal effects** are the *most* ***proven.*** It is for this reason that it is analyzed on these pages. The smooth creaminess of its pulp has helped cherimoya to conquer markets and palates throughout the world.

Sugar apple

Annona squamosa L.

Sugar apple

These are grown primarily in the Far East. They are heart-shaped with very pronounced scales on their rind. Their pulp is creamy like the cherimoya, but somewhat sweeter and with a flavor reminiscent of cinnamon. They are used in deserts, ice cream, and beverages.

Soursop

Soursop

Annona muricata L.

This is the ***largest*** of the annonas, reaching up to two kilos in weight. It is kidney-shaped and is covered with soft spines. Its pulp tends to be quite tart and is not usually eaten fresh, but rather in juices, frozen desserts, and preserves.

The soursop is **astringent, cholagogic** (promotes bile discharge), and **promotes digestion.** It is recommended in cases of **constipation, obesity, hypertension, coronary disease,** and **diabetes.**

Cherimoya preparation

and other annonas

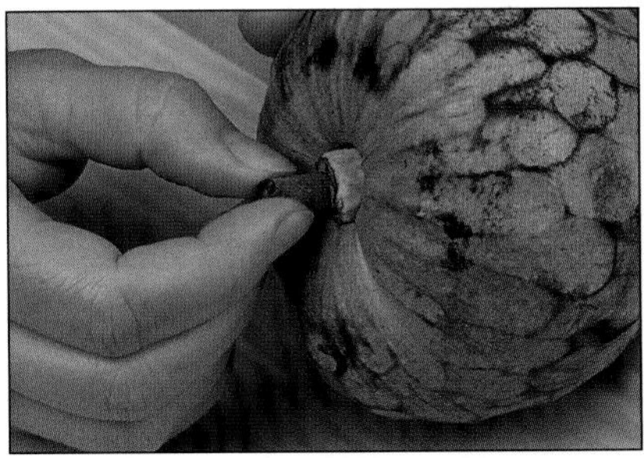

1. **Remove the stem** by pulling gently. These are easily removed from ripe fruit.

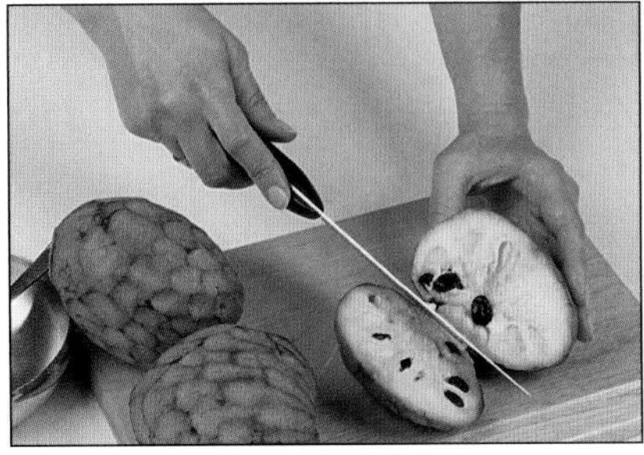

2. **Cut the fruit** in half with a knife.

3. Remove the pulp with a spoon and eat it just as it is or strain it into a puree (step 4).

4. Strain the pulp to prepare a **puree** for use in beverages, frozen desserts, or shakes.

It is possible to know when a cherimoya is ripe: just when it yields slightly to the touch. All annonas combine well with orange or lime. Beverages based on annona pulp blended with orange or lime juice are very refreshing and delicious. They are a healthful and delicious beverage for those suffering heart disorders.

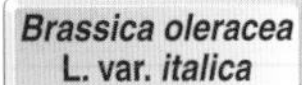

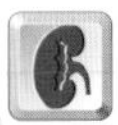

Broccoli

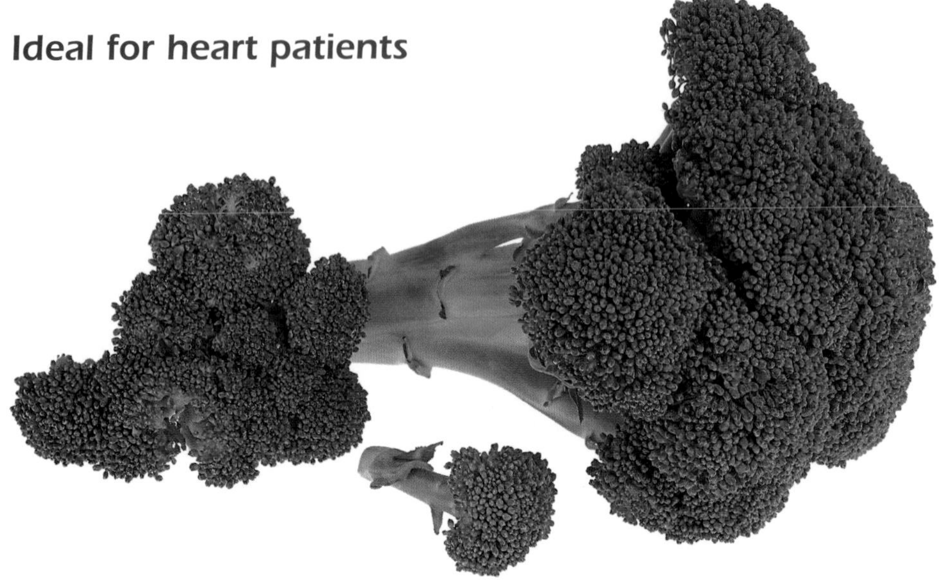

BROCCOLI Composition
per 100 g of raw edible portion

Energy	28.0 kcal = 116 kj
Protein	2.98 g
Carbohydrates	2.24 g
Fiber	3.00 g
Vitamin A	154 µg RE
Vitamin B_1	0.065 mg
Vitamin B_2	0.119 mg
Niacin	1.12 mg NE
Vitamin B_6	0.159 mg
Folate	71.0 µg
Vitamin B_{12}	—
Vitamin C	93.2 mg
Vitamin E	1.66 mg α-TE
Calcium	48.0 mg
Phosphorus	66.0 mg
Magnesium	25.0 mg
Iron	0.880 mg
Potassium	325 mg
Zinc	0.400 mg
Total Fat	*0.350 g*
Saturated Fat	*0.054 g*
Cholesterol	—
Sodium	*27.0 mg*

1% 2% 4% 10% 20% 40% 100% 200% 500%

% Daily Value (based on a 2,000 calorie diet) provided by 100 g of this food

Synonyms: *Asparagus broccoli, Calabrese.*

French: *Brocoli;* ***Spanish:*** *Brécol, Bróculi.*

Description: *This is the inflorescence and stalks of the broccoli ('Brassica oleracea' L. var. 'italica'), a herbaceous plant of the botanical family Cruciferae that constitutes a variant of the cauliflower. In contrast to the cauliflower, the inflorescences of broccoli are formed of larger, less tightly packed flowers. Their color varies from green to violet.*

BROCCOLI CULTIVATION has experienced a significant increase in recent years in Europe as well as in America. More broccoli and less cauliflower is being eaten (see p. 154), possibly because broccoli produces less flatulence than cauliflower and for many it has a better flavor.

PROPERTIES AND INDICATIONS: Among all of the cabbages belonging to the Crucifer family, broccoli stands out as among the *richest* in ***proteins,*** calcium, ***provitamin A*** (beta-carotene), and ***vitamin C.*** It is also *rich* in ***potassium*** and *low* in ***sodium.*** It contains

All vegetables and greens, especially those of the 'Cruciferae family', provide phytochemical elements that protect against cardiovascular disease and cancer.

anticarcinogenic sulfurated ***phytochemicals***, as do all Crucifers. These are its most prominent diet therapeutic applications:

Preparation and use

❶ **Cooked** in a variety of ways similar to cauliflower. It should be boiled as little as possible to avoid the loss of its nutritional properties.

❷ Its **tender stalks** may be eaten raw or lightly steamed or boiled **in salads.** They are very flavorful, reminiscent of asparagus.

- **Coronary disease:** Because of its low calorie content, its paucity of fats, and above all its *optimal **sodium/potassium** balance,* broccoli is a very appropriate food for those suffering **heart failure** at any level. It promotes the elimination of excess liquid retained in the tissues (edema), operating as a decongestive to the circulatory system and the heart.
- **Obesity and diabetes:** Because it is very low in calories and sugars, and because it produces a certain feeling of satiety, it should be included in the diets of the obese and diabetics.
- **Cancer:** Its *high levels* of ***beta-carotene*** (provitamin A) and ***phytochemicals*** make broccoli, along with other Crucifers, a powerful **anticarcinogenic** food, whose effectiveness has been proven in a wide variety of scientific investigations.[9, 10, 11, 12]

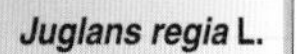

Walnut

Provides energy to the heart

Walnuts are a highly concentrated food containing high levels of essential fatty acids, vitamin B_6 and trace elements such as zinc, copper, and manganese.

WALNUT
Composition
per 100 g of raw edible portion

Energy	642 kcal = 2,686 kj
Protein	14.3 g
Carbohydrates	13.5 g
Fiber	4.80 g
Vitamin A	12.0 µg RE
Vitamin B_1	0.382 mg
Vitamin B_2	0.148 mg
Niacin	4.19 mg NE
Vitamin B_6	0.558 mg
Folate	66.0 µg
Vitamin B_{12}	—
Vitamin C	3.20 mg
Vitamin E	2.62 mg α-TE
Calcium	94.0 mg
Phosphorus	317 mg
Magnesium	169 mg
Iron	2.44 mg
Potassium	502 mg
Zinc	2.73 mg
Total Fat	*61.9 g*
Saturated Fat	*5.59 g*
Cholesterol	—
Sodium	*10.0 mg*

1% 2% 4% 10% 20% 40% 100%

% Daily Value (based on a 2,000 calorie diet) provided by 100 g of this food

Synonyms: *Persian walnut, Heartnut.*

French: *Noix;* ***Spanish:*** *Nuez.*

Description: *the walnut is the seed of the fruit of the walnut tree ('Juglans regia' L.), a tree of the botanical family Juglandaceae that grows to a height of 20 meters. The fruit is a drupe, whose fleshy portion (pericarp and mesocarp) is greenish; the seed or endocarp is woody and hard, but it contains a very nutritious dicotyledonous seed: the walnut.*

EVEN THOUGH it is believed that the walnut originated in Central Asia, it has adapted very well to the countries surrounding the Mediterranean. It may be said that for millennia the walnut has formed part of the **Mediterranean diet,** which is praised for its beneficial effects on health in general and on the heart in particular.

PROPERTIES AND INDICATIONS: The walnut is, together with other oil-bearing nuts, one of the most *concentrated* food sources of nutrients provided by nature. Together with the Brazil nut (see p. 52), it is the nut with the *highest* caloric content (642 kcal/100 g), due to its high fat content (oil). These are the characteristics of the walnut's nutrients:

✓ **Fats:** These make up three-fifths of the weight of the nut (61.9%), superior to almonds, hazelnuts, and peanuts (see pp. 58, 238, 320). These fats are formed *primarily* of ***unsaturated fatty acids,*** with a *preponderance* of ***polyunsaturated,*** in addition to ***lecithin.*** Among the two fatty acids found in walnuts, these two stand out:

- ***Linoleic*** acid (31.8%), with 18 carbon atoms and two double bonds. This is an essential fatty acid that the body cannot be without, particularly during infancy. It *lowers* **cholesterol** level and is involved in the formation of **nerve** tissue and in the production of **antibodies.**
- ***Linolenic*** acid (6.8%), with 18 carbon atoms and three double bonds. This is an ***Omega-3*** series fatty acid, the same as those found in fish. It reduces cholesterol and triglyceride levels in the blood, prevents the formation of clots in the blood vessels, and stops inflammatory processes.

  The walnut is one of the best vegetable sources of linolenic acid, together with wheat germ, primrose, and canola.

✓ ***Carbohydrates:*** The walnut is the *lowest* of any oil-bearing nut in this nutrient (13.5%). From a chemical point of view these are ***oligosaccharides (dextrins)*** and a small amount of sugars ***(saccharose*** and ***dextrose).*** Because of this, walnuts are well tolerated by **diabetics.**

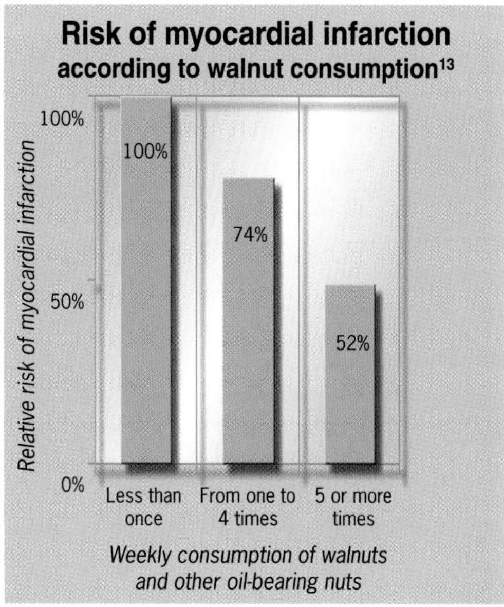

The risk of myocardial infarction diminishes as the consumption of walnuts and other oil-bearing nuts increases. Eating whole-grain bread instead of white bread also protects the heart and reduces the risk of heart attack.

✓ ***Proteins:*** Walnuts contain up to 14.3% of high quality protein, more than peanuts, and about the same as almonds. They are somewhat deficient in the essential amino acid me-

Preparation and use

❶ **Raw and whole:** Raw walnuts must be chewed very well. If they are indigestible, elimination of the thin yellow skin may help.

❷ **Ground:** Ground walnuts are easily assimilated by those with chewing difficulty.

❸ **Cooked:** A great variety of delicious vegetarian dishes can be made from walnuts including meat analogues, "meat" balls, and many others.

❹ **Walnut oil:** This is very flavorful and nutritious, but is seldom available commercially because it becomes rancid very easily.

Walnuts against heart attack

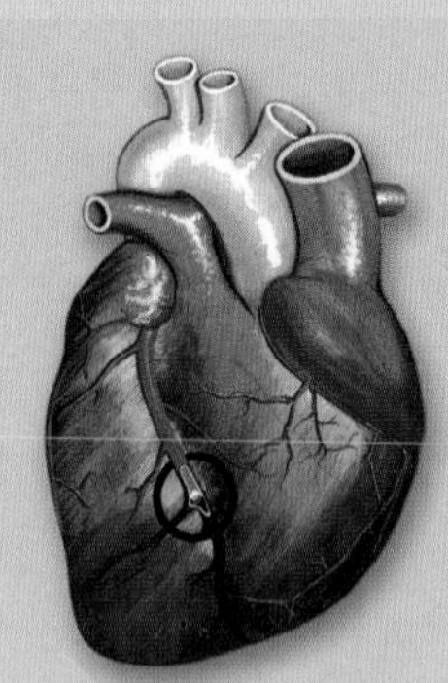

A study conducted in California known as the Adventist Health Study, analyzed the dietary habits of more than 25,000 Seventh-day Adventist Christians, universally recognized for their healthy lifestyle.

The results showed that heart attack risk among Adventists is considerably lower than that of the general population.

Additionally, those that ate walnuts five or more times a week, had an even lower risk of heart attack: approximately half of the Adventists in the study ate walnuts at least once a week.[13]

thionine, which is solved by *combining* them with whole **grains** (wheat, oats, rice, etc.), which are very rich in ***methionine.***

The mixture of nuts and grains is doubly beneficial because grains are deficient in ***lysine*** and ***threonine,*** two other essential amino acids that walnuts contain in abundance. Because of this, mixing **walnuts and grains** (bread, for example) provides *complete* ***proteins*** that are equal or superior to those of meat.

✓ ***Vitamins:*** Walnuts are a good source of vitamins B_1, B_2, B_3 (niacin), and particularly B_6. Vitamin B_1 or ***thiamin*** is necessary for the function of the heart as well as the stability of the nervous system. They are relatively poor in vitamins A and C.

Walnuts are one of the *richest* sources of ***vitamin B_6,*** also known as pyridoxine. ***Vitamin B_6*** is involved in proper **brain** function as well as **red blood** cell production.

✓ ***Minerals:*** Walnuts are *rich* in ***phosphorous*** and ***potassium,*** while they are *low* in ***sodium,*** which promotes cardiovascular health. They also contain a significant amount of ***iron*** (2.44 mg/100 g), ***magnesium,*** and ***calcium,*** although almonds and hazelnuts are richer in calcium.

Walnuts, along with other nuts, are one of the *best sources* of ***TRACE ELEMENTS.***

- ***Zinc:*** Walnuts contain 2,730 µg (=2.73 mg) of zinc per 100 g, an amount superior to all meats and fish, except liver. Zinc *deficiency* leads to a *weakening* of the **immune system** and *slow* **wound** healing.
- ***Copper:*** Walnuts contain 1,390 µg (=1.39 mg) of copper per 100 g, greater than most plant-based and animal-based foods. This trace element *facilitates* the *absorption* of ***iron*** in the intestine and helps *prevent* **anemia.**
- ***Manganese:*** Walnuts contain 2,900 µg (=2.9 mg) of this trace element per 100 g, surpassed only by hazelnuts, soy, beans, and whole grains. Meat, fish, eggs, and milk are poor in manganese, which is necessary for reproductive functions. Manganese *deficiency* produces **sterility** in both sexes.

With this rich and varied nutritional composition, walnuts have the following therapeutic applications:

• **Coronary disease:** Walnuts are an excellent food for those suffering from coronary disease for three reasons:

1st Because of their *richness* in ***fatty acids:*** these constitute the primary *energy* source for the cells of the **heart,** in contrast to other cells, neurons among others, which use glucose as their principal fuel.

2nd Because of its ***vitamin*** B_1 content, which, in spite of being moderate, contributes sufficiently to adequate muscle function, including the heart.

3rd They *inhibit* obstructive buildup of **cholesterol** on artery walls by reducing blood cholesterol levels. The less cholesterol there is in the blood, the *lower* the *risk* of **arteriosclerosis** (obstruction of the arteries), and **blood circulation** is *improved*.

Walnuts are heart-friendly for these three reasons, and should be *included regularly* in the diets of those suffering from **heart failure** for any reason, **angina,** or **heart attack** *risk*. Their consumption is particularly recommended for those who have suffered a myocardial infarction and are in rehabilitation.

• **Elevated cholesterol:** Up until not long ago the consumption of oil-bearing nuts, and walnuts in particular, was discouraged for those with elevated cholesterol levels. However, investigations conducted by Dr. Joan Sabaté at Loma Linda University (California), demonstrate[13] that daily consumption of 80 g of walnuts for two months, reduces the level of LDL (harmful cholesterol) by 16%.

• **Disorders of the nervous system:** Walnuts are highly recommended for neurological disorders in general because of their *richness* in ***essential fatty acids*** directly involved in the metabolism of the neurons, and in ***lecithin, phosphorous,*** and ***vitamin*** B_6.

Because they improve mental performance and restore tone and balance to the nervous system, they should form a part of the diets of **students and knowledge workers.** Those suffering from **irritability, depression, stress,** or **nervous exhaustion** should eat at least a good handful of walnuts a day, preferably at breakfast.

• **Sexual disorders and sterility:** Walnut consumption has a positive effect on sexual performance: it *increases* a ***man's*** **potency** and *improves* a ***woman's*** **sexual response.**

It cannot be said that walnuts are an aphrodisiac in the strict sense of the word since walnuts do not really increase sexual desire, but they do facilitate the complex physiological reactions produced during sexual activity in both men and women.

• **Diabetes:** Because of their low carbohydrate content and high nutritional value, walnuts are one of the foods best tolerated by diabetics.

Walnuts must replace other foods rich in calories (margarine, butter, sausage) and not supplement them in order to reduce cholesterol and avoid obesity.

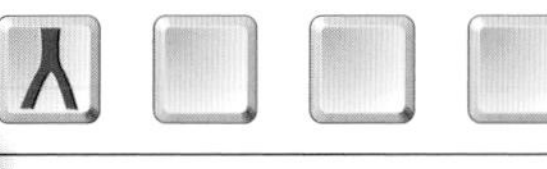

Macadamia

A heart-friendly nut

Scientific synonym: *Macadamia ternifolia* F. v. Muell.

Synonyms: *Macadamia nut, Australian nut, Queensland nut.*

French: *Noix de Queensland;* ***Spanish:*** *Macadamia.*

Description: *These are the seed of the fruit of the macadamia tree, which is an evergreen of the botanical family Proteaceae that grows to a height of 9 meters.*

MACADAMIA NUT
Composition
per 100 g of raw edible portion

Energy	702 kcal = 2,936 kj
Protein	8.30 g
Carbohydrates	4.43 g
Fiber	9.30 g
Vitamin A	—
Vitamin B_1	0.350 mg
Vitamin B_2	0.110 mg
Niacin	5.69 mg NE
Vitamin B_6	0.196 mg
Folate	15.7 µg
Vitamin B_{12}	—
Vitamin C	—
Vitamin E	0.410 mg α-TE
Calcium	70.0 mg
Phosphorus	136 mg
Magnesium	116 mg
Iron	2.41 mg
Potassium	368 mg
Zinc	1.71 mg
Total Fat	*73.7 g*
Saturated Fat	*11.0 g*
Cholesterol	—
Sodium	*5.00 mg*

1% 2% 4% 10% 20% 40% 100% 200% 500%

% Daily Value (based on a 2,000 calorie diet)
provided by 100 g of this food

THE MACADAMIA TREE was discovered and identified in Australia in the mid-19th century. Among the ten known species only one is of dietary importance because of the quality and properties of its nuts.

Its tough, thick shell encloses a cream-colored oil-rich nut somewhat larger than a hazelnut.

PROPERTIES AND INDICATIONS: The seeds of the macadamia fruit, known as macadamia nuts, contain up to 73.7% ***fat.*** Its ***proteins*** (8.3%) are quite complete, although lacking in ***methionine***[14] (this is easily compensated by combining them with whole grains).

Cholesterol alone is not enough to harm the arteries

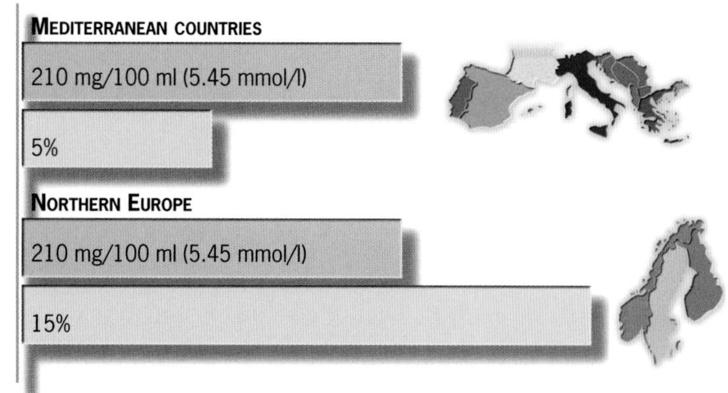

The so-called "Seven Countries Study" was conducted by following 12,467 males between the ages of 40 and 59 years in seven countries to determine the relationship between blood cholesterol level and coronary disease mortality.[15]

This broad international study found:

- *The higher the blood cholesterol level, the greater the risk of arteriosclerosis and coronary disease.*
- *With the same cholesterol level, heart attack risk is much higher among inhabitants of countries that typically eat fewer fruits and vegetables, such as Scandinavians, and lower among those that follow a Mediterranean diet as is done in Southern European countries.*

Preparation and use

❶ **Raw:** Macadamias must be ripe to be eaten raw, and they must be well chewed. Some have a bitter taste due to the presence of cyanogenetic glucosides similar to those in bitter almonds.

❷ **Toasted:** When toasted, macadamias are very tasty and easier to digest. They usually contain added salt, which is not advised for those suffering from coronary disease.

❸ **Macadamia oil:** Excellent for frying and desserts.

Macadamia nuts are one of the most oil-rich of the oil-bearing nuts.

Macadamias are also a good source of calcium, phosphorous, iron, vitamins B_1 and B_2, and niacin.[14] They also provide antioxidant polyphenolic flavonoids that prevent arteriosclerosis.[15]

The **OIL** extracted from macadamias is similar in composition to olive oil. It is formed of 58.2% monounsaturated fatty acids,[16] and has *no* ***trans fatty acids,*** which, according to recent studies, have a negative effect on the heart. This oil is *excellent* for **frying** because of its heat stability and very high evaporation point (198°C).

Macadamias and their oil are heart-friendly foods because of the characteristics of their fats, which *lower* **cholesterol** and *improve* blood **circulation** through the **coronary** arteries.

Banana

Very rich in potassium

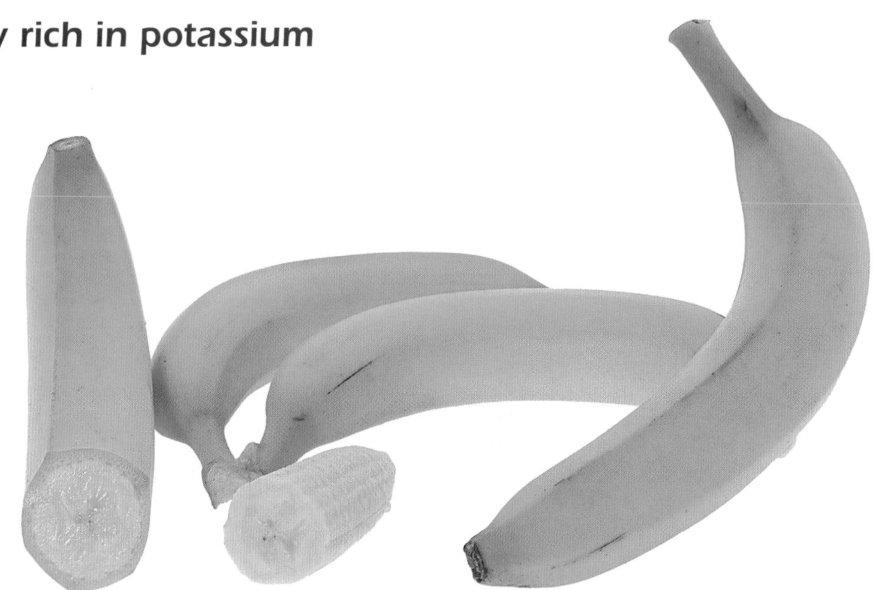

BANANA Composition
per 100 g of raw edible portion

Energy	92.0 kcal = 384 kj
Protein	1.03 g
Carbohydrates	21.0 g
Fiber	2.40 g
Vitamin A	8.00 µg RE
Vitamin B_1	0.045 mg
Vitamin B_2	0.100 mg
Niacin	0.740 mg NE
Vitamin B_6	0.578 mg
Folate	19.1 µg
Vitamin B_{12}	—
Vitamin C	9.10 mg
Vitamin E	0.270 mg α-TE
Calcium	6.00 mg
Phosphorus	20.0 mg
Magnesium	29.0 mg
Iron	0.310 mg
Potassium	396 mg
Zinc	0.160 mg
Total Fat	*0.480 g*
Saturated Fat	*0.185 g*
Cholesterol	—
Sodium	*1.00 mg*

1% 2% 4% 10% 20% 40% 100%

% Daily Value (based on a 2,000 calorie diet)
provided by 100 g of this food

French: *Banane;* ***Spanish:*** *Plátano, banana.*

Description: *This is the aggregate fruit of the banana tree ('Musa x paradisiaca' L. var. 'sapientum'), a hybrid species formed from two others. It is a bush of the botanical family Musaceae that reaches a height of three to five meters.*
The bananas grow in bunches that may weigh as much as 50 kg and contain as many as 300 pieces.

AFTER THE APPLE, the banana is the most consumed fruit in the world. The fact that it is on tables on the five continents may be due to its ease of use: a banana can be eaten anywhere without need for a napkin or a knife. It even comes wrapped in its own natural hygienic "packaging"—its peel—that protects it from contamination.

But more than anything, the banana is one of the *most* **nutritious and medicinal** fruits that exist.

PROPERTIES AND INDICATIONS: ***Carbohydrates*** are prominent in the banana's composition (up to 21%). *Unripe* bananas are made up primarily of ***starch.*** As they ripen, this starch converts to sugars such as ***saccharose, glucose,*** and ***fructose.*** About 1% starch remains in a ripe banana, which poses no difficulty if it is well chewed.

However, unripe or green bananas contain significant amounts of starch that is difficult to digest and can cause flatulence (intestinal gas) and dyspepsia (indigestion).[17]

Bananas contain a small amount of ***proteins*** (1%) and very little fat (less than 0.5%).

Bananas *stand out* for their ***vitamin B6*** content. About three medium-sized bananas provide the recommended daily allowance of this vitamin for an adult male. Bananas also contain significant amounts of ***vitamins C, B1, B2,*** and ***E,*** as well as ***folates.***

Bananas are also quite rich in ***minerals,*** *prominent* among which are ***potassium, magnesium,*** and ***iron.*** Their rich potassium content makes them one of the *best* fresh fruit sources of this mineral: only the avocado and the date (see pp. 112, 148) surpass the banana in ***potassium.***

Both types of ***vegetable fiber,*** soluble and insoluble, are present in significant amounts in bananas, as fruit is concerned: 2.4 g/100 g. This fiber contributes to the banana's hypolipidemic (lipid and cholesterol-lowering)[18] and intestinal-soothing effects.

Bananas contain small amounts of ***SEROTONIN.*** This substance, which is derived from the amino acid tryptophan, performs various functions within the nervous system such as arterial vasodilation, inhibition of pain in the spinal cord, and sedation of the nerves. The effect on the body of the small amounts of serotonin found in bananas is still being studied.

The banana's medicinal applications are as follows:

The digestion of the banana begins in the mouth. Its starch content is difficult to digest, especially when the banana is unripe, and can produce flatulence.
Proper digestion is facilitated by chewing the banana well, mixing it with saliva.

Preparation and use

❶ **Raw:** This is the ***ideal*** way to consume it. We must bear in mind that all bananas consumed in non-producing countries are collected unripe and artificially ripened in chambers. This process causes them to have fewer sugars and vitamins than those ripened on the tree.

❷ **Cooked** in different ways: *Most **vitamins*** are *lost* this way, although carbohydrates, minerals, and other nutrients remain. The variety most often cooked is **plantain,** which is very rich in starch.

• **Coronary disease:** Bananas are an ***ideal*** fruit for those suffering from coronary disease (angina, myocardial infarction, arrhythmia, heart failure) or circulatory system disorders (arterial hypertension, arteriosclerosis) because of its exceptional composition:

- ***Their richness in potassium and the absence of sodium:*** With 396 mg of potassium and 1 g of sodium per 100 g of edible portion, bananas have the *highest* ***potassium/sodium quotient*** of any fruit or vegetable (meat, fish, and dairy products have much less potassium and more sodium). A diet rich in potassium and low in sodium prevents arterial hypertension,[19] arrhythmia, stroke,[20] and even cancer.[21]
- The presence of significant amounts of ***B*** group ***vitamins,*** necessary for energy production within the heart muscle, as well as ***magnesium,*** which *inhibits* the progress of **arteriosclerosis** and *prevents* **heart attack.**
- Abundant ***vegetable fiber*** that lowers **cholesterol** level.
- Small amounts of ***serotonin*** acting as a **vasodilator.**

• **Intestinal disorders:** Bananas alone or with **apples** (see p. 216) are effective in relieving **diarrhea** in children as well as in adults. They are also effective for those suffering from **celiac** disease (poor intestinal absorption accompanied by diarrhea and undernourishment produced by allergy to gluten) and may be eaten abundantly or even exclusively for some days. Bananas are an ideal food for those who

Individuals taking medications for the heart or arterial hypertension (potassium-wasting diuretics and digitalis-type cardiotonics) need a greater supply of potassium, which may be healthfully obtained from bananas.
Two large bananas (about 4 ounzes each) provide one gram of potassium (1,000 mg), a daily amount that more than meets the need for individuals under medical treatment. They also help avoid hypertension and maintain a healthy heart.

Banana varieties

Plantain

It is cultivated in many Central and South American regions, as well as in Africa. It is larger and much less sweet, but *rich* in ***starch.*** Its ***potassium*** content is also *very high.*

It should ***not*** be eaten **raw.** It lends itself to all types of cooked dishes, similar in use to potatoes. It is also used to produce **flour** that may be used even in bread making. This type of banana is a staple food in many tropical regions.

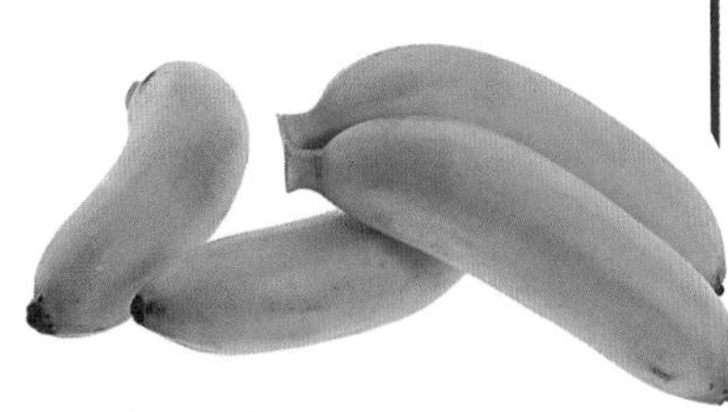

Dwarf banana

These are smaller, sweeter, and more flavorful than the common banana. They are raised in the Canary Islands, in Africa and in Southeast Asia.

Red banana

This variety of banana from Malaysia has a dark red peel and flavor very similar to the common banana. It is eaten raw.

suffer from this disorder, along with corn and rice (see p. 198).

• **Uric arthritis and gout:** Bananas **alkalize** the blood, which helps neutralize and eliminate the excess uric acid that causes arthritis and gout.

• **Low sodium diet:** Bananas are the *ideal fruit* whenever a low sodium diet is called for, since they provide calories, vitamins, and other minerals. Their use is recommended in cases of cirrhosis, ascites (accumulation of fluid in the peritoneal cavity), edema (retention of watery fluid in the tissues) caused by cardiac or renal nephritis, nephrosis, or kidney failure.

• **Diabetes:** Bananas are not contraindicated for diabetics, although the use of the carbohydrates they contain in the form of sugars must be controlled. In contrast to refined sugars (white sugar), those found in bananas are absorbed more slowly and do not produce a sharp rise in blood glucose (sugar) level.

Peas

The heart's friends

PEAS
Composition
per 100 g of raw edible portion

Energy	81.0 kcal = 339 kj
Protein	5.42 g
Carbohydrates	9.36 g
Fiber	5.10 g
Vitamin A	64.0 µg RE
Vitamin B_1	0.266 mg
Vitamin B_2	0.132 mg
Niacin	2.71 mg NE
Vitamin B_6	0.169 mg
Folate	65.0 µg
Vitamin B_{12}	—
Vitamin C	40.0 mg
Vitamin E	0.390 mg α-TE
Calcium	25.0 mg
Phosphorus	108 mg
Magnesium	33.0 mg
Iron	1.47 mg
Potassium	244 mg
Zinc	1.24 mg
Total Fat	*0.400 g*
Saturated Fat	*0.071 g*
Cholesterol	—
Sodium	*5.00 mg*

1% 2% 4% 10% 20% 40% 100%

% Daily Value (based on a 2,000 calorie diet)
provided by 100 g of this food

Synonyms: *Garden peas, Chickling vetches, Green peas.*

French: *Pois, petit pois;* ***Spanish:*** *Guisante, Arveja, Chícharo.*

Description: *These are the seeds of the garden pea plant ('Pisum sativum' L.), a herbaceous vine of the botanical family Leguminosae. The seeds are found enclosed in green pods approximately 10 cm in length. Each pod usually contains from 7 to 9 seeds.*

YOU MAY HAVE BEEN ONE of those children that carefully separated peas from other foods on your plate to avoid eating them. If so, there is still time to give these little seeds another try, particularly if you suffer from coronary disease.

PROPERTIES AND INDICATIONS: Raw peas contain 78.9% water. There are various noteworthy nutrients in peas:

✓ ***Carbohydrates:*** Peas contain a significant amount (9.63%), although less than the potato (16.4%). These are primarily constituted of starch with a small amount of saccharose.

✓ ***Proteins:*** Their content (5.42%) is greater than that of potatoes (2.07%) and is close to that of grains such as rice (6.61%), although much less than other legumes such as beans (23.4%). The proteins in peas are quite complete, although there is a relative lack of the essential amino acid methionine, and excess lysine. On the other hand, grains are very rich in methionine and lacking in lysine. Therefore the combination of **peas and grains** provides the body with *all* of the **amino acids** necessary to produce its own proteins.

✓ ***B complex vitamins:*** One hundred grams of peas supplies 0.266 mg of ***vitamin B_1,*** which represents 18% of RDA for an adult male. Additionally, peas are a good source of vitamins B_2, B_6, niacin, and folates, all of which are necessary for the proper function of the heart and nervous system.

✓ ***Vitamin C:*** Peas supply 40 mg for each 100 g, almost as much as lemon (53 mg).

✓ ***Potassium:*** Peas contain 244 mg per 100 g of potassium, an essential mineral for cardiac health.

Preparation and use

❶ **Raw:** When they are tender, peas may be eaten raw. They are very flavorful and healthful.

❷ **Frozen:** These are eaten after they have been thawed and briefly heated.

❸ **Cooked:** Peas should ***not*** be cooked for more than ***5-10 minutes*** (longer cooking times destroy almost their entire vitamin content). Very brief boiling or steaming is ideal.

❹ **Dried:** While dried peas may be stored for a very long time, they contain very little provitamin A and vitamin C. Cooking them for a few minutes is sufficient.

❺ **Canning:** Canned peas may be eaten as they are. Vitamin loss is between 15% and 30%.

Additionally, peas are a *good source* of ***iron*** (1.47 mg/100 g), ***zinc, folates*** and ***fiber.*** They also provide significant amounts of ***provitamin A*** (beta-carotene), ***vitamin E,*** and ***magnesium.*** Because of this, they are particularly useful in the following cases:

- **Cardiac disease:** As we have seen, peas have everything necessary to be a **heart-healthy food.** Additionally, they contain practically no ***fat*** or ***sodium,*** two substances that are antagonistic to coronary health if consumed in excess. They are appropriate in the diet of those suffering from heart failure, heart valve lesions, myocardiopathy (degeneration of the heart muscle), and, of course, coronary heart disease.
- **Nervous system disorders:** Peas are a very nutritious food rich in B group vitamins and minerals necessary for the proper functioning of the nervous system. They are appropriate in cases of a debilitated nervous system, neurasthenia, irritability, depression, insomnia, and other functional disorders.
- **Pregnancy and lactation:** Because of their protein richness (particularly when combined with grains), vitamins, and minerals, peas are a very appropriate food for pregnant or lactating women. They are also *rich* in ***folates,*** which prevent fetal nervous system malformations.
- **Diabetes:** The starch in peas is slowly transformed to glucose during digestion, which makes them well tolerated by diabetics.

Peas, with or without corn or another grain, are ideal food for those suffering from coronary heart disease.

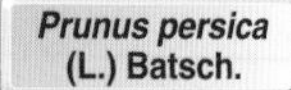

Peach

Ideal for the heart

Synonym: *Persian apple.*

French: *Pêche;* ***Spanish:*** *Melocotón.*

Description: *The peach is the fruit of the peach tree ('Prunus persica' [L] Batsch.), a tree of the botanical family Rosaceae. The fruit is a typical drupe: fleshy pulp with a hard stone in the center.*

PEACH
Composition
per 100 g of raw edible portion

Energy	43.0 kcal = 180 kj
Protein	0.700 g
Carbohydrates	9.10 g
Fiber	2.00 g
Vitamin A	54.0 µg RE
Vitamin B_1	0.017 mg
Vitamin B_2	0.041 mg
Niacin	1.02 mg NE
Vitamin B_6	0.018 mg
Folate	3.40 µg
Vitamin B_{12}	—
Vitamin C	6.60 mg
Vitamin E	0.700 mg α-TE
Calcium	5.00 mg
Phosphorus	12.0 mg
Magnesium	7.00 mg
Iron	0.110 mg
Potassium	197 mg
Zinc	0.140 mg
Total Fat	0.090 g
Saturated Fat	0.010 g
Cholesterol	—
Sodium	1.00 mg

1% 2% 4% 10% 20% 40% 100%

% Daily Value (based on a 2,000 calorie diet)
provided by 100 g of this food

THE PEACH is a well-traveled tree. The oldest orchards are in China. From there it was taken to Persia (Iran) several centuries before the birth of Christ. After spreading throughout the Mediterranean more than two thousand years ago, it was introduced in the Americas by the Spaniards. The peach has adapted well to each region where it has been taken. Today more than half of the world's peach production is from the Americas.

PROPERTIES AND INDICATIONS: The composition of the peach is a *balanced combination* of ***provitamin A*** (beta-carotene), B group ***vitamins,*** vitamin C, vitamin E, ***potassium, magnesium,*** and vegetable ***fiber,*** all in moderate amounts. Peaches contain virtually *no* ***sodium*** or ***fat.*** They do contain 9% ***fructose*** and other ***sugars*** and less than 1% proteins.

It may be said that the ***composition*** of the peach is almost perfect for a healthy **heart.** ***Vitamins A, C,*** and ***E*** are nature's *best* **antioxidants,** and few foods contain all three in such balance. The antioxidant effect of these vitamins maintains artery health in general, and those that nourish the heart in particular.

The ***B*** group ***vitamins*** (B_1, B_2, niacin, and B_6), which are found in peaches in significant quantities, are necessary for heart muscle cell contraction utilizing the energy of fatty acids and sugars.

Potassium, *very abundant* in peaches, and **magnesium** are minerals *essential* to maintain normal, strong **heartbeat** rhythm.

Not only is the peach the lowest of any fruit in fat, its ***sodium*** content is also among the *lowest*, with only one milligram (mg) per 100 g of edible portion. A low sodium diet helps avoid arterial hypertension and aids the heart's activity.

Peaches are medically indicated in the following cases:

- **Heart disease:** Eating peaches is of benefit whenever there is any degree of heart failure, any impairment in the heart's capacity to perform effectively its pumping activity. Even though peaches are not a direct heart stimulant, they do aid the work of this organ.

- **Digestive disorders:** Peaches are easy to digest when they are ripe. They contain soluble vegetable fiber that acts as an emollient in the digestive tract. It is a mild laxative.

- **Kidney disorders:** Peaches are mildly diuretic, which, together with very low sodium and protein content, make them excellent for those with renal failure.

- **Obesity:** Peaches are among the best fruits for creating a sensation of satiety, thus reducing the appetite. Their caloric content is quite low: 43 kcal/100 g. Additionally, its depurative action facilitates the removal of the acidic metabolic waste that frequently accompanies obesity.

Preparation and use

❶ **Fresh:** The peach's velvety peel may produce an allergic reaction in sensitive individuals, thus they should be peeled. The peel may also carry pesticide residuals. While it is true that the peel contains vitamins, eating a little more peeled peach easily compensates for this loss.

❷ **Canned:** While canned peaches provide somewhat fewer vitamins and minerals, they have the advantage of being available year-round. Peaches canned in as little sugar as possible are preferable.

❸ **Marmalade** and **juice.**

The peach's shape is reminiscent of that of the heart, possibly as a reminder of its many benefits for this organ.

Grapes

Invigorates the heart and improves blood flow

GRAPES
Composition
per 100 g of raw edible portion

Energy	71.0 kcal = 297 kj
Protein	0.660 g
Carbohydrates	16.8 g
Fiber	1.00 g
Vitamin A	7.00 µg RE
Vitamin B_1	0.092 mg
Vitamin B_2	0.057 mg
Niacin	0.350 mg NE
Vitamin B_6	0.110 mg
Folate	3.90 µg
Vitamin B_{12}	—
Vitamin C	10.8 mg
Vitamin E	0.700 mg α-TE
Calcium	11.0 mg
Phosphorus	13.0 mg
Magnesium	6.00 mg
Iron	0.260 mg
Potassium	185 mg
Zinc	0.050 mg
Total Fat	*0.580 g*
Saturated Fat	*0.189 g*
Cholesterol	—
Sodium	*2.00 mg*

1% 2% 4% 10% 20% 40% 100%

% Daily Value (based on a 2,000 calorie diet) provided by 100 g of this food

French: *Raisin;* ***Spanish:*** *Uva.*

Description: *Fruit of the vine ('Vitis vinifera' L.), a climbing vine of the botanical family Vitaceae. Grapes are an aggregate fruit that grows in clusters from few to as many more than one hundred.*

GRAPES ARE, after the orange, the most cultivated fruit in the world. Unfortunately only a small percentage of the crop is eaten as fruit; most is destined for the production of alcoholic beverages, particularly wine.

Grapes constitute an essential component of the Mediterranean diet, and even of the regional culture. It is for good reason that they have been cultivated in the warm lands surrounding the sea for thousands of years.

Recent scientific discoveries attribute the good cardiac health of Mediterranean peoples specifically on some of the substances found in grapes.

PROPERTIES AND INDICATIONS: Two types of nutrients *stand out* in the grape's composition: ***sugars*** and ***B*** complex ***vitamins.*** On the other hand, grapes supply few proteins and fats. Grape proteins, although scarce, contain all essential amino acids. Minerals are present in moderate amounts. These are the grape's components that merit special discussion:

✓ ***Sugars*** are present in proportions that vary between 15% and 30%. Grapes grown in cold regions tend to have lower sugar content, while those from hot dry climates are much sweeter.

The two most abundant sugars in grapes are ***GLUCOSE*** and ***FRUCTOSE.*** From a chemical standpoint, these are ***MONOSACCHARIDES*** or simple sugars that are capable of passing directly to the bloodstream without need for digestion.

✓ ***Vitamins:*** With 0.11 mg/100 g of ***vitamin*** B_6, grapes are among the richest fresh fruit in this vitamin, surpassed only by tropical fruits such as avocados, bananas, cherimoyas, guavas, and mangoes. ***Vitamins*** B_1, B_2, and B_3 or ***niacin*** are also present in amounts that are greater than those of most fresh fruits.

All of these ***vitamins*** are responsible, among other things, for **metabolizing *sugars,*** thus facilitating their chemical "combustion" within the cells to provide energy. Here nature gives yet another example of intelligent design by providing a great deal of sugars within the grape together with the vitamins needed to convert them to energy.

Grapes also contain significant amounts of provitamin A (7 µg RE/100 g) and vitamins C (10.8 mg/100 g), and E (0.7 mg/100 g).

✓ ***Minerals:*** Potassium and iron are the most abundant minerals in grapes, although they also contain calcium, phosphorous and copper.

✓ ***Fiber:*** Grapes contain around 1% soluble vegetable fiber (pectin), a significant amount for a fresh fruit.

✓ ***Non-nutritive substances:*** Grapes contain numerous chemical substances that do not fit into any of the classical groups of nutrients, but exercise a great deal of functions within the body, many of which are still not understood. These substances are also known as ***PHYTOCHEMICALS:***

- ***Organic acids:*** These give a slight tart flavor to grapes. These acids have a paradoxical effect in the blood, producing alkalinization. ***ALKALIZATION*** of the blood and urine facilitates the elimination of metabolic wastes, which are mostly acidic, such as **uric acid.**
- ***Flavonoids:*** It has recently been shown that they act as *powerful* **antioxidants,** which impede the oxidation of the **cholesterol** that causes arteriosclerosis. Flavonoids also avoid the formation of blood clots in the arteries.
- ***Resveratrol:*** Impedes the progress of **arteriosclerosis.**[22] It has recently been shown to be a powerful **anticarcinogen.**
- ***Anthocyanidines:*** These are vegetable pigments present in the skins of white, and particularly black grapes. They are *powerful* **antioxidants** able to *prevent* **coronary heart** disease.

In essence it may be said that grapes provide energy to the cells and promote the health of the arteries, particularly those that nourish the heart. They are also laxative, antitoxic, diuretic, anti-anemic, and anti-tumor. These are their primary medical indications:

• **Cardiovascular disease in general:** Grapes are highly recommended for any cardiac conditions because:

- They provide ***energy*** in the form of simple sugars that the heart muscle uses to contract. Although the primary sources of energy for the heart are fatty acids, it also utilizes glucose.
- Grapes are *rich* in ***potassium*** and also contain ***calcium*** and ***magnesium,*** minerals involved in cardiac contractions.
- Additionally, grapes contain virtually *no* ***sodium*** or ***saturated fat,*** the two primary enemies of the cardiovascular system.

How to prepare delicious natural grape juice

1. Place whole grapes in a **blender.** While it is more time consuming, the seeds can be removed for better flavor. This method is indicated:
   - To take *full advantage* of all of the medicinal properties of the skin on the **heart** and **arteries.**
   - To take advantage of the **anti-carcinogenic** effect of the ***resveratrol*** found *primarily* in the **skin** of the grape.

   In this case black or red grapes are preferable.
2. Use a **strainer** to eliminate skin and seeds. This gives a delicious, fine textured juice appropriate for all other indications of grapes.

Unfermented grape juice contains the same cardio-protective substances found in wine, but in higher concentrations and without the drawback of ethyl alcohol. Additionally, grapes and grape juice provide energy-producing sugars and vitamins that wine lacks.

• **Coronary artery disease:** The phenolic non-nutritive substances present in grapes (***flavonoids*** and ***resveratrol***) produce the following beneficial effects on circulation through the arteries in general, and the coronary arteries in particular:

- **Vasodilatation,** thus overcoming arterial spasms and increasing blood flow.
- *Reduction* in tendency of blood platelets to form clots, which reduces the risk of arterial occlusion caused by arteriosclerosis. Ethyl alcohol also produces this effect, but only at high blood-alcohol levels (2 g per liter) incompatible with good health.
- *Inhibition* of the **oxidation of the cholesterol** transported by low-density lipoproteins (LDL). The oxidation of this type of cholesterol (harmful) initiates the process of creating deposits on the artery walls, giving rise to arteriosclerosis.

In summary, investigations regarding grapes and grape juice demonstrate that both are capable of dilating the arteries, improve blood flow without forming clots, and impede the deposit of cholesterol on arterial walls. What else might be expected of a food that protects the heart and the circulatory system?

RED WINE (not white) also exercises the same actions since it retains some of the active substances present in grapes. However, it has *drawbacks* compared to the grapes or grape juice. Wine has few sugars or vitamins, and it contains a toxin **ethyl alcohol** that the body must eliminate from the blood by "burning" it in the liver.

Because of this, **grapes** or **grape juice** are far *better* than **wine** as protectors of the cardiovascular system and they have *no* ***undesirable side effects.***

The cardiac patient that eats grapes regularly during the summer and autumn and raisins or grape juice the rest of the year will note how the heart improves in its response to small efforts. Those recovering from heart attack should include grapes in their diet to stop the progress of coronary arteriosclerosis.

- **Thrombosis:** The blood's tendency to form clots within arteries and veins can be reduced by consumption of grapes, grape juice, or raisins. This is particularly important for those who have suffered a stroke or are at risk of one.

Raisins

*They provide less than 300 kcal/100 g. They are **very rich** in **iron:** 100 g covers one-fourth of the RDA for this mineral. Raisins are also rich in **potassium** (825 mg/100 g), and in vegetable **fiber** (6.8%). Their fat content is about the same as fresh grapes (0.54%). B complex **vitamins** are found in higher concentrations, but there is less vitamin C and vitamin A is almost absent.*

- **Anemia:** Grapes are one of the *richest* **fresh fruits** in iron (0.26 mg/100 g). Raisins, because they are more concentrated, are much richer in iron (2.59 mg/100 g), higher even than lamb (2-2.5 mg/100 g).

The ***iron*** in grapes is ***nonheme,*** and by itself is more difficult to absorb that the iron in meat. However, its absorption is greatly enhanced when facilitated by the presence of vitamin C found in the grape itself or in other plant-based foods.

All who tend toward anemia will notice improvement with the regular consumption of grapes during the summer and autumn months and with raisins during the rest of the year.

- **Liver disorders:** Grapes *activate* the **detoxifying** effect of the liver, increasing bile production (choleretic action). Additionally, grapes facilitate blood circulation in the portal system and thus are of value in cases of **cirrhosis** and **ascites** (accumulation of fluid in the peritoneal cavity) due to portal hypertension.
- **Intestinal disorders:** Grapes are a mild laxative that *relieves* **chronic constipation** due to lazy intestine. They also *balance* **intestinal flora** and *avoid* **putrefaction** caused by a diet rich in animal proteins.
- **Renal disorders:** Because of their diuretic and decongestive action, as well as their mineral composition and low levels of proteins, grapes are *highly recommended* in cases of **renal failure** due to nephritis, nephrosis, or other causes.
- **Gout and excess uric acid:** Grapes are excellent for eliminating uric acid in the kidneys due to their **alkalizing** and **diuretic** effects. Regular grape consumption as well as grape treatment is particularly beneficial for arthritics, the obese, and those with a diet rich in meat products.
- **Cancerous processes:** The ***RESVERATROL*** found in grapes, particularly in the skin, has been shown experimentally to possess anti-tumor properties. Although the use of this substance in cancer cases is still under investigation, abundant grape consumption is advised as a complement to other treatments for those who have been diagnosed with cancer or who are at high risk of it.

5

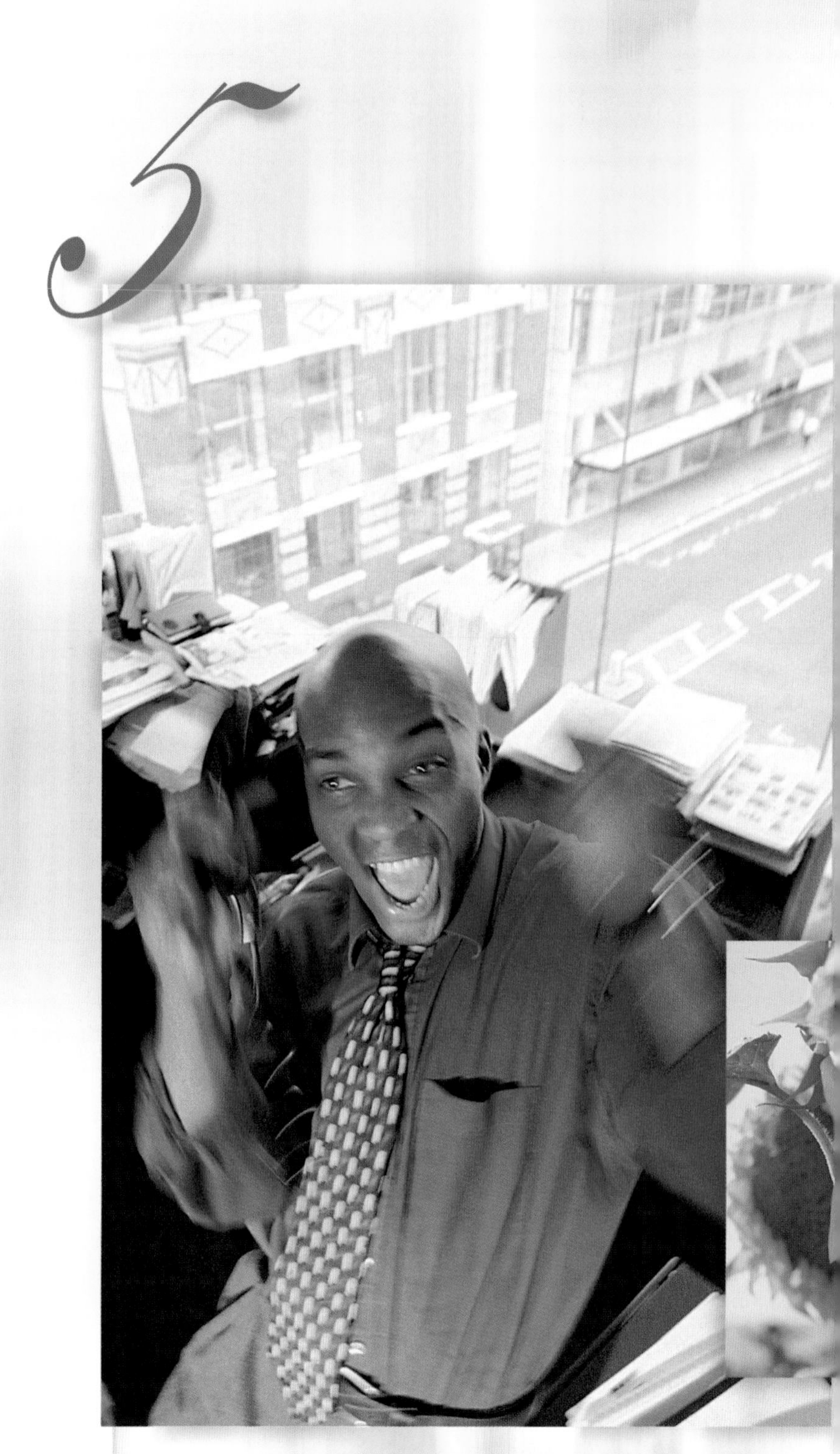

Foods for the Arteries

THE HEALTH of the arteries is intimately intertwined with the diet. Some food components are *injurious* to the arteries, while others *benefit* them:

• ***Injurious*** substances: ***Sodium,*** (primarily from table salt), ***saturated fat,*** and ***cholesterol,*** which is found only in animal-based foods.

• ***Beneficial*** components: **Antioxidants** (found primarily in fruits and vegetables), soluble **fiber** (fruits, vegetables, and legumes), and **unsaturated fatty acids** (nuts, seeds, and vegetable oils).

Cholesterol, the artery's worst enemy

• Cholesterol is ***necessary*** within the body, and should not be considered a toxic substance in and of itself.

The body is capable of producing sufficient cholesterol for its needs without recourse to consuming it from external sources.

• Cholesterol is harmful only because it *adheres* to **arterial** walls causing **arteriosclerosis.** Above a certain level of blood cholesterol there is an increased risk of arteriosclerosis and heart attack.

• Cholesterol is necessary, but insufficient by itself to cause **arteriosclerosis.** This disease results from the combination of several factors:

- *Elevated* blood **cholesterol** level.
- *Lack* of **antioxidant** substances, such as provitamin A, vitamins C and E, flavonoids, and other phytochemicals, due to a diet that is lacking in fruits, vegetables, whole grains, and nuts.
- *Excess* **saturated fats** because of a diet rich in milk, eggs, shellfish, meats, and meat derivatives.
- Lack of physical exercise, tobacco, stress, hormones, genetic makeup.

• Therefore, it is not enough to be concerned with just achieving a certain cholesterol level. Some doctors prescribe drugs and recommend diets to lower cholesterol levels, but such half-measures are not enough to avoid arteriosclerosis and its complications. In fact, there are many cases of heart attack where cholesterol levels are normal.

• There are **two types** of cholesterol in the blood depending on the lipoproteins that transport it:

- **LDL** or ***harmful*** **cholesterol** is combined with low-density lipoproteins and fosters arteriosclerosis.
- **HDL** or ***beneficial*** **cholesterol** is combined with high-density lipoproteins that protect against arteriosclerosis. Olive oil and physical exercise increase the levels of HDL cholesterol.

  The expression "blood cholesterol level" refers to the ***total*** amount of **cholesterol,** the sum of both fractions.

• To have **healthy arteries** and reduce the risk of arteriosclerosis and its complications (heart attack, stroke, poor circulation), it is necessary to:

- ***Reduce*** total **cholesterol** level.
- ***Increase*** the level of **antioxidants** in the blood.

• The above requisites are easily met with a **diet** that is ***high*** in **fresh plant-based foods.**

NORMAL BLOOD CHOLESTEROL LEVEL

Total cholesterol:
5-6 mmol/l (193-231 mg/dl).

HDL cholesterol:
1 mmol/l (38 mg/dl).

LDL cholesterol:
the difference between total cholesterol and HDL (4-5 mmol/l = 155-193 mg/dl).[3]

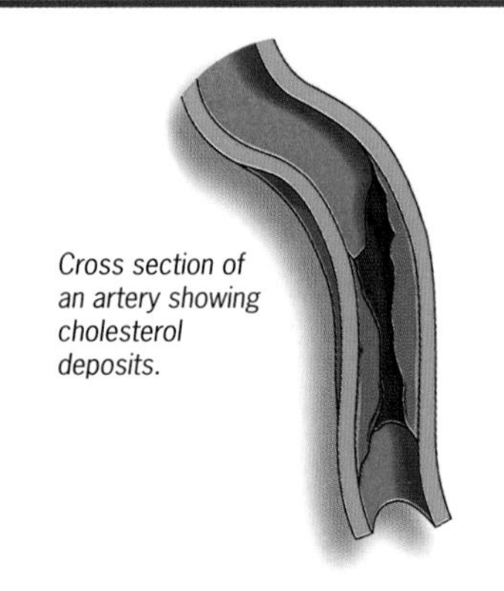

Cross section of an artery showing cholesterol deposits.

ARTERIOSCLEROSIS

Definition

This is a degenerative process that can affect all of the arteries of the body. It begins with **cholesterol** deposits in their inner lining, called the intima.

The thickening and hardening of the arteries coupled with a reduction of their inner diameter reduces blood circulation through them. Less blood flow, less life.

Diet

Diet is possibly the most influential factor in arteriosclerosis, which is considered one of the great evils of civilization. Among primitive or less developed groups whose diet is unrefined and natural there is virtually no arteriosclerosis. By contrast, it is becoming more frequent in Western countries as consumption of refined and artificial foods increases.

Causes

Tobacco, together with an inadequate diet, is a main cause of arteriosclerosis.

Increase

FRUIT
WHOLE GRAINS
LEGUMES
VEGETABLES
NUTS
FIBER
GARLIC
OILS
ANTIOXIDANTS
FOLATES

Reduce or eliminate

CHOLESTEROL
SATURATED FAT
TRANS FATTY ACIDS
MEAT
CURED CHEESES
EGGS
DAIRY PRODUCTS
PROTEINS
ALCOHOLIC BEVERAGES
COFFEE
WHITE SUGAR
SALT

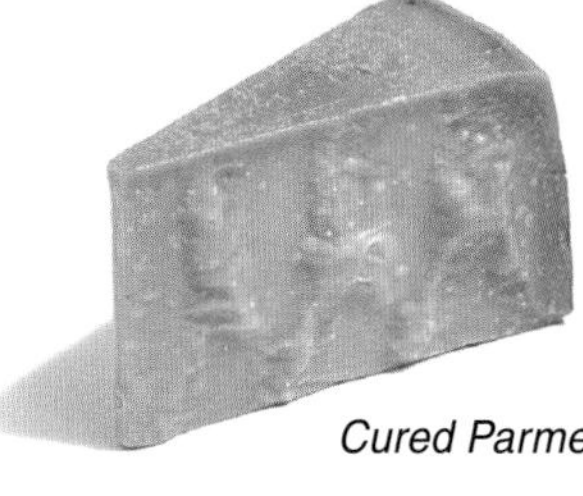

Cured Parmesan cheese

Cured cheese, like this Parmesan, is rich in salt, saturated fat, and cholesterol: three enemies of arterial health.

STROKE

Definition

Also referred to as **ictus** or **cerebrovascular accident.**

This results when a portion of the brain is suddenly deprived of blood circulation due to:

- The **bursting** of an **artery,** which produces a cerebral hemorrhage.
- The **blockage** of an **artery** by a blood clot at the site of the blockage in the brain or an embolism (a blockage caused by a clot anywhere in the body that has broken loose and traveled to the blockage site).

Causes

Arteriosclerosis is the primary cause of stroke since it fosters arterial rupture and the formation of clots. Other factors such as **hypertension, tobacco,** and **diabetes** increase stroke risk.

Increase

FRUIT
VEGETABLES
GARLIC
OLIVE OIL
FISH OIL
SELENIUM

Reduce or eliminate

THE SAME AS FOR ARTERIOSCLEROSIS

Olives

Olive oil prevents blood clotting.

VASCULAR FRAGILITY

Definition and symptoms

Weakness in tiny blood vessels, which lead to **hemorrhages** or **hematomas** resulting from minor traumas.

Causes

It is caused by a generally hereditary weakness of the conjunctive tissue that makes up the walls of arteries and veins. The deficiency of certain vitamins like C can aggravate it.

Increase

LEMON
CITRUS FRUITS
VITAMIN C
FLAVONOIDS

Flavonoids protect and strengthen the walls of capillaries and small blood vessels. The most effective flavonoid is hesperidin, which is found in lemons.

HYPERTENSION

Definition

The blood must maintain a certain pressure in the arteries to properly circulate to all tissues. Hypertension is said to exist when one or both of these conditions:

- Systolic (maximum) pressure exceeds 140 mm Hg.
- Diastolic (minimum) pressure exceeds 90 mm Hg.

Hypertension does not produce symptoms, but rather slowly deteriorates the arteries and various organs.

Diet

Diet can play an *important role* in maintaining blood pressure within healthy limits. The more simply prepared fruit and vegetables are eaten, the lower the hypertension risk.

Heat Counsels

Nicotine is a vasoconstrictor (contracts the arteries). Because of this, smoking causes an increase in blood pressure that can be detected after only one cigarette.

Increase

DIURETIC FOODS
FRUIT
LEAFY GREEN VEGETABLES
DEPURANT BROTH
LEGUMES
CELERY
SQUASH
GARLIC
GUAVA
PEAR
GRAPEFRUIT
FIBER
POTASSIUM
CALCIUM
MAGNESIUM
FISH OIL

Reduce or eliminate

SALT
SODIUM
HAM
SAUSAGES
MEAT
PROTEINS
ALCOHOLIC BEVERAGES
SATURATED FAT
COFFEE
STIMULANT BEVERAGES
PEPPER
MATURED CHEESES
EGG

Depurant vegetable broth

It is made by boiling various alkalizing and diuretic vegetables, primarily onions and celery, in abundant water. A small amount of olive oil may be added.

This broth is very healthful and constitutes one of the fundamental ingredients in a cleansing diet. One-half to one liter may be taken a day as a beverage in place of water. Some of its benefits are:

- **Depurant** or purifying action: It **alkalizes** the blood and urine, which improves the ***elimination*** of waste products, particularly **uric acid.**
- **Diuretic:** *Improves* **kidney function** and increases urine output.
- **Mineralizer:** It supplies a significant amount of ***minerals*** and ***trace elements***, particularly potassium, magnesium, and iron. Potassium prevents arterial hypertension.

Depurant broth

Garlic

Garlic is a vasodilator (dilates the arteries) and a hypotensor (lowers blood pressure), although it is necessary to eat a certain amount (several cloves) to achieve this effect.

RAYNAUD'S SYNDROME

Definition and symptoms

This is due to sudden spasms of the distal arteries, generally in the hands, which turn white, then purple, and finally red as the spasm passes.

Causes

This syndrome tends to occur more frequently in postmenopausal women.

Known circumstances that initiate the syndrome are:

- Smoking.
- Emotional stress.
- Cold.
- Handling appliances that vibrate, such as hair dryers or kitchen blenders.

Heath Counsels

Although on occasion it may require medical treatment or surgery, certain foods can contribute to avoiding its appearance.

Increase

GARLIC
NUTS
VITAMIN E
FLAVONOIDS
FISH OIL

Reduce or eliminate

ALCOHOLIC BEVERAGES
STIMULANT BEVERAGES

CHILBLAINS

Definition

Chilblains, or **erythema pernio,** are due to inadequate blood circulation in the tiny capillaries that supply the skin. Cold or tightfitting shoes can produce or aggravate them.

Symptoms

They manifest themselves as an inflammatory swelling of the skin of the hands or feet, which itch and burn. They generally disappear spontaneously, although on occasion they become ulcerated and infected.

Heath Counsels

In addition to local treatment using compresses of appropriate medicinal plants (see *EMP [Encyclopedia of Medicinal Plants]* p. 229), certain **foods** can improve the condition of the capillaries and blood circulation.

Tobacco fosters chilblains by constricting the arteries and reducing blood flow.

Increase

CITRUS FRUITS
GARLIC
VITAMIN C
VITAMIN E
FLAVONOIDS

Reduce or eliminate

ALCOHOLIC BEVERAGES
STIMULANT BEVERAGES

Sausage

Sausages are very high in sodium, both because of that which the meat naturally contains and that which is added with salt and additives (the nitrites and nitrates used to cure the meat are sodium salts). Sausages are also high in saturated fat, which promotes hardening of the arteries and hypertension.

Eating abundant amounts of natural or minimally processed fruits and vegetables is an effective means of avoiding hypertension.

Substituting
to reduce

By substituting each of these foods with the one to its right, it is possible to reduce cholesterol levels. The more substitutions are made, the greater the cholesterol reduction. Additionally, following the counsels regarding arteriosclerosis will prove of benefit.

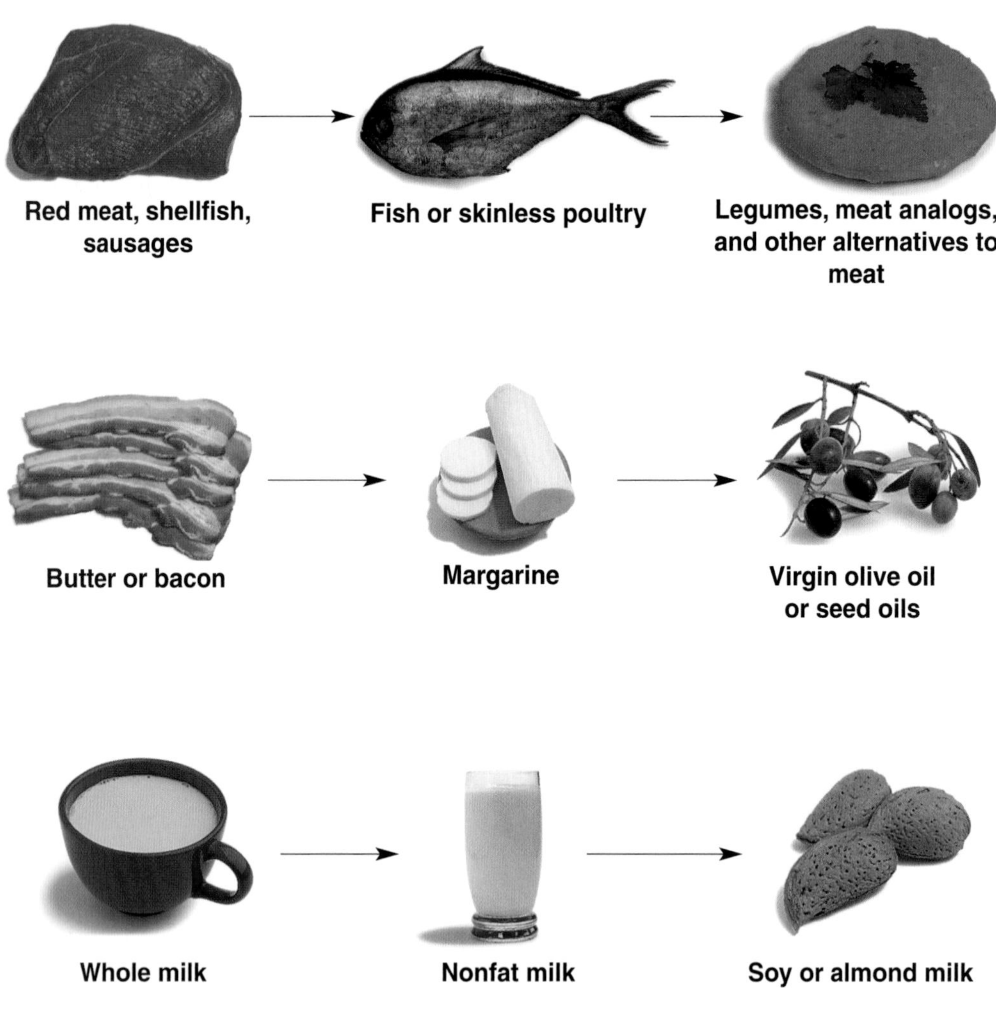

oods

cholesterol

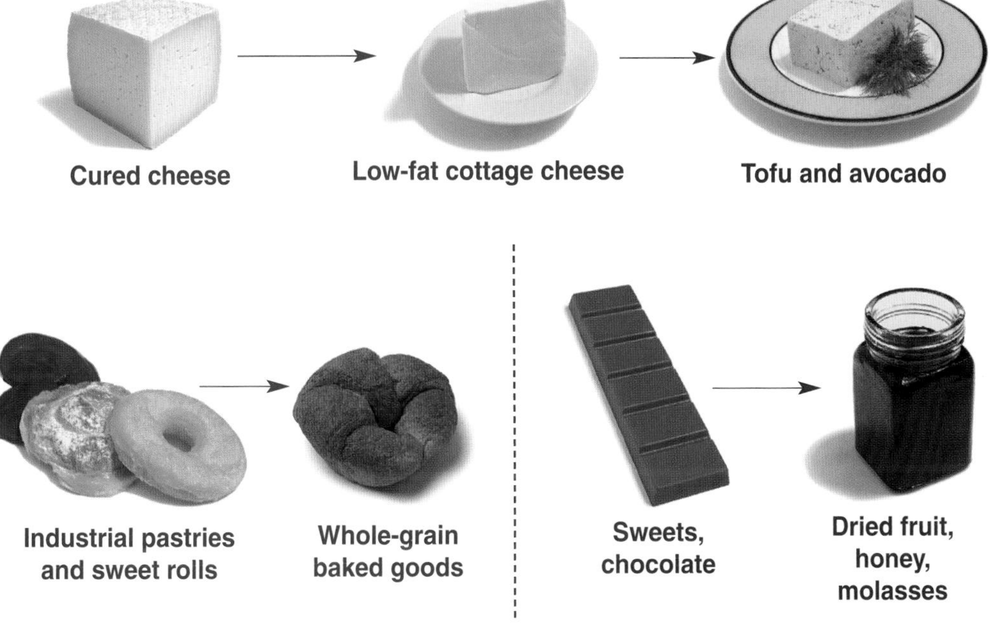

Cured cheese → Low-fat cottage cheese → Tofu and avocado

Industrial pastries and sweet rolls → Whole-grain baked goods

Sweets, chocolate → Dried fruit, honey, molasses

Types of fatty acids

- **Saturated fatty acids:** These are found in milk, egg yolk, and meat and its derivatives. They increase cholesterol production in the body.
- **Unsaturated fatty acids:**
  - ***Monounsaturated*** such as ***oleic*** acid found in olive oil: They *reduce* **LDL** (harmful) **cholesterol** and *increase* **HDL,** which *protects* against **arteriosclerosis** (see p. 95).
  - ***Polyunsaturated:*** These are found *primarily* in **seed oils.** They *reduce* **LDL** (harmful) **cholesterol.** ***Omega-3*** fatty acids are a special type of polyunsaturated fatty acid present specifically in fatty fish.
- **Trans fatty acids:** These are unsaturated fatty acids ***altered by*** **heat** or industrial processes. They are formed when **frying** with vegetable oils or when they are processed industrially by heating and **hydrogenation** to produce **semisolid fats** such as **margarine.**
  - Health **effects:** Trans fatty acids *increase* **LDL** (harmful) **cholesterol,** *reduce* **HDL** (beneficial) **cholesterol,** *foster* **arteriosclerosis,** and *increase* the risk of **coronary heart disease.**[1,2] However, their effect is ***not as injurious as*** the **saturated fat** in **milk, cheese, egg yolk, meat,** and **sausage.**[3]

Chickpea

Just the thing for modern men and women

CHICKPEA
Composition
per 100 g of raw edible portion

Energy	364 kcal = 1,525 kj
Protein	19.3 g
Carbohydrates	43.3 g
Fiber	17.4 g
Vitamin A	7.00 µg RE
Vitamin B_1	0.477 mg
Vitamin B_2	0.212 mg
Niacin	4.62 mg NE
Vitamin B_6	0.535 mg
Folate	557 µg
Vitamin B_{12}	—
Vitamin C	4.00 mg
Vitamin E	0.820 mg α-TE
Calcium	105 mg
Phosphorus	366 mg
Magnesium	115 mg
Iron	6.24 mg
Potassium	875 mg
Zinc	3.43 mg
Total Fat	*6.04 g*
Saturated Fat	*0.626 g*
Cholesterol	—
Sodium	*24.0 mg*

1% 2% 4% 10% 20% 40% 100% 200% 500%
% Daily Value (based on a 2,000 calorie diet)
provided by 100 g of this food

Synonyms: *Ceci, Garbanzo [bean], Bengal gram, Calvance pea, Chick pea, Dwarf pea, Gram pea, Yellow gram.*

French: *Pois chiche;* ***Spanish:*** *Garbanzo, chícharo.*

Description: *The seed of the chickpea plant ('Cicer arietinum' L.), of the botanical family Leguminosae. Its fruit is an ovoid legume containing two seeds, chickpeas.*

PROPERTIES AND INDICATIONS: The noteworthy therapeutic properties of the chickpea make this humble legume a dietary food ideal for modern men and women: they help *reduce* **cholesterol** and *avoid* **constipation** while *strengthening* the **nervous system.**

Additionally, the chickpea is nourishing and balanced as it contains a great deal of energy (364 kcal/100 g). It is a good source of the most important nutrients except vitamin B_{12} (which is true of all plant-based foods). Even provitamin A and vitamins C and E are present, but only in small amounts. The remaining nutrients are well represented in the chickpea:

✓ ***Proteins:*** Chickpeas provide a significant amount (19.3%), equal or *superior* to **meat** and **eggs** but less than other protein-rich legumes such as soy, lentils, or beans (see pp. 130, 254, 330). The legume-grain combination produces a protein of excellent biological quality.[4]

✓ ***Carbohydrates:*** Chickpeas are very rich in carbohydrates (43.3%), ***starch*** being predominant. Starch is transformed slowly to glucose during digestion, but it must be well chewed and salivated.

✓ ***Fat:*** Chickpeas are 6.04% fat. This is considerably more than lentils or beans, but less than soy. Most of these fats are ***polyunsaturated.***

✓ ***Vitamins:*** Chickpeas are a good source of vitamins B_2 and B_6. ***Folates,*** which are also involved in proper nervous system function and the reduction of heart attack risk, are *very abundant*: One hundred grams of chickpeas supply almost *triple* the RDA (Recommended Dietary Allowance) of this nutrient.

✓ ***Minerals:*** The most noteworthy are ***iron*** (6.24 mg/100 g, almost *three times* that of **meat**), phosphorous (366 mg /100 g), potassium (875 mg /100 g), magnesium (115 mg /100 g), calcium (105 mg/100 mg), and ***zinc*** (3.43 mg /100 g).

Preparation and use

❶ **Cooked:** This is the most common manner of preparing and eating chickpeas in the West. They can be added to soups and stews. They combine very well with rice dishes.

❷ **Oven toasted or fried:** When prepared in this way they are somewhat indigestible since a part of the starch becomes resistant to gastric juices.[5]

❸ **Chickpea flour:** This is widely used in India to make a variety of culinary items such as ***falafel.***

Chickpeas are an almost complete food whose nutritional proportions are quite well balanced. For this reason, they can be used as the main dish of a meal, as is the case in a traditional Mediterranean diet. Eating chickpeas regularly is recommended in the following situations:

- **Increased cholesterol:** Chickpeas contain a moderate amount of high-quality (mono and polyunsaturated) fats (6.04%) that aid in lowering blood cholesterol level. Chickpeas' ***fiber*** also impedes the absorption of cholesterol from other foods in the intestine (chickpeas contain no cholesterol). Consequently, eating more chickpeas and fewer meat products reduces cholesterol levels and improves arterial health. Finally, eating chickpeas *prevents* **arteriosclerosis** in all of its manifestations, including heart attack.
- **Constipation:** The fiber in chickpeas naturally stimulates intestinal peristaltic action thus moving the feces through the lower digestive tract.
- **Functional disorders of the nervous system** due to B vitamin deficiency, such as irritability, nervousness, and lack of concentration. Chickpeas are *highly recommended* for those suffering from **stress** or **depression.**
- **Pregnancy:** For pregnant women this legume is an ideal food because it is *rich* in ***folates,*** which prevent nervous system defects in the fetus. Additionally, chickpeas have a *very high* content of ***proteins, iron,*** and other minerals.

Zinc deficit

*Some nutrition specialists emphasize the fact that **plant-based food** can be lacking in zinc. However, 100 g chickpeas contains more zinc (3.43 mg) than the same quantity of **meat** (2.97 mg). Chickpeas, the same as lentils and soy, are an excellent source of **zinc.***

Grapefruit

Unblocks the arteries and cleanses the blood

There are varieties of grapefruit with yellow, orange, and even pink pulp. The latter two have the additional advantage of being particularly rich in carotenoids of preventive action against cancer.

GRAPEFRUIT
Composition
per 100 g of raw edible portion

Energy	**32.0 kcal = 134 kj**
Protein	**0.630 g**
Carbohydrates	**6.98 g**
Fiber	**1.10 g**
Vitamin A	**12.0 µg RE**
Vitamin B_1	**0.036 mg**
Vitamin B_2	**0.020 mg**
Niacin	**0.283 mg NE**
Vitamin B_6	**0.042 mg**
Folate	**10.2 µg**
Vitamin B_{12}	—
Vitamin C	**34.4 mg**
Vitamin E	**0.250 mg α-TE**
Calcium	**12.0 mg**
Phosphorus	**8.00 mg**
Magnesium	**8.00 mg**
Iron	**0.090 mg**
Potassium	**139 mg**
Zinc	**0.070 mg**
Total Fat	***0.100 g***
Saturated Fat	***0.014 g***
Cholesterol	—
Sodium	—

1% 2% 4% 10% 20% 40% 100%

% Daily Value (based on a 2,000 calorie diet)
provided by 100 g of this food

Scientific synonyms: *Citrus maxima* (Burm.) Merr., Citrus decumanus L.

Synonyms: *Marsh grapefruit, Shaddock.*

French: *Pamplemousse;* ***Spanish:*** *pomelo.*

Description: *The grapefruit is the fruit of the tree 'Citrus paradisi' MacFad., from the botanical family Rutaceae. It is shaped like an orange, although somewhat larger, and is lemon-like in color. Some varieties are pink or green.*

PROPERTIES AND INDICATIONS: grapefruit pulp contains a moderate amount of carbohydrates and very few proteins and lipids. Among its ***vitamins*** the most prominent is ***C*** (34.4 mg/100 g), although *less* than the **orange** (53.2 mg/100 g), or the **lemon** (46 mg/100 g). As for mineral salts, its *virtual lack* of ***sodium*** is noteworthy, as is its *rather elevated* ***potassium*** content, in addition to a certain amount of calcium and magnesium.

Since the ***nutritional*** content of the grapefruit is fairly *low*, most of its therapeutic properties are attributed to non-nutritive components of the fruit.

✓ ***PECTIN:*** This is a type of soluble vegetable ***fiber*** found in many fruits such as citrus and apples (see p. 216). Vegetable fiber was the first non-nutritive food component to be studied because of its medicinal effects. Grapefruit pectin is found in the fiber forming its pulp and in the whitish layer just below the skin and between the sections. This fiber *stands out* for its **arterial** *protection* and its **anti-cholesterol** effects as *demonstrated* in numerous scientific experiments.

✓ ***Flavonoids:*** It improves **blood flow,** and has **antioxidant** and **anticarcinogen** properties.

✓ ***Carotenoids:*** **PINK GRAPEFRUIT** are a good source of ***beta-carotene,*** the precursor to vitamin A.

Preparation and use

❶ **Fresh:** It is advantageous to eat the whole grapefruit including the white layer just beneath the peel and between the sections with its pectin-rich fiber.

❷ **Juice:** Grapefruit juice is a good alternative to that of orange or lemon, or mixed with either of them. It may be sweetened with honey.

❸ **Grapefruit treatment:** This may be done either with the whole fruit or the juice. This treatment begins by eating a grapefruit on an empty stomach (whole fruit or juice), two the next day, and so forth up to five. When five a day has been reached, reduce the dose by one each day down to one.

For the next five days continue eating one grapefruit a day until completing the **two-week course** of the treatment.

✓ ***Limonoids:*** These are terpenoids that constitute the ***essence*** of citrus fruits. Grapefruit is *particularly rich* in one of these, ***limonene,*** which gives the fruit its bitter taste, and a large portion of its *proven* **anti-carcinogenic properties.**

Both the grapefruit's nutrients and its non-nutritive components explain its medical applications:

- **Arteriosclerosis:** The grapefruit serves to *protect* arterial walls from the hardening and thickening associated with the deposit of **cholesterol** and its consequent **calcification,** the process known as arteriosclerosis.
- **Other cardiocirculatory disorders:** The *virtual absence* of ***sodium*** and ***fat*** in grapefruit, as well as its *high level* of ***potassium,*** make it very suitable for those suffering from heart disease, particularly **heart failure.** Those suffering from **hypertension** should also eat abundant amounts of grapefruit, since it has a *mild* **diuretic** effect that helps decongest the circulatory system. In these cases the juice [❷] is adequate, although eating the whole fruit including the pulp [❶] provides better access to the benefits for the circulatory system.
- **Excess uric acid,** in any of its forms: **gout, uratic arthritis, kidney stones,** etc.
- **Depurative treatments:** Whenever one wishes to "cleanse the blood," thus *promoting* the body's **detoxifying** functions (particularly in the liver), one may drink a glass of grapefruit juice on an empty stomach each morning.
- **Infections:** The grapefruit *stimulates* the functions of the **immune system** much as does the orange because of its ***vitamin C*** and ***flavonoid*** content (see p. 346).
- **Obesity:** Because of its **depurative** and **detoxifying** properties, it is an *excellent complement* to the diet of anyone wishing to lose weight.
- **Protection against cancer:** The grapefruit's specific *combination* of ***vitamin C, pectin,*** and ***limonoids*** help *protect* against cancer by impeding the activity of many carcinogenic substances. *Regular consumption* of grapefruit and other citrus fruits is a good way to prevent cancer (see p. 345).

Squash

A great ally of the arteries

SQUASH
Composition
per 100 g of raw edible portion

Energy	26.0 kcal = 109 kj
Protein	1.00 g
Carbohydrates	6.00 g
Fiber	0.500 g
Vitamin A	160 µg RE
Vitamin B_1	0.050 mg
Vitamin B_2	0.110 mg
Niacin	0.800 mg NE
Vitamin B_6	0.061 mg
Folate	16.2 µg
Vitamin B_{12}	—
Vitamin C	9.00 mg
Vitamin E	1.06 mg α-TE
Calcium	21.0 mg
Phosphorus	44.0 mg
Magnesium	12.0 mg
Iron	0.800 mg
Potassium	340 mg
Zinc	0.320 mg
Total Fat	0.100 g
Saturated Fat	0.052 g
Cholesterol	—
Sodium	1.00 mg

1% 2% 4% 10% 20% 40% 100%

% Daily Value (based on a 2,000 calorie diet) provided by 100 g of this food

Related species: *Cucurbita maxima* L.

Synonyms: *Pumpkin, Courge, Calabaza, Coyote Melon, Gourd.*

French: *Courge;* ***Spanish:*** *Calabaza, Zapallo, Chayote.*

Description: *These are fruits of various vines ('Cucurbita pepo' L.) of the botanical family Cucurbitaceae. Squash come in a wide variety of shapes, predominantly spherical, flattened, ovoid, and bottle-shaped. Their rinds vary in color from orange, yellow, green, white, black, or even purple. Their pulp or flesh is generally orange or yellow and the center area is filled with seeds.*

PROPERTIES AND INDICATIONS: It may be said that the remarkable nutritional value of the reddish pulp of the squash is due in part to its composition, but also for what it does not contain. These are among the *lowest* of any foods in ***fat*** and ***sodium,*** both antagonistic to healthy arteries and heart.

The nutrient content of squash is quite low: 6% carbohydrates, 1% proteins, and virtually no fat. On the other hand, it stands out for its *richness* in ***beta-carotene*** (provitamin A) and minerals such as ***potassium*** and ***calcium.*** Its soluble ***fiber*** content is also significant, which gives squash a satiating effect on the appetite.

All varieties of squash have the same hypotensive, diuretic, laxative, and anticarcinogenic properties. As a result, their primary medical indications are:

• **Hypertension:** Squash are remarkable for their *very low* **sodium** and *very high* ***potassium*** contents. Sodium-rich diets promote hypertension, while a diet rich in potassium acts to prevent hypertension and its negative consequences (arterial blood clots and stroke).[6, 7] Those with hypertension may eat squash daily in any form, but with no added salt, which would negate its properties. A daylong treatment based on pureed squash is also of great benefit **[❸]**.

Preparing squash for cooking

1. After **cutting** the squash into appropriately sized sections with a large knife, **remove the seeds** and the fibrous interior with a spoon.

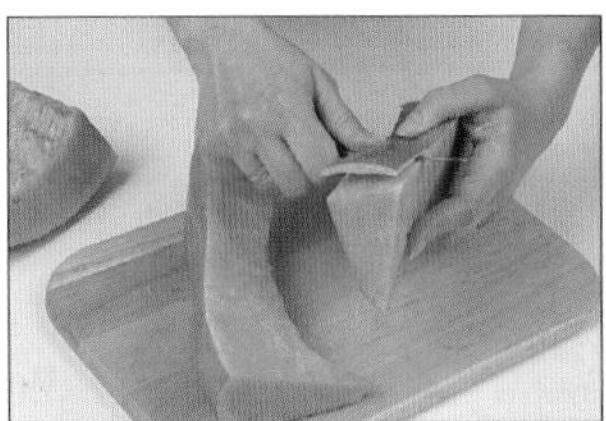

2. **Remove the rind.**

3. **Cut into pieces** according to the culinary need.

• **Coronary affections and arteriosclerosis:** Those suffering from coronary heart disease (**angina pectoris** or **myocardial infarction**) should not fail to eat squash at least three times a week.

Preparation and use

❶ **Baked:** The squash is cut in half or into various pieces and baked in the oven until golden brown. It is eaten with honey or combined with fruit.

❷ **Cooked:** Squash is used in soups and stews.

❸ **Puree:** After cooking, the squash is blended with milk or soy beverage. It may be sweetened to taste, preferably with honey.

• **Renal disorders:** Squash acts as a *mild* **diuretic** in the kidneys, increasing urine production and encouraging the elimination of liquids from the body.

• **Stomach disorders:** Squash pulp is capable of *neutralizing* excess stomach **acid** because of its rich content of alkalizing mineral salts. It also has an **emollient** and **protective** effect on the stomach mucosa (lining). Its consumption, particularly pureed with milk or soy beverage **[❸]**, is particularly indicated in case of excess stomach **acid, dyspepsia** (indigestion), **pyrosis** (heartburn), and, of course, cases of gastroduodenal **ulcer.**

• **Constipation:** Squash fiber is of the soluble type acting as a *mild* **laxative** *not irritatant* to the intestine.

• **Cancer prevention:** Squash contains three of the ***most*** effective, *proven* **anticarcinogenic** vegetable-based substances: beta-carotene, vitamin C, and vegetable fiber. Because of this, the **squash** family, together with that of the **cabbages** (see p. 186), constitute the foods with the *highest* level of **anticarcinogenic** effect.

Yam

Nourishes and lowers triglycerides

YAM
Composition
per 100 g of raw edible portion

Energy	118 kcal = 494 kj
Protein	1.53 g
Carbohydrates	23.8 g
Fiber	4.10 g
Vitamin A	—
Vitamin B_1	0.112 mg
Vitamin B_2	0.032 mg
Niacin	0.752 mg NE
Vitamin B_6	0.293 mg
Folate	23.0 µg
Vitamin B_{12}	—
Vitamin C	17.1 mg
Vitamin E	0.160 mg α-TE
Calcium	17.0 mg
Phosphorus	55.0 mg
Magnesium	21.0 mg
Iron	0.540 mg
Potassium	816 mg
Zinc	0.240 mg
Total Fat	*0.170 g*
Saturated Fat	*0.037 g*
Cholesterol	—
Sodium	*9.00 mg*

1% 2% 4% 10% 20% 40% 100%

% Daily Value (based on a 2,000 calorie diet) provided by 100 g of this food

French: *Igname;*
Spanish: *Ñame, Papa, Batata de China.*

Description: *Tubers of various vines of the genus Dioscorea, particularly 'Dioscorea alata' L., all belonging to the botanical family Dioscoreaceae. The various types of yams differ in shape, size, and color, but the most common weigh between 2 and 5 kilos and have whitish flesh.*

ALTHOUGH THIS article deals only with the **common** or **white yam,** there are many other edible tubers that bear the name "yam":

- Other species of the genus *Dioscorea.*
- **Jicama,** a tuber similar to the yam of the botanical family Convolvulaceae.
- **Taro** and **tania** of the botanical family Araceae, which are found in Southeast Asia.

Properties and indications: Common or **white yams,** as well as other similar tubers

Cassava

Another healthy and nutritious tuber

Scientific syn.: *Manihot esculenta, Manihot utilissima.*
Syn.: *Yuca, Manioc.*

This is the tuber of a bush that is grown in tropical regions of America, Africa, and Asia. It is eaten cooked like potatoes, and constitutes a **staple** in the diets of many in the Third World.

It is ***very rich*** in ***carbohydrates*** (25.3%), ***B vitamins, vitamin C*** (48.2 mg/100 g), ***magnesium, potassium, iron,*** and ***calcium.*** It does not contain provitamin A or vitamin B_{12}, and contains very little fat. It has **anti-thyroid** effects (slows thyroid function).[8]

Caution: The **tubers** and **raw leaves** of the cassava are **toxic** due to the prussic acid that they contain. They ***must be* washed** in water and **boiled** or **dried** before they are edible.[9]

Tapioca is the **flour** obtained from this and other species of cassava. It can be cooked with milk or vegetable broth. It contains 88% ***carbohydrates*** (***starch***) and very **little** ***protein*** or ***fat.*** It is very easily **digested** and *rich* in ***calories.*** It is particularly beneficial is cases of:

Tapioca

- **Digestive disorders:** Tapioca flour retains a great deal of water due to its ***mucilage*** (soluble fiber) content and it is an ***excellent* emollient** (softener) and protector of the digestive lining. It is recommended in cases of excess stomach acid, gastritis, gastroduodenal ulcer, and all types of colitis.
- **Celiac disease:** Contains no gluten.
- **Liver disease:** Tapioca provides easily assimilated carbohydrates and virtually no fat or protein. This facilitates liver function.
- **Convalescence** from serious disease or surgery and reinitiating solid foods after a period of fasting.

called yams, are a staple food in many tropical regions because of their richness in ***carbohydrates*** in the form of ***starch*** (23.8%). However, because they require much effort to grow and are rather *poor* in ***proteins*** (1.53%), the yam is being progressively replaced by **sweet cassava** and **sweet potatoes** (see p. 288).

The yam contains considerable energy (118 kcal/100 g), and contains moderate amounts of B group vitamins, vitamin C, and minerals, among which ***potassium*** is significant (816 mg/100 g). However, yams lack provitamin A.

It has been proven[10] that the yam contains a steroid that stops the peroxidation of blood lipids (the principal cause of arteriosclerosis) and *lowers* the level of **triglycerides,** which are a type of fat in the blood. All of this, together with their low fat content and their richness in potassium, makes yams *very appropriate* for **cardiovascular disorders,** particularly **arteriosclerosis.**

Preparation and use

❶ **Raw:** Although mature yams may be eaten raw, this is not recommended when they are unripe since they contain small amounts of a toxin that disappears when heated. This toxic substance is found primarily in wild yams and causes digestive disturbances.

❷ **Cooked:** Yams can be baked, boiled, or fried, the same as potatoes. In West Africa, cooked yams are used to prepare a much-appreciated type of puree.

Strawberry

The most antioxidant fruit

Related species: *Fragaria virginiana* Duch., *Fragaria chiloensis* Duch.

French: *Fraise [sauvage];* ***Spanish:*** *Fresa, frutilla.*

Description: *False fruit of the strawberry plant 'Fragaria vesca' L. or related species, of the botanical family Rosaceae. The true fruits are the small grains adhered to the surface of the strawberry, which contain the seeds. The strawberry is in reality a kind of fleshy thalamus formed in flowers by the union of the male and female parts.*

STRAWBERRY
Composition
per 100 g of raw edible portion

Energy	30.0 kcal = 127 kj
Protein	0.610 g
Carbohydrates	4.72 g
Fiber	2.30 g
Vitamin A	3.00 µg RE
Vitamin B_1	0.020 mg
Vitamin B_2	0.066 mg
Niacin	0.347 mg NE
Vitamin B_6	0.059 mg
Folate	17.7 µg
Vitamin B_{12}	—
Vitamin C	56.7 mg
Vitamin E	0.140 mg α-TE
Calcium	14.0 mg
Phosphorus	19.0 mg
Magnesium	10.0 mg
Iron	0.380 mg
Potassium	166 mg
Zinc	0.130 mg
Total Fat	*0.370 g*
Saturated Fat	*0.020 g*
Cholesterol	—
Sodium	*1.00 mg*

1% 2% 4% 10% 20% 40% 100%

% Daily Value (based on a 2,000 calorie diet)
provided by 100 g of this food

PROPERTIES AND INDICATIONS: The strawberry is among the fruits with the *lowest* **calorie** content (30 kcal/100 g), lower even than melon (35 kcal/100 g), or watermelon (32 kcal). Its ***protein, fat,*** and ***sodium*** content is also *very low.*

Sugars are the *most significant* ***nutrient*** in strawberries, together with modest amounts of vitamin C, folates, potassium, and iron, which amount to about 5% of their weight.

The color of strawberries comes from vegetable pigments known as anthocyanidines, which are similar to ***bioflavonoids.*** The ***ANTHOCYANIDINES*** found in certain fruits such as strawberries act as *powerful* **antioxidants,** in addition to reducing the synthesis of cholesterol in the liver.

A study carried out at Tufts University in Boston (USA) demonstrated that strawberries have the *greatest* ***antioxidant*** *capacity* of any fruit,[11] followed by plums, oranges, and grapes. The antioxidant effect of a fruit was evaluated in terms of its ability to neutralize oxidizing ***FREE RADICALS.***

The **antioxidant** *capability* of strawberries is due *primarily* to their vitamin C, bioflavonoid, and antocyanidine content.

Strawberries' composition, as well as their antioxidant and alkalizing properties, makes them particularly indicated in the following cases:

- **Arteriosclerosis:** Because their *great* **antioxidant** *capability*, which *neutralizes* the effect of **free radicals,** strawberries are an effective means of avoiding arteriosclerosis (the depositing of cholesterol on artery walls, which later thicken and become narrow). Strawberries also contribute to arterial health by their *lack* of ***fat*** and ***sodium,*** and their *richness* in ***potassium,*** a mineral that prevents hypertension.

Eating strawberries regularly during the spring and the first months of summer helps prevent arteriosclerosis and avert its further development. Strawberries should be included in the diet of those who have suffered a **heart attack** or **angina pectoris,** as well as when there is **poor circulation** to the cerebral arteries or to those of the lower limbs.

- **Excess uric acid:** Strawberries are **diuretic** (they increase urine production) and facilitate the elimination of uric acid with the urine because of their alkalizing effect. Because of this, strawberries are recommended in cases of gout and uratic arthritis.

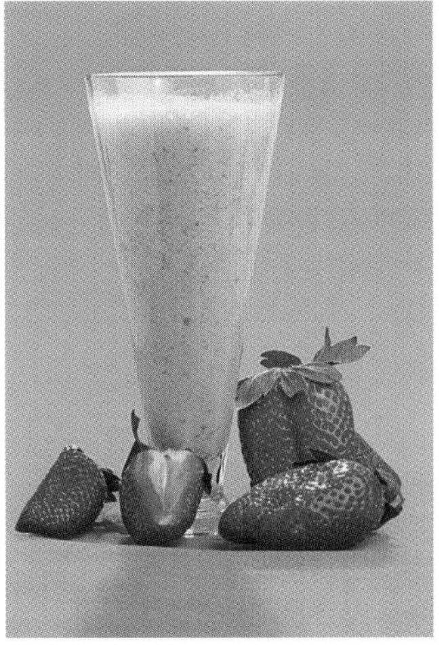

Strawberries are particularly appropriate for those working to improve blood circulation in the arteries.

- **Constipation:** Because of their richness in soluble vegetable ***fiber,*** strawberries facilitate passage of the feces through the intestines. They also *decongest* **venous circulation** in the portal system (veins in the bowel), thus they are useful in cases of **hemorrhoids, ascites** (fluid in the abdomen), and liver disorders such as chronic **hepatitis** and cirrhosis.
- **Cancer:** Because of its antioxidant effect.

Preparation and use

❶ **Fresh:** Fresh strawberries should be washed just before eating. They go well with apples, orange juice, grains, and yogurt.

❷ **Strawberry shake:** This is made by blending strawberries with orange juice, nonfat milk, or soy beverage.

❸ **Jam and compote:** Strawberries prepared in this way retain almost all of their nutrients and active elements, although they lose vitamin C. They represent a means of having them available out of season, with the drawback, however, of a very high sugar content (around 50%).

❹ **Frozen:** Frozen strawberries are very popular since they make the fruit available year-round and virtually everywhere. Frozen strawberries tend to contain less added sugar (0%-20%) than jam, and retain most of their nutrients and active elements, including vitamin C.

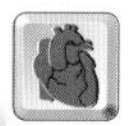

Sunflower seeds

Combating arteriosclerosis

SUNFLOWER SEED
Composition
per 100 g of raw edible portion

Energy	570 kcal = 2,386 kj
Protein	22.8 g
Carbohydrates	8.26 g
Fiber	10.5 g
Vitamin A	5.00 µg RE
Vitamin B_1	2.29 mg
Vitamin B_2	0.250 mg
Niacin	10.3 mg NE
Vitamin B_6	0.770 mg
Folate	227 µg
Vitamin B_{12}	—
Vitamin C	1.40 mg
Vitamin E	50.3 mg α-TE
Calcium	116 mg
Phosphorus	705 mg
Magnesium	354 mg
Iron	6.77 mg
Potassium	689 mg
Zinc	5.06 mg
Total Fat	*49.6 g*
Saturated Fat	*5.20 g*
Cholesterol	*—*
Sodium	*3.00 mg*

1% 2% 4% 10% 20% 40% 100% 200% 500%

% Daily Value (based on a 2,000 calorie diet)
provided by 100 g of this food

French: *Graine du tournesol;*
Spanish: *Semillas de girasol.*

Description: *Seeds from the sunflower ('Helianthus annuus' L.), an annual plant of the botanical family Solanaceae Compositae that grows to a height of two meters.*

PROPERTIES AND INDICATIONS: Sunflower seeds are composed of up to 49.6% ***fat,*** which provides an *excellent* culinary ***oil;*** 22.8% ***proteins,*** an amount similar to meat; and up to 8.3% ***carbohydrates.***

Sunflower seeds are almost completely lacking in vitamins A and C. But they are one of the *richest* sources of ***vitamin E*** (double than almonds, p. 58) and ***vitamin*** $\boldsymbol{B_1}$ (surpassed only by brewer's yeast).

They are *very rich* in such minerals as ***magnesium, iron*** (6.8 mg/100 g, equal to lentils, p. 130), ***calcium*** and ***phosphorous.***

It is possible to deduce from this that sunflower seeds are among the *most* ***nutritionally*** *concentrated* foods offered by nature, particularly in fats, minerals, and vitamins B_1 and E. Even with all of this nutritional richness, they are easily digested provided they are well chewed.

Eating sunflower seeds regularly (unsalted, of course) is particularly indicated in the following situations:

- **Arteriosclerosis and coronary heart disease:** The ***essential fatty acids*** in sunflower seeds (*particularly* ***linoleic*** acid) impede the progress of arteriosclerosis by lowering the level of cholesterol in the blood.

Vitamin E, which sunflower seeds contain in abundance, is a *powerful* **antioxidant** that prevents arterial deterioration. It also *reduces* **platelet stickiness,** which helps *prevent* **blood clots** and **heart attacks.**[12, 13]

- **Excess cholesterol:** Eating sunflower seeds, *particularly* as a *substitute* for *other* **fatty** or **calorie-rich foods,** causes a significant reduction in cholesterol level.[14] This same effect is gained by using sunflower seed oil.
- **Skin and related disorders:** ***Linoleic acid*** and **vitamin E** improve the elasticity of the skin, protecting its cells *from* the effects of **aging** (antioxidant action). Eating sunflower seeds is recommended for **eczema, cracked, dry skin,** and **dermatitis** in general. They also *strengthen* the **nails** and **hair,** *reducing* the number of **gray hairs.**

The humble sunflower seed is particularly rich in linoleic acid and vitamins B_1 and E, which give it healing power in cases of arteriosclerosis and excess cholesterol.

Preparation and use

❶ **Raw:** Sunflower seeds are best eaten raw after they have been spread on a flat surface and dried for a few days.

❷ **Toasted:** These are very flavorful, but if they are toasted for a long period their nutritional value suffers.

❸ **Ground to a paste:** Once shelled, the seeds are ground to a homogeneous paste, which is excellent for children, the elderly, and those with deteriorated teeth.

- **Nervous disorders:** Sunflower seeds contain as much ***vitamin B_1*** as wheat germ (see p. 296). Those suffering from **stress, depression, insomnia,** or **nervousness** will find real help in these humble seeds.
- **Diabetes:** Sunflower seeds are well tolerated by diabetics and constitute a nutritious food that should be included in their diet.
- **Increased nutritional needs:** Sunflower seeds are a ***high-calorie*** *food,* as well as being *rich* in ***essential nutrients.*** They are appropriate for **pregnant** or **lactating women, athletes,** those with **anemia,** those that are **undernourished,** and those **recovering** from debilitating diseases, and in general, anyone needing a greater supply of nutrition.
- **Cancer:** Numerous epidemiological and experimental studies show that ***vitamin E*** exercises an *anticarcinogenic* effect, as well as offering a possible *cure* in some instances.

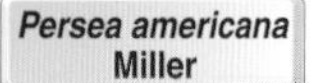

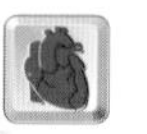

Avocado

Lowers cholesterol and fights anemia

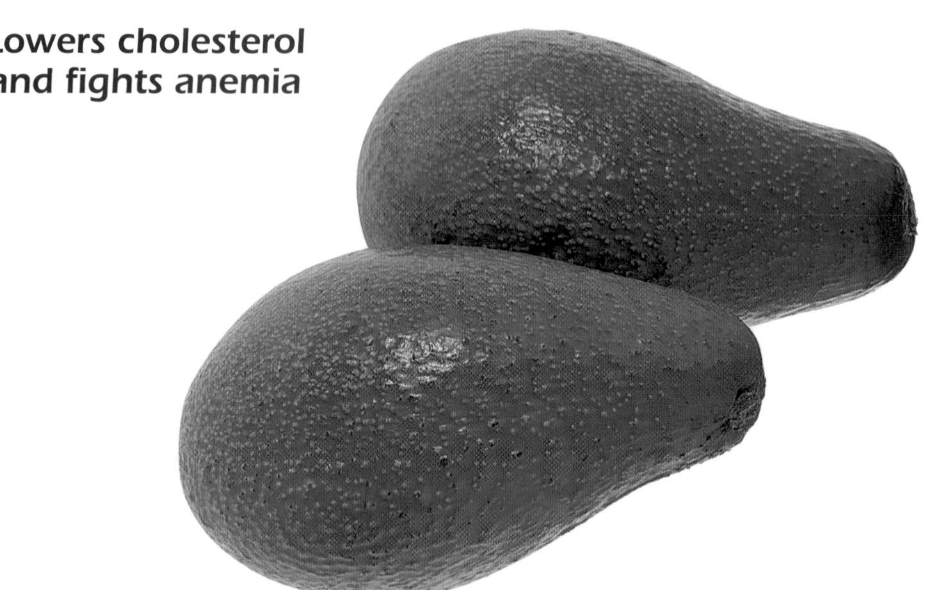

AVOCADO
Composition
per 100 g of raw edible portion

Energy	161 kcal = 674 kj
Protein	1.98 g
Carbohydrates	2.39 g
Fiber	5.00 g
Vitamin A	61.0 µg RE
Vitamin B_1	0.108 mg
Vitamin B_2	0.122 mg
Niacin	2.27 mg NE
Vitamin B_6	0.500 mg
Folate	61.9 µg
Vitamin B_{12}	—
Vitamin C	7.90 mg
Vitamin E	2.30 mg α-TE
Calcium	11.0 mg
Phosphorus	41.0 mg
Magnesium	39.0 mg
Iron	1.02 mg
Potassium	599 mg
Zinc	0.420 mg
Total Fat	*15.3 g*
Saturated Fat	*2.44 g*
Cholesterol	—
Sodium	*10.0 mg*

1% 2% 4% 10% 20% 40% 100%

% Daily Value (based on a 2,000 calorie diet) provided by 100 g of this food

Scientific synonym: *Persea gratissima* Gaertn.

Synonyms: *Alligator pear, Zuttano, Fuerte.*

French: *Avocat;* ***Spanish:*** *Aguacate, palta, avocado.*

Description: *The fruit of the avocado tree ('Persea americana' Miller), evergreen tree of the botanical family Lauraceae that grows to a height of 16 meters.*

PROPERTIES AND INDICATIONS: The avocado's composition has several noteworthy features:[15]

✓ ***Water:*** The avocado contains a *very low* proportion of water (74.2% or less) compared to what is usual for fresh fruit. Other than bananas and olives, no other fruit has less. This indicates that the avocado is a concentrated fruit with *high* **nutritional** and **caloric** *capacity* that can reach as high as 200 kcal /100 g of edible portion in certain varieties.

✓ ***Fats:*** Together with the olive, the avocado is among the *richest* fruits in fats (up to 20% depending on the variety).

The composition of the fats in avocados is as follows:

- Neutral lipids or ***glycerides*** formed by the union of a glycerin molecule with one, two, or three fatty acid molecules. These are then referred to as mono, di, or triglycerides respectively. Triglycerides are by far the most common of these. ***Oleic*** acid is the *most abundant* of the fatty acids in avocados, as is the case with olive oil.
- ***Phospholipids:*** These are fats containing phosphorous in their molecule. They perform very important functions in the nervous system.
- **Free fatty acids,** in other words, not united to glycerin. These are present in very small amounts, and are partly responsible for the typical aroma of the fruit.

As can be seen, the ***fats*** in avocados are of *high* **biological value** and are *primarily* **unsaturated.** Of course, they contain *no* **cholesterol,** as is the case with all plant-based foods.

✓ ***Proteins:*** Avocados are among the *most* ***protein-rich*** of fresh fruits, which, depending on variety, can reach 2% of their weight. They contain all of the ***essential amino acids,***[16] although their proportion is not optimal, as is usually the case with plant-based foods with the exception of soy (see p. 254). In spite of this, avocado proteins are of *great value,* as much for their amount as for their quality. This value is multiplied if these proteins are combined with other vegetable proteins thanks to the phenomenon of **supplementation.**

✓ ***Vitamin E:*** With its 2.3 mg per 100 g of α-TE (*alpha*-tocopherol equivalents), the avocado is the *richest* fresh **fruit** in this vitamin. No animal-based food approaches this amount, not even eggs (1.05 mg α-TE) or butter (1.58 mg α-TE). Among plant foods, oil-bearing **nuts, wheat germ,** and **olives** surpass the avocado in vitamin E.

This important vitamin not only promotes reproductive functions, but because it is a *powerful* **antioxidant** it *protects* against **cancer and** cellular **aging.**

✓ ***Vitamin B_6:*** The avocado is, together with the banana, the *richest* fresh **fruit** in this vitamin: 0.5 mg/100 g, an amount superior, even, to beef, which has 0.37 mg/100 g.

✓ ***Iron:*** The avocado has the *highest* iron content (1.02 mg/100 g) of any fresh **fruit.**

By studying the composition of the avocado one can deduce that this is one on the ***most nutritious*** fruits extant. This together with their delicate flavor and culinary versatility explains the important role that they played in the diets of pre-Columbian Americans, for whom it was used as a *substitute* for **meat.**

✓ ***Fiber:*** With 5% or more, the avocado is the richest of any fresh fruit in fiber. Today, the av-

Preparation and use

❶ **Fresh:** The avocado is not a fruit in the culinary sense of the word, since it lacks the sweetness and acidity that characterize fruits. Thanks to this, avocado combine very well with all types of salads and dishes, whether sweet or not.

Preferably avocados are eaten raw with lemon juice, which also keeps them from turning black because of the oxidation of the iron salts they contain. They can be spread on bread as an effective substitute for butter or margarine.

❷ **Guacamole:** Although there are various recipes, authentic Mexican guacamole is prepared with mashed avocado, chopped onion, lemon juice, salt, and chile.

As a fresh fruit, avocado is one of the richest in high-value nutritional fats, proteins, vitamins E and B_6, iron, as well as vegetable fiber. It mixes together very well with all kinds of salads and other vegetable dishes.
When avocado is used **in place of cheese** in salads, the result is a significant **reduction** in **calories, saturated fat, cholesterol,** and **sodium.**

ocado is one of the most valued of fruits for its nutritional value, as well as for its dietary and therapeutic properties. Avocado consumption is particularly recommended in the following cases:

• **Excess cholesterol:** An avocado paradox was revealed in 1960 when W. C. Grant[17] discovered that eating this fruit, so rich in fats, actually *lowered* blood cholesterol levels. These first studies were conducted by feeding 16 males aged 27 to 72 various amounts of avocado (one-half to one and a-half a day). Half of the subjects showed a reduction in cholesterol level. No subject showed any increase.

More recently, in 1992 a similar study was conducted at the General Hospital of Morelia (Mexico).[18] The diet used in this case contained 30% of its calories in the form of fats, of which 75% were from avocado. After two weeks there was a significant *reduction* in **cholesterol** level, particularly in the LDL fraction (cholesterol united with low density lipoproteins, commonly known as harmful cholesterol). The plasma triglyceride level was also *lowered* (**triglycerides** are a type of fat that circulates in the blood, see p. 275).

It is curious, almost paradoxical, that eating avocados, a fruit rich in triglycerides, actually lowers this type of fat in the blood. This is one of the pleasant surprises found in plant-based foods.

The avocado's **hypolipidemic action** (reduction of fat level in the blood) is possibly due to the balanced composition of its fatty acids, or its *rich* vegetable ***fiber*** content, although there may be other reasons, as yet unknown.

Because of all of this, eating avocados regularly is *highly recommended* for those with excess cholesterol or triglycerides in the blood, as well as any other type of hyperlipemia (increase in fats in the blood).

• **Circulatory disorders:** Avocados cannot be more *highly recommended* for cases of **arteriosclerosis, hypertension,** and coronary **heart** disease in general. This is due, in addition to their interesting hypolipidemic (reduction of fat level in the blood) action, to the fact that they contain *very little* ***sodium*** and *abundant* ***potassium.***

• **Anemia:** The ***iron*** in avocados is relatively well assimilated. Therefore eating them is encouraged for all those needing additional iron, such as **adolescents** (particularly girls) and **pregnant** women.

Avocados should be included in the diet of all who are anemic because of blood loss or lack of iron.

Normally the ***IRON*** found in plant-based foods, called ***nonheme iron,*** is absorbed with greater difficulty than the ***heme iron*** from animal sources. However, the iron in avocados is *absorbed* ***better*** than that of other plant-based

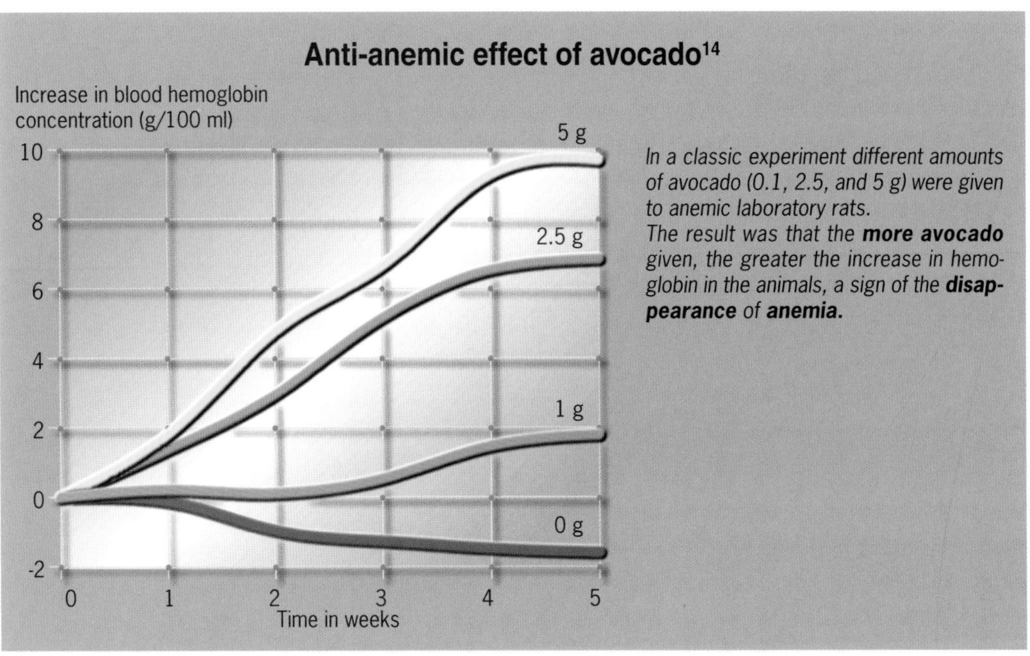

*In a classic experiment different amounts of avocado (0.1, 2.5, and 5 g) were given to anemic laboratory rats. The result was that the **more avocado** given, the greater the increase in hemoglobin in the animals, a sign of the **disappearance** of **anemia.***

foods, possibly due to their ***vitamin C*** content, which facilitates its absorption.

• **Nervous disorders:** Avocados contain fats that are very important to the metabolism of the nervous system such as ***linoleic acid*** and ***phospholipids.*** Additionally, they are very rich in ***vitamin B6,*** one of the most important for proper neuron function. Based on this, avocados are very appropriate for those suffering from **nervousness, irritability,** or **depression.**

• **Digestive disorders:** Avocados are appropriate for the diet of those suffering from stomach **ulcers** or **gastritis** because of their **alkalinity** and the **emollient** and protective effects of their fats on the mucosa.

• **Diabetes:** Up until a few years ago diabetics were discouraged from eating avocados since they contain a monosaccharide sugar consisting of seven carbon atoms called ***mannoheptulos,*** which seemed to produce **hyperglycemia**[19] (elevated glucose in the blood) in experimentally high doses.

More recent studies[20] show that eating avocados is *particularly beneficial* to diabetics. They not only help maintain an appropriate glycemia level (blood glucose), it also lowers cholesterol and improves the lipid profile (the composition of fats) in the blood.

• **Invigorating diets:** Because of their great nutritional value, their ease of digestion, and their ***vitamin E*** content, avocados should be a regular part of the diets of children, adolescents during periods of rapid growth, athletes, exhausted or stressed adults, the elderly, and of all those wishing to naturally and healthfully ***increase*** their **vitality.**

Pear

Effective blood pressure controller

French: *Poire;* ***Spanish:*** *Pera.*

Description: *Fruit of the pear tree ('Pyrus communis' L.), a tree similar to the apple tree of the botanical family Rosaceae.*

PEAR
Composition
per 100 g of raw edible portion

Energy	59.0 kcal = 247 kj
Protein	0.390 g
Carbohydrates	12.7 g
Fiber	2.40 g
Vitamin A	2.00 µg RE
Vitamin B_1	0.020 mg
Vitamin B_2	0.040 mg
Niacin	0.100 mg NE
Vitamin B_6	0.018 mg
Folate	7.30 µg
Vitamin B_{12}	—
Vitamin C	4.00 mg
Vitamin E	0.500 mg α-TE
Calcium	11.0 mg
Phosphorus	11.0 mg
Magnesium	6.00 mg
Iron	0.250 mg
Potassium	125 mg
Zinc	0.120 mg
Total Fat	0.400 g
Saturated Fat	0.022 g
Cholesterol	—
Sodium	—

1% 2% 4% 10% 20% 40% 100%

% Daily Value (based on a 2,000 calorie diet) provided by 100 g of this food

Properties and indications: Pears are noted for their content of ***sugars*** (12.7%), while they are lacking in proteins (0.39%) and fats (0.4%). The most abundant of these sugars is ***fructose*** or levulose, which makes them well *tolerated* by **diabetics.**

Pears contain small amounts of vitamins C, E, and B. The most important of the ***minerals*** they contain are potassium, magnesium, and iron. They are also a good source of ***trace elements*** such as copper and manganese, and, in lower proportion, zinc. The pear's vitamin and mineral content is slightly greater than that of apples (see p. 216).

The pear is also a good source of vegetable ***fiber*** (2.4%), an amount that is slightly less than the apple (2.7%). In contrast to the apple, the pear contains a greater amount of insoluble fiber rich in lignin (the material that makes wood and wheat bran hard).[21]

Soluble fiber is more effective against cholesterol, while the insoluble is a more effective laxative.

In terms of non-nutritive components, the pear contains a lower proportion of ***organic acids*** than the apple and a greater proportion of ***tannins.*** These are responsible for the absorbent and anti-inflammatory effect of pears.

The pear is also diuretic, remineralizing, a mild astringent, and refreshing. These are its primary medical indications:

- **Hypertension:** The pear's capacity to lower blood pressure has been known since antiquity. This is attributed to its diuretic effect. Today it is known, as well, that the pear contains *no* ***sodium,*** a mineral that tends to retain water within the body, thus increasing blood pressure.

Additionally, the pear is *very rich* in ***potassium,*** a mineral with the opposite effect of sodium. There are studies[22] demonstrating that the *higher* the ***potassium*** *intake,* the lower the risk of hypertension. New studies are constantly appearing that relate diet to hypertension of apparently unknown causes.

Preparation and use

❶ **Raw:** It is important to chew pears well, particularly those that are hard and gritty-textured. They should generally be peeled (because of potential external contamination). However, in the case of the pear, the peel is of dietary value because of its diuretic value. Of course, they must be well washed, and, if possible, organically grown.

❷ **Cooked:** Cooked pears are easier to digest but the cooking process destroys most of their vitamins while the sugars and minerals remain intact.

❸ **Compotes and jams.**

Although a diuretic, and preventer of hypertension, the pear is a very luscious fruit and is more thirst-quenching than ice cream.

- **Renal failure:** The pear stimulates renal function, thus it is a highly recommended fruit in cases of renal failure due to nephritis or nephrosis. In addition to containing *no* ***sodium*** and being *very low* in ***proteins,*** the pear is a *good source* of ***potassium*** and produces a mild diuretic effect, all of which benefit renal disorders.

Abundant pear *consumption* is recommended in cases of cardiac, as well as renal **edema** (fluid retention).

- **Excess uric acid:** Pear consumption promotes the elimination of uric acid and other nitrogenated substances through the urine. It has an **alkalizing** effect on the blood, which is of benefit in detoxifying diets used to neutralize excess acid residues produced by a high-meat diet.
- **Obesity:** The pear should be included in weight loss diets because of its mild diuretic action and its depurative effect.
- **Digestive disorders:** When it is ripe and tender, the pear is digested rapidly and easily. There is evidence that shows that within 90 minutes of eating, it has been digested and has arrived in the large intestine. It has a *mild* **astringent** action and *works against* the **intestinal putrefaction and flatulence** occurring in case of colitis (inflammation of the large intestine) and intestinal dyspepsia (indigestion at the intestinal level).

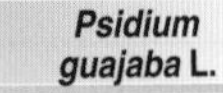

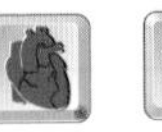

Guava

Reduces hypertension and cholesterol

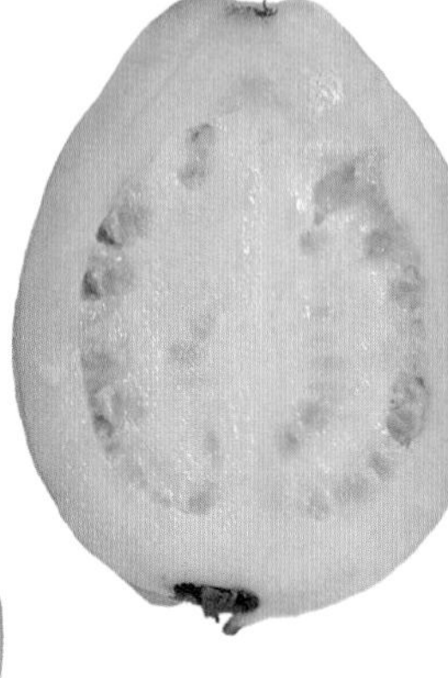

Synonyms: *Common guava, Goyave, Guayaba, Guyaba, Mountain guava.*

French: *Goyave;* ***Spanish:*** *Guayaba, guava.*

Description: *Fruit of the guava tree ('Psidium guajaba' L.), a tree of the botanical family Myrtaceae that reaches 6 meters in height.*

GUAVA
Composition
per 100 g of raw edible portion

Energy	51.0 kcal = 211 kj
Protein	0.820 g
Carbohydrates	6.48 g
Fiber	5.40 g
Vitamin A	79.0 µg RE
Vitamin B_1	0.050 mg
Vitamin B_2	0.050 mg
Niacin	1.32 mg NE
Vitamin B_6	0.143 mg
Folate	14.0 µg
Vitamin B_{12}	—
Vitamin C	184 mg
Vitamin E	1.12 mg α-TE
Calcium	20.0 mg
Phosphorus	25.0 mg
Magnesium	10.0 mg
Iron	0.310 mg
Potassium	284 mg
Zinc	0.230 mg
Total Fat	*0.600 g*
Saturated Fat	*0.172 g*
Cholesterol	—
Sodium	*3.00 mg*

1% 2% 4% 10% 20% 40% 100% 200% 500%

% Daily Value (based on a 2,000 calorie diet)
provided by 100 g of this food

Properties and Indications: The guava is *low* in ***proteins, fats*** (less than 1% each) and ***carbohydrates*** (6%), but is noteworthy because of its supply of:

✓ ***Vitamin C:*** With 183 mg/100 g, the guava is among the *richest* fruits in this vitamin. Only the acerola (see p. 354) and the brier hip (*EMP* p. 762) are richer. The guava also contains small quantities of organic ***acids*** such as ***citric*** acid and ***malic*** acid, which *facilitate* the absorption of the ***vitamin C*** and give the fruit its typical acidic taste.

✓ ***Carotenoids:*** These are substances that transform to vitamin A and have a *powerful* **antioxidant** *effect* within the cells. The guava's richness in carotenoids is 79 µg RE, which means that 100 g of pulp supplies 8% of the daily need of vitamin A. Those varieties with reddish pulp are the richest in carotenoids, and contain ***lycopene,*** the same carotenoid found in tomatoes.

✓ ***Vegetable fiber:*** Most of the 5.4% of fiber in the guava is soluble, composed of ***pectin*** and ***mucilage.***

The guava also contains significant amounts of B group vitamins (except B_{12}), and vitamin E, as well as calcium, phosphorous, magnesium, and iron. Its most abundant mineral is potassium. It is also *relatively rich* in ***trace elements*** such as zinc, copper, and manganese.

The guava's medicinal applications are the following:

• **Hypertension:** A study conducted in India and published in the *American Journal of Cardiology,*[20] found that adding guava to the daily diets of 61 hypertensive volunteers lowered their systolic blood pressure by 9 mm/Hg and the diastolic by 8 mm/Hg (the equivalent of moving from 150/90 mm Hg to 141/82 mm /Hg). These results were obtained over a three-month period of regular guava consumption. Although the results are not spectacular, they provide yet another tool in the treatment of hypertension.

Just which component of the guava is responsible for this gentle hypertensive effect is not known, but it is undoubtedly affected by the fact that this fruit is *very low* in ***sodium*** and *high* in ***potassium*** and vegetable ***fiber.***

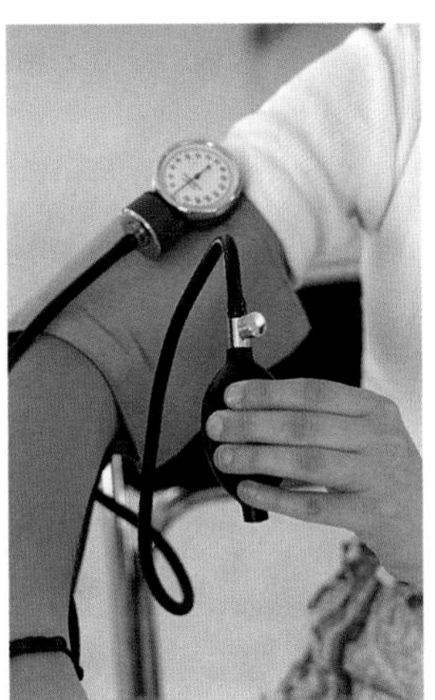

Guava lowers blood pressure, cholesterol, and blood fats. It also neutralizes the effect of nicotine because of its rich vitamin C content.

One guava, which may weigh about 100 g, provides three times the RDA for vitamin C for an adult.

• **Excess cholesterol:** This same experiment,[23] produced a 9.9% overall cholesterol reduction and 7.7% reduction in triglycerides (see p. 275) in the blood. This hypolipidemic (lipid-reducing) effect is due to the guava's *rich* content of soluble ***fiber*** (***pectin***), which "sweeps" the intestine and facilitates the elimination through the feces of cholesterol and the biliary salts from which it is synthesized.

• **Arteriosclerosis:** The guava is an excellent fruit for maintaining good arterial health. Its consumption *prevents* the risk factors that cause arteriosclerosis: **hypertension** and high **cholesterol.**

• **Nicotine addiction:** This is another important factor in the hardening of the arteries. The *large amount* of ***vitamin C*** found in guavas is a *great help* to those in treatment for **nicotine addiction** since this vitamin *neutralizes* **nicotine.** Two or three guavas a day make an excellent dessert for those wishing to stop smoking.

• **Physical fatigue:** The guava has an **invigorating** effect on the body. They are beneficial, in addition to specific circumstances, for those convalescing from infectious illnesses and in cases of fatigue and weakness provoked by chronic disease.

Preparation and use

❶ **Fresh:** The seed-containing interior of the guava must be well chewed or strained. The external portion of the fruit lacks seeds and is softer. Overripe fruit loses vitamin C and fiber.

❷ **Manufactured products:** The guava is used to produce all types of delicious syrups, jellies, and jams.

❸ **Guava paste:** A typical Brazilian product prepared by adding sugar to guava pulp, and concentrating the mixture by cooking. It is similar to quince jelly.

Rye

Provides flexibility to the arteries

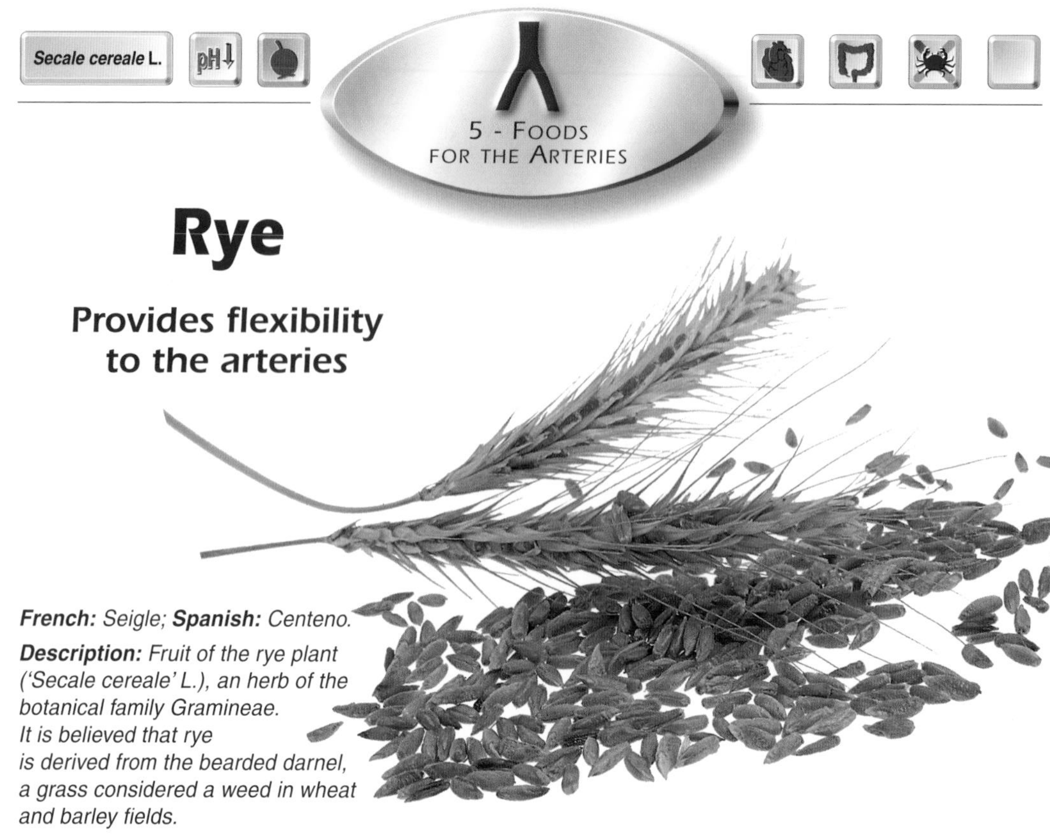

French: *Seigle;* ***Spanish:*** *Centeno.*

Description: *Fruit of the rye plant ('Secale cereale' L.), an herb of the botanical family Gramineae. It is believed that rye is derived from the bearded darnel, a grass considered a weed in wheat and barley fields.*

RYE
Composition
per 100 g of raw edible portion

Energy	335 kcal = 1,403 kj
Protein	14.8 g
Carbohydrates	55.2 g
Fiber	14.6 g
Vitamin A	—
Vitamin B_1	0.316 mg
Vitamin B_2	0.251 mg
Niacin	6.84 mg NE
Vitamin B_6	0.294 mg
Folate	60.0 µg
Vitamin B_{12}	—
Vitamin C	—
Vitamin E	1.87 mg α-TE
Calcium	33.0 mg
Phosphorus	374 mg
Magnesium	121 mg
Iron	2.67 mg
Potassium	264 mg
Zinc	3.73 mg
Total Fat	*2.50 g*
Saturated Fat	*0.287 g*
Cholesterol	—
Sodium	*6.00 mg*

1% 2% 4% 10% 20% 40% 100%

% Daily Value (based on a 2,000 calorie diet) provided by 100 g of this food

PROPERTIES AND INDICATIONS: Rye is similar to wheat in composition, but with more proteins and fiber. Its energy content is 331 kcal/100 g, which is also similar to wheat (335 kcal/100 g).

Although it lacks provitamin A, and vitamins C and B_{12} as do all grains, it has a good proportion of other nutrients, except fats and calcium, which are not as abundant as others:

✓ **Carbohydrates:** These form most of the grain (55.2%) with starch being its primary constituent. The starch granules in rye, more than other grains, are encapsulated in cellulose. This makes rye digestion slower, thus releasing the glucose molecules little by little.Because of this, rye does not provoke sudden increases in blood glucose levels; it is satiating and well tolerated by diabetics.

✓ **Proteins:** Rye is quite protein-rich (14.8%); for example higher than wheat (10.4%), although it contains less glutelin and gliadin, proteins that form gluten. Because of this, rye bread is heavier than bread made from wheat flour.

✓ ***Vitamins:*** Rye is a good source of vitamins B_1, B_2, B_6, E, niacin, and folates. Since it lacks provitamin A, and vitamin C, rye should be combined with fresh fruits and vegetables that are rich in these vitamins.

✓ ***Minerals:*** Rye is quite rich in phosphorous, magnesium, and iron, as well as zinc, selenium, and other trace elements. However, it is deficient in calcium, another good reason to eat it with milk or dairy products.

Each 100 g of rye satisfies more than a fourth of the daily need for ***iron,*** and more than a *third* of that of ***magnesium;*** all of this with *virtually no* ***sodium.***

Rye is as much or more nutritious than wheat, although not as easy to digest. Its use is particularly indicated in these cases:

- **Arteriosclerosis and coronary heart disease:** Rye makes the arterial walls more elastic, the blood more fluid, and it improves circulation. In reality, this prevention of arterial degeneration is a common feature of whole grains,[21] although it seems that rye's effect is more pronounced.

"Pumpernickel" is a whole rye bread typical of Germany. It is very rich in B group vitamins and cellulose.

Rye's content of **antioxidants** such as ***vitamin E*** and selenium, as well as its high cellulose ***fiber*** content explains this property in part.

Those suffering from arteriosclerosis in any part of the body, particularly in the coronary arteries, which manifests as angina pectoris or heart attack, will benefit from eating rye regularly.

- **Hypertension:** Because of its favorable effect on the arteries and its *very low* ***sodium*** content, rye is also of benefit to those suffering from hypertension. If rye is eaten as bread, it is preferable that it be unsalted.

- **Constipation:** Rye's rich cellulose ***fiber*** content, which is primarily insoluble, makes it of value in the diet of those suffering from constipation.

- ***Prevention*** of ***colon cancer:*** Besides helping avoid constipation, which is a colon cancer risk factor, it has been shown that rye bread, more than any other, reduces the concentration of the bile acids, lithocholic acid and deoxycholic acid in the intestine.[24] These acids, which are eliminated with the bile, act as carcinogens on the intestinal mucosa, in addition to potentiating other cancer precursors that may be found in the intestine, particularly those from meat.

In this manner, regular use of rye is highly recommended for those at high colon cancer risk, as well as those who have been operated to avoid recurrence.

Preparation and use

❶ **Whole grain:** Although the outer layer (bran) is very hard, rye may be eaten as flakes by soaking the raw grains to make muesli.

❷ **Cooked:** After soaking for several hours, rye may be cooked like rice. It should be cooked in a pressure cooker to keep it from becoming hard.

❸ **Flour:** Rye flour is not as gluten-rich as that of wheat, however it is still used for bread. Rye bread is denser than that of wheat since it contains less gluten and the dough does not rise. Normally rye flour is mixed with that of wheat.

❹ **Rye crackers:** These are light, crunchy, and very tasty. They are typical of Germany and the Scandinavian countries.

Foods for the Blood

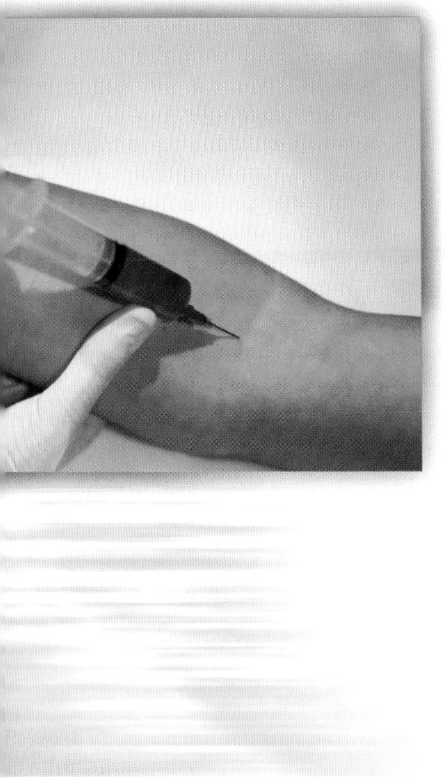

MOST **dietary *iron*** is in the form of ferric salts (***nonheme iron***) that come from fruits, vegetables, and eggs. However, this chemical form of iron is absorbed with some difficulty in the intestine. The iron found in meat and fish, called ***heme iron,*** is more easily absorbed.

Numerous experiments have shown that ***vitamin C,*** particularly that from lemon juice, can *double* or *triple* the **absorption** rate of ***nonheme iron*** in the intestine.[1] This can *even* ***compensate*** for the *negative effects* of **phytates** (a component of bran) or polyphenols (**tannins**) have on iron absorption.[2]

Most cases of **anemia** are caused by a *lack* of the **iron, *folic acid,*** and ***vitamin B12*** that the body needs to produce red **blood cells.** Using **lemon** together with *iron-rich* **plant-based** foods, such as legumes (beans, lentils, soy and its derivatives), certain green leafy vegetables (spinach, leeks), or grains (wheat, rice), *significantly* ***increases*** the **utilization** of this important mineral.

The current recommendation is that ***each meal*** includes 25 mg of ***vitamin C*** because of its beneficial effect on iron absorption.[3] This amount of vitamin C is provided by half a lemon.

Meat is not essential to blood formation. Blood developed from plant-based foods is of a better quality than that from foods of animal origin.

THROMBOSIS

Definition

Blood has the tendency to clot spontaneously. Thanks to this property, hemorrhages are stopped. But when this clotting takes place within the blood vessels a solid clot or thrombus is formed that blocks free circulation of blood through the vessel. This process is called thrombosis and can occur in the arteries or the veins. Its consequences are always serious, for example heart attack or stroke.

Causes

Factors that ***promote*** thrombosis are:

- **Arteriosclerosis.**
- A diet high in **saturated fat** and **salt.**
- Excess **toxins** or waste material in the blood.
- **Tobacco** and *lack* of **physical exercise.**

Diet

Certain foods, *particularly* **fruits,** can go a long way toward reducing the tendency to the formation of thrombi in the blood vessels.

Increase

GARLIC
LEMON
ORANGE
ONION
GRAPE
FRUIT
SOY
OLIVE OIL
FISH OIL

Reduce or eliminate

SATURATED FAT
CHOLESTEROL
SALT

Soy milk

Soy is the most iron-rich of legumes. Its derivatives are also good sources of this mineral. For example, "tofu" contains 5.36 mg /100 g of iron (about three times more than meat or soft cheese) and soymilk or soy beverage contains 0.58 mg/100 g (about 10 times that of cow's milk).

Oranges

Lemon or orange consumed together with soy or its derivatives facilitates the absorption of the iron contained in soy.

ANEMIA

Definition

The word anemia literally means, "lack of blood." However, it is used to describe a reduction in erythrocyte (red blood cell) count in the blood. These cells are those that give blood its red color and those that transport life-giving oxygen to all of the body's cells.

Diet

Anemia may be caused by various mechanisms as described on the next column.

Diet plays an ***essential*** role since foods provide the necessary nutrients for blood cell production:

- Iron, proteins, vitamin B_{12}, and folates or folic acid are the ***most* important** of these nutrients.
- Vitamins B_1, B_2, B_6, C, E and copper are also necessary nutrients for blood production.

Causes

- **Insufficient blood production:** Erythrocytes (red blood cells) live approximately one hundred days, and the bone marrow is constantly producing new blood cells. To do this, the marrow requires iron, proteins, folic acid, and a variety of vitamins. The scarcest nutrient is iron, and the anemia produced under these circumstances is called **iron deficiency** anemia.
- **Blood loss,** whether from acute hemorrhage or from smaller hemorrhages. In some cases these hemorrhages may go unnoticed, such as stomach or intestinal bleeding.
- **Destruction of blood cells:** This produces **hemolytic** anemia, in which the red blood cells are destroyed for various causes and diseases.

Increase

LEGUMES
SOY
FRUIT
LEAFY GREEN VEGETABLES
ALFALFA
WATERCRESS
RED BEET
SPINACH, AVOCADO
SUNFLOWER SEEDS
PISTACHO, GRAPE
PASSION FRUIT
APRICOT
LEMON
SPIRULINA
MOLASSES
IRON, MEAT
VITAMIN B_{12}
FOLATES
VITAMINS B, E AND C

Reduce or eliminate

TEA
WHEAT BRAN
ALCOHOLIC BEVERAGES
MILK

Alfalfa sprouts

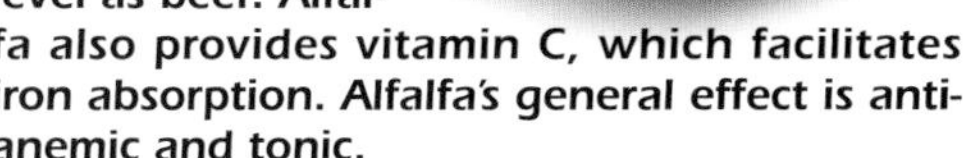

Alfalfa sprouts contain almost 1 mg/100 g of iron, approximately the same level as beef. Alfalfa also provides vitamin C, which facilitates iron absorption. Alfalfa's general effect is anti-anemic and tonic.

The practice of dressing and seasoning dishes with lemon (for example vegetables and legumes) is doubly beneficial:

- **It aids the assimilation of the iron in the foods;**
- **It reduces the need for salt to bring out the flavors of the food.**

The current recommendation is that each meal provide at least 30 mg of vitamin C because of its beneficial effect on iron assimilation.[4] The juice from one-half lemon provides this amount.

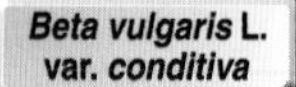

Its red juice combats anemia

RED BEET
Composition
per 100 g of raw edible portion

Energy	**43.0 kcal = 179 kj**
Protein	**1.61 g**
Carbohydrates	**6.76 g**
Fiber	**2.80 g**
Vitamin A	**4.00 µg RE**
Vitamin B1	**0.031 mg**
Vitamin B2	**0.040 mg**
Niacin	**0.651 mg NE**
Vitamin B6	**0.067 mg**
Folate	**109 µg**
Vitamin B12	—
Vitamin C	**4.90 mg**
Vitamin E	**0.300 mg α-TE**
Calcium	**16.0 mg**
Phosphorus	**40.0 mg**
Magnesium	**23.0 mg**
Iron	**0.800 mg**
Potassium	**325 mg**
Zinc	**0.350 mg**
Total Fat	***0.170 g***
Saturated Fat	***0.027 g***
Cholesterol	—
Sodium	***78.0 mg***

1% 2% 4% 10% 20% 40% 100%

% Daily Value (based on a 2,000 calorie diet) provided by 100 g of this food

French: *Betterave;* ***Spanish:*** *Remolacha.*

Description: *The tuberous root of the red beet ('Beta vulgaris' L. ssp. 'vulgaris' var. 'conditiva' Alef.), a herbaceous plant of the botanical family Chenopodiaceae.*

THE BLOOD-RED color of beets gives a cheerful note to salads and potato dishes. Could it be that red beets truly contain blood?

Those who have passed blood-red urine or feces a few hours after eating beets might think so. What a fright! But it is not blood, but rather a pigment specific to this plant called ***betacyanin.***

According to a study carried out at the University of Sheffield (UK), red urine or feces after eating beets occurs in 10% to 14% of the population, and it is more frequent in individuals with iron deficiency or difficulty with intestinal absorption of iron. So if one is surprised by red elimination, he or she should be grateful that

this plant has warned of a possible lack of iron or digestive problems.

However, one should not worry excessively: Beets not only warn of the problem, but aid in its solution, thanks to their anti-anemic and regulating effects on the digestive system.

PROPERTIES AND INDICATIONS: ***Carbohydrates*** (sugars) such as ***saccharose*** and ***fructose*** are prominent in beets' composition. These can reach 10% of their weight. This makes the red beet one of the *most* ***sugar-rich*** vegetables, surpassed only by other varieties of beets. These are beets' most notable characteristics:

- **Anti-anemic:** The anti-anemic action of red beets is well known, and has been described by Doctor Schneider[10] among others. Their iron content (1.80 mg/100 g) and vitamin C (30 mg /100 g) which facilitates the absorption of that mineral are quite modest and alone do not explain red beets' **anti-anemic** effect. It is probably some unidentified component that stimulates **hematopoiesis** (production of blood cells in the bone marrow).

Drinking 50 to 100 ml of ***raw,*** *freshly prepared* beet ***JUICE*** **[❶]** before meals twice a day provides the *greatest* **anti-anemic effect.** This is particularly indicated when the patient does not respond well to iron treatment, which is the case in anemia caused by low blood production in the bone marrow (**hypoplastic anemia**).

- **Alkalizer:** Beet's high levels of mineral salts, particularly ***potassium, calcium,*** and ***magnesium,*** explain their alkalizing effect on the blood. They are highly recommended in case of **gout,** increase in **uric acid** levels in the blood, and a **high-fat** low vegetable diet.
- **Hypolipidemic:** The beet root contains considerable vegetable ***FIBER,*** which has the property of facilitating intestinal action and, above all, decreasing blood cholesterol level by reducing the amount absorbed in the intestine. It is highly recommended, then, that red beets frequently be included in the diet of individuals wishing to reduce cholesterol levels **[❷,❸]**.
- Mild **laxative** due to its fiber content.
- **Aperitif:** Beets increase gastric juice production and tone the stomach.
- **Anticarcinogen:** Doctor Schneider[5] refers to various experiences that took place in Hungary and Germany in which cancerous tumors were reduced or eliminated by administering a daily dose of 250 g of shredded beets or 300-500 ml of juice. These effects were produced even when the juice was boiled and concentrated to make it more tolerable to the stomach, which suggests that whatever the anticarcinogenic substance is, it is heat resistant.

Preparation and use

❶ **Fresh juice:** The flavor of beet juice is unpleasant and may be mixed with other juices or sweetened with honey to make it more palatable. No more than 50 to 100 ml should be drunk at a time to avoid indigestion.

❷ **Grated raw:** Beets prepared in this way may be dressed with lemon and oil.

❸ **Boiled:** Cooked beets are more digestible. They should be boiled for at least an hour. They are easier to peel if dipped in cold water while they are still hot.

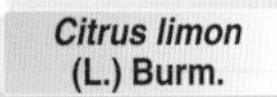

Lemon

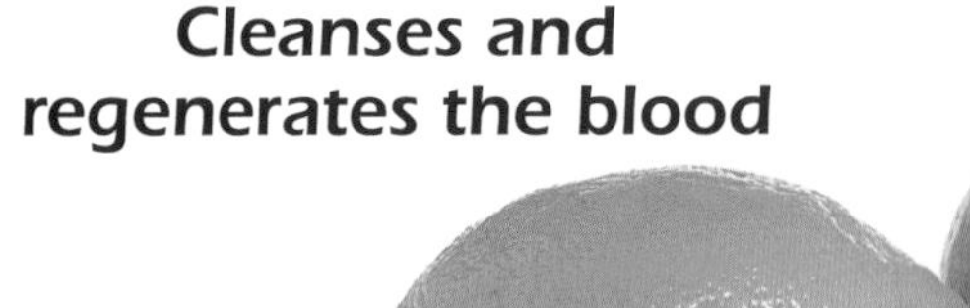

Cleanses and regenerates the blood

A **medium-sized lemon** that weighs about 150 grams provides the **RDA** (recommended dietary allowance) of **vitamin C** for an adult nonsmoker (about 60 mg). **Smokers** require about **50% more** of this vitamin.

Synonyms: *Bearss, Eureka lemon.*

French: *Citron;* ***Spanish:*** *Limón, limón agrio.*

Description: *The lemon is the aggregate fruit of the lemon tree ('Citrus limon' Burm.), a spiny evergreen of the botanical family Rutaceae that reaches 3 to 6 meters in height.*

LEMON
Composition
per 100 g of raw edible portion

Energy	29.0 kcal = 123 kj
Protein	1.10 g
Carbohydrates	6.52 g
Fiber	2.80 g
Vitamin A	3.00 µg RE
Vitamin B_1	0.040 mg
Vitamin B_2	0.020 mg
Niacin	0.100 mg NE
Vitamin B_6	0.080 mg
Folate	10.6 µg
Vitamin B_{12}	—
Vitamin C	53.0 mg
Vitamin E	0.240 mg α-TE
Calcium	26.0 mg
Phosphorus	16.0 mg
Magnesium	8.00 mg
Iron	0.600 mg
Potassium	138 mg
Zinc	0.060 mg
Total Fat	*0.300 g*
Saturated Fat	*0.039 g*
Cholesterol	—
Sodium	*2.00 mg*

1% 2% 4% 10% 20% 40% 100%

% Daily Value (based on a 2,000 calorie diet)
provided by 100 g of this food

PROPERTIES AND INDICATIONS: ***Vitamin C*** stands out in the lemon's composition, only slightly less than the orange. Lemons have virtually no proteins or fats and about 8.23% carbohydrates.

However, the most interesting components of lemons from a dietary and therapeutic standpoint are not its nutrients, but rather its so-called accompanying substances or ***PHYTOCHEMICALS.*** These are substances that lack any calories, and they are neither vitamins nor mineral salts, so they cannot be qualified as nutrients.

✓ ***Organic acids*** (between 6 and 8%), among which ***citric acid*** is predominant, followed by *lesser* amounts of ***malic*** acid, ***acetic*** acid, and ***formic*** acid. These acids potentiate the action of ascorbic acid or ***vitamin C,*** and have a *significant* **antiseptic** *effect.*

✓ ***Flavonoids,*** among which ***hesperidin*** and ***diosmin*** predominate. These are found in the peel and pulp of the lemon. They perform physiological roles:

- **Antioxidants**
- **Protecting the capillaries**
- **Anticarcinogens**

✓ ***Terpenes:*** These are the substances that give citrus fruits their unique aroma. They are found primarily in the peel. The most abundant of these is ***d-limonene*** with its *proven* **detoxifying** and **anticarcinogenic** effects.

Although the lemon affects the entire body, its clinical applications derive particularly from its effect on the blood:

- **Anti-anemic:** It improves iron absorption.
- **Improves blood fluidity,** thus preventing thrombosis.
- **Depurant,** facilitating the elimination of toxins from the blood.

For these reasons, lemons are specifically recommended in the following cases:

• **Anemia:** Lemons should form a regular part of the diet of anyone suffering from anemia. Although its iron content is very low, it is *a very potent* **anti-anemic** since it *increases* the *absorption* of ***iron*** supplied in other plant-based foods.

• **Circulatory disorders:** ***Hesperidin*** and the other ***flavonoids*** found in lemons strengthen the capillary walls, improve the elasticity of arteries and reduce the blood's tendency to excessive clotting.

Lemon use is highly recommended in case of **arteriosclerosis,** tendency to **thrombosis, edema** (retention of fluid in the tissues), and whenever there is a need to improve blood fluidity and circulation.

• **Excess uric acid:** the lemon is *highly* effective in *eliminating* uric acid, which is a waste product generated constantly within the body and must be eliminated in the urine. Excess uric acid is deposited in the joints causing **arthritis** and **rheumatic** pain. It produces **nephritis** (inflammation) in the kidneys.

• **Kidney stones:** Lemon treatment **[❸]** is very effective in helping dissolve kidney stones, particularly when these are formed of uric acid salts (urates).

• **Infections:** Because of their ***vitamin C*** and ***phytochemical*** content, lemons *improve* the body's **immune system's** ability to resist infections. Lemon use is appropriate for all types of infectious disease, whether viral or bacterial.

• **Anticarcinogen:** ***D-limonene,*** an aromatic terpene found in the lemon, *particularly* in the ***PEEL,*** has been shown capable of neutralizing certain carcinogens.[6]

Preparation and use

❶ **Fresh juice:** Because of their high acidity, lemons are not usually eaten as fruit; only their juice is consumed. It is *important* to include the **peel** (if it is pesticide-free) because many of the aromatic terpenes, which have great medicinal value, are concentrated in it.

❷ **Dressing** and seasoning for various dishes: Lemon juice improves the flavor, digestibility, and properties of all green leafy vegetables, rice, and legumes.

❸ **Lemon treatment:** This treatment is conducted over a two-week period. The first day one drinks the juice of one lemon diluted in water one-half hour before breakfast. On consequent days one lemon is added everyday up to seven lemons. From that point the order is reversed back down to one lemon on the last day.

Children, the **elderly**, those with **low calcium, renal failure** or **anemia** should ***not use*** this lemon treatment. Large amounts of lemon are not recommended in these conditions.

Lentils

Iron and fiber-rich

Scientific synonyms:
Lens esculenta Moench., *Ervum lens* L.

French: *Lentille;* ***Spanish:*** *Lenteja.*

Description: *The seed of the lentil plant ('Lens culinaris' Medik.), herbaceous plant of the botanical family Leguminosae. The fruit of this plant consists of two pods containing one or two seeds, lentils.*

LENTIL
Composition
per 100 g of raw edible portion

Energy	338 kcal = 1,413 kj
Protein	28.1 g
Carbohydrates	26.6 g
Fiber	30.5 g
Vitamin A	4.00 µg RE
Vitamin B_1	0.475 mg
Vitamin B_2	0.245 mg
Niacin	6.80 mg NE
Vitamin B_6	0.535 mg
Folate	433 µg
Vitamin B_{12}	—
Vitamin C	6.20 mg
Vitamin E	0.330 mg α-TE
Calcium	51.0 mg
Phosphorus	454 mg
Magnesium	107 mg
Iron	9.02 mg
Potassium	905 mg
Zinc	3.61 mg
Total Fat	*0.960 g*
Saturated Fat	*0.135 g*
Cholesterol	—
Sodium	*10.0 mg*

1% 2% 4% 10% 20% 40% 100% 200% 500%

% Daily Value (based on a 2,000 calorie diet)
provided by 100 g of this food

PROPERTIES AND INDICATIONS: Lentils are a highly concentrated food, being only 11.2% water by weight. This makes them a remarkable energy source, which supplies 338 Cal/100 g. Most of this energy comes from proteins and carbohydrates since lentils contain virtually no fat (less than 1%).

One hundred grams of raw lentils (enough to prepare one large dish of this legume, or two small ones) meet most or even all of the nutritional needs of an adult male for various nutrients:

✓ ***Proteins*** (28.1 g): more than half (53% of RDA).

✓ ***Fiber*** (30.5 g): supplies almost 125%.

✓ ***Vitamin*** B_1 (0.475 mg): almost one-third (32%).

✓ ***Vitamin*** B_6 (0.535 mg): more than one-fourth (27%).

✓ ***Folates*** (433 mg): more than double (216%).

✓ ***Magnesium*** (107 mg): almost one-third (31%).

✓ ***Iron*** (9 mg): 90%.

✓ ***Potassium*** (905 mg): almost half (45%).

✓ ***Zinc*** (3.61 mg): almost one-fourth (24%).

✓ ***Copper*** (0.852 mg): more than half (57%).

All of this is supplied in a dish of lentils. It is no wonder that Esau sold his birthright to his brother Jacob, the Biblical patriarch, for a pot of these nutritious legumes.

However, even though lentils represent such a high concentration of nutrients, they are ***deficient*** or completely lacking in others:

- polyunsaturated fatty acids, since they have virtually no fat at all;
- provitamin A and vitamins C and E;
- calcium;
- vitamin B_{12}, as is the case with all plant-based foods.

Lentils are particularly recommended in these cases:

Preparation and use

❶ **Cooked:** This is the usual way to eat lentils. The heat of cooking breaks down and softens the cellulose fibers, improving digestibility. It also destroys the lectin (toxic protein) that is present in all raw legumes. It is more effective to soak lentils for some hours before cooking.

❷ **Puree:** Lentil puree is easier to digest than whole lentils, particularly if the skin is removed during the process. This skin contains indigestible polysaccharides that cause intestinal flatulence.

❸ **Flour:** This is used in North African and Middle and Near Eastern countries. It is mixed with grain flours to increase dietary protein.

Lentils are very rich in folates and iron, two nutrients that are particularly important to young women and those planning to become pregnant. Iron and folates contribute to avoiding anemia.

• **Anemia:** Lentils are an ***excellent source*** of ***iron,*** since they supply 9 mg/100 g. This is much more than meat (about 2 mg/100 g) and eggs (1.44 mg/100 g).

But in addition to iron, lentils provide large amounts of other nutrients that contribute to erythrocyte (red blood cell) production: ***folates*** (a vitamin factor of the B group) and ***copper*** (a trace element).

• **Constipation:** Lentils' *high* ***fiber*** content, excessive in some cases of sensitive intestines, acts to stimulate peristalsis in the intestine.

• **Diabetes:** Although lentils are rich in carbohydrates, their glucose atoms are released slowly in the intestine and do not provoke sudden increases in blood sugar levels. Because of this, they are recommended for diabetic diets,[7] as are all legumes, in spite of earlier held beliefs and prohibitions.

• **Elevated cholesterol:** The fiber in lentils collects cholesterol from other foods, as well as bile acids, which are the prime materials for cholesterol synthesis in the body, and eliminates them through the feces. Therefore, lentil consumption is convenient for those whishing to reduce their cholesterol level.

• **Pregnancy:** By eating lentils, pregnant women can get *abundant* ***iron*** to avoid pregnancy-related anemia, ***fiber*** to aid evacuation, and large amounts of ***folates*** that prevent fetal nervous system malformations.

(See the chart "Foods that belnd well with lentils" p. 135.)

Passion fruit

Iron-rich fruit

The yellow passion fruit is also appreciated for its delicate flavor. It is ripe when the skin is somewhat wrinkled and a deep yellow color.

The purple passion fruit has a rather wrinkled skin and a deep purple color when it is ripe.

Synonyms: *Granadilla, Wild watermelon.*

French: *Grenadille;* *Spanish:* *Fruta de la pasión, Pasionaria, Maracuyá.*

Description: *Fruit of different varieties of 'Passiflora edulis' Sims., a climbing plant of the botanical family Passifloraceae. It is approximately the size and shape of an egg. Its color varies according to variety, from purple to yellow. It has a gelatinous pulp full of black seeds.*

PASSION FRUIT (GRANADILLA)
Composition
per 100 g of raw edible portion

Energy	97.0 kcal = 408 kj
Protein	2.20 g
Carbohydrates	13.0 g
Fiber	10.4 g
Vitamin A	70.0 µg RE
Vitamin B_1	—
Vitamin B_2	0.130 mg
Niacin	1.50 mg NE
Vitamin B_6	0.100 mg
Folate	14.0 µg
Vitamin B_{12}	—
Vitamin C	30.0 mg
Vitamin E	1.12 mg α-TE
Calcium	12.0 mg
Phosphorus	68.0 mg
Magnesium	29.0 mg
Iron	1.60 mg
Potassium	348 mg
Zinc	0.100 mg
Total Fat	*0.700 g*
Saturated Fat	*0.059 g*
Cholesterol	—
Sodium	*28.0 mg*

1% 2% 4% 10% 20% 40% 100%

% Daily Value (based on a 2,000 calorie diet) provided by 100 g of this food

THERE ARE various species of the genus *Passiflora* that provide edible fruit, all very aromatic with a tart flavor. The most widespread and utilized are those known as passion fruit, also called **granadilla.**

PROPERTIES AND INDICATIONS: Passion fruit pulp is gelatinous and very aromatic. The following nutrients stand out:

✓ ***Sugars:*** Although it may not seem so because of their acid taste, they contain a *considerable* amount of sugar (13%), constituted of almost equal parts of glucose, fructose, and saccharose.

✓ ***Proteins:*** With 2.2% it is one of the most protein-rich fresh **fruits.**

✓ ***Iron:*** This is possibly the most iron-rich fresh fruit (1.6 mg/100 g), followed far back by the quince (0.7 mg), lemon (0.6 mg), raspberry (0.57 mg), and cherimoya (0.5 mg). Passion fruit surpasses even the egg's iron content (1.41 mg) and is close to that of meat (about 2 mg per 100 g). Even though this iron is ***nonheme*** of vegetable origin, and is absorbed with greater difficulty than that of animal origin, the simultaneous presence of ***vitamin C*** in the passion fruit significantly *enhances* the absorption of this mineral.

✓ ***Other minerals:*** Passion fruit is quite rich in magnesium, calcium, phosphorous, and potassium.

✓ ***Vitamins:*** One hundred grams of passion fruit pulp provides 30 mg of ***vitamin C,*** half of the **RDA** (recommended dietary allowance). It also contains provitamin A, vitamins B_2, B_6, and E, as well as niacin and folic acid.

✓ ***Fiber:*** Passion fruit pulp is one or the richest **vegetable** products in ***soluble*** fiber (pectin and mucilage).

✓ ***Aromatic non-nutritive substances:*** The pleasant aroma of the passion fruit is due to the combination of more than one hundred chemical substances.[8] The slightly sedative effect of this fruit may be due to some of these aromatic substances, which are present in much higher concentrations in the passion flower's leaves and blossoms (*Passiflora incarnata* L.) used as a medicinal plant.

How to extract passion fruit juice:
1. Remove the pulp with a spoon.
2. Strain it to remove the seeds.
3. Blend it to a homogenous consistency.

The pulp as well as the juice from the passion fruit are refreshing, stimulate the digestive function, and are mildly sedating, although their most important medicinal use is as an anti-anemic. These are their medical indications:

- **Iron deficiency anemia:** Due to its very high iron content as well as the vitamin C that facilitates the absorption of this mineral, passion fruit is excellent for **anemics.**
- **Constipation:** The gelatinous pulp [❶], and to a lesser degree, the juices made from it, exercise a mild laxative action and also protect the lining of the intestine.
- **Nervousness and anxiety:** Even though its sedating effect is much more mild than the leaves and blossoms of the passion flower,[9] it is appropriate for those wishing to relax the nervous system.

Preparation and use

❶ **Fresh:** The gelatinous pulp is eaten with a spoon using the peel as a bowl. Separating the seeds from the pulp in the mouth is somewhat inconvenient.

❷ **Juice:** The pulp is filtered through a strainer, then placed in a blender.

❸ As a **complement** that gives an exotic note to fruit dishes and a variety of fresh or frozen desserts.

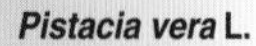

Pistachio

The most iron-rich nut

Polyunsat. **7.32 g** Saturated **6.13 g**

Monounsat. **32.7 g**

Percentage distribution of **fatty acids**

Synonyms: *Pistachio nut, Pistache.*

French: *Pistache;* ***Spanish:*** *Pistacho.*

Description: *The seed of the pistachio tree ('Pistacia vera' L.), a small evergreen tree of the botanical family Anacardiaceae.*

PISTACHIO NUT
Composition
per 100 g of raw edible portion

Energy	**577 kcal = 2,416 kj**
Protein	**20.6 g**
Carbohydrates	**14.0 g**
Fiber	**10.8 g**
Vitamin A	**23.0 µg RE**
Vitamin B_1	**0.820 mg**
Vitamin B_2	**0.174 mg**
Niacin	**5.80 mg NE**
Vitamin B_6	**0.250 mg**
Folate	**58.0 µg**
Vitamin B_{12}	—
Vitamin C	**7.20 mg**
Vitamin E	**5.21 mg α-TE**
Calcium	**135 mg**
Phosphorus	**503 mg**
Magnesium	**158 mg**
Iron	**6.78 mg**
Potassium	**1093 mg**
Zinc	**1.34 mg**
Total Fat	***48.4 g***
Saturated Fat	***6.13 g***
Cholesterol	—
Sodium	***6.00 mg***

1% 2% 4% 10% 20% 40% 100%

% Daily Value (based on a 2,000 calorie diet) provided by 100 g of this food

SOME 1,700 years before Christ pistachios were already considered "some of the best products of the land," together with honey and almonds, according to the words of the Patriarch Jacob, who was living in Palestine.[10] Since then they have spread throughout the Mediterranean, and recently to North America.

PROPERTIES AND INDICATIONS: The shape and composition of the pistachio are similar to that of the pine nut (see p. 56), but with more ***proteins*** (up to 20.6% of their weight), and fewer ***fats*** (48.4%). Its carbohydrate content is also considerable (up to 14%).

Its ***provitamin A*** and ***vitamin C*** content is relatively poor. It is *very rich* in ***minerals,*** supplying potassium, magnesium, phosphorous, and calcium.

But pistachios truly stand out because of their high iron content (6.8 mg /100 g), which equals

Preparation and use

➊ **Toasted:** Pistachios are usually eaten lightly toasted. Excess salt must be avoided.

➋ Pistachios are very much appreciated preparing **desserts** and **ice-cream** because of their exquisite flavor.

or surpasses lentils (see p. 130). They contain valuable trace elements such as copper (1.2 mg /100 g) that, according to recent investigations, facilitates the absorption and assimilation of the iron.[11] The iron/copper combination produces an anti-anemic effect that is far superior to any pharmaceutical preparation based solely on iron.

The pistachio's **anti-anemic** effect is *potentiated* when they are eaten *together with* ***vitamin C-rich*** fresh **fruits** and **vegetables.** It is well known that vitamin C greatly *enhances* the *absorption* of ***iron*** in the intestine.

Those suffering from **iron deficiency anemia** can benefit from regular pistachio consumption.

continued from page 130

Foods that blend well with lentils

These foods compensate for lentils' nutritional deficiencies and blend very well with them as a result.

Lemon

Lemons provide **vitamin C,** which increases absorption of lentils' iron in addition to improving their flavor.

Grains

These are rich in the essential amino acid **methionine,** lacking in legumes in general. Rice is the grain that best blends with lentils.

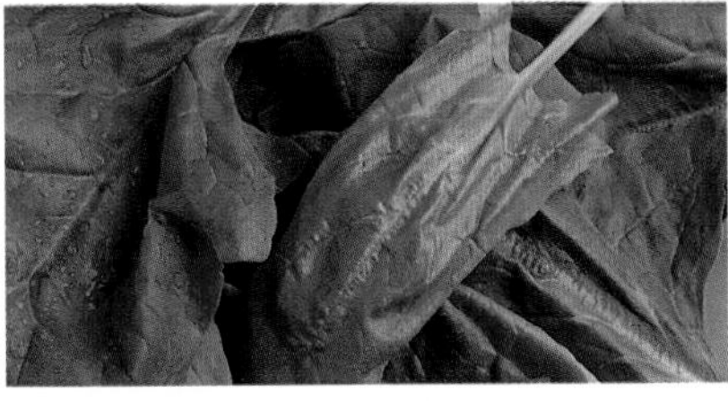

Cabbages, spinach and dairy products

These are rich in **calcium,** which is very scarce in lentils.

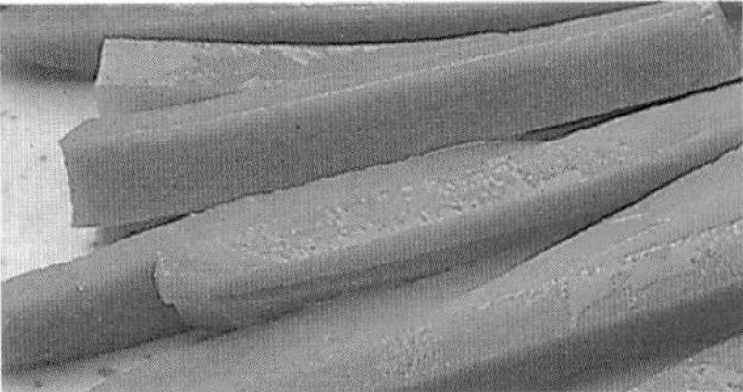

Carrots

Carrots provide **provitamin A** not found in lentils.

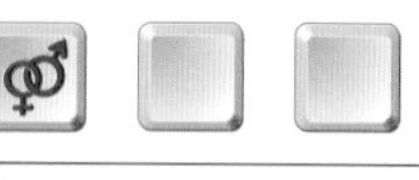

Fava bean
(Broad bean)

Nutritious and iron-rich

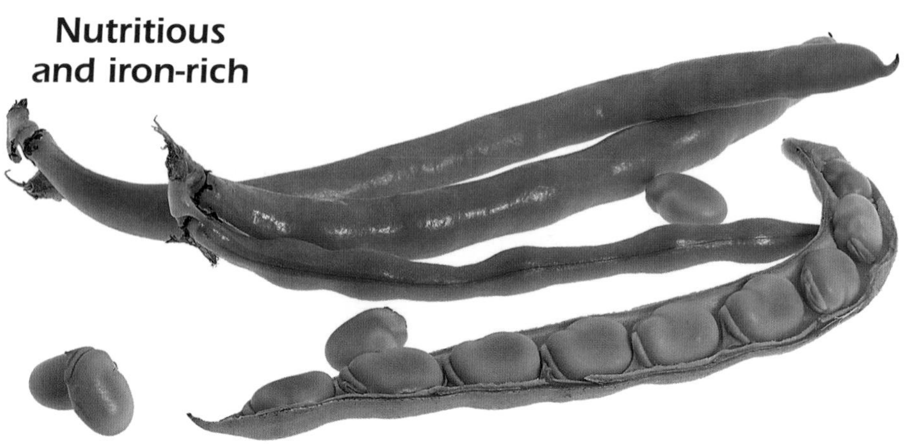

Synonyms: *Faba bean, Horse-bean, Field-bean, Tick-bean, Windsor bean.*

French: *Fève;* ***Spanish:*** *Haba.*

Description: *Seeds of the fruit of the broad bean plant ('Vicia faba' L.), a herbaceous plant of the botanical family Leguminosae whose stalks reach about a meter in height. From a botanical point of view, the fruit is a legume formed of a fleshy green pod 15 to 25 cm long containing six or seven seeds (the beans themselves).*

FAVA BEAN
Composition
per 100 g of raw edible portion

Energy	341 kcal = 1,425 kj
Protein	26.1 g
Carbohydrates	33.3 g
Fiber	25.0 g
Vitamin A	5.00 µg RE
Vitamin B_1	0.555 mg
Vitamin B_2	0.333 mg
Niacin	6.95 mg NE
Vitamin B_6	0.366 mg
Folate	423 µg
Vitamin B_{12}	—
Vitamin C	1.40 mg
Vitamin E	0.090 mg α-TE
Calcium	103 mg
Phosphorus	421 mg
Magnesium	192 mg
Iron	6.70 mg
Potassium	1,062 mg
Zinc	3.14 mg
Total Fat	*1.53 g*
Saturated Fat	*0.254 g*
Cholesterol	—
Sodium	*13.0 mg*

1% 2% 4% 10% 20% 40% 100%

% Daily Value (based on a 2,000 calorie diet) provided by 100 g of this food

HUMANITY has been eating broad beans for millennia. It is possibly the oldest domesticated legume.

PROPERTIES AND INDICATIONS: Fresh broad beans contain a considerable amount of ***protein*** of *high* biological *quality* (5.6%), carbohydrates primarily in the form of starch (7.5%), virtually no fat (0.6%). Among its vitamins, vitamin B_1 (0.17 mg/100 g), folates (96.3 mg/100 g), as well as vitamin C (33 mg /100 g) of which they contain about half that of the lemon, predominate.

Iron is the *most abundant* ***mineral*** in broad beans (1.9 mg/100 g), almost as much

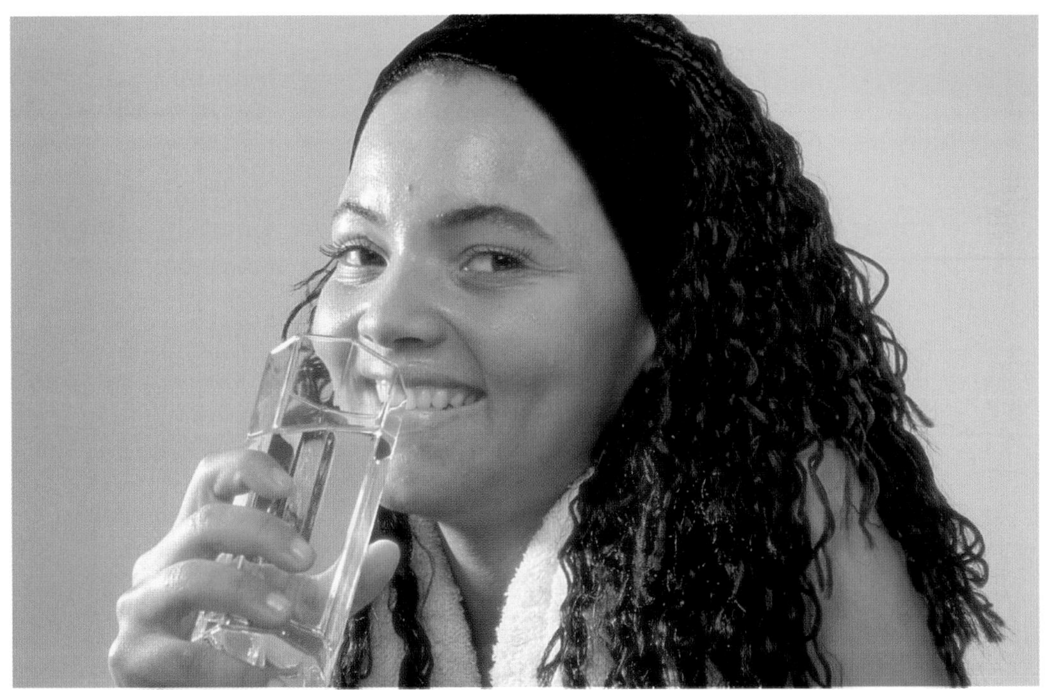

Fava beans are a good source of iron, so they are ideal for athletes and young people to foster blood production.

Preparation and use

❶ **Raw:** They may be eaten this way when they are fresh and tender, although they are not always well tolerated. Removing the skin can help prevent flatulence and digestive disturbances.

❷ **Cooked:** This is the recommended way to eat broad beans. The heat and water deactivate the small amounts of lectin (a toxic protein; see page 84) that they may contain, the same as all other legumes. Brief boiling or steaming is more than sufficient to destroy any toxin and make them perfectly digestible.

❸ **Dried:** Drying is the traditional means of storing broad beans, although they lose a significant portion of their vitamin content (not minerals). Dried broad beans require a rather long cooking time.

as meat. This is ***nonheme*** iron, whose **absorption** is *enhanced* by the simultaneous presence of ***vitamin C.***

Broad beans are recommended in cases of iron deficiency **anemia,** as well as during pregnancy, for adolescents, athletes, and those convalescing from infectious diseases or surgery.

Favism

A small percentage of the population of Mediterranean countries suffers ***intolerance*** *to broad beans for genetic reasons. When these individuals eat broad beans they suffer hemolysis (destruction of the blood cells) and various other disturbances known as favism.*

7

Foods for the Respiratory System

DIET influences the condition of the respiratory system more than one might think. Certain foods such as milk and eggs can precipitate asthmatic crises. Others such as onions or garlic resist bronchitis. Fruits and vegetables rich in beta-carotene protect against lung cancer.

An investigation conducted in England and Wales shows that **children** who eat ***two or more*** pieces of fruit a day **breathe *better*** and have a ***lower*** *risk* of **dyspnea** (respiratory difficulty). On the other hand, **pulmonary function** is ***worsened*** in those who eat processed **meats** (ham, sausage, etc.).[1]

COUGH

Definition

Cough is the *most common* **symptom** of respiratory disease. In reality, coughing is the body's **defense mechanism** to expel foreign or irritating substances from the bronchial tubes.

Diet

Certain foods can help eliminate the causes of cough and help relieve it, while others make it worse.

Increase

ONION
HONEY
LEMON
VITAMIN A
VITAMIN C

Reduce or eliminate

SALT
DAIRY PRODUCTS

Milk

It is possible that dairy products increase mucus production in the respiratory tract, which can trigger or aggravate cough.

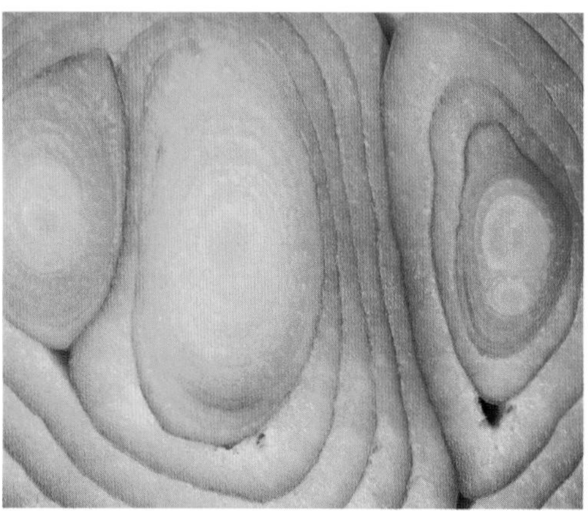

Simply breathing the essence released by raw onions is often enough to relieve a cough. The onion's sulfur compounds produce antispasmodic, sedating, mucolytic (facilitate the elimination of mucus), and antibiotic effects.

BRONCHITIS

Definition

This is the inflammation of the mucosa lining the bronchial passages. It is usually caused by infection and is *exacerbated* by the inhalation of irritant fumes such as **tobacco** smoke.

Diet

Various foods have healing properties that are apt for cases of bronchitis:

- **Mucolytics:** these soften and promote the expulsion of mucus. Examples are onions and radishes.
- **Emollients:** These, such as okra, dates, and figs, soften and reduce inflammation in the respiratory mucosa.
- **Antibiotics** and **antiseptics:** Foods such as garlic and propolis combat bacteria and viruses that cause or aggravate bronchitis.

Increase

ONION
GARLIC
RADISH
HORSERADISH
LEEK
WATERCRESS
JUJUBE
DATE
BORAGE
FIG
OKRA
HONEY
PROPOLIS
VITAMIN A

Reduce or eliminate

SALT
ALCOHOLIC BEVERAGES
SATURATED FAT

Dates

Radishes contain a piquant sulfurated essence that facilitates removal of excess bronchial mucus.

ASTHMA

Definition

Asthma is manifested by attacks of *dyspnea* (respiratory difficulty) accompanied by wheezing, cough, expectoration, and chest pressure. Asthma is a result of spasms and inflammation of the bronchial tubes, usually caused by an **allergic** mechanism.

Diet

Abundant use of certain foods can contribute to reducing bronchial sensitivity and predisposition to asthma attacks.

Reducing salt consumption and eliminating foods known to most frequently cause allergic reactions can do a great deal to reduce the frequency and intensity of crises.

Other factors

In addition to certain allergenic foods, other factors can trigger asthma attacks such as environmental **pollution, dust,** and physical or psychological **stress.**

Increase

ONION
ORANGES
HORSERADISH
OIL
HONEY
YOGURT
VEGETABLES
MAGNESIUM
B VITAMINS
ANTIOXIDANTS

Reduce or eliminate

SALT
ADDITIVES
WINE
BEER
FISH
SHELLFISH
CURED CHEESES
EGGS
BREWER'S YEAST
ROYAL JELLY
MILK
NUTS

Prawn

Shellfish are a frequent cause of allergic reactions that can initiate or aggravate asthma attacks.

SMOKING CESSATION

Diet

Diet plays an important role in smoking cessation. When stop smoking, one must carefully chose foods capable of achieving these three goals:

- **Eliminate nicotine** and other poisons from the body: Water, fruits and vegetables with depurant qualities contribute to this.
- **Repair the damage:** Plant-based foods that are rich in **antioxidants** protect the cells from the chemical aggression caused by tobacco and contribute to the restoration of the damage already done.
- **Reduce the desire to smoke:** Avoid foods or products that stimulate the desire.

Increase

WATER
FRUIT
VEGETABLES
VITAMIN C
WHEAT GERM
ANTIOXIDANTS

Reduce or eliminate

ALCOHOLIC BEVERAGES
STIMULANT BEVERAGES
SATURATED FAT
MEAT
SPICES

Wheat germ

Wheat germ is very rich in the B vitamins and minerals necessary for the proper function of the nervous system and to overcome the stress involved in giving up tobacco.

Fruit

Fruit provides antioxidant vitamins and phytochemicals that neutralize part of the poisons in tobacco.

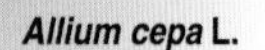

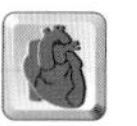

Onion

Effective against bronchitis and asthma

ONION
Composition
per 100 g of raw edible portion

Energy	38.0 kcal = 158 kj
Protein	1.16 g
Carbohydrates	6.83 g
Fiber	1.80 g
Vitamin A	—
Vitamin B_1	0.042 mg
Vitamin B_2	0.020 mg
Niacin	0.431 mg NE
Vitamin B_6	0.116 mg
Folate	19.0 µg
Vitamin B_{12}	—
Vitamin C	6.40 mg
Vitamin E	0.130 mg α-TE
Calcium	20.0 mg
Phosphorus	33.0 mg
Magnesium	10.0 mg
Iron	0.220 mg
Potassium	157 mg
Zinc	0.190 mg
Total Fat	*0.160 g*
Saturated Fat	*0.026 g*
Cholesterol	—
Sodium	*3.00 mg*

1% 2% 4% 10% 20% 40% 100%

% Daily Value (based on a 2,000 calorie diet)
provided by 100 g of this food

French: *Oignon;* ***Spanish:*** *Cebolla.*

Description: *The bulb of the onion plant ('Allium cepa' L.), of the botanical family Liliaceae.*
The bulb is not the root of the plant, but rather an underground thickening of the stalk. The true roots are formed of filaments on the lower portion of the bulb.

IT SAYS in the fourth book of Moses, the one called Numbers, that while the Israelites wandered in the Sinai desert they yearned for the foods they had eaten in Egypt. Specifically, they mentioned onions, garlic, and leeks.[2] It is plausible, then, that onions, together with other vegetables, made up an important part of the diet of these pyramid-building slaves of more than 3,500 years ago.

However, onions provide few calories to the diet, particularly when one is engaged in intense physical labor; nor can it be said that they have a particularly delicious flavor. Therefore, it seems that this group of rough slaves valued and missed onions primarily for their medicinal value. How many of them must have come down with bronchitis or pneumonia while sloshing in the cold mud to make adobe bricks!

In the onion, as in other allium (garlic and leeks), the Israelites possibly found a medicinal food that helped them avoid and cure respiratory disorders and also gave them vigor and health.

Today, onions continue as one to nature's most healing foods.

PROPERTIES AND INDICATIONS: No particular nutrient stands out when one examines the composition of the onion. The 38 kcal/100 g that it provides comes primarily from its glucose, saccharose and other ***carbohydrates*** (6.83%). ***Proteins*** are present in a small proportion (1.16%), but noteworthy for a vegetable. Its ***fat*** content is negligible (0.16%).

All ***vitamins*** are present (except B_{12}), although in small amounts. The same is the case with ***minerals,*** among which only potassium (157 mg/100 g) is worth mentioning. Among trace elements the most abundant is ***sulfur,*** which forms part of the onion's volatile essence.

The onion's mineral salts are converted to carbonates of alkaline reaction when passed to the blood,[3] which explains the *remarkable* **alkalizing effect** of this bulb. Alkalizing foods facilitate the elimination of waste products from the body, which are all acidic.

In contrast to its rather unimportant nutrient content, the onion is rich in non-nutritive substances of major physiological activity:

✓ ***Essential oil:*** This oil is responsible for the onion's typical odor. It is highly volatile, and evaporates easily. Its composition is very complex since it is formed from a mixture of more than one hundred different substances, among which ***allyl disulfide*** and ***thiosulfinate*** stand out.

✓ ***FLAVONOIDS:*** These glycosides improve blood circulation, prevent blood clots (reduce platelet stickiness), and block the oxidation of low-density lipoproteins (a type of fat in the blood) that causes arteriosclerosis. Onions are *rich* in ***quercetin,*** one of the *most active* **flavonoids.** A study conducted at the University of Wageningen (The Netherlands) demonstrates that quercetin is well absorbed in the intestine regardless of whether the onion is raw or cooked.[4]

The flavonoids and the substances that form this essential oil are attributed with most of the onion's properties: **antibiotic, decongestant, anti-asthmatic, heart** and arterial *protector*, **diuretic,** and **anticarcinogenic.**

Preparation and use

❶ **Raw:** This is the best way to eat onions, but for this, they must be fresh. The piquancy is attenuated somewhat by washing them for a few minutes and adding lemon. Those suffering from gastric ulcer or gastritis should eat onions either boiled or baked.

❷ **Boiled in water:** Their piquancy disappears and they are better tolerated, but their medicinal effects are also diminished. Cooking time should be short, less than a minute, and the resulting broth should be used, as well.

❸ **Baked:** Baked onions are very tasty; although the longer they are in the oven, the less effective they are as a medicine.

❹ **Onion syrup:** Boil several slices of onion. After mashing them to a paste, add a few spoonfuls of honey or brown sugar.

❺ **Onion water:** This is prepared by soaking a chopped raw onion in a glass of water for several hours.

Eating raw onion can stop or relieve an asthma crisis because of its anti-allergic and bronchodilator properties. These effects last up to twelve hours. Inhaling the onion's essential oil is also beneficial, and is more appropriate for children.

Onions contain many other non-nutritive substances whose actions are not as well defined as the previous two groups. Among them are:

✓ ***Enzymes:*** The onion is rich in enzymatic substances such as oxidase and diastase,[3] which have an invigorating effect on digestive processes.

✓ ***Glycoquine:*** Dr. Schneider[5] defines this as a ***"vegetable hormone"*** that reduces the blood glucose level. This explains the onion's desirable effects on **diabetics.**

✓ ***Vegetable fiber*** (1.8%): Fiber contributes to the onion's lipid-lowering (diminishes the absorption of cholesterol) and anti-diabetic action (delays the passage of sugar into the bloodstream).

Many medicinal properties of onions have been described, and they have been recommended for various disorders. Since the essential oil is very volatile and rapidly impregnates all the tissues of the body, it is logical to believe that it works on multiple organs and systems. However, this work will describe only those dietary and therapeutic applications that have been ***scientifically*** investigated and proven.

• ***Respiratory disorders:*** The sulfur compounds that form the onion's essential oil pass rapidly to the bloodstream from the stomach. They are first released in the lungs. This explains why after only a few minutes of eating onions, the breath has its characteristic odor. Onions are **mucolytic** (able to break down heavy mucus), expectorant (facilitating the expectoration of bronchial mucus), and **antibiotic** on gram-positive germs.[6, 7]

All respiratory infections, from sinusitis to pneumonia, improve with onion consumption, preferably raw **(❶)**, although also boiled **(❷)**, baked **(❸)** or in syrup **(❹)**.

• **Bronchial asthma:** In the pediatric clinic of the University Ludwig-Maximilians in Munich (Germany), it was proven that thiosulfinate, one of the components of the onion's essential oil, is capable of stopping bronchial allergic reaction in asthma cases.[8, 9]

It was also shown that thiosulfinate from onions acts on the respiratory center of the brain stem as well, producing dilation of the bronchial passages.[10]

These investigations plainly justify the use of raw onion for bronchial asthma because of its anti-allergenic and bronchodilator effects. The positive effects of onions on the bronchial tubes are felt in only a few minutes after eating them.

• **Arteriosclerosis and coronary heart disease:** More evidence is constantly becoming known that onions *prevent* **arteriosclerosis** and **thrombosis** (formation of clots within the arteries and veins) and improve the circulation of the blood in the coronary arteries. In 1989 a study conducted at the University of Limburg (Maastricht, the Netherlands),[11] stated that the onion's cardiovascular benefits had not been sufficiently demonstrated. However, in 1996 various investigations[12, 13] showed that those who eat more **onions** and **apples** (two of the foods richest in the flavonoid quercetin) have a lower risk of dying from a heart attack.

Regular onion consumption in any form **(❶,❷,❸)** prevents arteriosclerosis, improves blood flow in all arteries, and reduces the risk of suffering a serious complication such as a heart attack.

• **Elevated blood triglycerides:** Triglycerides, formed from fatty acids and glycerin, are a type of fat that circulates in the blood. A high triglyceride level promotes arteriosclerosis and heart disease. It has been shown that consuming the liquid extract from onions **(❺)**) reduces triglycerides in the blood and liver.[14] Onion also increases the HDL (beneficial) cholesterol level, helping to prevent arteriosclerosis.

• **Kidney disorders:** Onion increases urine volume, facilitating the elimination of waste material because of its **alkalizing** effect. It is appropriate in the diets of those suffering from **kidney stones,** urinary **infections,** or any degree of **renal failure.**

• **Diabetes:** Onions reduce the blood glucose level. They are therefore *indicated* for diabetics.

• **Liver disorders:** Onions stimulate the detoxifying function of the liver as well as improving the activity of other digestive juice-producing glands. *Highly recommended* in cases of hepatic failure caused by chronic hepatitis or cirrhosis.

• **Cancer:** A study conducted in China, sponsored by the National Cancer Institute of the United States, found that those who eat more onions and garlic have a *much lower* **risk** of developing **stomach cancer.**[15, 16] Other studies[17] demonstrate the onion's capacity, as well as that of garlic, to prevent the development of tumor cells and to neutralize carcinogens.

Therefore, abundant onion consumption is fully justified as a cancer preventive and as a complement to the treatment of certain types of cancer, such as that of the stomach and the colon. However, other studies carried out in The Netherlands show that onions have no significant effect on breast or lung cancers.[18, 19]

Eating raw onion can stop or relieve an asthma crisis because of its anti-allergic and bronchodilator properties. These effects last up to twelve hours. Inhaling the onion's essential oil is also beneficial, and is more appropriate for children.

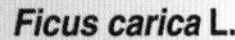

Figs

Soothe the bronchial passages and invigorate the body

FIG
Composition
per 100 g of raw edible portion

Energy	74.0 kcal = 310 kj
Protein	0.750 g
Carbohydrates	15.9 g
Fiber	3.30 g
Vitamin A	14.0 µg RE
Vitamin B_1	0.060 mg
Vitamin B_2	0.050 mg
Niacin	0.500 mg NE
Vitamin B_6	0.113 mg
Folate	6.00 µg
Vitamin B_{12}	—
Vitamin C	2.00 mg
Vitamin E	0.890 mg α-TE
Calcium	35.0 mg
Phosphorus	14.0 mg
Magnesium	17.0 mg
Iron	0.370 mg
Potassium	232 mg
Zinc	0.150 mg
Total Fat	*0.300 g*
Saturated Fat	*0.060 g*
Cholesterol	—
Sodium	*1.00 mg*

1% 2% 4% 10% 20% 40% 100%

% Daily Value (based on a 2,000 calorie diet) provided by 100 g of this food

Synonyms: *Common fig, Poor-man's-food.*

French: *Figue;* ***Spanish:*** *Higo, breva.*

Description: *The sweet, fleshy, hollow, pear-shaped, multiple fruit of the fig tree, a deciduous plant ('Ficus carica' L.), having numerous tiny seedlike fruits. It is of the botanical family Moraceae. Certain types of fig trees give two crops a year: the early figs in spring are very tender and juicy. Later figs are harvested in late summer or fall.*

Properties and indications: ***Carbohydrates*** are the most significant component in figs, composing 15.9% by weight. Most of these are made up of monosaccharides or simple sugars (glucose and fructose), and a small portion of disaccharides (saccharose). Their proportion of proteins does not reach 1%, and their fat content is only 0.3%.

Figs are quite rich in ***vitamins*** E, B_6, B_1, and B_2. On the other hand, they are deficient in vitamins A and C. Their more prominent ***minerals*** are potassium, calcium, magnesium, and iron. ***Trace elements*** such as zinc, copper, and manganese are present in significant quantities.

Dried figs concentrate most of their nutrients, with the exception of vitamins E and C, which practically disappear. Dried figs' medicinal effects on the bronchial passages and the digestive tract are even superior to those of fresh figs.

Figs are easily digested, and have an **emollient** (soothing) effect on the bronchial passages and the digestive tract. They are also **laxative** and **diuretic.** Fig consumption is particularly indicated in the following cases:

- **Bronchial disorders:** Figs, regardless of how they are prepared, but particularly dried figs that have been rehydrated [❷] or boiled with milk [❸], have a pectoral action that fights infections.[20] They relieve cough, facilitate expectoration, and soothe the respiratory tract. Their use is recommended in cases of chronic bronchitis, as well as acute respiratory infections caused by colds or flu.
- **Constipation:** Fresh figs [❶] and rehydrated dried figs [❷] are *particularly useful* in cases of slow intestinal peristalsis. They act much in the same way as prunes. They soothe the digestive tract and stimulate peristalsis in the intestine, thus moving the feces.
- **Increase in nutritional need:** Figs in any form are a highly desirable food in cases of anemia or fatigue from physiological or psychological causes because of their invigorating effect.

Pregnant or lactating women, adolescents, and all who are involved in physical (athletes) or psychological (students) activities will find in the fig a highly nutritious, easily digested, and high-energy food.

Preparation and use

❶ **Fresh:** Figs must be **tree-ripened** to truly enjoy their sweetness and flavor. If they are harvested green, they will never fully ripen. Fresh figs are only available in the market for a few weeks a year because they are difficult to transport and store.

❷ **Dried:** Dried figs have lost two thirds of their water content, which highly concentrates their sugars, vitamins, and minerals. They are available year-round. Soaking them overnight rehydrates them before eating.

❸ **Boiled in milk** (preferably non-dairy): A half-dozen dried figs cooked in a half-liter of milk is an excellent cough remedy and expectorant, particularly if a few spoonfuls of honey are added.

❹ **Fig cakes:** These are prepared from dried figs, almonds, and aromatic herbs. They provide a great deal of energy and are invigorating to the whole body.

Dates

Relieve cough and soothe bronchial passages

Synonyms: *Date palm, Deglet Noor date, Bahri date.*

French: *Datte;* ***Spanish:*** *Dátil, támara.*

Description: *Dates are the fruit of the date palm ('Phoenix dactylifera' L.), a tree of the botanical family Palmaceae, reaching a height of 20 meters.*

DATES
Composition
per 100 g of raw edible portion

Energy	275 kcal = 1,151 kj
Protein	1.97 g
Carbohydrates	66.0 g
Fiber	7.50 g
Vitamin A	5.00 µg RE
Vitamin B_1	0.090 mg
Vitamin B_2	0.100 mg
Niacin	3.03 mg NE
Vitamin B_6	0.192 mg
Folate	12.6 µg
Vitamin B_{12}	—
Vitamin C	3.00 mg
Vitamin E	0.100 mg α-TE
Calcium	32.0 mg
Phosphorus	40.0 mg
Magnesium	35.0 mg
Iron	1.15 mg
Potassium	652 mg
Zinc	0.290 mg
Total Fat	*0.450 g*
Saturated Fat	*0.191 g*
Cholesterol	—
Sodium	*3.00 mg*

1% 2% 4% 10% 20% 40% 100%

% Daily Value (based on a 2,000 calorie diet)
provided by 100 g of this food

THE ARABS of the desert consider the date palm to be "the source of life." Not only does it provide the traveler with its nutritious fruit, dates, but it also provides a sugary beverage when the tree trunk is tapped, textile fibers to make garments and rope, and refreshing shade.

PROPERTIES AND INDICATIONS: Dates are one of the most energy-rich fruits: 100 g (about 10 dates) provides 275 calories. This represents 11% of the daily energy needs of an adult male involved in average physical activity. The most significant of dates' nutrients are:

✓ ***Sugars*** (66%), comprised *primarily* of ***glucose*** and ***fructose.*** Dates are one of the *most sugar-rich* fruits.

✓ ***B group vitamins,*** particularly B_1, B_2, niacin, and B_6. These vitamins, among other functions, *facilitate* the **utilization** of ***sugars*** by the body's cells. Dates provide significant amounts of these vitamins, which contributes to their **invigorating** effect.

✓ ***Minerals:*** Dates are among the richest of all fruits in minerals. Among those present, ***potassium, iron, magnesium, phosphorous,*** and ***calcium*** are prominent in order of importance. ***The trace*** elements copper, manganese, and zinc are also present in significant quantities.

✓ ***Vegetable fiber:*** One hundred grams of dates provide almost one-third of RDA (Recommended Dietary Allowance) of vegetable fiber. These are predominantly soluble fibers in the form of ***pectin*** and ***gums,*** although they also contain insoluble or cellulose fiber. Both types of fiber have a favorable, complementary effect on the intestine.

Dates, then, are a highly nutritious and energy-producing fruit. Their protein content, which barely reaches 2%, is quite low but higher than most fresh fruit, except the avocado (see p. 112). These quite complete ***proteins*** are easily assimilated by the body. Their ***fat*** content is around 0.5%.

The most important dietary and therapeutic applications of dates are:

• **Respiratory disorders:** Dates have been traditionally used to relieve excessively dry **cough** and to fight **bronchial colds.** They have a proven soothing effect on the bronchial passages, as well as being antitussive. This is possibly due to their richness in sugars and some other component that has yet to be identified.

Dates boiled in milk (preferably non-dairy) are a traditional remedy for cough and respiratory disorders.

The most effective manner to use them for this purpose is boiled in milk **[❸]**.

• **Low protein diets:** Dates contain very few proteins in proportion to their richness in energy. This is useful when it is necessary to limit protein intake, as occurs, for example, in cases of renal failure.

• **High-energy diets:** Dates have an **invigorating** effect. They are useful in cases of fatigue or weakness at any age. Because of their richness in sugars, vitamins, and minerals (including iron), they are particularly beneficial to **adolescents, young athletes,** and **pregnant** and **lactating** women.

Preparation and use

❶ **Fresh:** Fresh dates are softer and more pleasant than dried. In many cases, dates are frozen in their country of origin after harvest, and are thawed immediately prior to export to market. Although the freezing process affects them very little due to their relatively slight water content, fresh dates are better—and more expensive.

❷ **Dried:** Drying is the traditional way of preserving dates. To avoid their tough texture, they may be soaked in water or milk before eating.

❸ **Boiled in milk** (preferably non-dairy): One hundred grams of dates are placed to boil for a few minutes in a half-liter of cow's milk or soy milk. The dates are then eaten with the milk to take full advantage of their **effect** on the **respiratory system.** A spoonful of honey may be added.

8

Foods for the Digestive System

THIS CHAPTER will discuss those diseases of the digestive tract that do not specifically affect the liver, the gall bladder, the stomach, or the intestines since each of these will be reviewed in their own dedicated chapters.

The first sections of the digestive tract

The mouth, pharynx, esophagus, and stomach are the first sections or stages of the digestive process that food passes through. In the process the foods themselves act upon these sections because of the food's own characteristics:

• **Chemical composition:** Sugar promotes dental caries; carcinogenic substances found in certain types of meat, as well as alcoholic beverages, foster cancer of the mouth, esophagus, and the stomach (see pp. 364, 365).

• **Physical texture:** Tough foods that must be chewed vigorously, strengthen the gums and teeth. However, if they are not well chewed, they can irritate the esophagus and the stomach.

• **Temperature:** Very hot and very cold foods irritate the digestive mucosa and may be a factor in cancer.

MOUTH SORES

Definition

Also referred to as **cold sores** or canker sores. These small painful ulcerations that appear in the oral mucosa are white in the center with a red border.

Causes

They have a wide variety of causes:

- **Nutritional deficiencies,** particularly iron, B vitamins, including folates. They can be the first manifestation of iron deficiency anemia.
- **Allergy** to some, often unknown, food.
- **Depressed immune** system.
- **Stress** and emotional **tension.**
- Viral **infections.**

 **Increase**

IRON
B VITAMINS
FOLATES
ZINC
YOGURT
ACIDIFIED WHEY

 **Reduce or eliminate**

ALCOHOLIC BEVERAGES
VINEGAR
SALT

The papaya aids all of the digestive processes due, among other reasons, to its papain content. This enzyme digests proteins and can partially supplement a lack of digestive juices.

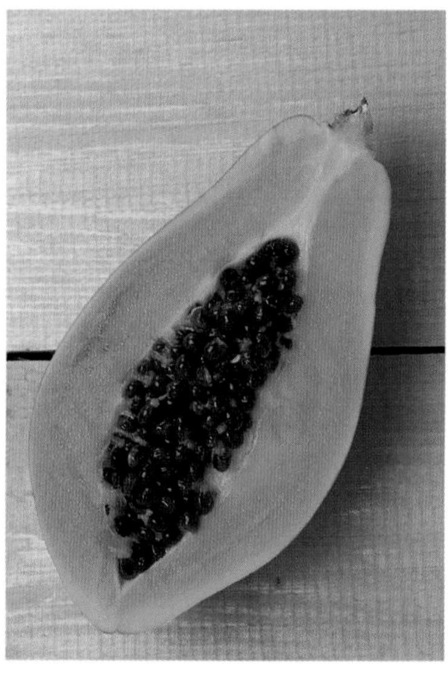

HALITOSIS

Definition

This is defined as **bad breath.** Inadequate oral hygiene, poor digestion, constipation, consumption of alcoholic beverages, and smoking are the most common causes.

Diet

A diet of plant-based foods promotes proper digestion and abstaining from alcoholic beverages and tobacco can resolve many cases of halitosis.

 **Increase**

WHEAT BRAN
APPLE
YOGURT
WATER

 **Reduce or eliminate**

ALCOHOLIC BEVERAGES
SUGARS
SOFT DRINKS

Apples

Apples regulate the intestine and balance the intestinal flora because of their pectin (soluble fiber) content, thus aiding with halitosis.

DENTAL CARIES

Definition

It is well known that dental caries are caused by a certain type of oral **bacteria,** which proliferate in the presence of sugar.

Diet

The acids in soft drinks, as well as those in fruit, can erode dental enamel, leaning to caries.

Proper dental and **oral hygiene,** in addition to a low-sugar diet, are essential in preventing dental caries.

 **Increase**

CARROTS
WHOLE GRAINS

 **Reduce or eliminate**

SUGAR
CHOCOLATE
SOFT DRINKS
FRUIT JUICES
CITRUS FRUITS

GINGIVITIS AND PERIODONTITIS

Definition

Gingivitis is the inflammation of the gums, which also bleed easily. If the problem is not corrected promptly, the periodontal tissues (all of the tissues surrounding teeth) can be affected leading to periodontitis.

Periodontitis deteriorates the alveolar bone, which is part of the jaw structure supporting the teeth. The result is loosening and finally loss of teeth.

Diet

Lack of certain nutrients can cause or aggravate gingivitis or periodontitis. The consumption of certain foods has the same effect.

Increase

- FRUIT
- VITAMIN C
- FOLATES
- VITAMIN A
- COENZYME Q10

Reduce or eliminate

- SUGARS
- ALCOHOLIC BEVERAGES
- PHOSPHOROUS
- MEAT

Kiwis

Kiwis provide folates and vitamin C, both of which foster healthy gums.

LACK OF APPETITE

Definition

Inappetence, or lack of appetite, can be due to multiple causes. It is *always* convenient to ***diagnose*** as soon as possible the cause of inappetence, because occasionally it can be due to malignant conditions such as cancer.

Diet

The foods mentioned here can improve appetite and facilitate digestion.

Increase

- CONDIMENTS AND SEASONINGS
- OLIVES
- HORSERADISH
- RHUBARB
- SCURVY GRASS
- SLOEBERRY
- POLLEN

Lemons

Natural seasonings stimulate the appetite and prepare the stomach for digestion. Recommended are garlic, lemon, and aromatic herbs.

Abundant intake of fruit is a guarantee of a healthy diet, one that promotes health and which, thanks to its different textures and tastes, is pleasant to the most demanding palate.

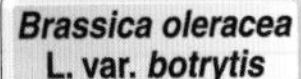

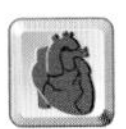

Cauliflower

The most digestible cabbage

The cauliflower is considered the most delicate and digestible of the cabbages (see p. 186), although it produces flatulence in some individuals. Its flavor adapts well to any cuisine, American, European, Asian, or Arabic.

CAULIFLOWER
Composition
per 100 g of raw edible portion

Energy	25.0 kcal = 105 kj
Protein	1.98 g
Carbohydrates	2.70 g
Fiber	2.50 g
Vitamin A	2.00 µg RE
Vitamin B_1	0.057 mg
Vitamin B_2	0.063 mg
Niacin	0.959 mg NE
Vitamin B_6	0.222 mg
Folate	57.0 µg
Vitamin B_{12}	—
Vitamin C	46.4 mg
Vitamin E	0.040 mg α-TE
Calcium	22.0 mg
Phosphorus	44.0 mg
Magnesium	15.0 mg
Iron	0.440 mg
Potassium	303 mg
Zinc	0.280 mg
Total Fat	*0.210 g*
Saturated Fat	*0.032 g*
Cholesterol	—
Sodium	*30.0 mg*

1% 2% 4% 10% 20% 40% 100%

% Daily Value (based on a 2,000 calorie diet)
provided by 100 g of this food

French: *Chou-fleur;*
Spanish: *Coliflor, brécol de cabeza.*

Description: *The inflorescence (unopened buds) of the herbaceous plant 'Brassica oleracea' L. var 'botrytis,' of the botanical family Cruciferae.*

THE EDIBLE portion of the cauliflower is precisely its inflorescence (blossoms) before it fully flowers. It is formed of thousands of tiny buds. Botanically, cauliflower, as well as broccoli (see p. 72) and all cabbages (see p. 186) are varieties of the same species.

Farmers maintain the bright white of the cauliflower by binding the plant's heavy outer leaves over the top, protecting it from sunlight.

When sunlight reaches the buds, the result is cauliflowers in a variety of colors depending on the variety: **green,** like the **Romanesque** cauliflower, due to the presence of chlorophyll, or **purple** caused by their anthocyanin content.

Although the most common variety of cauliflower is white, others are green and purple. Cauliflower is known for producing flatulence, but often this is due to the heavy recipes used in their preparation, rather than the cauliflower itself. They are most healthful and digestible when they are steamed and served with a few drops of lemon and oil.

PROPERTIES AND INDICATIONS: The cauliflower contains small amounts of carbohydrates and proteins, and practically no fat. It contains provitamin A (beta-carotene), ***vitamins*** B, C, and E, of which C *stands out* with 46.4 mg /100 g. As for minerals, it is *very rich* in ***potassium*** and *low* in **sodium.** It also contains significant amounts of calcium, magnesium, phosphorous, and iron.

Cauliflower is *rich* in ***trace elements*** such as chromium, zinc, manganese, copper, and selenium.

Preparation and use

❶ **Raw:** in salad, when young and tender.

❷ **Cooked** in a great variety of manners: boiled, steamed (these are the most healthful means of preparation), baked, fried, stewed, au gratin.

As with other crucifers, the cauliflower is *very rich* in ***phytochemical*** **anticarcinogens,** which give it its cancer preventive properties.

The medicinal applications of the cauliflower are as follows:

- **Digestive disorders:** Cauliflower is an excellent supplier of vitamins, minerals, and trace elements that vitalize digestive processes. It acts on the digestive tract in general, from the stomach to the colon. Because it is highly **digestible,** more so than other crucifers, it is preferred for those with stomach ailments (**gastritis, ulcer, dyspepsia**). It *regulates* transit through the intestine both in cases of constipation, as well as diarrhea. Because of this, it is indicated for **constipation, colitis,** and **diverticulosis.**

Cauliflower is, together with carrots (see p. 32) and asparagus (see p. 234), one of the best vegetables for patients after an acute bout of **gastritis** or **gastroenteritis.**

- **Cardiovascular** disorders: Its *low* ***sodium*** content, *abundant* ***potassium,*** and virtual *lack* of ***fat*** make the cauliflower one of the *most effective* foods for those suffering with

continued on page 157

Cauliflower preparation

1. Cut the base of the cauliflower with a large knife.

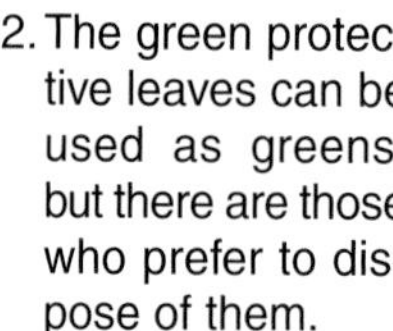

2. The green protective leaves can be used as greens, but there are those who prefer to dispose of them.

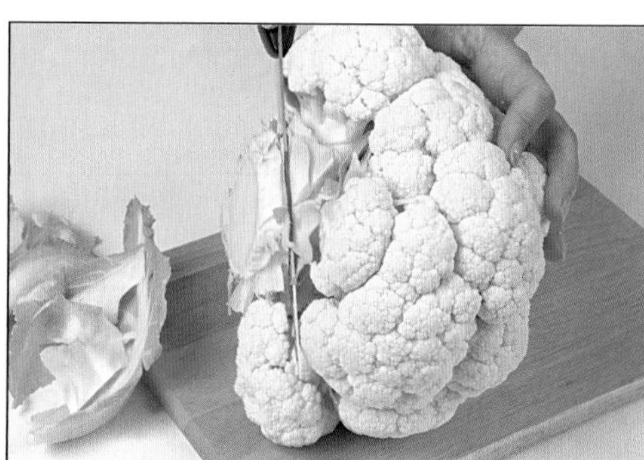

3. Cut the small branches of inflorescences.

4. Wash these fragments in running water.
5. They may be eaten raw {❶}, or cooked in a variety of ways.{❷}

continued from page 155

disorders of the heart or circulatory system. It should be included in the diets of those with any form of **heart disease, hypertension,** or **arteriosclerosis** in any of their manifestations.

- **Obesity and diabetes:** Cauliflower contains a minimum of calories: only 28 kcal/100 g; however, it produces a sense of satiety. Boiled or steamed, cauliflower is the perfect supper for those wishing to lose weight and for diabetics due to their low carbohydrate content.

- **Kidney disorders:** Cauliflower is **diuretic and depurant,** facilitating the elimination of excess water retained in the tissues (edema) and waste materials such as urea. Its use is indicated in cases of **renal failure, arthritis, gout, edema** related to renal issues, and kidney **stones.**

- **Cancer:** Beginning in recent years, a variety of experimental and statistical studies are being conducted that demonstrate the anticarcinogenic effect of cauliflower, broccoli, cabbage and other **cruciferous** plants (see p. 361). This effect is due to two types of ***phytochemicals: sulfurated glycosides,*** and ***indole-derived*** compounds.[1, 2] Administrated orally, both substances are capable of inhibiting the formation of malignant tumors in laboratory animals that had been previously treated with carcinogens such as benzopyrene.[3]

Thus, abundant use of cauliflower and other crucifers is indicated for persons at higher risk of cancer due to genetic predisposition, consumption of toxic substances such as tobacco, or other reasons. Those who have already been diagnosed with some type of **cancer,** and are in *treatment* should include some vegetable of the crucifer family, such as cauliflower, broccoli (see p. 72), cabbage (see p. 182), or radish (see p. 174) in their *daily diet.*

Caution

Although cauliflower is recommended for gastric and intestinal disorders, its use should be restricted in the following cases:

- ***Cholelithiasis*** *(gallstones), since it can produce bile-related heaviness and dyspepsia.*
- ***Intestinal flatulence:*** *Cauliflower increases the production of intestinal gas in individuals with this propensity because of its cellulose content.*

The Romanesque or minaret is a yellow-green cauliflower. It is much sought after in Germany. Its distinguishing characteristic is its little tower or minaret-shaped inflorescences. It is usually boiled and served whole.

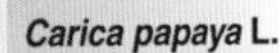

Papaya

Activates the digestive process

Synonyms: *Pawpaw, Melon fruit, Papaw, Melon pawpaw.*

French: *Papaye;* **Spanish:** *Papaya, Lechosa, Mamao, melón zapote.*

Description: *Fruit of 'Carica papaya' L, a fast-growing branchless herb-like tree 3-6 meters in height of the botanical family Caricaceae. The fruit usually weighs 0.5 to 2 kilos, although there are some that reach 6 kilos. The green or yellow rind encloses a delicate yellow or orange pulp. Its center is filled with sour black seeds.*

PAPAYA
Composition
per 100 g of raw edible portion

Energy	39.0 kcal = 161 kj
Protein	0.610 g
Carbohydrates	8.01 g
Fiber	1.80 g
Vitamin A	175 µg RE
Vitamin B_1	0.027 mg
Vitamin B_2	0.032 mg
Niacin	0.471 mg NE
Vitamin B_6	0.019 mg
Folate	38.0 µg
Vitamin B_{12}	—
Vitamin C	61.8 mg
Vitamin E	1.12 mg α-TE
Calcium	24.0 mg
Phosphorus	5.00 mg
Magnesium	10.0 mg
Iron	0.100 mg
Potassium	257 mg
Zinc	0.070 mg
Total Fat	*0.140 g*
Saturated Fat	*0.043 g*
Cholesterol	—
Sodium	*3.00 mg*

1% 2% 4% 10% 20% 40% 100% 200% 500%

% Daily Value (based on a 2,000 calorie diet) provided by 100 g of this food

Properties and indications: The papaya in 88.8% water, almost as much as a melon (92%). This is why some call it the "tropical melon." However, the papaya and the melon belong to distinct botanical families with completely different characteristics.

Its content of ***energy*** producing ***nutrients*** is quite reduced in carbohydrates (8%), proteins (0.61%) and fats (0.14%). Most of its carbohydrates are formed from sugars: saccharose, glucose, and fructose.

Its ***vitamin*** content, however, is striking: 100 g of pulp provides 103% of the RDA of ***vitamin C*** and 18% of ***vitamin A*** for an adult.

The B vitamins are also present in small amounts except for ***folates,*** which, with 38 µg /100 g, is as much as the mango (see p. 326) or the feijoa (see p. 252), the richest fresh fruits in these substances.

Where minerals are concerned, the papaya is *rich* in potassium (257 µg/100 g), and significant amounts of calcium, magnesium, phosphorous, and iron. ***Pectin*** (soluble vegetable fiber) makes 1.8%.

PAPAIN is a proteolytic enzyme (one that digests proteins), similar to the pepsin in gastric juice. Its primary source is the leaves of the papaya tree or its unripe fruit. Papain is greatly reduced in ripe papayas.

Papaya is very easy to digest and contributes to the digestion of other foods. These are its primary therapeutic indications:

- **Stomach disorders:** Papaya is recommended in cases of difficult digestion, gastric ptosis (gastric prolapse), gastritis, and anytime digestion is affected by inflammation of the gastric mucosa.

Preparation and use

❶ **Fresh:** This is the ***best*** way to eat papaya. The fruit sold in nontropical countries is normally picked green to facilitate its transport. Consequently, it loses quality and flavor. Papaya makes an excellent breakfast or dessert, although it also goes well in a lettuce salad with lemon juice.

❷ **Other methods of preparation:** The papaya lends itself well to **soft drinks, shakes,** and **ice cream.** Papaya **jam** is a popular dessert in the American tropics.

❸ **Canned:** Canned papaya allows it to be enjoyed throughout the world.

Papaya is considered the perfect breakfast throughout the tropics. Perhaps this is because of its digestibility and vitamin richness. A papaya shake is one of the most pleasant ways of eating this fruit.

Papaya helps *neutralize* excess ***gastric acid.*** Consequently, it is beneficial in cases of gastroduodenal **ulcer, hiatal hernia,** and **pyrosis** (heartburn).

- **Biliary dyspepsia and chronic pancreatitis:** Papaya is of value because of its effect on all digestive processes and its very low fat content.

- **Intestinal disorders:** The papaya's emollient and antiseptic effect on the digestive mucosa makes it useful in any type of case of gastroenteritis or colitis: infectious, ulcerous, or spastic (irritable bowel).

Studies carried out in Japan,[4] show that papaya, particularly when it is slightly green, has **bacteriostatic** properties, impeding the development of many enteropathogens that cause intestinal infections. Papaya is highly recommended for **infectious diarrhea.**

- **Intestinal parasites:** Papaya sap or latex,[5] and to a lesser extent the pulp, have anthelminthic and vermifuge properties against intestinal parasites, particularly tenia (tapeworm).

- **Skin disorders:** Papaya is a part of the suggested diet for those with skin disorders such as eczema, furunculosis, and acne because of its richness in provitamin A.

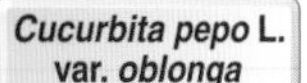

Zucchini

Soothes the digestive tract

ZUCCHINI
Composition
per 100 g of raw edible portion

Energy	14.0 kcal = 60.0 kj
Protein	1.16 g
Carbohydrates	1.70 g
Fiber	1.20 g
Vitamin A	34.0 µg RE
Vitamin B_1	0.070 mg
Vitamin B_2	0.030 mg
Niacin	0.567 mg NE
Vitamin B_6	0.089 mg
Folate	22.1 µg
Vitamin B_{12}	—
Vitamin C	9.00 mg
Vitamin E	0.120 mg α-TE
Calcium	15.0 mg
Phosphorus	32.0 mg
Magnesium	22.0 mg
Iron	0.420 mg
Potassium	248 mg
Zinc	0.200 mg
Total Fat	*0.140 g*
Saturated Fat	*0.029 g*
Cholesterol	—
Sodium	*3.00 mg*

1% 2% 4% 10% 20% 40% 100%

% Daily Value (based on a 2,000 calorie diet) provided by 100 g of this food

Related species: *Cucurbita pepo* L., var. *giromontina.*

Synonyms: *Courgette, Vegetable marrow, Golden zucchini, Italian squash.*

French: *Courgette;* ***Spanish:*** *Calabacín, Zapallo.*

Description: *Fruit of the zucchini plant ('Cucurbita pepo' L. var. 'oblonga'), a botanical variety of the squash ('Cucurbita pepo' L., see p. 104). This is an annual herbaceous plant of the botanical family Cucurbitaceae, whose vine reaches a meter in length.*

THE ZUCCHINI is very similar to the cucumber (see p. 324), although botanically it is much closer to the squash (see p. 104). All varieties of zucchini have a white or yellowish pulp similar to the cucumber, but with a more solid consistency. Its delicate flavor (reminiscent of the walnut), and its dietary and therapeutic properties have given the zucchini a well-deserved reputation among vegetables.

PROPERTIES AND INDICATIONS: Although the zucchini is a species of squash, it has its

Zucchini combines very well with tomato. Provided they are not fried, both are highly digestive and slightly diuretic. They are ideal in slimming diets.

own characteristics. For example, it has very little beta-carotene, while other squash are very rich in this important vitamin precursor. On the other hand, the zucchini contains 1.16% protein, an amount similar to other squash.

Both squash and zucchini are *very low* in ***fat, sodium,*** and ***calories,*** although squash is the lower in the two nutrients.

Zucchini is *remarkable* for its **emollient** or soothing properties because of its mucilage content. It is also *slightly* **diuretic.** All of these properties make it of value in these cases:

- **Dyspepsia** (indigestion), **gastritis, irritable bowel, colitis** (inflammation of the colon).
- **Weight-loss treatments:** It provides very little fat and calories, but is relatively high in protein.
- **Cardiovascular disease,** such as hypertension, arteriosclerosis, and coronary disease.

Preparation and use

❶ **Cooked** in a variety of dishes. It is delicious fried but retains a great deal of oil.

❷ **Puree:** Finely chopped zucchini is boiled in somewhat diluted milk or soy beverage, and then placed in a blender. Cornstarch may be added as a thickener.

Barley

Eases digestion

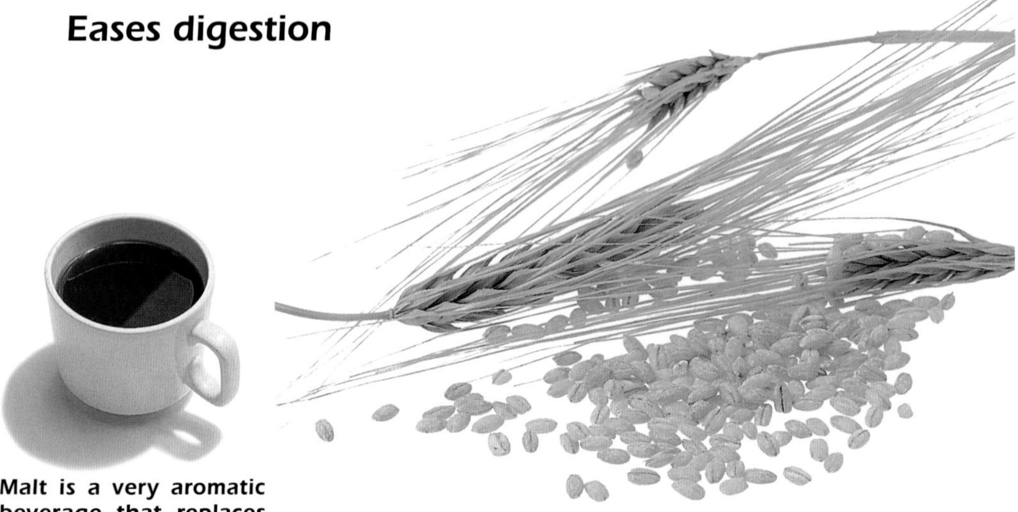

Malt is a very aromatic beverage that replaces coffee with advantage, as it is digestive, healthy, and nutritious.

__Synonyms:__ Barleycorn, Barley flakes, Malt.

__French:__ Orge; __Spanish:__ Cebada.

__Description:__ Fruit of the barley plant ('Hordeum vulgare' L.), a herbaceous plant of the botanical family Gramineae.

BARLEY
Composition
per 100 g of raw edible portion

Energy	354 kcal = 1,481 kj
Protein	12.5 g
Carbohydrates	56.2 g
Fiber	17.3 g
Vitamin A	2.00 µg RE
Vitamin B_1	0.646 mg
Vitamin B_2	0.285 mg
Niacin	8.07 mg NE
Vitamin B_6	0.318 mg
Folate	19.0 µg
Vitamin B_{12}	—
Vitamin C	—
Vitamin E	0.600 mg α-TE
Calcium	33.0 mg
Phosphorus	264 mg
Magnesium	133 mg
Iron	3.60 mg
Potassium	452 mg
Zinc	2.77 mg
Total Fat	*2.30 g*
Saturated Fat	*0.482 g*
Cholesterol	—
Sodium	*12.0 mg*

1% 2% 4% 10% 20% 40% 100%

% Daily Value (based on a 2,000 calorie diet)
provided by 100 g of this food

Properties and indications: Barley, whole-grain or polished, is very similar in composition to wheat (see p. 292), with some significant differences:

✓ ***Proteins:*** Barley's percentage of proteins is somewhat higher (12.5%) than that of wheat (11.3%), while containing less gluten. Because of this, barley bread is more compact and less spongy than that made with wheat.

Barley proteins are also deficient in lysine. However, this lack is minimized by combining barley with legumes or dairy products, which are rich in lysine.

✓ ***Carbohydrates:*** Barley contains 56.2%, somewhat less than wheat (61.7%). The carbohydrates of both grains are in the form of ***starch.*** This is digested more easily when it has been ground to fine flour, as opposed to the whole grain[6] (cooked barley, flakes). However, barley is *most* **digestible** when it has been malted, either as grain or as flour **[❻]** or as liquid malt **[❼]**.

✓ ***Vitamins:*** Barley contains more vitamins B_1 and B_2 than wheat, but only half as much vitamin E. As is the case with all grains, it lacks provitamin A, vitamin C, and vitamin B_{12}.

✓ ***Minerals:*** Its composition is similar to that of wheat: rich in phosphorus, magnesium, and iron, as well as zinc and other ***trace elements.*** However, like wheat, it is poor in calcium.

✓ ***Fiber:*** Barley contains 17.3 g of cellulose fiber per 100 g; this is about 5 g more than wheat.

Barley is indicated in the following cases:

• **Digestive disorders:** Pearl barley **[❷]**, barley flour **[❺]**, and primarily malt granules and flour **[❻]**, are well tolerated by frail stomachs. They are beneficial in cases of gastritis dyspepsia (indigestion), gastroduodenal ulcer, gastroenteritis, and colitis.

Barley water **[❸]** and malt beverage **[❼]**, are also of great value in cases of digestive distress.

As is the case with wheat and rye, barley should be avoided by those who suffer from celiac disease.

• **Excess Cholesterol:** Eating barley in any form: whole grain (polished) **[❶]**, flakes **[❹]**, whole-grain flour **[❺]**, or partially whole-grain (malted grain and flour **[❻]**) produces a reduction in total cholesterol level, LDL (harmful) cholesterol level, and triglycerides.

Barley consumption, as with that of all whole grains, has been shown effective in preventing **arteriosclerosis.** It should be included in the diet of those at high risk of **coronary disease.**

• **Diabetes:** Diabetic laboratory animals that were fed barley showed lower blood glucose levels than those fed on wheat.[7] This effect is attributed to some hypoglycemic factor in barley that is still being investigated.

• **Intestinal disorders:** Barley fiber helps prevent constipation and all of its complications, including colon cancer.[8]

Preparation and use

❶ **Polished barley (whole-grain):** Barley that has had its outer indigestible shell (glume), and part of the bran removed by abrasion. After soaking in water, it is boiled for an hour with vegetables or it is cooked as a soup.

❷ **Pearl Barley (refined):** Barley that has been polished until the glume, the bran, and most of the germ have been removed. The result is a polished round uniform grain. It is boiled as if it were rice, although its flavor is more intense. It requires a minimum of 45 minutes of cooking.

❸ **Barley water:** See preparation instructions on the following page.

❹ **Flakes:** These are prepared with grain that has been soaked, boiled, and pressed. It is used as a part of muesli, or cooked for ten minutes in milk or vegetable broth.

❺ **Flour:** This can be made from either polished (whole-grain) or pearl (refined) barley.

❻ **Malted barley and flour.**

❼ **Malt:** This is an aqueous extract of barley that has been germinated and roasted.

Olive

A Mediterranean pearl

French: *Olive;* ***Spanish:*** *Aceituna, oliva.*

Description: *The olive, fruit of the olive tree ('Olea europaea' L.), of the botanical family Oleaceae. Green olives are harvested at the beginning of fall, while black olives are harvested beginning in December, when they are ripe.*

OLIVES, RIPE
Composition
per 100 g of raw edible portion

Energy	115 kcal = 480 kj
Protein	0.840 g
Carbohydrates	3.06 g
Fiber	3.20 g
Vitamin A	40.0 µg RE
Vitamin B_1	0.003 mg
Vitamin B_2	—
Niacin	0.037 mg NE
Vitamin B_6	0.009 mg
Folate	—
Vitamin B_{12}	—
Vitamin C	0.900 mg
Vitamin E	3.00 mg α-TE
Calcium	88.0 mg
Phosphorus	3.00 mg
Magnesium	4.00 mg
Iron	3.30 mg
Potassium	8.00 mg
Zinc	0.220 mg
Total Fat	*10.7 g*
Saturated Fat	*1.42 g*
Cholesterol	—
Sodium	*872 mg*

1% 2% 4% 10% 20% 40% 100%

% Daily Value (based on a 2,000 calorie diet)
provided by 100 g of this food

IF THERE IS a tree that symbolizes Mediterranean civilization, it is the olive. Its fruit has been part of the human diet from the remotest of times as a food in itself as well as for its oil.

Properties and indications: Olives are an oleaginous fruit, *very rich* in ***fats,*** and as a result, ***calories.*** They are also noted for their ***protein*** content, which is higher than most fruits. These proteins are of high biological value since they contain all essential amino acids.

The *skin* of the olive is rich in vegetable pigments (anthocyanins) and volatile substances that give olives their unique aroma. The *pulp* is rich in vegetable fiber and fatty substances called triglycerides (up to 30% of their weight). Triglycerides are composed of the union of one molecule of glycerin and three of fatty acids.

Olives contain significant amounts of ***provitamin A*** and ***vitamins B and E.*** As for minerals, ***calcium*** is the most abundant, but with significant amounts of ***potassium, iron*** and ***phosphorous,*** as well. The olive's *elevated* ***sodium*** content is due to the **salt** added during its soaking in brine.

These are the olive's more important indications:

- **Lack of appetite:** Olives stimulate the digestive processes and the appetite. Eating two or three olives before a meal is a natural aperitif that increases the flow of gastric juices and improves digestion.

However, because olives contain so much fiber, they must be *chewed well* to prevent indigestion.

- **Gallbladder disorders:** Olives, as well as olive oil, act as a **cholagogue,** facilitating the emptying of the gallbladder. They are useful in case of **biliary dyskinesia** (disorder that interferes with gallbladder drainage) and ***biliary dyspepsia*** (indigestion caused by disturbances in the drainage of the gallbladder). In cases of **cholelithiasis** (gallstones), they may be used, but carefully.

- **Constipation:** Because of their oil and vegetable fiber content, olives have a mild but effective laxative effect. Olives are among the fruits *highest* in ***fiber.***

Olive oil, the authentic juice of the olive, is ideal for seasoning any vegetable or salad.

Preparation and use

❶ **Natural:** In their natural state, olives, both green and black, are hard and bitter.

To make them edible, they are first **soaked**, changing water daily until they lose their **bitterness.** This process is accelerated by making small cuts in the olives' skin or by pounding them.

❷ **Treated:** To speed the process further 10-20 g of sodium hydroxide (caustic soda) is added to the water. In this way, 24 to 36 hours of soaking are sufficient. The olives are then washed in clean water, changing it every two hours three or four times.

Once the olives have been debittered using one of the two methods described, they are put in **brine** (20-30 g of salt per liter of water), along with **aromatic herbs:** savory, oregano, thyme, laurel, or rosemary. After 15 days, they are ready to eat.

❸ **Olive paté:** This is prepared from ripe black olives, mashing them to a consistent paste. Its exquisite flavor has caused some to refer to it as "vegetable caviar."

9

Foods for the Liver

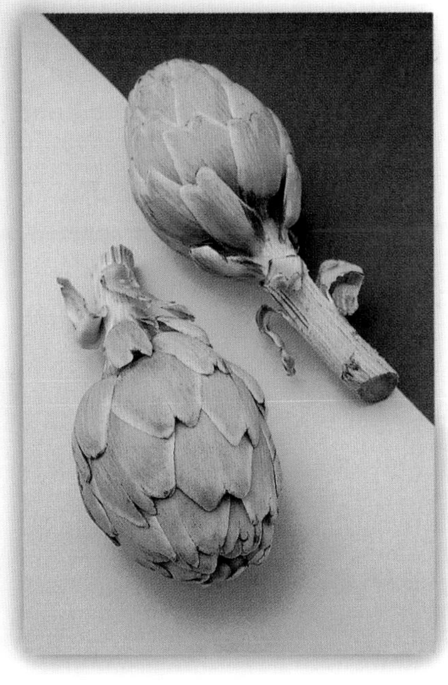

WEIGHING 1,500 grams, the liver is the ***largest*** of the internal organs and the one responsible for the ***most*** chemical **processes** and metabolic **functions.**

Before the blood from the intestine, which circulates through the **portal venous system,** is distributed throughout the body, it must pass through the liver. There it undergoes:

- The **processing** of **nutritive substances** carried in the portal blood from the intestine. For example, *part* of the ***glucose*** is transformed to *reserve* **glycogen; *amino acids*** are joined in specific sequences, providing the *unique* **proteins** for each body; ***fatty acids*** are joined with ***glycerin*** to form *stored* **fat.**
- **Neutralization** of **toxins** and **foreign substances** from the digestive tract.

The liver performs another important role: it *secretes* the **bile** necessary for digestion (approximately one liter daily), which is stored in the **gallbladder.**

HEPATOPATHIES

Definition

These are **diseases of the liver** in general that affect some function of this essential organ.

Diet

Healthful **foods** can do a great deal to ***facilitate*** the **recuperation** of liver function. In contrast, **alcoholic beverages** and foods *rich* in **animal protein** and **fat** are the *primary* ***threats*** to the liver.

The liver is the ***first*** **processing and purifying** station for the substances that the blood brings from the intestine. As a result, the following are particularly important in case of liver disease:

- *Choose* **foods** *carefully*, avoiding those that overwork the liver.
- *Avoid* **alcoholic beverages.** There is a type of hepatopathy caused primarily by the consumption of alcoholic beverages.
- **Avoid,** to the extent possible, *chemical-based* **medications, food contaminants** such as pesticides, and **chemical additives,** all of which must be neutralized or eliminated by the liver.

Increase

WHOLE GRAINS
FRUIT
LEAFY GREEN VEGETABLES
GRAPE
APPLE
PLUM
CHERRY
LOQUAT
ARTICHOKE
CARDOON
ONION
SAUERKRAUT
RADISH
TAPIOCA
TAMARIND
HONEY
LECITHIN
BREWER'S YEAST
OLIVE OIL

Reduce or eliminate

ALCOHOLIC BEVERAGES
TOTAL FAT
PROTEINS
SALT
BACON
SAUSAGES
SHELLFISH
MEAT
CREAM
BUTTER
FRIED FOODS
SPICES

Plums

HEPATITIS

Definition

This is an **inflammation** or **infection of the liver,** caused by a virus, alcohol, a medication or another toxin.

Diet

In cases of hepatitis, the **diet** must be **light and healthful,** but **nutritious.** In addition to the foods described in the section ***"Hepatopathies"***, particular attention should be given to those in this section.

Increase

VEGETABLES
VITAMIN C
B VITAMINS
FOLATES
ANTIOXIDANTS

Reduce or eliminate

ALCOHOLIC BEVERAGES
SATURATED FAT
PROTEINS
SUGARS
COFFEE
VITAMIN A

CHOLELITHIASIS

This is the presence of **calculi** or **stones** in the **gallbladder.** They are typically formed primarily of **cholesterol.** This is one of the components of bile and is characterized by its semi-insolubility and its tendency to crystallize and precipitate forming calculi or stones.

In addition to the foods described in the section entitled ***"Gallbladder disorders"*** (see next page), those described here should also be considered in an effort to ***avoid*** the formation of gallstones, as well as to ***prevent*** **complications** such as **gallbladder attack** and **cholecystitis,** or gallbladder inflammation, once they have been formed.

Increase

FRUIT
LEGUMES
ARTICHOKE
APPLE
RADISH
SOY BEVERAGE OR SOYMILK
LECITHIN
FIBER
VITAMIN C

Reduce or eliminate

TOTAL FAT
DAIRY PRODUCTS
SUGARS
PROTEINS

Lecithin contributes to avoiding the formation of gallstones.

Lecithin

CIRRHOSIS

Definition

This serious disease permanently destroys liver cells. The destroyed cells are replaced by a fibrous tissue that proliferates, impeding blood flow through the liver. Its consequences are:

- **Increased pressure** in the **portal** venous system, which collects blood from the intestine.
- Fluid retention in the abdomen (**ascites**).
- **Deterioration** of the liver's **detoxifying capabilities.**

Diet

Certain foods can help minimize the consequences of cirrhosis, while others aggravate it to the point of complete liver failure. Alcohol and animal proteins, together with fats, are the most detrimental nutrients in cases of cirrhosis.

In addition to the foods described in ***"Hepatopathies"*** (see p. 168), those described on this page should also be considered.

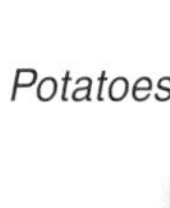

Increase

CARBOHYDRATES
B VITAMINS
FRUIT
VEGETABLES
ARTICHOKE
APPLE
GRAPE
LOQUAT
BANANA
STRAWBERRY
ONION

Reduce or eliminate

ALCOHOLIC BEVERAGES
TOTAL FAT
SODIUM
MEAT
CURED CHEESES
DAIRY

Potatoes

Complex carbohydrates such as starch are the nutrient most easily metabolized by a diseased liver. Whole grains, potatoes, tapioca and other tubers are the best sources.

GALLBLADDER DISORDERS

Definition

The gallbladder is a reservoir for bile that must empty at the appropriate time (as fats pass through the duodenum) and with the appropriate intensity.

For a variety of reasons, such as **gallstones, inflammation** or excessively **thick bile,** it is possible that the gallbladder does not empty at the appropriate time or intensity. These disorders are known as **biliary dyskinesia** or **lazy gallbladder.**

Symtoms

They are manifested by abdominal heaviness, pain on the right side or headache.

Diet

Certain foods can help avoid functional disorders. They are both **choleretic** (increasing bile production) and **cholagogic** (more or less gently stimulating the emptying of the gallbladder). Foods high in fat, however, exacerbate them.

Increase

ARTICHOKE
CHICORY
BELGIAN ENDIVE
ESCAROLE
RADISH
EGGPLANT
RHUBARB
TAMARIND
OLIVE
PAPAYA

Reduce or eliminate

TOTAL FAT
CITRUS FRUITS
VEGETABLES

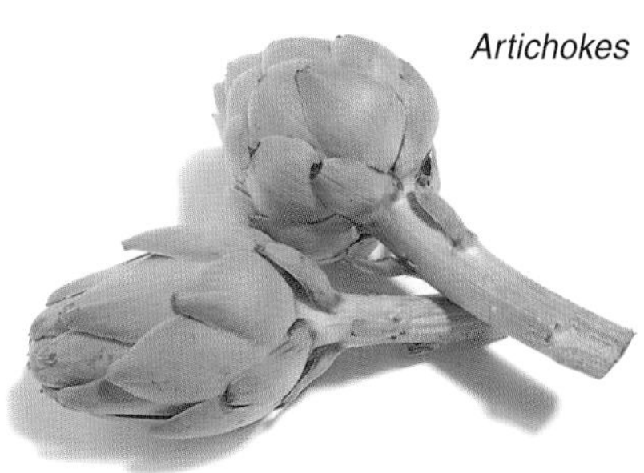

Artichokes

Artichokes increase bile secretion and improve its drainage into the intestine. It alleviates the bad taste in the mouth and difficult digestion associated with biliary dyskinesia (poor gallbladder function).

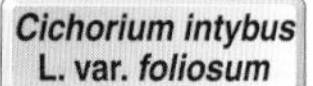

Belgian Endive

Eases digestion for gallbladder patients

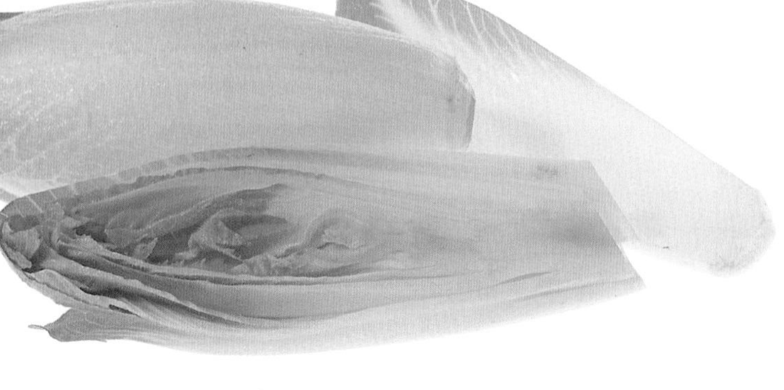

The white tenderness of the Belgian endive is the result of depriving it of sunlight. This makes it poorer in vitamins and other nutrients than the green leaves of other varieties of chicory.

Synonyms: *Witloof, French endive, Endive.*

French: *Endive;* ***Spanish:*** *Endivia, achicoria blanca.*

Description: *The leaves of the Belgian endive ('Cichorium intybus' L. var. 'foliosum'), a herbaceous plant of the botanical family Compositae. This is a variety of chicory, derived by sprouting its roots in a dark, hot, humid place.*

BELGIAN ENDIVE
Composition
per 100 g of raw edible portion

Energy	17.0 kcal = 72.0 kj
Protein	0.900 g
Carbohydrates	0.900 g
Fiber	3.10 g
Vitamin A	3.00 µg RE
Vitamin B_1	0.062 mg
Vitamin B_2	0.027 mg
Niacin	0.427 mg NE
Vitamin B_6	0.042 mg
Folate	37.0 µg
Vitamin B_{12}	—
Vitamin C	2.80 mg
Vitamin E	—
Calcium	19.0 mg
Phosphorus	26.0 mg
Magnesium	10.0 mg
Iron	0.240 mg
Potassium	211 mg
Zinc	0.160 mg
Total Fat	*0.100 g*
Saturated Fat	*0.024 g*
Cholesterol	—
Sodium	*2.00 mg*

1% 2% 4% 10% 20% 40% 100%

% Daily Value (based on a 2,000 calorie diet) provided by 100 g of this food

IT IS SAID that to find the perfect endive, one cannot leave Brussels and must keep the three requirements of the forced cultivation of the vegetable in mind: humidity, heat, and darkness.

PROPERTIES AND INDICATIONS: Belgian endive has a very pleasant texture and flavor. As it is an artificially grown plant, however, it has fewer nutrients and active substances than other chicory varieties, including wild chicory. However, refined Western palates find the white endive more acceptable than other varieties.

Belgian endive is 94.5% ***water. Proteins*** make up 0.9% of its weight, which is significant since this is a fresh vegetable. Its ***carbohydrates***, the most abundant of which is ***in-***

Endive

Endive

The **endive** belongs to the same genus *Cichorium* as the Belgian endive, but it constitutes a different species. There are two varieties of endive:

- **escarole** (*Cichorium endivia* L. var. *latifolium*),
- **curly** endive (*Cichorium endivia* L. var. *crispum*).

Both are rich in ***provitamin A*** (205 µg RE/100 g), ***folic acid*** (142 µg/100 g), and ***zinc*** (0.79 mg/100 g), a trace element that is usually scarce in plant-based foods.

The escarole, as well, contains a bitter substance that stimulates the digestive organs and facilitates the drainage of the gallbladder. In addition to being **choleretic** and **cholagogic,** it is **alkalizing** and mildly diuretic. It is usually eaten in salad and is *particularly* useful in **gallbladder disorders** and **obesity.**

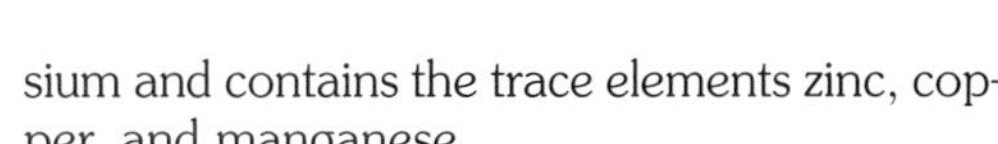

ulin, do not reach 1%. Its ***fat*** content is practically *nonexistent* (0.1%). Taken together the Belgian endive provides **17 kcal /100 g,** one of the lowest figures of any food.

Belgian endive is a good source of ***folic acid*** (37 µg/100 g), as well as ***vitamin*** B_1 (thiamin). Vitamins B_2, B_6, and niacin are also present. It contains very little vitamin A or C, as opposed to green-leafed chicory, which is quite rich in these vitamins.

As far as ***minerals*** are concerned, it contains small amounts of calcium, phosphorous, magnesium, and iron. It is quite rich in potassium and contains the trace elements zinc, copper, and manganese.

Preparation and use

❶ **Raw:** This is the ideal form to eat them. Seasoned with olive oil and lemon, it is a healthful and highly digestible dish.

❷ **Cooked,** either boiled (served with mayonnaise, as asparagus) or baked in the oven as a part of various dishes.

Belgian endive contains the same bitter substances that are found in green chicory, but in lower amounts. This is what gives it a slightly bitter taste. These substances act on the liver, increasing bile production (**choleretic** action) and facilitating the drainage of the gallbladder (**cholagogic** action). It also serves as an **aperitif** and a **tonic** for the stomach and digestive functions. This makes Belgian endives useful in the following cases:

- **Gallbladder disorders** due to the presence of calculi (cholelithiasis) or disruption of its proper drainage (biliary dyskinesia). The beneficial action of the bitter substances in the Belgian endive, together with its virtual lack of fat, makes it very easy to digest.
- **Diabetes:** Belgian endive is a perfect food for diabetics since it contains very few carbohydrates, and those that are present are primarily formed of ***fructose*** (***inulin*** is a polymer of fructose).
- **Obesity:** Belgian endives require a certain amount of chewing and contain very few calories. This makes them very appropriate for weight-loss diets.

Artichoke

Detoxifies the liver

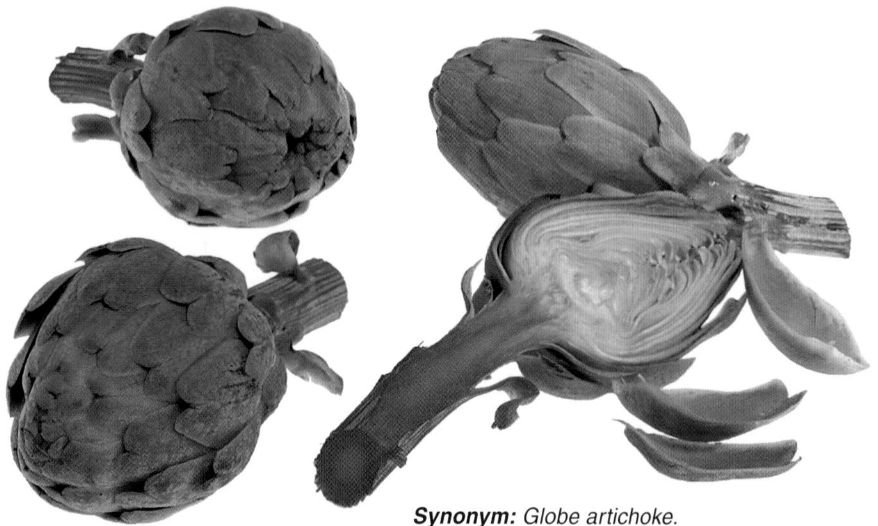

Synonym: *Globe artichoke.*

French: *Artichaut;* ***Spanish:*** *Alcachofa, alcaucil.*

Description: *The artichoke is the inflorescence of the artichoke thistle ('Cynara scolymus' L.), a herbaceous plant of the botanical family Compositae, which can reach a height of 2 meters.*

ARTICHOKE
Composition
per 100 g of raw edible portion

Energy	47.0 kcal = 196 kj
Protein	3.27 g
Carbohydrates	5.11 g
Fiber	5.40 g
Vitamin A	18.0 µg RE
Vitamin B_1	0.072 mg
Vitamin B_2	0.066 mg
Niacin	1.05 mg NE
Vitamin B_6	0.116 mg
Folate	68.0 µg
Vitamin B_{12}	—
Vitamin C	11.7 mg
Vitamin E	0.190 mg α-TE
Calcium	44.0 mg
Phosphorus	90.0 mg
Magnesium	60.0 mg
Iron	1.28 mg
Potassium	370 mg
Zinc	0.490 mg
Total Fat	*0.150 g*
Saturated Fat	*0.035 g*
Cholesterol	—
Sodium	*94.0 mg*

1% 2% 4% 10% 20% 40% 100%

% Daily Value (based on a 2,000 calorie diet)
provided by 100 g of this food

PROPERTIES AND INDICATIONS: The artichoke is *virtually* ***fat-free,*** while its ***carbohydrate*** (5.11%) and ***protein*** (3.27%) content is significant. However, the most noteworthy aspect of its composition is a series of substances that are present in minute quantities, but have remarkable physiological effects. These are:

✓ ***CYNARINE:*** This is 1.5-dicaffeoylquinic acid, which acts on the cells in the liver to increase **bile** production, as well as on the cells of the kidneys, increasing **urine** production.

✓ ***Cynaroside:*** This is a glycosidic flavonoid derived from luteolin with **anti-inflammatory** properties.

✓ ***Cynaropicrin:*** This is an aromatic substance responsible for the artichoke's bitter taste.

✓ **Organic acids:** Malic, lactic, citric, glycolic, and glyceric, among others. Although their function is still not well understood, it is known that they *potentiate* the activity of ***cynarine*** and ***cynaroside.***

✓ **STEROLS: *Beta-sitosterol*** and ***stigmasterol.*** These substances are similar to cholesterol in their chemical structure, but of vegetable origin. They have the interesting effect of *limiting* the absorption of **cholesterol** in the intestine.

The artichoke is a highly digestible and well-tolerated vegetable by healthy and ill alike. Its components make it a true **medicinal food,** particularly indicated in the following cases:

• **Liver disorders: *CYNARINE,*** potentiated by the other components of the artichoke, produces an ***intense* choleretic** (increase in bile production) effect. Normally the liver secretes approximately 800 ml of bile a day, but the consumption of one-half kilo of artichokes can raise that amount to as much as 1,200 ml (1.2 liters).

• **Gallbladder disorders: *CYNARIN*** also acts as a **cholagogue** (facilitates the emptying of the gallbladder) but with less intensity than its choleretic effect. Consequently, it is appropriate in cases of **biliary dyspepsia** provoked by cholelithiasis (gallstones) or other gallbladder dysfunction.

To keep the artichokes from turning dark because of the oxidation of its mineral salts being exposed to the air, moisten them with lemon juice or rub them against half a lemon.

The bile secreted after eating artichokes is less dense and more fluid, thus decongesting the liver. In this manner, it aids the **detoxifying** function of **this organ** in eliminating along with the bile many of the foreign and toxic substances circulating in the blood, including medications, additives, and other chemical substances.

The bitter taste in the mouth and slow digestion associated with eating high fat foods improve considerably after an artichoke treatment (eating one-half kilo of artichokes daily for 3 to 4 days).

• **Kidney disorders: *CYNARIN*** and the substances that accompany it in the artichoke, produce an *increase* in **urine production,** but, more importantly, of urea in the urine.

• **Elevated cholesterol:** Artichokes reduce cholesterol's tendency to deposit on arterial walls,[1] which leads to hardening of the arteries (arteriosclerosis).

• **Diabetes: *CYNARIN*** and its accompanying substances gently *reduce* the **level of glucose** in the blood.

• **Skin disorders:** It is a clinically proven fact that many cases of **dermatitis,** including **eczema** and **allergic** skin reactions, disappear or significantly improve when the detoxifying functions of the liver are working properly. The abundant consumption of artichokes can have surprising results on **chronic** skin conditions.

Preparation and use

❶ **Raw:** Tender artichoke hearts may be used in salad, prepared with lemon and oil. They are very pleasant tasting, and this is the best way to take full advantage of their vitamin and trace element content.

❷ **Roasted** either on a grill or in the oven. In either case, the tips of the outer leaves should not be removed since they help maintain internal moisture during the cooking process.

❸ **Cooked:** Ideally, artichokes should be steamed. They are placed whole in a basket in a cooking pot. Cooking in this way they retain most of their mineral salts and trace elements. If artichokes are cooked in water, the water should be saved for broths or soups.

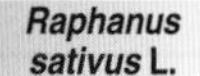

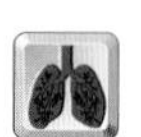

Radish

Promotes bile production

RADISH
Composition
per 100 g of raw edible portion

Energy	17.0 kcal = 69.0 kj
Protein	0.600 g
Carbohydrates	1.99 g
Fiber	1.60 g
Vitamin A	1.00 µg RE
Vitamin B_1	0.005 mg
Vitamin B_2	0.045 mg
Niacin	0.367 mg NE
Vitamin B_6	0.071 mg
Folate	27.0 µg
Vitamin B_{12}	—
Vitamin C	22.8 mg
Vitamin E	0.001 mg α-TE
Calcium	21.0 mg
Phosphorus	18.0 mg
Magnesium	9.00 mg
Iron	0.290 mg
Potassium	232 mg
Zinc	0.300 mg
Total Fat	*0.540 g*
Saturated Fat	*0.030 g*
Cholesterol	—
Sodium	*24.0 mg*

1% 2% 4% 10% 20% 40% 100%

% Daily Value (based on a 2,000 calorie diet) provided by 100 g of this food

Related species: *Horseradish (Armoracia rusticana).*

Synonym: *Clover radish.*

French: *Radis cultivé;* **Spanish:** *Rábano, rabanete, nabón.*

Description: *This is the root of the radish plant ('Raphanus sativus' L.), a herbaceous plant of the botanical family Cruciferae that may reach one meter in height. The root can be spherical, conical, or cylindrical. They are usually bright red but there are also black and white radishes.*

WHILE the Romans spread radishes throughout Europe, it is in the Far East where they are truly appreciated. While the Germans eat an average of 250 g of radishes per person per year, the Japanese eat up to 13 kilos, and in Korea it may be as much as 30.[2]

The liver is the filter where most of the toxins and foreign chemical substances such as ethyl alcohol, pesticides, and most medications are neutralized.
Although the liver is capable of neutralizing these toxins, it requires an extreme effort that can damage this organ. It is best to avoid as many of these substances as possible.
On the other hand, fruits such as the grape and vegetables such as the artichoke or the onion facilitate the liver's detoxifying function.

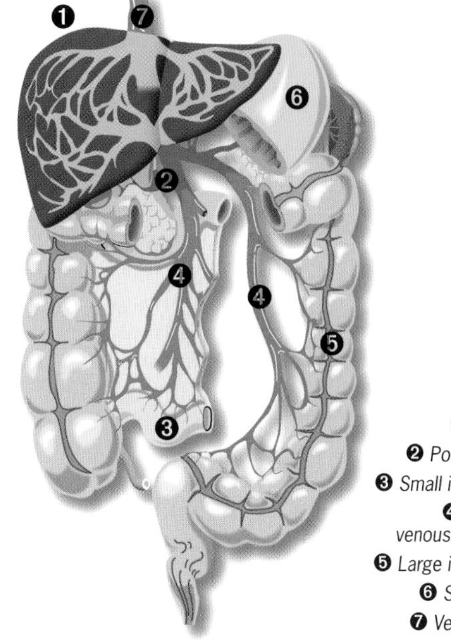

❶ Liver
❷ Portal vein
❸ Small intestine
❹ Portal venous system
❺ Large intestine
❻ Stomach
❼ Vena cava

PROPERTIES AND INDICATIONS: The radish is almost 95% water. It contains very little protein (0.6%) and fat (0.54%), and its percentage of carbohydrates is also low (1.99%). It is also poor in provitamin A and B group vitamins, except ***folates*** (27 µg/100 g). It does not provide vitamin E. ***Vitamin C*** is the most abundant (22.8 mg/100 g). Minerals are present in small amounts, except ***potassium.*** From a nutritional point of view, they are of little value: they provide only 17 kcal/100 g.

All varieties of radish contain a ***sulfurated essence*** that gives them a sharp, piquant taste, and also is attributed with **choleretic** (increases bile production), **cholagogic** (facilitates gallbladder drainage), **digestive, antibiotic,** and **mucolytic** (softening mucus) properties. Their applications are as follows:

- **Liver and gallbladder disorders.**
- Functional **digestive disorders** (slow or difficult digestion) because of their aperitif and tonic effects.
- **Sinusitis,** and **bronchitis.**
- **Cancer *prevention:*** The Chinese radish, and possibly the common radish as well, impedes cellular mutations that lead to cancer.[3]

Preparation and use

❶ **Raw:** This is typically how radishes are eaten. Red radishes add a vivid note to salads. Their piquant flavor is an aperitif and digestive.

❷ **Canned:** In some Far Eastern countries radishes are preserved in vinegar or fermented in a variety of other substances. These methods greatly reduce their vitamin content and medicinal properties.

10

Foods for the Stomach

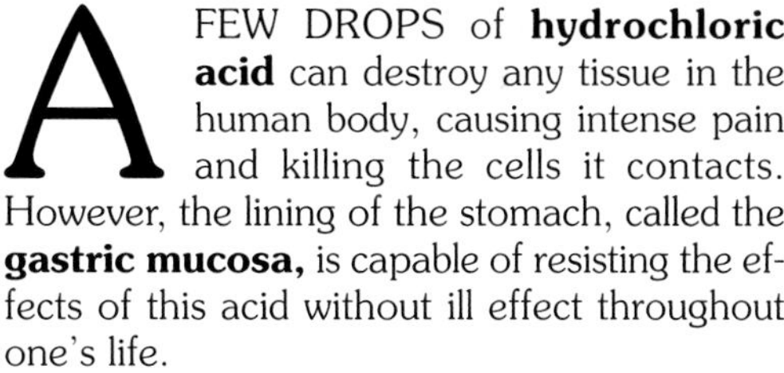

A FEW DROPS of **hydrochloric acid** can destroy any tissue in the human body, causing intense pain and killing the cells it contacts. However, the lining of the stomach, called the **gastric mucosa,** is capable of resisting the effects of this acid without ill effect throughout one's life.

Hydrochloric acid, together with **pepsin,** is necessary in initiating the process of digesting foods, particularly proteins.

How does the stomach protect itself from the corrosive action of the acid it produces?

There is a true ***protective barrier,*** formed primarily of **mucus,** which protects the internal lining of the stomach. Largely, the health of this important organ depends on keeping this barrier in proper condition.

Gastritis and **gastroduodenal ulcers** are two of the *most common* ***consequences*** of ***damage*** to the stomach's ***mucus barrier.***

DYSPEPSIA

Definition

This is **difficult** and **painful digestion.** Dyspepsia is known commonly as **indigestion.**

Symptoms

Its manifestations include eructation, flatulence, discomfort or abdominal distension and acidity.

Causes

In some cases, dyspepsia has an **organic** cause, and may even be an early symptom of serious illness. However, it is more usual that it be **functional,** due to inappropriate diet or unhealthy habits. It is essential to correct these causes in order to cure functional dyspepsia. If this is not done, it may evolve to gastritis and stomach ulcer.

These factors can ***produce*** or ***aggravate*** dyspepsia:

- **Chewing** food **insufficiently** (eating too fast).
- Eating at **irregular** hours.
- **Stress** or nervous tension.
- A diet rich in **fried** foods, **preserves,** and **pickled** foods (preserved in vinegar), as is usually the case with "junk food."
- **Excess fat** and consumption of foods that often cause **digestive intolerance** such as milk.
- **Excess liquid,** particularly carbonated soft drinks and beer.

Increase

SPROUTS
WHOLE GRAINS
SALADS
SQUASH
PAPAYA
FENNEL
MALT BEVERAGE

Reduce or eliminate

FRIED FOODS
HOT SPICES
ALCOHOLIC BEVERAGES
COFFEE
VINEGAR
SOFT DRINKS
TOTAL FAT
SHELLFISH
CHOCOLATE
MILK

Soft drink

GASTRITIS

Definition and causes

This is the **inflammation of the gastric** mucosa, usually caused by inappropriate dietary habits or by aggressive substances to the stomach such as:

- **Alcoholic beverages** and coffee.
- Certain **drugs,** particularly anti-inflammatories such as aspirin.
- Foods or drinks **excessively hot** (such as tea) or cold (such as beer or ice cream).
- **Tobacco:** Smoking releases **nicotine** and **tars** that dissolve in the saliva and move to the stomach where they can cause gastritis.

Diet

Dietetic treatment of gastritis requires a soft, bland diet that will not irritate the stomach. It is ***essential*** to *avoid* ***anything*** that may irritate the gastric mucosa such as **tobacco** or **nervous tension.**

Drugs

Antacid drugs commonly prescribed for gastritis are of little effect unless unhealthful lifestyle and dietary habits are corrected.

Increase

POTATOES
OATS
RICE
TAPIOCA
CARROTS
AVOCADO
SQUASH
SAUERKRAUT
CHERIMOYA
APPLE

Reduce or eliminate

BEER
ALCOHOLIC BEVERAGES
STIMULANT BEVERAGES
COFFEE
SOFT DRINKS
HOT SPICES
SHELLFISH
MEAT
SUGARS
ICE CREAM
CITRUS FRUITS

Oat flakes

Oats contain mucilage that acts to soothe and protect the gastric mucosa. Oatmeal is a food specifically recommended for gastritis.

GASTRODUODENAL ULCER

Definition

This is a discontinuity of the mucous membrane lining the interior of the stomach or duodenum.

Causes

It may have multiple **causes** such as the following:

- **Excess** of stomach **acid.**
- **Irritants** (spices, alcoholic beverages, coffee, carbonated beverages, aspirin, tobacco, etc.).
- Certain **microorganisms** such as Helicobacter pylori that can cause gastritis and ulceration of the stomach and duodenum.
- **Stress** or nervous tension, which cause vasoconstriction, and reduce the blood supply to the gastric mucosa, leaving it unprotected.

Treatment

In recent years it has been found that some of the **traditional remedies** for ulcers are ***without basis.***[1] For example:

- Drinking large amounts of **milk** helps cure ulcers. Today it is known that milk can raise acid levels.
- It is necessary to **eat often and small amounts:** This keeps the stomach in a state of near-continual stimulation, which increases acid production even more and is counterproductive as an ulcer cure. Three meals a day are preferable to five or six.
- One should **avoid eating fiber or raw foods:** If they are well chewed, they protect against ulcers.

Increase

CABBAGE
POTATO
OATS
TAPIOCA
OKRA
CHERIMOYA
OILS
HONEY
FIBER
VITAMIN A
VITAMIN C

Reduce or eliminate

ALCOHOLIC BEVERAGES
COFFEE
SPICES
SHELLFISH
MEAT
MILK
WHITE SUGAR

Potato

Potatoes are nutritious, antacid, soothing and sedating. Thus, they are specifically indicated as a basic food in cases of gastroduodenal ulcer.

HIATAL HERNIA

Definition

This type of hernia occurs when the *upper part of the stomach passes to the thoracic* cavity through the esophageal hiatus of the diaphragm.

This anatomical disorder impedes the function of the sphincter or valve between the esophagus and the stomach in keeping stomach contents from returning to the esophagus.

Symptoms

The most common symptom of hiatal hernia is **reflux** of gastric content, which is usually highly acidic, into the esophagus. This acid attacks the esophagus and produces the typical burning sensation known as **pyrosis** or **heartburn.**

Diet

The **dietetic treatment** for hiatal hernia consists primarily in ***avoiding:***

- Foods that further **relax** the **esophageal sphincter.**
- Foods that **stimulate the production of acid** in the stomach.

Lifestyle

Proper posture that avoids pressure on the upper portion of the abdomen, as well as **abstaining** from **tobacco,** *helps **mitigate*** the **progress** of hiatal hernia and the **stomach inflammation** that accompanies it.

Increase

POTATO
CARROT
SEAWEED
POMEGRANATE

Reduce or eliminate

ALCOHOL
WINE
COFFEE
SPICES
CHOCOLATE
TOTAL FAT
MILK

Pomegranates

Pomegranate juice reduces stomach acid and esophageal reflux.

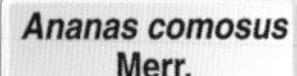

Pineapple

The stomach's friend

Scientific synonym: *Ananas sativus* Schult.

Synonyms: *Cayenne pineapple, Nana, Ananás.*

French: *Ananas;* ***Spanish:*** *Ananás, piña [tropical], piña americana.*

Description: *Compound fruit (formed by the union of the fruits of various blossoms around a central fleshy core) of the pineapple plant ('Ananas comosus' Merr.), a herbaceous plant of the botanical family Bromeliaceae that reaches a height of 50 cm.*

PINEAPPLE
Composition
per 100 g of raw edible portion

Energy	49.0 kcal = 207 kj
Protein	0.390 g
Carbohydrates	11.2 g
Fiber	1.20 g
Vitamin A	2.00 µg RE
Vitamin B_1	0.092 mg
Vitamin B_2	0.036 mg
Niacin	0.503 mg NE
Vitamin B_6	0.087 mg
Folate	10.6 µg
Vitamin B_{12}	—
Vitamin C	15.4 mg
Vitamin E	0.100 mg α-TE
Calcium	7.00 mg
Phosphorus	7.00 mg
Magnesium	14.0 mg
Iron	0.370 mg
Potassium	113 mg
Zinc	0.080 mg
Total Fat	*0.430 g*
Saturated Fat	*0.032 g*
Cholesterol	—
Sodium	*1.00 mg*

1% 2% 4% 10% 20% 40% 100%

% Daily Value (based on a 2,000 calorie diet)
provided by 100 g of this food

HISTORY tells that in 1493 the inhabitants of the Antillean island of Guadeloupe offered Christopher Columbus a pineapple, which he took to be a variety of artichoke. He brought it back to Spain, from where it spread to the tropical areas of Asia and Africa. It was first cultivated in Hawaii in the 19th century, which is now one of the primary world producers.

PROPERTIES AND INDICATIONS: Pineapple that has been properly matured contains approximately 11% carbohydrates, most of which are ***sugars.*** Their fat and protein contents are negligible.

The prevalent ***vitamins*** in pineapple are ***C, B1,*** and ***B6.*** It is also a good source of ***folates.*** Among the ***minerals*** it contains are manganese (1.65 mg /100 g), followed by copper, potassium, magnesium, and iron.

The pineapple's non-nutritive components are of utmost importance from a dietary and therapeutic standpoint:

✓ ***Citric and malic acids:*** These are responsible for the pineapple's acidic taste. As is the case with citrus fruits, they potentiate the action of ***vitamin C.***

✓ ***BROMELIN*** acts in the digestive tract by breaking down ***proteins*** and *facilitating* **digestion** in much the same way as the stomach's own pepsin.

The pineapple is a succulent, delicious fruit rich in certain vitamins and minerals. Many consider it a wonderful dessert as an *aid* to the **digestion** of other foods. Others prefer to eat it as an aperitif before a meal, particularly when the stomach is somehow weakened.

Its consumption is specifically indicated for the following conditions:

• **Hypochlorhydria** (scanty gastric juice), which is manifested by slow digestion and a sense of heaviness in the stomach.

• **Gastric ptosis** (prolapsed stomach) caused by the stomach's inability to empty itself (gastric atonia).

In both cases pineapple must be eaten **fresh** (not canned) and **ripe** either before or after a meal.

• **Obesity:** Pineapple or fresh pineapple juice consumed before meals reduces appetite and constitutes a good complement to weight-loss diets. It is also slightly diuretic (facilitates urine production).

• **Sterility:** This tropical fruit is one of the *richest* foods in ***manganese,*** a trace element actively involved in the formation of reproductive cells, both male and female. It is therefore recommended for those suffering from sterility due to insufficient production of germinal cells (sperm in men and ova in women).

• **Stomach cancer:** It has been shown[2] that pineapple is a *powerful* ***inhibitor*** of the formation of ***nitrosamines.*** These carcinogenic substances form in the stomach as a chemical reaction between nitrites and certain proteins contained in foods.

Preparation and use

❶ **Natural:** Pineapple is an ideal dessert, improving digestion. It also is an excellent aperitif, preparing the stomach for a meal.

❷ **Juice:** Pineapple juice must be drunk slowly because of its acidity.

❸ **Canned:** Canned pineapple retains most of its vitamins, minerals, and fiber. However, it is poor in the enzyme bromelin, which is easily degraded. As a result, canned pineapple has little effect as a digestive aid.

Pineapple only ripens properly on the plant. If it is harvested early to meet the needs of transport, it is very acid and poor in nutrients.

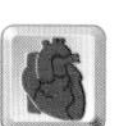

Cabbage

Heals ulcers

A cabbage head is a more or less spherical cluster of leaves from a botanical standpoint. Most cabbages are heads, although some, such as cauliflower and broccoli are inflorescences (see pp. 154, 72). White cabbage is also called a head cabbage.

CABBAGE
Composition
per 100 g of raw edible portion

Energy	25.0 kcal = 105 kj
Protein	1.44 g
Carbohydrates	3.13 g
Fiber	2.30 g
Vitamin A	13.0 µg RE
Vitamin B_1	0.050 mg
Vitamin B_2	0.040 mg
Niacin	0.550 mg NE
Vitamin B_6	0.096 mg
Folate	43.0 µg
Vitamin B_{12}	—
Vitamin C	32.2 mg
Vitamin E	0.105 mg α-TE
Calcium	47.0 mg
Phosphorus	23.0 mg
Magnesium	15.0 mg
Iron	0.590 mg
Potassium	246 mg
Zinc	0.180 mg
Total Fat	*0.270 g*
Saturated Fat	*0.033 g*
Cholesterol	—
Sodium	*18.0 mg*

1% 2% 4% 10% 20% 40% 100%

% Daily Value (based on a 2,000 calorie diet) provided by 100 g of this food

Description: *Cabbages are the leaves of diverse varieties of the species 'Brassica oleracea' L., a biannual or multi-annual herbaceous plant of the botanical family Cruciferae.*

ALL CURRENT varieties of cabbage are derived from the wild cabbage still found along the Atlantic coasts of France and England.

The different **varieties** of cabbage derive from the portion of the plant where its growth energy is concentrated:

- In the **leaves:** white cabbage, red cabbage, Savoy cabbage
- In the **inflorescence:** cauliflower, broccoli
- In the **base of the stalk:** kohlrabi
- In the **sprouts:** Brussels sprouts

Cabbage was already an important food in the Greco-Roman period. The Greeks, in addition to enjoying them as food, discovered their medicinal properties. Hippocrates, Galen, and Dioscorides praised the therapeutic value of cabbage. Kato the Elder, a Roman philosopher of the second century before Christ, declared that "if the Romans had endured the previous six centuries without physicians, it had to be attributed to the use of cabbage."

Throughout history the cabbage has been considered a food of the poor. This rather insulting view of cabbages changed dramatically some decades ago when their *great* **anticarcinogenic** *potential* was discovered: cabbage contains substances capable of *preventing* the formation of malignant **tumors** and can even *stop* their growth.

In addition to this anticarcinogenic property, cabbages have many other dietary, therapeutic, and medicinal properties such as those described below.

PROPERTIES AND INDICATIONS: Cabbage leaves contain a great variety of nutrients:

✓ ***Proteins:*** A fairly good proportion that varies between 3.38% in Brussels sprouts and 1.39% in red cabbage. These are incomplete proteins, as is the case with many vegetable proteins, because they do not contain all amino acids in the proper proportions. However, when they are *combined* with other vegetable proteins such as those in whole **grains** or **legumes,** they become high quality complete proteins.

✓ ***Fats*** or lipids are present in minimal, almost nonexistent amounts. Only Brussels sprouts reach 0.3%. Remaining varieties vary between 0.1% and 0.2% of their weight. This lack of fats makes cabbage a very appropriate food for those suffering from **coronary disease** and **obesity.**

The fats in cabbage, in spite of their scarcity, are of great preventive and healing importance. There are sulfurated substances dissolved in them that are responsible for most of their medicinal action. These are currently being identified as ***phytochemicals.***

✓ ***Carbohydrates:*** Most cabbages contain between 3% and 5%.

✓ ***Vitamins:*** Cabbages are *particularly rich* in ***beta-carotene*** (provitamin A) and ***vitamin C,*** although they also contain significant amounts of vitamins B, E, and K.

✓ ***Minerals*** and ***trace elements:*** All cabbages in general are *rich* in ***potassium*** and *very low* in ***sodium,*** which makes them of great value in cases of **hypertension** or fluid retention (**edema**). They also contain considerable calcium, phosphorous, iron, and mag-

Preparation and use

❶ **Raw:** Fresh leaves, finely shredded and seasoned with oil (preferably olive oil) and lemon makes an excellent salad.

❷ **Fresh juice:** This is prepared in the blender. Two or three spoonfuls to half a glass on an empty stomach before each meal three or four times a day.

❸ **Cooked:** Cabbage should be cooked carefully to protect its medicinal properties. Sulfurous phytochemicals are heat-sensitive, and disappear with prolonged cooking. The optimal cooking method is **steaming.**

Cabbage prevents cancer

Many experiments *have been conducted with laboratory animals (most commonly rats), which demonstrate the anticarcinogenic properties of cabbages, and, in general, all the plants of the* ***Crucifer*** *family.*[3, 4, 5] *All of these studies show that animals fed on cabbage, including those that have been submitted to potent carcinogens such as the benzopyrene found in tobacco smoke, do not develop tumors.*[6, 7]

To reduce the flatulent effect of cabbage, only the tenderest leaves should be chosen and then finely chopped, briefly cooked, seasoned with lemon, oil, and anti-flatulent herbs (fennel, cumin, caraway, etc.). It must be chewed slowly, mixing it well with saliva. It should not be eaten with other plant-based foods rich in cellulose fiber, as whole grains or bran.

nesium, as well as trace elements, the most notable of which is ***sulfur.***

Cabbages in general are a good *source* of ***calcium,*** as much for its quantity (35-77 mg /100 g, half that of milk), as for the ease with which it is absorbed. Studies have shown that the body absorbs the calcium in cabbage much better than that in milk.

✓ ***Vegetable fiber:*** Cabbages are rich in cellulose vegetable fiber. Thus they are **laxative,** which helps **regulate** passage through the intestine. Some individuals who have a propensity to formation of intestinal gas experience **flatulence** from eating cabbage.

✓ ***PHYTOCHEMICALS:*** These recently discovered substances found in fruits and vegetables in minute quantities play important roles within the body.

Of the phytochemicals found in cabbage, the *most important* and most studied **effect** is that of being **anticarcinogenic.** However, these surprising substances may have other medicinal **effects,** such as preventing or treating **ulcers** or **diabetes,** or may even have **antibiotic** properties.

With such a varied and scientifically intriguing composition, cabbages offer the following medicinal applications.

• **Gastroduodenal ulcer:** The **healing** capacity of applying cabbage leaves on the **skin** has been known for generations.[8]

Doctor Ernst Schneider describes experiments carried out at Stanford University that demonstrated the healing effect of cabbage juice on gastric and duodenal ulcers.[9] The healing time for those ulcer patients who drank a glass of fresh cabbage juice (200-250 ml) four or five times a day was shortened to two weeks. Their stomach pain also disappeared within a few days of beginning to drink this juice.

Subsequent experiments have shown that smaller amounts of cabbage juice (from two tablespoons to one-half glass) are equally effective **(❷)**.

• **Other stomach disorders:** A few spoonfuls of cabbage juice taken on an empty stomach five or ten minutes before meals are sufficient to relieve stomach **inflammation** after a few days of treatment. The typical symptoms of functional **dyspepsia,** heaviness, eructation, and stomach pain disappear.

• ***Intestinal disorders:*** Cabbage has a mild *laxative* and **regulating** effect on intestinal transit because of its cellulose ***fiber*** content. It is beneficial in cases of chronic **constipation** and **diverticulosis.**

The ***sulfurated substances*** contained in cabbage act as **antibiotics,** helping rebalance the **bacterial flora** within the intestine in cases of infection. Fresh cabbage juice **(❷)** (half a glass three or four times daily) may be used to *complement* the treatment of **colitis, fermentation,** and **bacterial imbalance** in the intestine.

• **Intestinal parasites:** Cabbage juice drunk on an empty stomach has also been used as a **vermifuge** to expel intestinal parasites. One drinks half a glass on an empty stomach each morning for five consecutive days.

• **Cardiovascular disorders:** Cabbages in general are *very rich* in ***potassium*** and *low* in ***sodium.*** The latter directly influences the genesis of hypertension because of its capacity to retain water and increase blood volume.

Cabbage has a mild **diuretic** effect and is very appropriate for those suffering from coronary **heart disease, hypertension** and **arteriosclerosis** (hardening and narrowing of the arteries). Cabbage's content of ***antioxidant vitamins*** (A, C, and E) contributes to the regeneration of arterial walls.

• **Obesity:** Cabbages provide very few calories (20-40 kcal/100 g, except Brussels sprouts, which may have up to 43 kcal/100 g). However, they provide a satisfyingly full feeling (relieve the appetite). Because of this, and its richness in vitamins and minerals, cabbage is ideal for the obese. It should be included in all weight-loss diets.

• **Osteoporosis and decalcification:** Cabbage's ***calcium*** *content is significant* (approximately half that of milk). This calcium is also particularly easily absorbed by the body. Consequently, cabbages are a food that must be carefully considered in cases of osteoporosis and decalcification, as well as any circumstance requiring greater levels of this mineral.

• **Diabetes:** Because cabbage contains few carbohydrates and is rich in vitamins and minerals, it is very well tolerated by diabetics.

• **Scurvy:** The ***vitamin C*** content of cabbages, similar to that of oranges (53 mg/100 g) has given these vegetables a reputation as a remedy for scurvy. In Central and Northern European countries, where, particularly in winter months, there may be a shortage of fresh fruits and vegetables (rich in vitamin C), cabbage is one of the best, if not the only, sources of this vitamin.

• **Cancer:** Many animal studies have shown that regular cabbage consumption can prevent the formation of cancers as described in the informative box on page 183 (see p. 361, as well).

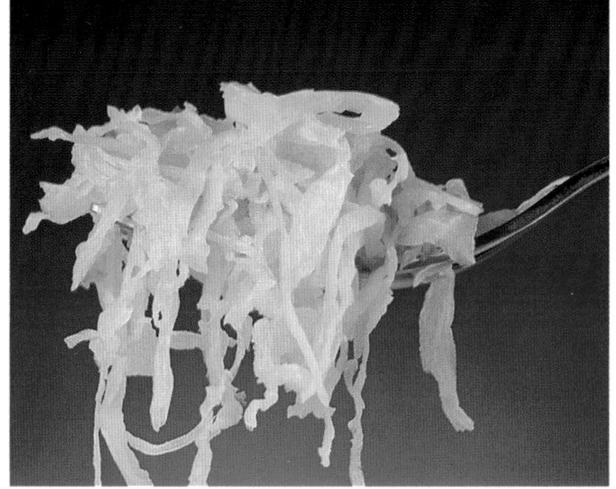

Fermented cabbage is an effective blood purifier (depurant) and it should be included in the diets of diabetics and the obese.
There are many ways to prepare fermented cabbage or sauerkraut:
▪ Raw: This method best preserves its healing properties. It may be prepared with olive oil, adding small pieces of pineapple or apple.
▪ Cooked: After cooking over low heat for 20 to 25 minutes, it is eaten with boiled potatoes, potato puree, or with soy products. These constitute healthful and nutritious dishes.

The cabbage family

All cabbages belong to the botanical family Cruciferae, and most are varieties of the same species: 'Brassica oleracea'. There are more than one hundred types of cabbages, only the best known of which are described here.

Collard

Brassica oleracea L. var. *acephala*

French: *Chou [commun];* ***Spanish:*** *Col común, berza.*

This variety of cabbage is among the *richest* in ***nutritive elements.*** Particularly noteworthy are its ***beta-carotene*** (provitamin A), ***vitamin C,*** and the minerals ***potassium, calcium,*** and ***manganese***. It is *rich* in ***chlorophyll*** and vegetable ***fiber.***

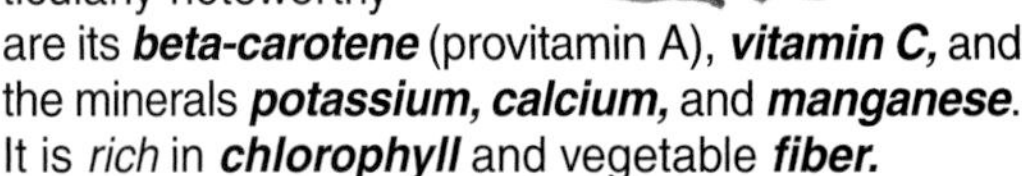

Its flavor is somewhat stronger than that of other cabbages. Due to its *high* ***cellulose*** *content,* its leaves are quite tough and not suited to eating raw. It is best eaten boiled, steamed, or roasted.

White cabbage

Brassica oleracea L. var. *capitata ssp. alba*

French: *Chou pommé;* ***Spanish:*** *Col blanca, repollo [blanco].*

The smooth, light-green leaves of the early varieties are delicious. It is ideal for making cabbage rolls, for all types of cooking, and to be consumed raw when shredded.

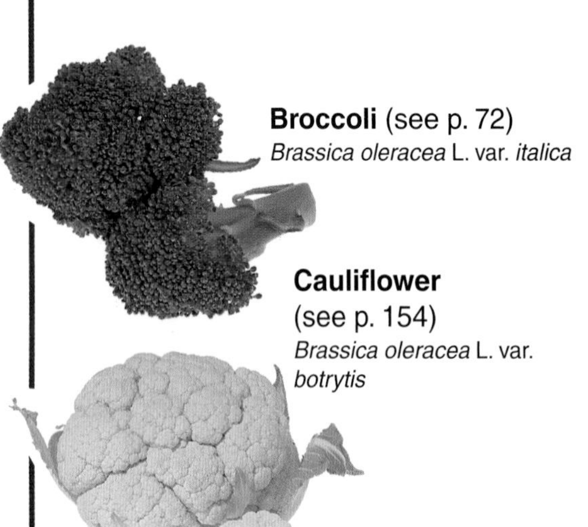

Broccoli (see p. 72)

Brassica oleracea L. var. *italica*

Cauliflower (see p. 154)

Brassica oleracea L. var. *botrytis*

Brussels sprout

Brassica oleracea L. var. *gemmifera*

French: *Chou de Bruxelles;* ***Spanish:*** *Col de Bruselas.*

Gastronomically, they are possibly the most valued variety of cabbage because of their intense, unique flavor. Brussels sprouts are *very rich* in ***vitamins*** (particularly A and C) and ***minerals*** (predominantly potassium, calcium, iron, and sulfur).

They are noteworthy among cabbages as being the variety with the *highest percentage* of ***carbohydrates*** and ***proteins.***

Red cabbage

Brassica oleracea L. var. *capitata ssp. rubra*

French: *Chou rouge;* ***Spanish:*** *Col roja, lombarda.*

Red cabbage has a slightly sweeter flavor than other cabbages. From a nutritional point of view, this variety is the *least rich* in ***proteins, vitamins,*** and ***minerals.*** However, it compensates by adding a note of bright color to the dishes in which it is used.

Chinese cabbage

Brassica pekinensis (Lour.) Rupr.

French: *Chou chinois;*
Spanish: *Col china.*

Its nutritional value is *very low* in terms of carbohydrates, fats, and proteins, and as a result, in ***calories*** (16 kcal/100 g). On the other hand, it contains a *great deal* of ***beta-carotene*** (provitamin A) and a *significant* amount of ***vitamin C.***

Kohlrabi

Brassica oleracea L. var. *gongylodes*

French: *Chou-rave;*
Spanish: *Colinabo, colirrábano.*

Kohlrabi leaves are rich in **vitamins** and **minerals,** the same as other cabbages. The most significant of its nutrients are **magnesium** and **beta-carotene** (provitamin A).

Savoy cabbage

Brassica oleracea L. var. *sabauda / bullata*

French: *Chou cloqué, chou de Milan, chou de Savoie;* ***Spanish:*** *Col rizada, berza, col de Milán.*

The earliest crop appears in spring and has the lightest, most tender leaves. These are usually cooked in oil, steamed, or even eaten raw. The summer crop, on the other hand, is intense green and has a stronger flavor. It is used in vegetable soups and stews.

These are generally *less* ***nutritious*** than other varieties of cabbage.

Pepper

Aperitif and tonic

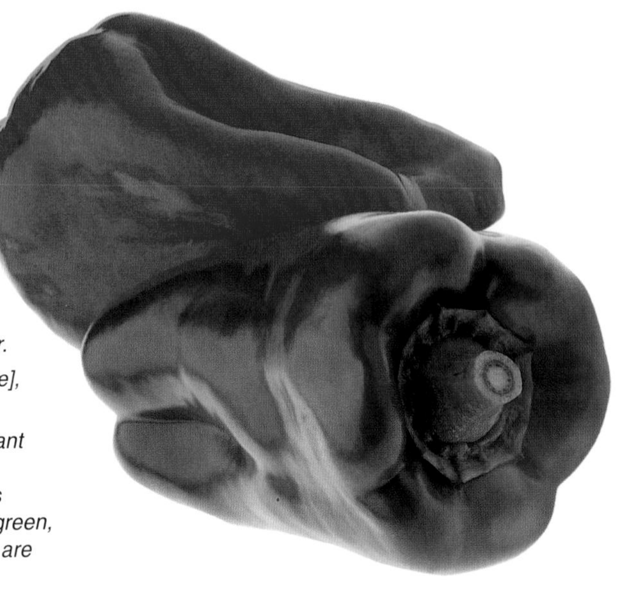

Synonyms: *Sweet pepper, Paprika, Bell pepper, Sweet bell pepper, Green pepper.*

French: *Piment;* ***Spanish:*** *Pimiento, ají [dulce], chile [dulce].*

Description*: This is the fruit of the pepper plant ('Capsicum annuum' L.), a herbaceous plant of the botanical family Solanaceae that grows to height of 60 cm. The fruit tends to be red, green, or yellow. However, there are specimens that are orange, purple, and even black.*

PEPPER, SWEET
Composition
per 100 g of raw edible portion

Energy	27.0 kcal = 112 kj
Protein	0.890 g
Carbohydrates	4.43 g
Fiber	2.00 g
Vitamin A	570 µg RE
Vitamin B_1	0.066 mg
Vitamin B_2	0.030 mg
Niacin	0.692 mg NE
Vitamin B_6	0.248 mg
Folate	22.0 µg
Vitamin B_{12}	—
Vitamin C	190 mg
Vitamin E	0.690 mg α-TE
Calcium	9.00 mg
Phosphorus	19.0 mg
Magnesium	10.0 mg
Iron	0.460 mg
Potassium	177 mg
Zinc	0.120 mg
Total Fat	*0.190 g*
Saturated Fat	*0.028 g*
Cholesterol	—
Sodium	*2.00 mg*

1% 2% 4% 10% 20% 40% 100% 200% 500%

% Daily Value (based on a 2,000 calorie diet) provided by 100 g of this food

Properties and indications: Peppers contain very little protein (0.89%) and carbohydrates (4.43%), and virtually no fat (0.19%). Because of this, they contain only 27 kcal /100 g. They also contain small amounts of B group vitamins, vitamin E, and all dietary minerals. However, two vitamins are particularly noteworthy:

✓ ***Provitamin A*** (beta-carotene), with 570 µg ER/100 g (sweet red pepper), which represents *more* than ***half*** of the daily requirement of this vitamin for an adult male.

In addition to beta-carotene, which transforms into vitamin A in the body, peppers also provide other carotenoids such as ***lycopene.*** This carotenoid is also very abundant in tomatoes. While it does not transform into vitamin A, it is a potent **antioxidant** that protects against the cancerous degeneration of the cells.

✓ ***Vitamin C:*** Red peppers provide almost four times as much vitamin C as lemons or oranges: One hundred grams of red peppers con-

Preparing peppers

The **skin** of the pepper may be difficult to digest for those with sensitive stomachs. To remove it, roast the whole pepper in the oven until the skin begins to separate. Immediately place it in cold water, thus facilitating removal of the skin.

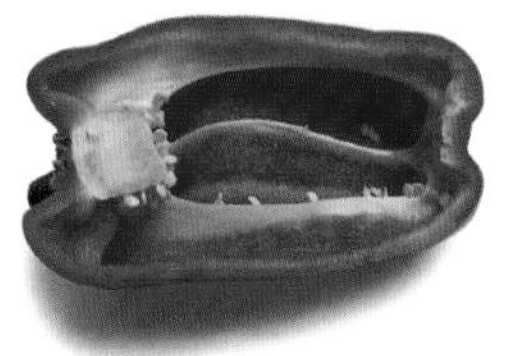

Once roasted, peppers may be seasoned with oil, a little salt, lemon, garlic, and parsley.

The **seeds** and particularly the membranes that cover them can give the fruit a bitter taste and should be **eliminated.**

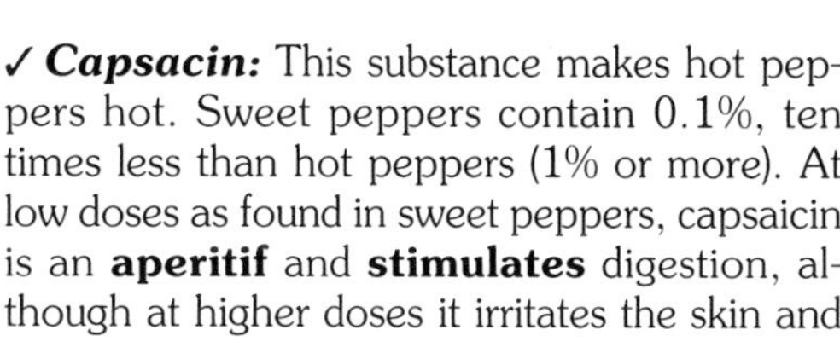

tain more than ***triple*** the RDA (Recommended Dietary Allowance).

Peppers are also significant for other non-nutritive substances:

✓ ***Flavonoids:*** These are *potent* anti-inflammatory **antioxidants** that protect the circulatory system.

Preparation and use

❶ **Raw:** When peppers are young and tender that may be eaten raw in salad, which provides maximum nutritional benefit. In this case they must be thinly sliced and well chewed.

❷ **Cooked:** The ***most healthful*** way to cook peppers is **to roast** them in the **oven. Fried** peppers are quite ***indigestible*** because of the large amount of oil that they absorb. Peppers form part of a variety of culinary recipes, particularly sauces and "pisto" (a Spanish dish of cooked peppers, tomatoes, zucchini, and others vegetables).

❸ **Paprika:** This is powdered dried red pepper. It may be sweet or slightly piquant. It is very rich in ***provitamin A,*** and gives a pleasant red color to sauces, potatoes, rice, and a variety of other dishes; thus, it is used as a healthful culinary coloring.

✓ ***Capsacin:*** This substance makes hot peppers hot. Sweet peppers contain 0.1%, ten times less than hot peppers (1% or more). At low doses as found in sweet peppers, capsaicin is an **aperitif** and **stimulates** digestion, although at higher doses it irritates the skin and mucosa.

✓ ***Vegetable fiber:*** Peppers contain approximately 2%. This, along with capsaicin, contributes to their laxative action.

The dietary and therapeutic applications of peppers are the following:

- **Stomach disorders:** Peppers are beneficial for those suffering with **dyspepsia** (indigestion) due to **scanty digestive juices** or digestive **atonia** because they work as an aperitif, stimulating the flow of gastric juice and reducing inflammation.
- **Constipation:** Peppers are a mild laxative, and are anti-flatulent.
- **Diabetes and obesity:** Because they contain very few carbohydrates or calories, peppers are well tolerated by diabetics and suitable for the diets of the obese.
- **Prevention of cancer of the digestive system:** Because of their *extraordinary richness* of ***antioxidant vitamins*** (A and C), which protect the cells from the mutagenic action of carcinogens,[10] regular pepper consumption contributes to the prevention of cancer, particularly of the digestive organs (stomach and colon).

Potato

The stomach's best friend

Synonyms: *White potato, Irish potato.*

French: *Pomme de terre;*
Spanish: *Patata, papa, criadilla de tierra.*

Description: *Tuber of the potato plant ('Solanum tuberosum' L.), a herbaceous plant which belongs to the botanical family Solanaceae. These tubers are not roots, but underground thickening of the stalks. The weight and size of potatoes may vary from a few grams to more than a kilo.*

POTATO
Composition
per 100 g of raw edible portion

Energy	79.0 kcal = 331 kj
Protein	2.07 g
Carbohydrates	16.4 g
Fiber	1.60 g
Vitamin A	—
Vitamin B_1	0.088 mg
Vitamin B_2	0.035 mg
Niacin	2.02 mg NE
Vitamin B_6	0.260 mg
Folate	12.8 µg
Vitamin B_{12}	—
Vitamin C	19.7 mg
Vitamin E	0.060 mg α-TE
Calcium	7.00 mg
Phosphorus	46.0 mg
Magnesium	21.0 mg
Iron	0.760 mg
Potassium	543 mg
Zinc	0.390 mg
Total Fat	*0.100 g*
Saturated Fat	*0.026 g*
Cholesterol	—
Sodium	*6.00 mg*

1% 2% 4% 10% 20% 40% 100%

% Daily Value (based on a 2,000 calorie diet)
provided by 100 g of this food

IT WAS THE Spanish conquistador Francisco Pizarro, who landed in Seville in 1534 and unloaded the first sack of potatoes from Peru. Because they were easy to grow, potatoes soon spread throughout the old continent.

The truth is, however, that potatoes were not well received. In Spain they were scornfully referred to as "edible rocks." The French rejected them under the false assumption that they carried the plague. The Germans only used them to feed livestock. Moreover, the English censured them because they are not mentioned in the Bible.

Potato skin

Concentrates the vitamins, but also the toxins

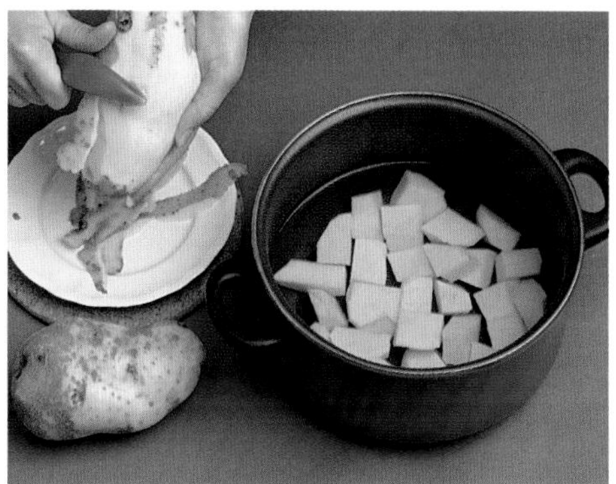

Potatoes should be peeled before they are cooked since any toxic substances that may be present in the skin can contaminate them during cooking.

If one wants to enjoy a delicious baked potato with the peel intact, avoid contaminants by using organically grown potatoes.

More than 200 years would pass before the humble potato would prove its ability to satisfy people's hunger. It was in the years leading up to the French Revolution when the potato's value as food became known.

From then on, the potato has had a place on the European table, and by extension, has spread to all the inhabitants of the earth.

With more than 1,300 varieties, the potato is the most cultivated vegetable in the world today (approximately 270 million metric tons per year). In Germany, for example, each inhabitant eats an average of 70 kilos (about 150 pounds) of this tuber a year.

Preparation and use

❶ **Steamed:** This is the ideal preparation method because it preserves the most nutrients. If they have not been organically grown, they should be peeled (see the box above).

❷ **Boiled,** alone or with other vegetables.

❸ Baked, possibly accompanied by onions or peppers.

❹ **Fried:** This is the least suitable method of preparation (see p. 193).

❺ **Raw juice:** This is used as an antacid (see next page).

One of the most digestible ways to prepare potatoes is in puree or mashed. These are particularly beneficial in cases of stomach disorders.

Raw potato juice

Neutralizes stomach acid

Dr. Schneider[11] recommends a popular German remedy: Raw potato juice, because it is rich in alkaline substances. A few spoonfuls before a meal are sufficient to relieve acid stomach.

Of course, the potatoes must be peeled before extracting the juice.

Humble, scorned, and cheap, but always delicious and healthful, potatoes are essential to the dietary needs of today's world.

PROPERTIES AND INDICATIONS: The potato is quite complete as a food, which provides high quality carbohydrates and proteins. It is only deficient in the following nutrients: fats, provitamin A, vitamin E, calcium, and vitamin B_{12}. Everything else is well represented:

✓ ***Carbohydrate:*** Potatoes contain 16.4 g /100 g (16.4%), of which most (approximately 16 g) is ***starch.*** The rest (0.4 g) is glucose, fructose, and saccharose. The starch in potatoes digests easily and does not produce flatulence.

✓ ***Proteins:*** Potatoes are a ***good source*** of proteins, although from a strictly quantitative standpoint their level may seem modest (2.07%). The proteins in potatoes have the following characteristics:

- They are of *high* **biological value,** providing all of the ***amino acids*** needed by the body in an *adequate* **proportion** to *foster* **growth.**
- The proteins in potatoes are *rich* in ***lysine,*** an amino acid that is deficient in grains.[11] From this point of view, potatoes are appropriately combined with grains (particularly corn).

✓ ***Vitamins:*** Potatoes are a good source of vitamin C, although some of this vitamin is lost during the cooking process. The least amount of vitamin C is lost when potatoes are steamed; the most, when they are fried. Potatoes contain virtually no provitamin A or vitamin E. On the other hand they are quite rich in B complex vitamins, particularly B_1 and B_6.

✓ ***Minerals:*** Potatoes are noted for their *richness* in ***potassium*** and their *low* ***sodium*** *content,* which makes them very appropriate for those suffering with hypertension and cardiovascular disease. They are poor in calcium, but quite rich in iron, phosphorous and magnesium, as well as zinc, copper, manganese, and other trace elements.

✓ ***Vegetable fiber:*** Potatoes contain about 1.6% soluble vegetable fiber. Two medium-sized potatoes (300 g) contain almost one-fifth of the daily fiber need.

This tuber is a food that is very useful in a variety of disorders and diseases. Among these are:

• **Stomach disorders:** It has been said that potatoes are the **stomach's** *best* **friend** because of the sense of well-being that one experiences after eating them. This beneficial effect is due to at least three factors:

- **Antacid effect:** Potatoes are a relatively alkaline food and are capable of neutralizing excess acid. This alkalizing action is produced locally in the stomach as well as in the blood and urine.

- **Physical consistency:** The potato's soft texture reduces the need for digestive effort in the stomach and provides relative rest.
- **Content of sedating substances:** Various investigations carried out in the Hoffman-La Roche laboratories in Basel, Switzerland,[12] and at Göttingen University (Germany)[13] have found that potatoes contain small amounts of various benzodiazepines, sedative substances widely used in pharmaceuticals. One of the substances found in potatoes is diazepam,[12] the same active element used in the well-known medication Valium®. These natural sedatives may also act locally in the stomach, relaxing this organ.

All of these reasons make potatoes, specially prepared as puree, *particularly beneficial* in cases of gastric hyperacidity, gastritis, stomach ulcer, gastric ptosis (stomach prolapse), gastric neurosis (nervous stomach), and any case of **problems with digestion** or **stomach conditions in general.**

Of course, one must be careful not to negate the healing effects of potatoes by improperly preparing them (fried with excess oil or condiments) or accompanying them with foods with negative effects on the stomach (fried foods, meats etc.).

• **Cardiovascular disease:** Because potatoes are low in fats and sodium, they are ***ideal*** in cases of arteriosclerosis, heart failure, angina or heart attack, and hypertension. The fact that they are **so rich** in ***potassium*** (543 mg /100 g) contributes to reducing blood pressure.

• **Kidney disease:** Potatoes **alkalize** the blood and urine, aiding the elimination of toxic acids. In this manner, they relieve the kidneys' work and purify the blood. A diet rich in potatoes, or the so-called ***"potato diet"*** is beneficial in cases of metabolic acidosis, excess uric acid, uric arthritis, and kidney stones.

• **Diabetes:** Potatoes contain complex carbohydrates (starch) that slowly transform to glucose during the three or four hours of digestion in the intestine. Thus, they do not cause abrupt changes in blood glucose level (as happens with simple carbohydrates or sugars), and are quite well tolerated by diabetics.

• **Obesity:** Potatoes alone do not cause obesity. Quite the contrary, they are useful in combating it for at least two reasons:

- They produce a sense of satiety that reduces the desire to keep eating. For example, 350 g of potatoes (two medium potatoes) contain the same calories as a small hamburger (about 270 kcal), but they are much more filling.
- They contain an abundance of B group vitamins that help metabolize carbohydrates, as well as minerals that prevent fluid retention in the tissues, which contributes to obesity.

Fried potatoes

When potatoes are fried, they lose water through evaporation and gain oil. From 15% to 20% of their weight is made up of fats.

Fried potatoes contain 500 to 600 kcal/100 g (raw potatoes contain only 79 kcal/100 g). They also tend to contain abundant **salt.** All of this makes them rather undesirable from a dietary standpoint.

The best **oil** for frying potatoes is **olive oil** since it is the most resistant to high temperatures. Still, care must be exercised not to overheat it. In other words, it must not smoke.

Fried potatoes are tasty, but not very healthful.

11

Foods for the Intestine

THE INTESTINE is a channel through which food passes. As it advances through the small intestine, most of the primary nutrients they contain are absorbed.

What is left is moved to the large intestine and is concentrated there as feces, which are finally expelled from the body.

The two most common intestinal disorders are related to the speed with which food travels through the intestine:

- **Too rapidly** results in ***diarrhea,*** with its consequent loss of water, mineral salts, and other nutrients that the body does not absorb.
- **Too slowly** results in ***constipation.*** The feces putrefy and produce toxic substances. These are absorbed into the blood resulting in a state of autointoxication in the body.

Avoiding constipation

Constipation is defined as *difficulty in defecation.* It is accompanied by:

- Expulsion of a small amount of hard feces.
- Reduction in defecation to less than three or four times a week.

Avoiding constipation is ***essential*** to enjoying good health.

1. Drink enough water

If the body is not properly hydrated, the large intestine extracts water from the feces. This dries them and makes them difficult to expel.

2. Eat a proper diet

Avoiding constipation requires a *proper* **diet**, increasing the intake of fiber (see p. 197). The foods that contribute most to constipation prevention are:

- **Fresh fruits** (except quince, persimmon, pomegranate, and loquat, which are astringents). **Dried fruits** such as prunes and raisins are also effective.
- **Vegetables.**
- **Whole grains** and products made from them such as whole grain bread and pasta.

3. Consume enough fiber

Plant-based foods are the ***only*** ones that contain the fiber necessary to, among other things, move the feces normally through the intestine.

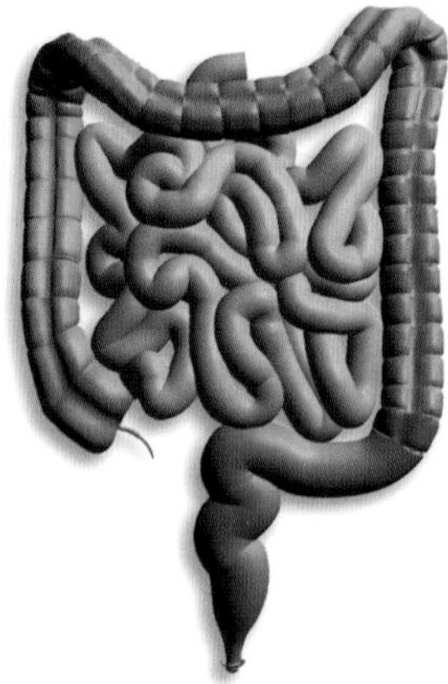

4. Educate the bowel

Laxatives (natural vegetable fiber and pharmaceutical preparations), enemas, glycerin suppositories, and other remedies may relieve an acute case, but not chronic constipation.

However, persistent functional constipation is not cured by these measures, which only provide temporary relief.

Avoiding constipation requires the learning of good toilet habits ***from* childhood** and educating the bowel.

- Do ***not* ignore** the physiological need to defecate.
- Try to evacuate at the ***same* time** of the day.
- Perform some type of **physical exercise.**

How to increase fiber intake

Fiber is a component of plant-based foods that has the following characteristics:

- It is ***necessary*** for proper intestinal function.
- It is ***not*** **digested** ***nor*** does it pass to the **bloodstream.** It remains in the intestine and forms part of the feces.
- It **retains water,** increasing fecal volume.
- Although it is not acted on by digestive enzymes, as are other carbohydrates, proteins and fats, it is partially fermented by bacterial flora in the colon. This results in various intestinal **gases.**
- Its consumption (at least 25 g daily for adults) contributes to the ***prevention*** of various diseases such as:
  - **Constipation**
  - **Diverticulosis**
  - **Colon cancer**
  - Excess **cholesterol** and **diabetes**

Eat whole-grain bread instead of white bread

Whole-grain bread contains approximately three times the fiber of white bread.

Increase the consumption of legumes and vegetables

- They *prevent* **constipation** by increasing the intensity of the intestine's **peristaltic action.**
- They *protect* against **colon cancer.**
- They *reduce* **cholesterol** levels.

Consume bran or other fiber-rich supplements

The *ideal* is to consume them in their **natural** state, forming part of grains or whole grain bread. However, it can be consumed as a supplement as long as no more than ***30 g*** are used daily. This amount of bran provides almost ***13 g*** of ***pure fiber.***

Eat fruit with all of its pulp instead of drinking fruit juice

Fruit juice contains virtually no fiber since it is found in the pulp.

CELIAC DISEASE

Definition

This is also referred to as **celiac sprue.** It is the result of **intolerance to gluten,** the ***protein*** found in **wheat, barley, rye,** and to some extent, **oats.**

Causes

This disease is *generally* of genetic **origin.** However, there are factors that precipitate its development such as early introduction of cow's milk or grains into an infant's diet.

Symptoms

The first manifestations are generally seen during lactation or infancy, although it may appear in the adult. Diagnosis is made by means of an intestinal biopsy. The most common **symptoms** are:

- Diarrhea: Celiac feces are foamy because of the fats they contain, which the body has not absorbed.
- Abdominal distension and discomfort, flatulence.
- Fatigue, depression, general discomfort.
- Mouth sores.

All of the symptoms disappear when gluten is removed from the diet.

Gluten intolerance that does not reach the stage of true celiac disease is much ***more common*** than is commonly believed.

Increase

RICE
CORN
LEGUMES
TAPIOCA
GREEN LEAFY VEGETABLES
FRUITS
BUCKWHEAT
OATS
MILLET
SORGHUM
VITAMINS, SUPPLEMENTS

Reduce or eliminate

GLUTEN
FLOURS
DAIRY PRODUCTS
TOTAL FAT
SAUSAGES
BEER

Rice

Rice, regardless of method of preparation, is the best tolerated by those with celiac disease.

CONSTIPATION

Definition

This is the *slow, difficult* ***transit*** of the contents of the intestine, with *infrequent* ***evacuations*** and **excessively *firm* feces.**

Causes

Most cases of constipation are **functional** in nature and are due to an atony or weakness in the musculature of the large intestine. **Organic** causes appear only in *very concrete* cases, with cancer of the colon or rectum being the most serious.

From ***two evacuations a day to once every other day*** is considered *normal.* If it is less frequent, it is considered constipation.

The factors that **precipitate** or **predispose** to atonic functional constipation are these:

- An improper diet, with *insufficient* **water** and/or ***fiber*** intake. Consequently, the intestinal lining is not stimulated and is weakened.
- **Irregular** bowel **habits:** If, because of nervous tension or hurry, one ignores the biological call to defecate, it is possible to lose the intestinal reflex.
- **Abuse of laxatives:** This produces a perpetual state of inflammation in the intestinal mucosa, which results in desensitizing it to normal stimuli.
- ***Lack*** of **physical exercise** necessary to stimulate the reflex to defecate.

  Once these four causes are corrected, most cases of functional atonic constipation are corrected, as well. A **proper diet** is ***essential*** to the solution.

Increase

WATER
FIBER
WHOLE GRAINS
WHOLE-GRAIN BREAD
WHEAT BRAN
FRUIT
VEGETABLES
LEGUMES
PRUNES
FLAXSEED
APPLE
GRAPE
FIG
RHUBARB
HONEY

Reduce or eliminate

INDUSTRIAL BAKED GOODS
WHITE BREAD
SHELLFISH
CHOCOLATE
MEAT
FISH

Fruit

IRRITABLE BOWEL

Definition

This is a **functional syndrome** characterized by malaise, abdominal distension and ***sudden* alternations** between episodes of **constipation** and **diarrhea.** Diagnosis is always made by a process of elimination, discarding intestinal pathologies.

Causes

In addition to the dietary recommendations provided here, it is important to bear the following things in mind that *can* ***bring* about** irritable bowel syndrome:

- Treatments with **medications that irritate** the bowel such as iron tablets or antibiotics.
- **Allergy** or **intolerance** to certain products such as lactose or gluten.
- **Stress, anxiety** or neurological **imbalance.**

Increase

OATS
FRUIT
CORN
PERSIMMON
PAPAYA
BILBERRY
FIBER
YOGURT
WATER

Reduce or eliminate

WHEAT BRAN
LEGUMES
MILK
CURED CHEESES
GLUTEN
MEAT

Milk

Whole-grain bread

An excess of fiber (bran, wholemeal grains, legumes), flour gluten, and milk lactose are some of the components of the worst-tolerated foods in case of irritable bowel.

DIARRHEA

Definition

This consists of expulsion of **soft** or **liquid feces** much **more frequently than normal.** This results in the *loss* of ***water*** and ***mineral*** salts that *must* be **replaced. Children** and the **elderly** are *most sensitive* to fluid imbalance.

Diet

In cases of **severe diarrhea, *only* water** and some of these **fluids** should be taken for 24 to 48 hours.

- **Vegetable broth** (rich in mineral salts).
- Oral rehydrating **serum** (this may be prepared by mixing a teaspoon of salt and four tablespoons of sugar in a liter of water).
- *Diluted* **lemon juice.**
- **Teas** made from **astringent** medicinal plants (see *EMP* [*Encyclopedia of Medicinal Plants*] p. 481).
- **Infant formulas** and/or **soymilk** for ***nursing infants.***

Causes

Causes of *all* diarrheas should be **diagnosed.** The *most frequent* are gastric **infections,** food **toxins,** food **allergies,** or food **intolerance.**

Treatment

In addition to specific treatment, once the acute phase has *passed,* one can give **foods** *mildly* **astringent** and **anti-inflammatory** for the intestinal mucosa, such as those described here.

Increase

SOYMILK (BEVERAGE)
ALMOND MILK
APPLE
QUINCE
POMEGRANATE
LOQUAT
BANANA
CARROT
PAPAYA
SAPOTE
RICE
OATS
TAPIOCA
CHESTNUT
CAROB
YOGURT

Reduce or eliminate

MILK
EGGS
CHICKEN
SHELLFISH
FRUIT JUICES

Yogurt

Many studies confirm that yogurt increases resistance to infections of the digestive tract.

COLITIS

Definition

This is **inflammation of the colon,** the most important portion of the large bowel.

Symptoms

It manifests itself in loose or diarrheic feces that may contain mucus or blood.

Causes

It is *usually* the result of **infection** but may be caused by **allergies** or **intolerance** to certain foods. **Antibiotics** or **laxatives** may play a role in its development, as well.

Diet

A gentle diet to the colon can contribute significantly to its cure. Therefore, the same foods that are useful in cases of diarrhea are recommended for colitis. **Wheat bran** *can cause* colitis in constipated individuals who use it ***excessively*** as a laxative.

Increase

THE SAME AS FOR DIARRHEA
VEGETABLES
ZUCCHINI
IRON
VITAMIN A

Reduce or eliminate

WHEAT BRAN
REFINED BAKED GOODS
MILK
COFFEE
HOT SPICES

CROHN'S DISEASE

Definition

This *special type of inflammation affects both the* ***small*** *and large* ***intestines.***

Causes

Its **causes** are ***not*** **well understood.** However Crohn's disease is related with the fiber and vegetable-poor, refined and processed food-rich diets common in Western societies. It is a disease that more frequently affects those whose diet is almost exclusively made up of ***"fast food."***

Increase

THE SAME AS FOR DIARRHEA
FIBER
OILS
FISH OIL
FOLATES
IRON

Reduce or eliminate

SUGARS
HAMBURGERS

Hamburger

ULCERATIVE COLITIS

Definition

This **serious form** of colitis *can* ***become*** **chronic** and *resist healing.*

Causes

Its **cause** is **unknown,** but is known to affect people in **Western societies** almost *exclusively.* A refined diet rich in meat and saturated fats, poor in fruits, vegetables, and grains, which makes up much of what is described as **"fast food,"** is a factor that increases the risk of ulcerative colitis.

Symptoms

It manifests itself through diarrhea, abdominal pain, occasional bloody feces, fatigue, and weight loss. It *can* ***degenerate*** into **colon cancer.**

Treatment

Although there is no specific treatment, a diet that protects the colon can improve the course of this disease.

Increase

THE SAME AS FOR DIARRHEA
CABBAGE
PRIMROSE OIL
FISH OIL

Reduce or eliminate

THE SAME AS FOR COLITIS
HAMBURGERS
MEAT

HEMORRHOIDS

Definition

Hemorrhoids are **varicose** veins situated in an anatomically sensitive area. Constipation requires effort during defecation that causes dilation of the veins of the anus resulting in hemorrhoids.

Treatment

Once these vein dilations take place, they do *not* spontaneously *recede.* Proper diet and hygiene may keep these tissues from becoming inflamed or blood clots forming in their interior (hemorrhoidal thrombosis), which can be very painful and may require surgical treatment.

Increase

THE SAME AS FOR CONSTIPATION
STRAWBERRY
BILBERRY

Reduce or eliminate

THE SAME AS FOR CONSTIPATION
HOT SPICES
WHITE SUGAR

FLATULENCE

Definition

This is **excess intestinal gas,** which causes intestinal spasms and abdominal distension. Intestinal gas comes from two sources: air that is swallowed while **eating,** and that which is naturally produced by the **bacteria** of the intestinal flora.

Causes

Excess gas *tends to be* the **result** of:

- **Disbacteriosis** or disturbance of the flora, which may be corrected by simple dietary means.
- *Abundant* **consumption** of **fiber-rich plant-based** foods: Flatulence can be more or less annoying, but is ***not* threatening.** These gases *tend to be* **odorless,** as opposed to those resulting from intestinal putrefaction derived from the consumption of meat and other animal proteins. Slowly increasing the consumption of fiber-rich foods, and abiding by simple culinary models spontaneously corrects flatulence.
- **Swallowing air** due to **stress** or **anxiety,** particularly when eating.

Treatment

In addition to the foods described, **charcoal** is very effective in reducing intestinal flatulence.

 Increase

SPROUTS
AROMATIC HERBS
YOGURT
PERSIMMON

 Reduce or eliminate

FIBER
LEGUMES
VEGETABLES
BREAD
PASTA
MILK

If legumes are soaked in boiling water without salt, and their skin is removed, the flatulent effect virtually disappears.

DIVERTICULOSIS

Definition

Also referred to as **diverticular disease of the colon,** this is the formation of a *large number of tiny sacs or diverticuli in the walls of the digestive tract, generally in the large intestine.*

Causes

Factors necessary for the formation of diverticuli are:

- **Weak** points in the intestinal wall.
- **Increased pressure** within the intestine. This can occur when the feces are small and hard, and the muscles of the intestine must contract strongly to move them.

Diet

The foods described here ***reduce*** the **risk** of the formation of diverticuli, or that keep them from increasing in size in the event that they already exist. What they ***cannot*** do is cause them **to disappear** once they have been formed.

Complication

When diverticuli become inflamed because of fecal material that has not been eliminated, it produces a serious disease called **diverticulitis.** This is a complication of diverticulosis that must be treated in **hospital** with a **strict diet** and, occasionally, by surgical means.

 Increase

WATER
FIBER
WHOLE GRAINS
FRUIT
VEGETABLES
LEGUMES

 Reduce or eliminate

REFINED BAKED GOODS
TOTAL FAT
MEAT

Refined baked goods

Baked products made with refined flour, including white bread, contain very little fiber. This promotes hard feces and the intestinal pressure that leads to diverticulosis.

Carambola

Mild laxative, delicate flavor

CARAMBOLA
Composition
per 100 g of raw edible portion

Energy	33.0 kcal = 138 kj
Protein	0.540 g
Carbohydrates	5.13 g
Fiber	2.70 g
Vitamin A	49.0 µg RE
Vitamin B_1	0.028 mg
Vitamin B_2	0.027 mg
Niacin	0.478 mg NE
Vitamin B_6	0.100 mg
Folate	14.0 µg
Vitamin B_{12}	—
Vitamin C	21.2 mg
Vitamin E	0.370 mg α-TE
Calcium	4.00 mg
Phosphorus	16.0 mg
Magnesium	9.00 mg
Iron	0.260 mg
Potassium	163 mg
Zinc	0.110 mg
Total Fat	*0.350 g*
Saturated Fat	*0.023 g*
Cholesterol	—
Sodium	*2.00 mg*

1% 2% 4% 10% 20% 40% 100%

% Daily Value (based on a 2,000 calorie diet) provided by 100 g of this food

Synonyms: *Star fruit, Belimbing, Bilimbi, Star apple, Five-angled fruit.*

French: *Carambole;* ***Spanish:*** *Carambola.*

Description: *The fruit of carambola or Chinese tamarind tree ('Averrhoa carambola' L.), a tree or bush of the botanical family Oxalidaceae that grows to a height of 2 m. The aggregate fruit is thin-skinned and golden-yellow, measuring from 6 to 12 cm in length.*

THE CARAMBOLA or star fruit, so called because of its five-pointed cross-section, is also a "star" because of its popularity in international markets.

Its pulp has a very delicate texture and its flavor is a pleasant bittersweet. It is used in restaurants to adorn a variety of special dishes. However, the carambola has other properties than its mere "good looks."

PROPERTIES AND INDICATIONS: The carambola contains 5.13% carbohydrates in the form of sugars, and small proportions of proteins (0.54%) and fats (0.34%), which supply 33 calories per 100 g (33 kcal/100 g). They contain a moderate amount of provitamin A (40 µg RE/100 g), B complex vitamins, as well as vitamins E and C, the latter being the most abundant (21.2 mg/100 g).

It provides all of the minerals necessary for the diet, but in small amounts, with the exception of ***potassium*** (163 mg/100 g).

The carambola's delicate pulp is rich in ***soluble*** vegetable ***fiber*** (2.7%), which explains its **soothing laxative** action.

These are its dietary and therapeutic applications:

- **Constipation** because of intestinal atony, which is the most frequent type. Two or three carambolas at breakfast facilitate evacuation.
- **Elevated cholesterol:** Carambolas help reduce intestinal absorption of cholesterol because of their *high **soluble fiber** content.*

Constipation, the most common intestinal disorder

Constipation is the most common intestinal disorder in the developed world. This is primarily due to a fiber-poor diet.

At times, modern life imposes so many restrictions that it is difficult to relieve oneself in a timely manner, which also contributes to constipation.

Many headaches, eczemas, allergies, increase in cholesterol level, rheumatism, apathy, and depression improve by simply preventing constipation.

Preparation and use

❶ **Fresh:** Large carambolas are the sweetest and most flavorful. The smaller specimens can be sour.

❷ **Preserves:** Carambola pulp lends itself very well to jellies and jams.

❸ **Beverages:** Carambolas are used to make "tropical" flavored beverages.

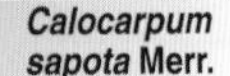

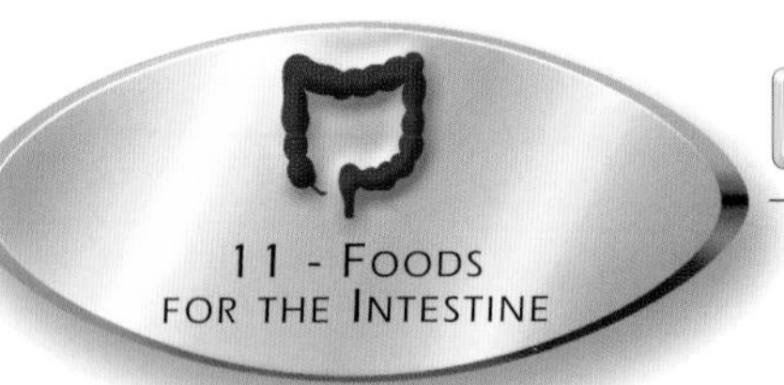

Sapote

Anti-anemic astringent

SAPOTE
Composition
per 100 g of raw edible portion

Energy	**134 kcal = 559 kj**
Protein	**2.12 g**
Carbohydrates	**31.2 g**
Fiber	**2.60 g**
Vitamin A	**41.0 µg RE**
Vitamin B_1	**0.010 mg**
Vitamin B_2	**0.020 mg**
Niacin	**2.18 mg NE**
Vitamin B_6	—
Folate	—
Vitamin B_{12}	—
Vitamin C	**20.0 mg**
Vitamin E	—
Calcium	**39.0 mg**
Phosphorus	**28.0 mg**
Magnesium	**30.0 mg**
Iron	**1.00 mg**
Potassium	**344 mg**
Zinc	—
Total Fat	***0.600 g***
Saturated Fat	—
Cholesterol	—
Sodium	***10.0 mg***

1% 2% 4% 10% 20% 40% 100%

% Daily Value (based on a 2,000 calorie diet) provided by 100 g of this food

Scientific synonym: *Pouteria sapota* L.

Synonyms: *Sapota.*

French: *Sapotille, sapote;* ***Spanish:*** *Zapote, mamey.*

Description: *The fruit of the sapote tree ('Calocarpum sapota' Merr.), of the botanical family Sapotaceae. The spherical or ovoid fruits may reach 20 cm in diameter and contain a rather large single seed.*

BENEATH its rough exterior, the sapote hides a delicate, sweet orange pulp without a hint of tartness.

PROPERTIES AND INDICATIONS: Sapotes provide a *considerable* amount of ***energy*** (134 kcal/100 g), because of their *high* ***carbohydrate*** content (31.2%), primarily from sugars. They are a good source of ***vitamin C*** (20 mg/100 g), and ***potassium*** (344 mg /100 g), ***iron*** (1 mg/100 g), and ***magnesium*** (30 mg/100 g). It lacks provitamin A (beta-carotene) and B group vitamins.

A breakfast of whole grains or whole-grain bread, with a few prunes and two pieces of fresh fruit can provide the 25 g of fiber that are needed daily. A breakfast like this makes preventing constipation easy.

It is a *good* intestinal **astringent** because of its richness in polyphenols (**tannins**), and is recommended in cases of **diarrhea** and **gastroenteritis.** It is also beneficial in cases of **anemia** and **malnutrition.**

Other sapotes

There are various other Central American fruits that bear the name sapote because of their similarity in appearance and composition to the true sapote. The most important are:

- **Sapodilla** (*Manilkara zapota* Van Royen = *Achras zapota* L.), also referred to as naseberry, curly dock, chico sapote, and marmalade plum. The pulp of this fruit is lighter than that of the sapote, and they contain three seeds instead of one. **Chicle** used for **chewing** gum is extracted from the tree on which this fruit grows.
- **Columbian sapote** (*Matisia cordata* Humb.-Bonpl.), also called "chupachupa" and red mamey. Its pulp is more fibrous than that of the true sapote.

Lucmo

Lucmo ('Pouteria lucuma') belongs to the botanical family of Sapoteaceae, as the sapote. It is grown in Chile, Peru and Ecuador. Its rind is dark green. Its pulp contains starch and is a good astringent in case of diarrea, as the sapote.

Preparation and use

❶ **Raw:** This is usually how sapotes are eaten. Their pulp has a creamy texture and is sweet and aromatic, without a hint of bitterness.

❷ **Preserves:** Sapote is used in jellies, jams, and ice creams.

Quince

Intestinal emollient and astringent

Quince jelly goes very well with tofu, cream cheese, cottage cheese.

QUINCE
Composition
per 100 g of raw edible portion

Energy	57.0 kcal = 240 kj
Protein	0.400 g
Carbohydrates	13.4 g
Fiber	1.90 g
Vitamin A	4.00 µg RE
Vitamin B_1	0.020 mg
Vitamin B_2	0.030 mg
Niacin	0.200 mg NE
Vitamin B_6	0.040 mg
Folate	3.00 µg
Vitamin B_{12}	—
Vitamin C	15.0 mg
Vitamin E	0.550 mg α-TE
Calcium	11.0 mg
Phosphorus	17.0 mg
Magnesium	8.00 mg
Iron	0.700 mg
Potassium	197 mg
Zinc	0.040 mg
Total Fat	*0.100 g*
Saturated Fat	*0.010 g*
Cholesterol	—
Sodium	*4.00 mg*

1% 2% 4% 10% 20% 40% 100%

% Daily Value (based on a 2,000 calorie diet)
provided by 100 g of this food

Synonyms: *Elephant apple, Pineapple quince.*

French: *Coing;* ***Spanish:*** *Membrillo, gamboa.*

Description: *Fruit of the quince tree ('Cydonia oblonga' Mill.), of the botanical family Rosaceae. The fruit is similar in appearance to the pear.*

THOSE UNFAMILIAR with the quince might think it is a variety of pear. However, they would be greatly disappointed with the first bite: it is so harsh and insipid that it is nearly impossible to eat. However, quince jelly is delicious and even appeals to children.

PROPERTIES AND INDICATIONS: Raw quince contains 13.4% carbohydrates in the form of sugars. But **QUINCE JELLY** is more than 50% ***sugar*** since it is made by adding its weight in sugar. Its protein and fat content is negligible (less than 1%).

Constipation, a symptom worth to be considered

*Constipation is a very common symptom, and is usually attributable to **functional disorders** or an **inadequate diet**. However, it **may be** the **early manifestation** of an intestinal tumor as colon cancer, or other **serious diseases.***

*Constipation that appears **without** an **evident cause** or that **persists** should **always be diagnosed by a physician.***

It is quite rich in vitamins C and E, as well as minerals such as potassium, iron, and copper.

The quince's **astringent** and **anti-inflammatory** effect on the intestine is due to two substances, apparently at odds with each other.

✓ ***Pectin:*** Soluble fiber that soothes the intestinal wall and facilitates bowel movement.

✓ **Astringent *tannins*** that dry the intestinal mucosa and reduce its inflammation.

As a desert or snack, it is beneficial for both children and adults with a tendency to loose feces or flatulence. It is highly recommended in cases of **diarrhea** caused by **gastroenteritis** or colitis, as a *first solid food* after the acute phase.

Its pectin content *helps* ***reduce*** blood **cholesterol** level.

Preparation and use

❶ **Raw:** The quince's harsh, acid taste makes it virtually inedible, even when ripe.

❷ **Quince jelly:** The traditional form in which quince is eaten. It is cooked in water, converted to a paste to which its own weight in sugar is added. There are manufactures that use brown (raw) sugar, which is richer in minerals and more healthful than white sugar.

Quince jelly is an astringent that is well tolerated by children and adults. It is one of the first solid foods that may be introduced after an episode of diarrhea.

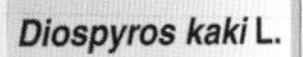

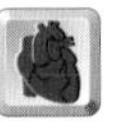

Persimmon

Stops diarrhea and reduces intestinal inflammation

PERSIMMON Composition
per 100 g of raw edible portion

Energy	70.0 kcal = 295 kj
Protein	0.580 g
Carbohydrates	15.0 g
Fiber	3.60 g
Vitamin A	217 µg RE
Vitamin B_1	0.030 mg
Vitamin B_2	0.020 mg
Niacin	0.267 mg NE
Vitamin B_6	0.100 mg
Folate	7.50 µg
Vitamin B_{12}	—
Vitamin C	16.0 mg
Vitamin E	0.590 mg α-TE
Calcium	8.00 mg
Phosphorus	17.0 mg
Magnesium	9.00 mg
Iron	0.370 mg
Potassium	161 mg
Zinc	0.110 mg
Total Fat	*0.190 g*
Saturated Fat	*0.020 g*
Cholesterol	—
Sodium	*1.00 mg*

1% 2% 4% 10% 20% 40% 100%

% Daily Value (based on a 2,000 calorie diet)
provided by 100 g of this food

Synonyms: *Kaki fruit, Sharon fruit, Chinese fig, Common persimmon.*

French: *Kaki;* ***Spanish:*** *Caqui, palosanto.*

Description: *the aggregate fruit of the persimmon tree ('Diospyros kaki' L.), a deciduous tree growing to 4 m of the botanical family Ebenaceae. The fruit is eaten almost overripe.*

WHETHER THEY are orange or bright red, persimmons are reminiscent of blazing flames. In fact, their scientific name, *Diospyros*, is Greek for "fire of Zeus."

However, once eaten, persimmons act completely contrary to what would be expected of a "blazing fire." They are an *exceptional* ***emollient*** for the digestive tract, particularly in the intestine.

PROPERTIES AND INDICATIONS: The persimmon's gelatinous pulp contains virtually no proteins or fats. However, the following substances are noteworthy:

✓ ***Sugars:*** Each 100 grams of persimmon pulp contain 15 g of sugars. The *most plentiful* is ***fructose,*** followed by ***glucose*** and **saccharose.**

✓ ***Pectin*** and ***mucilage:*** These complex carbohydrates are responsible for the gelatinous consistency of persimmon pulp. Persimmons, together with **apples** (see p. 216), are among the most ***pectin-rich*** fruits (1%). Pectin and mucilage comprise the most important component of what is known as ***soluble*** vegetable ***fiber,*** which represents 3.6% of the persimmon's weight.

PECTIN and ***MUCILAGE*** *retain* ***water,*** increasing fecal volume and facilitating evacuation. They also *retain* ***sugars,*** which keeps them from being rapidly absorbed (which is the case with pure sugar), but rather at a controlled pace. They also *retain* the **cholesterol** found in the digestive tract from animal-based foods, removing a portion through the feces.

But the immediate effect of this pectin and mucilage is **soothing** and **reducing inflammation** in the walls of the digestive tract, particularly toward the end, the large intestine.

✓ ***TANNINS:*** These phenolic compounds are *potent* **astringents.** They coagulate proteins, forming a dry resistant coating on the mucosa. Tannins are immediately recognized by their harsh taste. The more tannins, the greater the astringent effect.

Persimmon tannin content

This graph shows how tannin concentration varies with time in four varieties of persimmons.

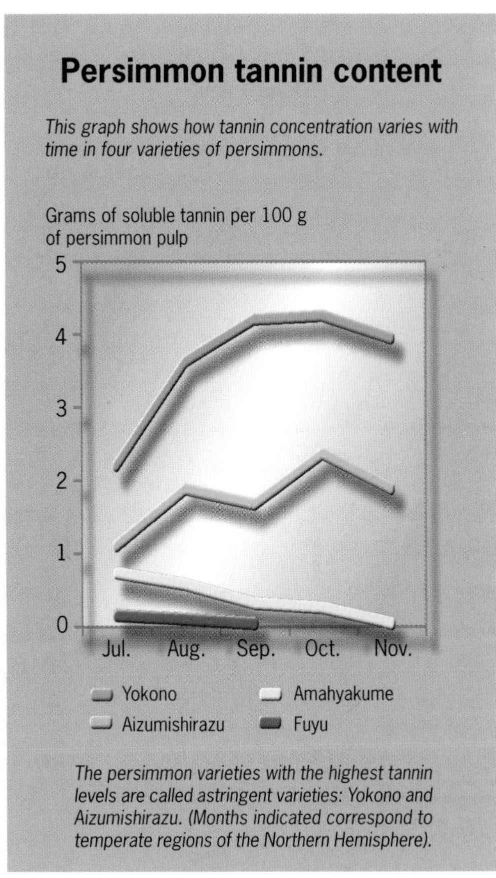

The persimmon varieties with the highest tannin levels are called astringent varieties: Yokono and Aizumishirazu. (Months indicated correspond to temperate regions of the Northern Hemisphere).

There are varieties of persimmon with higher tannin content than others. However, in all of them the tannin almost disappears during the final stages of **ripening.** The graph on the this page shows that the maximum tannin concentration in persimmons is in October, when the fruit still has not reached its peak ripeness, which is usually in November in the Northern Hemisphere.

✓ ***CAROTENOIDS:*** These are substances derived from beta-carotene, from which the body produces vitamin A. For this reasons they are called ***provitamin A.*** Contemporary interest in carotenoids is due to their *proven* **antioxidant** properties which prevent cellular aging, stop the process of arteriosclerosis and act to prevent cancer.

Preparation and use

❶ **Fresh:** Edible persimmons are only available in the fall, so it is necessary to take advantage of the opportunity to enjoy them in abundance. In case of diarrhea up to six a day may be eaten.

❷ **Persimmon puree:** This is a highly prized ingredient in cremes, jams, jellies, and compotes. It goes very well with tofu, cottage cheese, yogurt, and cream.

Persimmon preparation

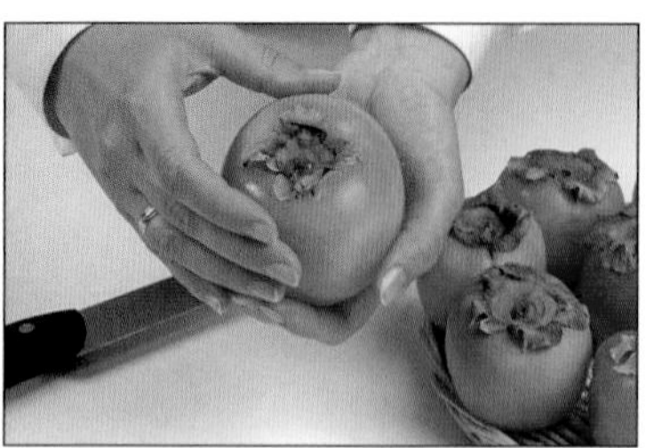

1. Test for ripeness with the fingers.

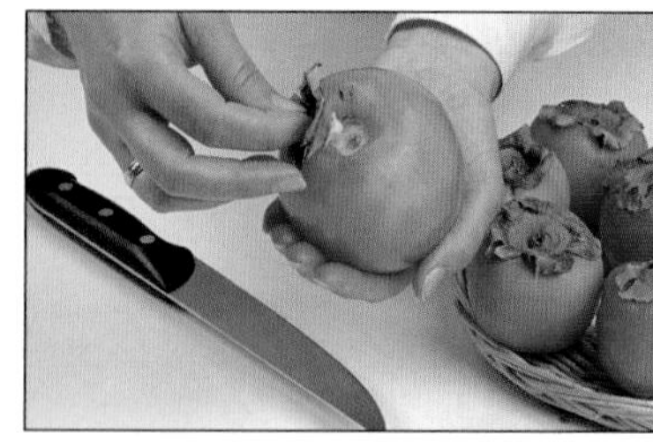

2. Remove the stem.

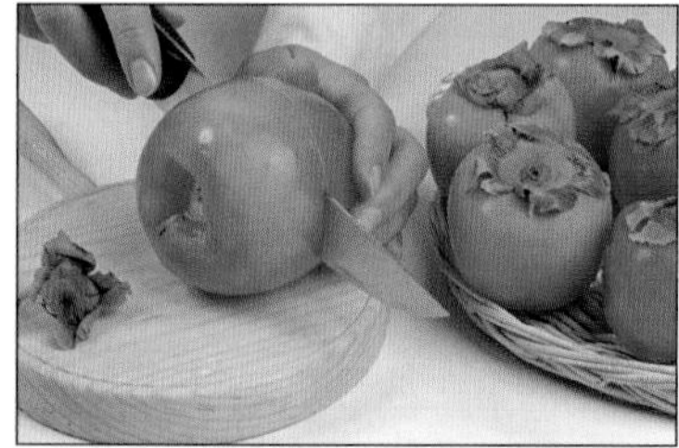

3. Cut the fruit in half with a knife.

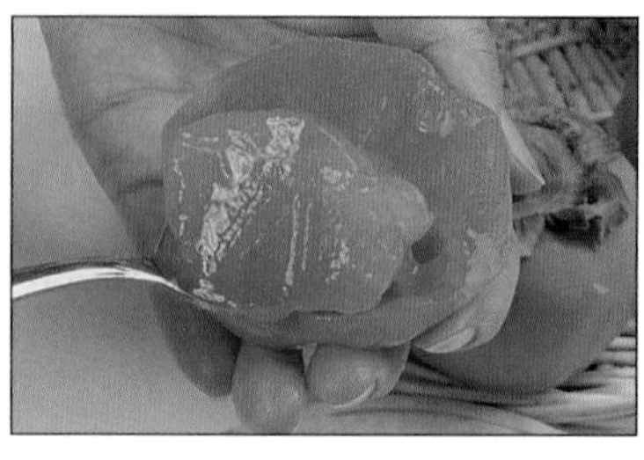

4. Eat it with a spoon. To prepare puree, grate the pulp or blend it to a uniform consistency.

Among the fifteen different carotenoids contained in persimmons ***lycopene,*** (also found in tomatoes, see p. 264) and ***cryptoxanthin*** predominate.[1] These carotenoids are responsible for persimmons' orange or reddish color.

Persimmons are among the *richest* fruits in ***carotenoids*** (provitamin A). Bearing in mind that 100 g of persimmon provides 22% of the adult daily need for vitamin A, one medium persimmon weighing 250 g is enough to provide half the RDA (Recommended Daily Allowance) for this vitamin.

✓ ***Vitamin C:*** Persimmons contain 16 mg per 100 g. One medium persimmon (250 g) supplies 40% of the daily need for this vitamin. While persimmons are not the richest fruit in vitamin C, but they do contain a significant amount, sufficient to *facilitate the absorption* of the ***iron*** that they also contain.

✓ ***Iron:*** This is the most abundant mineral (in terms of daily need) contained in the persimmon, after potassium. A 250-g persimmon provides 10% of the daily need for iron for an adult, which is considerable for a fresh fruit.

These components explain the medicinal applications of the persimmon:

• **Intestinal disorders:** Persimmons act to both soothe and dry the walls of the digestive system. This is due to the combined action of their tannins (**astringents**) and their pectin and mucilage (**emollients**). The astringent effect is more intense in certain varieties and in those that are not completely ripe.

In addition to their astringent effect, persimmons are **anti-inflammatory** because of their *considerable **pectin** and **mucilage** content.* The ***carotenoids*** they contain also contribute to this effect. They are beneficial in cases of **diarrhea** or **colitis** (inflammation of the large intestine) from any cause. Three to six persimmons a day aid in quickly regulating intestinal movement and in reducing inflammation in the digestive tract's mucosa.

Completely ripe persimmons of softer varieties contain very little tannin and are less astringent. These are characterized by a soft pulp with no harshness. This means that they are not as effective against diarrhea as varieties that are more astringent or those that are less ripe. However, they do retain their anti-inflammatory effect on the intestine, which is useful in cases of chronic colitis, intestinal spasms (cramps), excess gas, and irritable bowel.

• **Cardiovascular conditions:** Persimmons are *low* in ***fat*** and ***sodium,*** yet *rich* in ***carotenoids,*** which protect the arteries. They are highly recommended for those with **arteriosclerosis, hypertension,** and **cardiovascular conditions** in general.

• **Anemia:** Although persimmons' ***iron*** content is not particularly high, it is *highly absorbable* because the fruit also contains ***vitamin C.*** Eating ample amounts of persimmons is recommended in cases of **iron deficiency anemia,** which is the most common type of anemia.

• **Diabetes:** Although persimmons are a sweet fruit, diabetics tolerate them well for two reasons:

- More than half of their 15% sugars is ***FRUCTOSE,*** a ***natural sugar*** found in fruit. This type of sugar requires less insulin for utilization in the cells. Because of this, diabetics, whose pancreas produces less insulin, tolerate and absorb fructose better than other sugars.
- Persimmons' *abundant* ***soluble*** vegetable ***fiber*** in the form of ***pectin*** retains sugars in the intestine, releasing them little by little. Thus, the diabetic experiences no rapid burst of fructose and glucose into the bloodstream, which is harmful.

Persimmons can be safely eaten by diabetics, who may benefit from their positive action on the digestive system, as well as their carotenoid and iron content.

The ripest persimmons contain less astringent tannin, but they still provide their emollient and anti-inflammatory effects within the digestive system.

Rice

A diarrhea remedy that benefits hypertension

White rice boiled with a little oil and salt, is, together with apples and yogurt, one of the first solid foods that should be eaten after a bout of diarrhea from any cause.

RICE, WHITE
Composition
per 100 g of raw edible portion

Energy	360 kcal = 1,508 kj
Protein	6.61 g
Carbohydrates	79.3 g
Fiber	—
Vitamin A	—
Vitamin B_1	0.070 mg
Vitamin B_2	0.048 mg
Niacin	2.88 mg NE
Vitamin B_6	0.145 mg
Folate	9.00 µg
Vitamin B_{12}	—
Vitamin C	—
Vitamin E	—
Calcium	9.00 mg
Phosphorus	108 mg
Magnesium	35.0 mg
Iron	0.800 mg
Potassium	86.0 mg
Zinc	1.16 mg
Total Fat	*0.580 g*
Saturated Fat	*0.158 g*
Cholesterol	—
Sodium	*1.00 mg*

1% 2% 4% 10% 20% 40% 100%

% Daily Value (based on a 2,000 calorie diet)
provided by 100 g of this food

French: *Riz;* ***Spanish:*** *Arroz.*

Description: *The grain of the rice plant ('Oryza sativa' L.), of the botanical family Gramineae. The grains consist of the shell, pericarp, or glume, and the endosperm or grain itself.*

RICE has been called the ***"bread of Asia."*** Most of the world's rice production, some 500 million metric tons a year, is produced in tropical regions of the Far East: China, India, Bangladesh, and Indonesia. Rice is eaten every day in these countries; a meal without this grain is unthinkable.

The Greeks and Romans knew very little about rice. The Arabs introduced it to Europe through the Iberian Peninsula. The Dutch took it to North America in the 17th century, and later to Africa. Thus, it became the most widely cultivated grain in the world.

PROPERTIES AND INDICATIONS: In spite of the popularity of rice dishes, it is the *least **nutritious*** of all grains, particularly if it is refined (polished).

✓ ***Proteins:*** Rice's protein content is the lowest of any grain. No variety contains more than 7%. This is much less than oats' 16.9% or wheat's 13.7%. It is worth noting that rice contains no ***gliadin,*** the protein that constitutes wheat gluten. This characteristic makes rice suitable for those with **celiac** disease.

Rice ***protein*** is *deficient* in ***lysine*** and ***tryptophan,*** two essential amino acids. However, combining rice with **legumes,** which tend to have an excess of these substances, solves this problem. Rice and lentils, for example, provides the body with the necessary amino acids to produce a complete protein. Soy or cow's milk proteins also combine well with rice.

✓ **Fats:** White rice contains virtually no fat and the bulk that it does have is concentrated in the bran and germ. *Whole-grain rice* only contains 2.7% fats, considerably less than oats (6.9%) or corn (4.3%). Although they are scarce, rice's fatty acids are unsaturated and of great biological value.

Rice is the basis of many oriental recipes.

✓ ***Carbohydrates:*** These constitute four-fifths of the weight of a grain of rice. *Virtually all* of these carbohydrates are in the form of ***starch.***

✓ ***Vitamins:*** As is the case with other grains, rice lacks vitamins A and C. **Whole-grain** rice contains *significant amounts* of ***vitamins*** B_1 and ***E.*** However, **white** rice contains *very little* of these vitamins.

Eating *white rice* as a *staple* of the *diet* produces a serious vitamin B_1 deficiency that can lead to the serious disease of **beriberi.** When the diet is more varied and white rice is accompanied by other vitamin B_1-rich foods such as oil-bearing nuts or legumes, there is less risk of deficiency.

However, it is best to eat whole-grain or parboiled rice, which contains greater amounts of ***vitamin*** B_1 in addition to B_2, B_6, and ***niacin.***

Preparation and use

❶ **Cooked:** Rice cannot be eaten raw, but it is the primary ingredient in a wide variety of recipes. From a nutritional standpoint, it ***combines*** *particularly well* with **vegetables, legumes,** and cow's or soy **milk.**

❷ **Rice cereal:** Rice prepared in this way is used together with other grains in muesli. **Whole-grain** rice is used for this purpose.

❸ **Rice water:** This is prepared by boiling ***two tablespoons*** of rice in ***one liter*** of water until the rice begins to disintegrate. Let the liquid stand until cool, then strain. It may be flavored by adding a cinnamon stick and/or lemon peel, or a few drops of lemon.

✓ ***Minerals:*** With 1 mg/100 g of ***sodium,*** rice is among the foods lowest in this mineral. This makes it *particularly* appropriate for those with **hypertension** or **cardiovascular conditions.**

Whole-grain rice, as well as white rice, contains other minerals such as potassium, calcium, magnesium, and iron, although in relatively small amounts.

Nutritionally, rice may be *summarized* as a light food that is easy to digest and produces a feeling of satiety. However, white rice (refined) should not constitute the basis of the diet since it lacks many vitamins and minerals.

In any case, rice, whether white or whole-grain, *must be combined* with other foods such as **legumes, vegetables,** or **milk** to increase its nutritional capacity.

Rice is particularly useful in the following cases:

• **Any case of diarrhea:** Rice boiled with a little oil and salt is, together with the **apple** (see p. 216) and **yogurt,** one of the *first* ***solid foods*** after a case of diarrhea of any cause. Its ease of digestion, together with its mild astringent action, makes rice an exceptional food for restoration of the intestinal mucosa after **colitis** or **gastroenteritis.**

• **Diarrhea in infants:** Rice water **[❸]** is the *ideal* fluid for **oral rehydration** in case of diarrhea, *particularly* for **children.** It may be given as the only beverage, adding a few drops of lemon juice, if desired. In addition to providing necessary fluid (rehydration), rice water provides minerals salts, particularly potassium and complex carbohydrates (starch), which stop diarrhea.

• **Hypertension:** Because rice is a *very low* ***sodium*** food, it is very useful in cases of hypertension. ***SODIUM*** is a mineral with a great capacity for fluid retention (as occurs with common salt, sodium chloride). Excess sodium intake causes the body to retain fluid (edema) and increases blood volume. This causes an increase in blood pressure. The more sodium or salt taken in, the higher the risk of hypertension.

• **Cardiac disease:** When the heart does not perform its function (cardiac failure), fluids accumulate in the tissues and the kidneys do not eliminate sufficient urine. This situation is worsened by the consumption of sodium-rich foods, which retain even more fluid and produce more edema.

Rice maintains its greatness as the most widespread grain on earth.

Anemia and a rice-based diet

*Studies have shown that **rice-based diets,** as is the case in some Asian countries, can result in **anemia.** This fact is attributed to white rice's **very low iron** content.*

*However, there is **no** need to **fear** anemia in diets rich in rice, if it is eaten with **vitamin C-rich fresh fruits and vegetables. Vitamin C** enhances absorption of iron from vegetable sources. The practice of eating **rice with vegetables** and **lemon** is highly beneficial from a nutritional standpoint.*

Types of rice

Short grain white rice

The grains of this rice open during cooking, which makes it somewhat pasty. It is of great value in the **pastry** and confectionery, particularly for making **rice pudding.**

Shell rice

Also called *paddy* or raw rice. This is rice just as it comes from the field. Because it is so hard, it is *not appropriate* for human consumption.

Long grain white rice

The grains of this rice remain whole and fluffy during cooking. It is preferred for cold dishes such as rice **salads.**

Whole-grain rice

This type of rice is *richer* in ***vitamins*** and ***minerals*** than white rice, but takes longer to cook and is harder to chew. It is easier to prepare if it is **soaked** for some hours before cooking. A few drops of lemon juice in the cooking water also make it softer.

Parboiled rice

This hydro-thermically-treated whole-grain rice has been slightly refined. It is easier to eat than whole-grain rice and retains most of its ***vitamins***.

Because of this, in cases of **cardiac failure,** a ***low-sodium*** diet is required. **Rice** is an *ideal* food in this case. The fact that rice has *practically no* ***fat*** makes it even more beneficial in cases of coronary disease.

- **High cholesterol:** Whole-grain rice impedes the absorption of biliary acids in the intestine because of its ***fiber*** content. These acids are the raw material used by the liver to produce cholesterol. Since rice contains virtually no fat, and, naturally, no cholesterol, eating it in whole-grain form has the beneficial effect of lowering blood cholesterol level.

- **Excess uric acid:** Because of its *very low* ***protein*** content and its **alkalizing** effect, rice is highly recommended in cases of excess uric acid in the blood, which may manifest as **gout** or **arthritis.** Naturally, it must be eaten either *alone* or with *other plant-based* foods.

Apple

Cures both diarrhea and constipation

French: *Pomme;* ***Spanish:*** *Manzana.*

Description: *Fruit of the apple tree ('Pirus malus' L.), of the botanical family Rosaceae.*

APPLE
Composition
per 100 g of raw edible portion

Energy	59.0 kcal = 245 kj
Protein	0.190 g
Carbohydrates	12.6 g
Fiber	2.70 g
Vitamin A	5.00 µg RE
Vitamin B_1	0.017 mg
Vitamin B_2	0.014 mg
Niacin	0.110 mg NE
Vitamin B_6	0.048 mg
Folate	2.80 µg
Vitamin B_{12}	—
Vitamin C	5.70 mg
Vitamin E	0.320 mg α-TE
Calcium	7.00 mg
Phosphorus	7.00 mg
Magnesium	5.00 mg
Iron	0.180 mg
Potassium	115 mg
Zinc	0.040 mg
Total Fat	*0.360 g*
Saturated Fat	*0.058 g*
Cholesterol	—
Sodium	*1.50 mg*

1% 2% 4% 10% 20% 40% 100%

% Daily Value (based on a 2,000 calorie diet)
provided by 100 g of this food

EACH YEAR the world produces more than 40 million metric tons of apples, in fourth place after grapes, oranges, and bananas. Although not the most widely cultivated fruit, the apple is considered the ***"queen of fruits."*** This may be in view of the fact that in addition to its enormous culinary and medicinal virtues, it combines with practically all other foods.

Properties and indications: Aside from the 12.6% carbohydrates in the form of ***sugars,*** no other nutrient stands out in the apple's composition. The sugars are primarily ***fructose*** (fruit sugar, also called levulose) and lower proportions of glucose and saccharose. It contains *very small* amounts of ***proteins*** and ***fats.*** Among its ***vitamins*** are ***C*** and ***E,*** and its ***minerals*** include ***potassium*** and ***iron,*** although in limited amounts. Together, its nutrients provide 59 calories per 100 grams (59 kcal/100 g).

✓ ***Pectin:*** This hydrocarbon is not absorbed in the intestine, and forms most of what is called ***insoluble*** vegetable ***fiber.*** Most of the 2.4 g /100 g of fiber in the apple is pectin. Only one-fifth of the fruit's pectin is in the peel. Therefore, when it is removed only a small portion is lost. Pectin retains water and various waste products in the intestine, acting as an intestinal "broom" that facilitates the **elimination** of **toxins** with the feces.

✓ ***Organic acids:*** These represent 1% to 1.5% of the apple's weight, depending on variety. The most prevalent is malic acid, although citric, succinic, lactic, and salicylic acids are also present. As happens with citrus fruits, when these organic acids are metabolized they produce an **alkalizing** (antacid) effect in the blood and tissues. These acids also *renew* the **intestinal flora** and *prevent* intestinal **fermentation.**

✓ ***Tannins:*** The apple is, *after* the **quince** (see p. 206), one of the fruits *richest* in tannins, which are **astringent** and **anti-inflammatory.**

✓ ***Flavonoids:*** These constitute a group of ***phytochemicals*** present in many plant-based foods that are capable of *preventing* the *oxidation* of low-density lipoproteins (substances that carry cholesterol in the blood). In this way flavonoids *keep* **cholesterol** from depositing on arterial walls and stop the progress of **arteriosclerosis** (hardening and narrowing of the arteries). Apples contain a variety of flavonoids, the most active and important of which is ***quercetin,*** because of its **antioxidant** effect.[2] Apples, together with **onions** (see p. 142), are the richest plant-based foods in quercetin.

✓ ***Boron:*** this little-known mineral plays a variety of roles within the body that are currently being studied. One of these seems to be facilitating the assimilation of calcium and magnesium, meaning that boron *may* contribute to the *prevention* of **osteoporosis**. Apples are among the fruits *richest* in boron.

These substances partially explain the many medicinal properties of this simple but exceptional fruit: anti-diarrheic, laxative, diuretic, depurant, hypolipedemic (reduces blood lipid levels), choleretic, nerve tonic, alkalizer, and antioxidant. Because of this, **eating** them ***daily*** benefits both those who are healthy and the ill, particularly in these cases:

• **Diarrhea and colitis:** The pectin in apples acts as a sponge that absorbs and eliminates the toxins produced by the bacteria that cause gastroenteritis and colitis. Also, its ***tannins*** **dry** the intestinal mucosa and **reduce its inflammation.** The ***organic acids*** act as **antiseptics** and *restore* the normal bacterial **flora** in the intestine.

Preparation and use

❶ **Raw:** ***Peeling*** is recommended because, in spite of what many believe, the small amount of pectin and vitamins in the peel do not justify eating it. The peel can contain pesticides, and it is difficult to digest.

❷ **Applesauce:** A glass grater is best for this purpose because it is an inert material. However, modern stainless steel is adequate. Applesauce is recommended for children, the elderly, and those weakened by illness.

❸ **Baked:** This is a delicious and highly digestible way to eat apples.

❹ **Cooked:** Apples prepared in this way should be eaten with the cooking liquid. These are easy to digest and appropriate for children.

❺ **Juice:** Natural unprocessed juice is preferable to that prepared industrially.

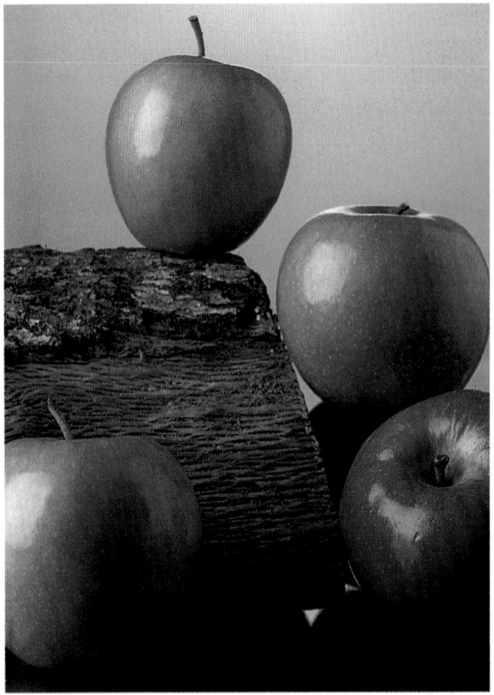

Apples are the quintessential fruit. They are well tolerated by everyone and combine well with any other food.

A diet based exclusively on apples is effective in any type of diarrhea. When the digestive organs are affected, apples are best prepared as applesauce, baked, or cooked **[❷,❸,❹]**.

• **Constipation:** Apples ***regulate*** intestinal function, and ***correct*** *both* **diarrhea** and **constipation.** Eating one or two apples on an empty stomach in the morning helps overcome intestinal hypotony, which is the most common cause of constipation.

• **Chronic skin eczema** caused by autointoxication due to constipation.

• **Hypertension:** Studies conducted in Japan, where the normal diet contains a great deal of salt, have shown that those who ***regularly*** eat apples have lower blood pressure than the rest of the population.[2]

Apples contain *virtually no* ***sodium,*** and are quite *rich* in ***potassium,*** which contributes to their hypertensive effect.

• **Excess cholesterol:** Eating two or three apples a day for several months has been shown *effective* in reducing cholesterol level. A partial explanation for this effect is that the pectin absorbs the biliary salts in the intestine, one of the basic ingredients from which the body makes cholesterol.

• **Arteriosclerosis:** Because of their richness in ***flavonoids,*** particularly ***quercetin,*** apples *help* ***prevent*** the deposit of cholesterol within the arteries and their subsequent narrowing. Flavonoids also *inhibit* **platelet stickiness** (the tendency of the platelets in the blood to form thromboses or clots). **Eating** apples ***regularly*** *prevents* narrowing of the coronary arteries, which leads to **heart attack.**[3]

• **Cholelithiasis** (gallstones): Studies conducted at the University of Toulouse (France) with laboratory animals[4] show that apples have a **choleretic** effect (increases bile production in the liver) which decongests the liver. It also *reduces* the **lithogenic index** of the bile, which measures the tendency to form biliary calculi.

It is reasonable, then, to recommend apples to patients who are at high risk of cholelithiasis (particularly women between 40 and 50 years old with more than two children), or those who have undergone surgery. Apples make the bile more fluid and prevent the formation of calculi, although they have no effect on those that are already formed.

• **Diabetes:** Diabetics tolerate apples very well for two reasons:

- A significant amount of their sugar is ***fructose,*** which does not require insulin to enter the cells;
- Second, ***pectin*** acts to regulate the release of sugars, allowing them into the bloodstream slowly and progressively.

• **Colon cancer:** Studies in Japan using laboratory animals[5] show that apple ***pectin*** is capable of preventing the growth of cancerous tumors of the colon.

This *preventive action* provides steady support for recommending abundant apple consumption to patients at high risk for colon cancer, as well as for those that have been diagnosed and/or treated, to avoid its relapse.

Indications for treatment using apples

A treatment with apples is done by eating two kilos of apples a day for 3 to 5 consecutive days. Water may be drunk. The apples may be eaten raw, as applesauce, baked, or cooked but without additional sweeteners. This treatment may be repeated several times a year.

Gastrointestinal and colitis-related diarrhea

Apple fiber (***pectin***) is a great absorbent that **cleanses** the intestine. It also **restores** the physiological bacterial **flora** acting in combination with the ***organic acids*** also found in apples.

Liver disease

Apples decongest the hepatic gland thanks to their choleretic and depurant effects. They are highly recommended in cases of **chronic hepatitis, fatty degeneration** of the liver due to the consumption of alcoholic beverages, and **cirrhosis.**

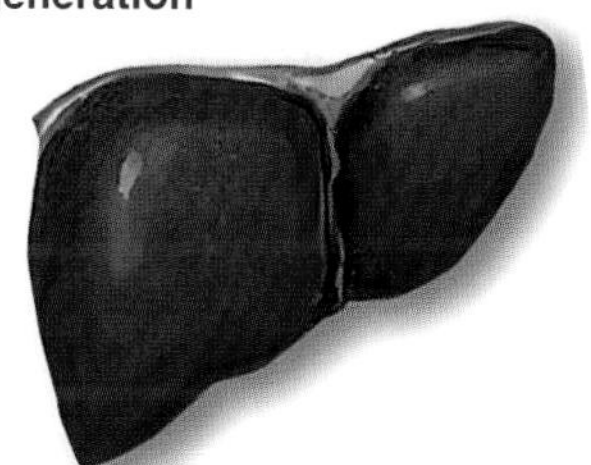

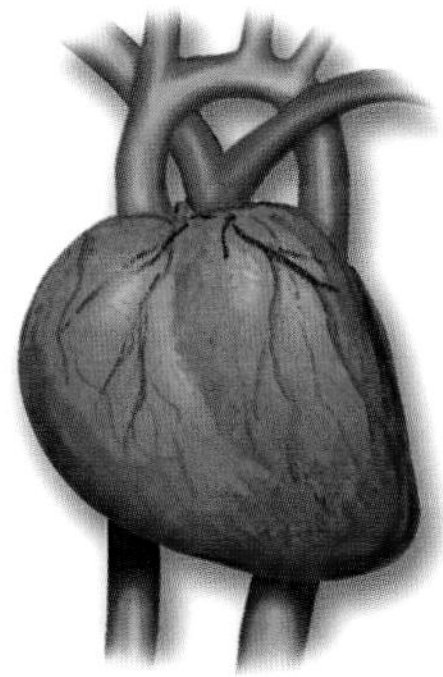

Hypertension

Apples *facilitate* the ***elimination*** of the **sodium** ions that cause the arteries to contract, increase in blood volume, and fluid retention in the tissues. They also *replace* the **sodium** ions with those of **potassium,** which normalize blood pressure and improve cardiac function.

Chronic eczema caused by autointoxication

Apples **absorb** intestinal **toxins,** thus facilitating the **purification** of the **blood** and the **skin.** Apples also *help relieve* **constipation** and promote *purification* of the **liver,** whose congestion results in many skin disorders.

Excess uric acid

An apple treatment **alkalizes** the blood and *facilitates* the **elimination** of uric acid through the urine.

High cholesterol and arteriosclerosis

Apples *reduce* the blood **cholesterol** level and *prevent* **arteriosclerosis.**

Colon cancer

Apples help avoid the cancerous degeneration of the colon.

Plum

Laxative that protects the intestine

Synonyms: *Prune, Prune plum, Greengage.*

French: *Prune;* ***Spanish:*** *Ciruela.*

Description: *Fruit of the plum tree ('Prunus domestica' L.), of the botanical family Rosaceae that reaches a height of 5 m. The fruit is a round or ovoid drupe that may reach 7 cm in diameter. It has a woody pit containing an inedible seed.*

PLUM
Composition
per 100 g of raw edible portion

Energy	55.0 kcal = 230 kj
Protein	0.790 g
Carbohydrates	11.5 g
Fiber	1.50 g
Vitamin A	32.0 µg RE
Vitamin B_1	0.043 mg
Vitamin B_2	0.096 mg
Niacin	0.500 mg NE
Vitamin B_6	0.081 mg
Folate	2.20 µg
Vitamin B_{12}	—
Vitamin C	9.50 mg
Vitamin E	0.600 mg α-TE
Calcium	4.00 mg
Phosphorus	10.0 mg
Magnesium	7.00 mg
Iron	0.100 mg
Potassium	172 mg
Zinc	0.100 mg
Total Fat	*0.620 g*
Saturated Fat	*0.049 g*
Cholesterol	—
Sodium	—

1% 2% 4% 10% 20% 40% 100%

% Daily Value (based on a 2,000 calorie diet)
provided by 100 g of this food

Properties and indications: All varieties of plums are similar in composition. They are only differentiated by their sugar content and their natural coloring, which determines the color of the skin and pulp.

Plums contain *scarcely any* ***proteins*** and ***fats*** (less than 1% of each of these nutrients). They contain a *balanced* proportion of all ***vitamins*** and ***minerals*** (except vitamin B_{12}), although in small amounts.

Plums' non-nutrient components are remarkable and explain this fruit's laxative action on the intestine:

✓ ***Vegetable fiber:*** This is ***soluble,*** *primarily* ***pectin.*** Fresh plums contain about 1.5%, while prunes can reach 7%. ***PECTIN*** is a *complex* ***carbohydrate*** that *absorbs* ***water*** in the intestine, *increasing* the volume of the **feces** and aiding evacuation. It also *absorbs* **cholesterol** and **biliary salts,** which are eliminated with the feces.

✓ ***Dihydroxyphenylisatin:*** This substance, also known as **oxyphenisatin**, has been chemically identified.[6] Its function is to *gently* **stimulate** the **peristaltic action** of the intestine, promoting movement of the feces.

Their healing applications are as follows:

- **Constipation:** The *combined action* of ***pectin*** and the ***substance*** that stimulates intestinal movement makes plums *gentle* and *effective* **laxatives.** In contrast to insoluble vegetable fiber such as bran, plums' ***soluble fiber*** **soothes** and **protects** intestinal walls.

Children and the **elderly** tolerate plums and prunes very well, making them the laxative of choice for constipation in both groups.

- **Elevated cholesterol:** The ***fiber*** in prunes, comprised *primarily* of ***pectin,*** reduces cholesterol levels in laboratory animals,[7] as well as in humans.

An ideal breakfast to fight constipation and protect the intestine should contain prunes, yogurt, honey and a few slices of whole-grain bread or rye bread.
One may increase the laxative effect of prunes by soaking them overnight and eating them the next morning for breakfast. Drink the water they have been soaking in for maximum benefit.

- **Chronic disorders:** Plums are *mildly* **diuretic, depurant,** and **detoxifying.** Their *extremely low* ***protein, fat,*** and ***sodium*** content makes them very suitable in cases of **arteriosclerosis,** excess **uric acid, gout,** degenerative conditions of the joints (**rheumatism** and **arthrosis**), and liver disease (**chronic hepatitis, cirrhosis,** etc.). In all of these situations, adding several plums or prunes to breakfast is a healthful practice.

- **Prevention of colon cancer:** The fact that the ***soluble fiber*** in certain foods *protects* against ***colon cancer*** has been an established scientific fact for years. Therefore, ***regular*** plum or prune **consumption** is a very appropriate *prophylactic* for all who are at risk of colon cancer, whether for genetic reasons (intestinal polyps) or lifestyle reasons (a diet lacking in vegetable fiber, chronic constipation, or diverticulosis).

Preparation and use

❶ **Fresh:** Raw plums must be at their **peak of ripeness** in order to be well tolerated by the stomach.

❷ **Prunes:** These may be eaten just as they are or **soaked** overnight. The normal dose is from 6 to 12 prunes, preferably in the morning.

❸ **Culinary preparations:** Plums and prunes are used to make a variety of delicious dishes, compotes and jams. These also have a laxative effect.

Pomegranate

Reduces intestinal inflammation and enriches the blood

Synonyms: *Chinese apple, Dalima, Grenade.*

French: *Grenade;* ***Spanish:*** *Granada.*

Description: *Fruit of the pomegranate tree ('Punica granatum' L.), an evergreen belonging to the botanical family Punicaceae that reaches 4 m in height. The fruit is formed of many sacs filled with a very juicy pink or reddish pulp. Each sac contains a seed.*

POMEGRANATE
Composition
per 100 g of raw edible portion

Energy	68.0 kcal = 283 kj
Protein	0.950 g
Carbohydrates	16.6 g
Fiber	0.600 g
Vitamin A	—
Vitamin B_1	0.030 mg
Vitamin B_2	0.030 mg
Niacin	0.300 mg NE
Vitamin B_6	0.105 mg
Folate	6.00 µg
Vitamin B_{12}	—
Vitamin C	6.10 mg
Vitamin E	0.550 mg α-TE
Calcium	3.00 mg
Phosphorus	8.00 mg
Magnesium	3.00 mg
Iron	0.300 mg
Potassium	259 mg
Zinc	0.120 mg
Total Fat	*0.300 g*
Saturated Fat	*0.038 g*
Cholesterol	—
Sodium	*3.00 mg*

1% 2% 4% 10% 20% 40% 100%

% Daily Value (based on a 2,000 calorie diet)
provided by 100 g of this food

Properties and indications: The pomegranate contains an amount of ***carbohydrates*** that surpasses most other fruits: 15.6% (bananas reach 21%). Its ***protein*** content is close to 1%, which is respectable bearing in mind that this is a fresh fruit. ***Fats*** are less than 0.3% of its weight.

The pomegranate is quite rich in ***vitamins C, E,*** and ***B_6,*** containing, as well, significant amounts of ***B_1, B_2,*** and ***niacin.*** It does not contain beta-carotene (provitamin A). The most abundant ***minerals*** are ***potassium, copper,*** and ***iron.***

Among its non-nutritive components the following are worth noting:

✓ ***Tannins,*** in small amounts. These are much more prevalent in the ***RIND*** of the fruit or in the ***MEMBRANES*** that separate the seed sacs. These tannins have an **astringent** and **anti-inflammatory** effect on the mucosa of the digestive tract.

✓ ***Citric acid*** and other organic acids which give the pomegranate its pleasant bittersweet taste and a portion of its beneficial effect on the intestine (it contributes to the *restoration* of the intestinal **bacterial flora**).

✓ ***Anthocyanins:*** These reddish or bluish vegetable pigments belonging to the ***flavonoid*** group act as **antiseptics** and **anti-inflammatory** substances in the digestive tract and as potent **antioxidants** within the cells, *halting* the **aging** process and **cancerous** degeneration. It also has a diuretic effect.

✓ ***Pelletierine:*** This alkaloid is an effective **vermifuge** (expulses intestinal parasites) that is found primarily in the bark of the ***ROOTS*** of the tree.

Together, these components give the pomegranate the following properties: astringent, anti-inflammatory, vermifuge (if the internal membranes are consumed), remineralizer, alkalizer, and depurant.

Its use is particularly indicated in the following cases:

The pomegranate is an intestinal astringent and anti-inflammatory. The hard residue that remains in the mouth should not be swallowed since it is indigestible.

- **Intestinal disorders:** The pomegranate is suitable in cases of **infectious diarrhea** caused by gastroenteritis or colitis because of its astringent and anti-inflammatory action on the digestive tract. It is also beneficial in cases of **flatulence** (excess gas) or intestinal **cramps.** Surprising results have been achieved in chronic cases such as ulcerative colitis or granulomatous colitis (Crohn's disease).
- **Excess stomach acid:** Because of its astringent action it reduces the production of gastric juice and reduces inflammation in an irritated stomach.
- Iron deficiency **anemia:** The pomegranate contains a significant amount of ***copper*** (70 µg /100 g), a trace element that *facilitates the absorption* of ***iron.***
- **Arteriosclerosis:** Because of its rich content of ***flavonoids*** and antioxidant vitamins (C and E), which halt the processes of arterial aging, the pomegranate is recommended in cases of reduced arterial blood flow. It is very beneficial in **heart attack** *prevention* and cardiac health in general.
- **Hypertension:** Because of their *richness* in ***potassium*** and *virtual absence* of **sodium,** pomegranates are appropriate for those suffering from hypertension. They help avoid excessive numbers of both systolic and diastolic pressure.
- **Metabolic disorders:** Pomegranates are of value in cases of **gout,** excess **uric acid,** and **obesity** because of its **alkalizing** and **depurant** effect.

Preparation and use

❶ **Natural:** The pomegranate is among the most easily stored fruits after harvest. It ripens well off the tree with little effect on its nutritive properties. Pomegranates stored in a cool, dry place can last up to six months.

If its **anti-parasitic effect** is undesired, the internal membranes that separate the sacs should be removed because of their bitter taste.

❷ **Juice:** Pomegranate juice is very refreshing and flavorful. It is easily extracted using a household juicer.

❸ **Grenadine:** This syrup is made by cooking pomegranate juice with sugar. It may be stored for months. It is used as a beverage, diluted with water, or to flavor fruit salads.

Corn

Soothes the intestine

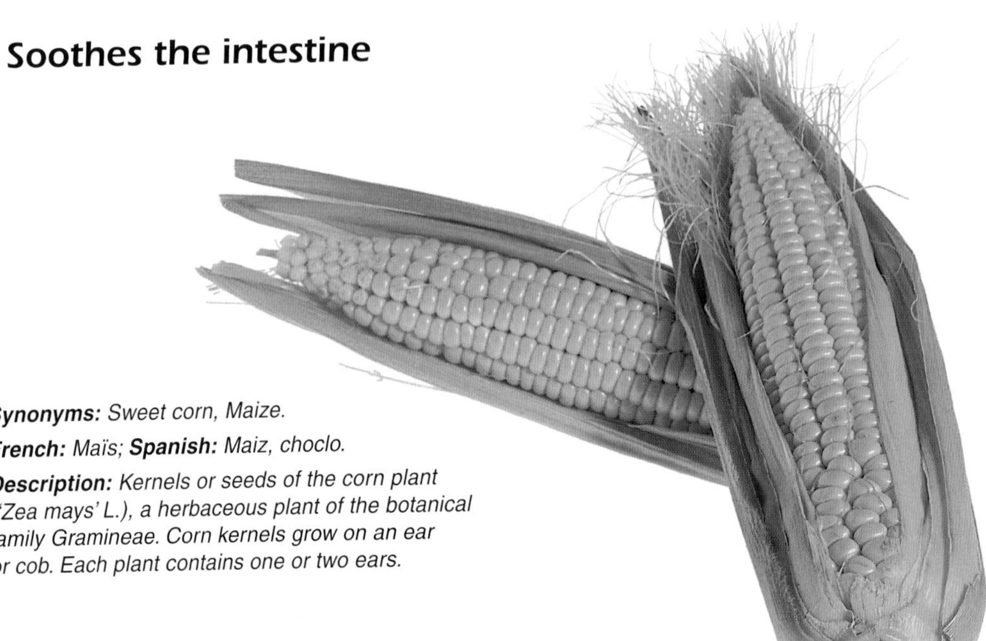

Synonyms: *Sweet corn, Maize.*

French: *Maïs;* ***Spanish:*** *Maiz, choclo.*

Description: *Kernels or seeds of the corn plant ('Zea mays' L.), a herbaceous plant of the botanical family Gramineae. Corn kernels grow on an ear or cob. Each plant contains one or two ears.*

CORN, SWEET
Composition
per 100 g of raw edible portion

Energy	86.0 kcal = 358 kj
Protein	3.22 g
Carbohydrates	16.3 g
Fiber	2.70 g
Vitamin A	28.0 µg RE
Vitamin B_1	0.200 mg
Vitamin B_2	0.060 mg
Niacin	2.08 mg NE
Vitamin B_6	0.055 mg
Folate	45.8 µg
Vitamin B_{12}	—
Vitamin C	6.80 mg
Vitamin E	0.090 mg α-TE
Calcium	2.00 mg
Phosphorus	89.0 mg
Magnesium	37.0 mg
Iron	0.520 mg
Potassium	270 mg
Zinc	0.450 mg
Total Fat	1.18 g
Saturated Fat	0.182 g
Cholesterol	—
Sodium	15.0 mg

1% 2% 4% 10% 20% 40% 100%

% Daily Value (based on a 2,000 calorie diet)
provided by 100 g of this food

ALL OF THE PRIMITIVE peoples of the American continent from Chile to Canada grew and ate corn from antiquity. Spaniards introduced it to Europe in the 16th century, from where it spread throughout the world.

Today corn is the third most cultivated grain in the world, after wheat and rice. However, nine out of every ten kilos harvested is destined as animal feed.

PROPERTIES AND INDICATIONS: Sweet corn contains 76% water, considerably more than other drier varieties of corn. This is because it is harvested before it is ripe; thus it contains a higher percentage of water, as well as sugars, which give it its pleasant tenderness and flavor.

Sweet corn provides 86 kcal/100 g, somewhat more than potatoes (79 kcal/100 g), but less than rice (360 kcal/100 g).

These are sweet corn's primary nutrients:

✓ ***Carbohydrates:*** These make up 16.3% of its weight. These are formed of a mixture of ***sugars*** and ***starch.*** Unripe kernels contain more sugar, while riper ones contain a higher proportion of starch. Both types of carbohydrates are easily digested and assimilated.

✓ ***Fat:*** This is found particularly in the **germ** and makes up 1.18 percent of its weight. It is rich in mono and polyunsaturated fatty acids, particularly ***linoleic acid.*** A highly nutritious **OIL** is extracted from this fat that is effective against excess **cholesterol.**

✓ ***Proteins:*** Sweet corn contains about 3.22% protein by weight, although when dried this reaches 10%. The most abundant protein in a kernel of corn is known as ***zein.*** Although it contains all essential amino acids, two are insufficient: lysine and tryptophan. This gives corn protein a biological value of 60%, relatively low compared with eggs (94%) or milk (85%).

Corn protein, although easily digestible, is insufficient to meet the amino acid needs of the body by itself, particularly during periods of growth. However, the *combination* of **corn** with **legumes** and **sunflower seeds** provides a ***complete protein.***

Preparation and use

❶ **Fresh sweet corn:** This may be heated in water or roasted over coals, and eaten directly from the cob.

❷ **Canned sweet corn:** This is typically canned or frozen. In either case it maintains its flavor and most of its nutritional properties. Canned or frozen corn is whole-grain, containing the germ and the bran of the grain.

❸ **Cornmeal:** This is as nutritious as the whole grain. Corn meal is used in Mexico to make the famous **tortillas.** In Italy, it is used to make **polenta,** a thick cornmeal mush.

❹ **Grits:** This is refined cornmeal, less nutritious than whole cornmeal because the germ and bran have been removed.

❺ **Cornflakes:** These are made by mashing and toasting corn, a process by which some of its vitamin content is lost. Consequently, industrially manufactured cornflakes are enriched with vitamins and minerals.

❻ **Popcorn:** See informational box on this same page.

❼ **Cornstarch:** This is highly refined, defatted corn flour. Therefore, it has very little nutritional value except for calories. It is used in sauces and confectionery and as a thickener in various food products.

Popcorn

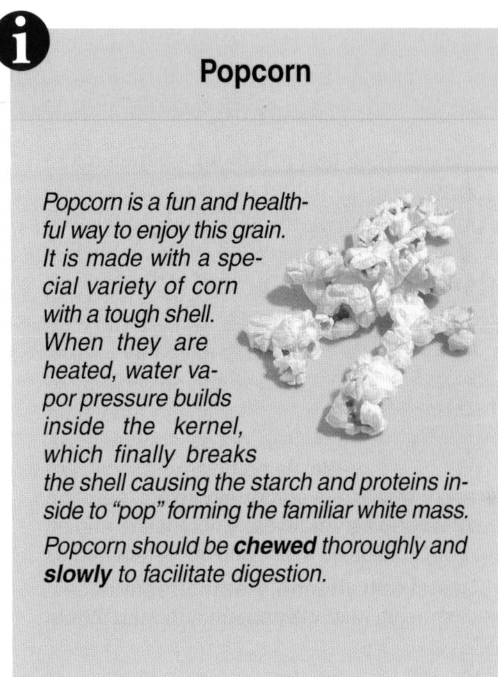

Popcorn is a fun and healthful way to enjoy this grain. It is made with a special variety of corn with a tough shell. When they are heated, water vapor pressure builds inside the kernel, which finally breaks the shell causing the starch and proteins inside to "pop" forming the familiar white mass.

*Popcorn should be **chewed** thoroughly and **slowly** to facilitate digestion.*

Corn soothes and protects the intestinal mucosa and is well tolerated by those with chronic colitis and irritable bowel syndrome.

✓ ***Vitamins:*** Yellow sweet corn contains a certain amount of provitamin A (28 µg RE /100 g), while white corn contains virtually none. Canned sweet corn loses 25% of its provitamin A in a year of storage.

Corn is a good source of vitamin B_1, and provides a moderate amount of vitamin C. Although it contains niacin, it cannot be utilized in the body if the corn is not treated with alkali.

✓ ***Minerals:*** Corn contains considerable potassium, phosphorous, magnesium, and iron, but very little calcium.

✓ ***Fiber:*** Sweet corn is a good source of fiber (2.7%) of both ***soluble*** and ***insoluble*** types.

Eating corn is especially recommended in the following cases:

- **Intestinal disorders:** Sweet corn **[❶,❷]** as well as cornmeal **[❸]** and other means of preparation have an emollient (soothing) effect on the intestinal mucosa. Additionally, corn contains *no* ***gluten,*** which makes it *easily tolerated* in **sensitive digestive systems.** It is recommended particularly in these cases:
  - Intestinal **dyspepsia** characterized by fermentation, gas, and pain (cramping).
  - **Irritable bowel** characterized by alternating between periods of constipation and diarrhea.
  - **Chronic colitis** (inflammation of the large intestine), particularly in the form of cornmeal mush **[❸]**.
  - **Weaning diet** for nursing infants, also in the form of flour.
  - **Celiac disease:** This disease is the result of intestinal intolerance of wheat gluten.
- **Chronic renal diseases** that result in kidney failure (chronic glomerulonephritis and nephrosis): Corn kernels have a slight **diuretic** effect (although much less than the silky styles[8]) and provide a limited amount of proteins in proportion to their caloric content. Because of all of this, corn is suitable for the diet of kidney patients.
- Excess cholesterol and fat in the blood: The bran that covers each kernel of corn, and which is present in sweet corn **[❶,❷]** as well as in corn meal **[❸]**, is capable of reducing blood cholesterol level.
- **Hyperthyroidism:** Corn has a slight retarding effect on the thyroid gland and on metabolism in general. Its consumption is appropriate in cases of hyperthyroidism, characterized by thinness and nervousness, among other symptoms.
- **Thinness in general:** Corn in any form is recommended for weight-gain diets.

Overcoming corn's nutritional deficiencies

Corn is a staple in the nutrition of many peoples, but it is insufficient by itself. It must be combined with other foods that compensate its nutritional deficiencies.

*The importance of corn for the human species is surpassed in importance only by **rice** and **wheat.** Many of the world's peoples, particularly in South America, depend primarily on corn to subsist.*

*Corn is used in developing countries to feed **weaned** infants for the following reasons:*

- *Corn is one of the **most productive** crops, yielding about six metric tons per hectare. Wheat, for example, only produces about two metric tones per hectare.*
- *Corn is the **most available source of calories and proteins** in many developing countries. Sometimes, it is virtually the only source.*
- *Cornmeal is **easy to store** without need for refrigeration.*
- *Cornmeal mush is **easily digested** by **young children.***
- *Corn **lacks gluten,** the protein of certain grains like wheat, which is the origin of certain intolerances in some children.*

In spite of all of these benefits, corn has three important nutritional deficits: Its proteins are of low quality, it does not provide sufficient niacin, and it is poor in calcium. These deficits are aggravated when corn is the primary element of the diet, particularly for babies.

Fortunately, these nutritional deficiencies can be corrected or ameliorated if corn is properly combined with other foods.

The famous Mexican tortillas combine very well with beans and legumes in general, which provide the lysine and calcium that are missing from corn. In contrast to other products made with corn, tortillas contain absorbable niacin that can be assimilated by the body. As a result, regular tortilla consumption does not raise the risk of niacin deficiency, which causes pellagra.

12

Foods for the Urinary Tract

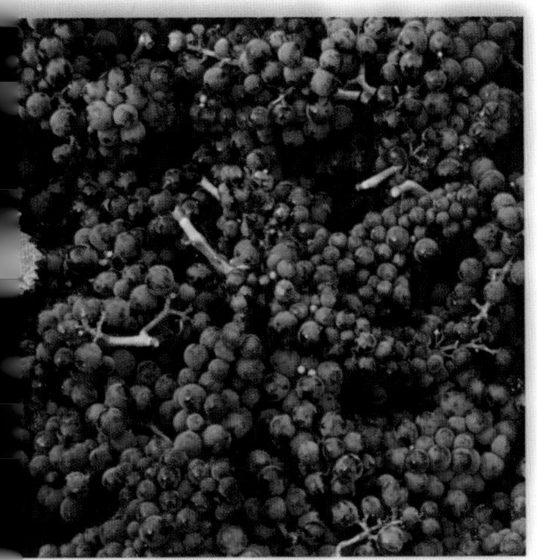

THE BLOOD not only conveys the oxygen and nutrients that are essential for life, but also assorted **toxic** and **foreign substances** that *must **be removed*** from the body. These substances come from:

• The body's own **metabolic processes.** When foods are utilized by the body, a series of toxins are generated that must be eliminated.

• **External contaminants** entering the body through food.

• **Medications** and foreign **chemical substances.**

The **kidneys** are the *primary* organs responsible for ***filtering*** and ***eliminating*** all of these toxic and foreign substances from the blood.

The kidneys' best allies

Fruits and **vegetables,** particularly those described in this chapter, are the foods that most facilitate the purifying function of the kidneys. Together with **water,** they are the kidneys' best allies.

Excess ***protein,*** particularly from animal sources, generates a great deal of waste products that must be eliminated, overloading the kidneys.

A diet of **plant-based** foods is the *most satisfactory* for ***preventing*** the formation of calculi or stones in the kidneys.[1]

The only precaution that must be taken is to *avoid* certain plant-based foods that are rich in ***oxalic acid,*** but *only* in cases where there is a ***tendency*** to form calcium oxalate stones.[2]

A study conducted at Washington State University (USA) formed a list of common foods that are rich in oxalic acid, increasing oxalate elimination through the urine. These are among those that should be avoided by those at risk of calcium oxalate stones: spinach, rhubarb, chard, nuts, chocolate, tea, bran, and strawberries.[3]

NEPHROSIS

Definition

This syndrome affecting the kidneys is characterized by the **loss of proteins** through the urine. This is due to excessive permeability of the **renal glomeruli** that filter the blood.

Nephrosis is usually one of the manifestations of a **variety** of kidney **diseases.** Its natural tendency is to evolve slowly toward **kidney failure** (see p. 231). It is accompanied by significant metabolic disorders, with increases in blood lipid and cholesterol levels.

Diet

A ***strict*** low-protein, low-sodium **vegetarian diet** has been shown to be the ***most effective*** means of controlling the progressive deterioration of the kidneys produced by nephrosis.

Increase

- FRUIT
- VEGETABLES
- WHOLE GRAINS
- SOY

Reduce or eliminate

- PROTEINS
- SHELLFISH
- MEAT
- TOTAL FAT
- SODIUM
- CHOLESTEROL

SCANTY URINE

All of these foods are **diuretic.** In other words, they ***stimulate* kidney** function and increase urine production. In reality, *most* **fruits** and **vegetables** are somewhat diuretic, but those described here are noted for this effect.

The increased urine output that these foods stimulate is *particularly beneficial* in ***reducing* edema** (fluid retention in the tissues) produced in cases of kidney and cardiac disease.

The diuretic effect of all of the foods described here is due to the ***phytochemicals*** that they contain, particularly ***flavonoids,*** non-nutritive components with healing powers.

One thing that all of these foods have in common is *very little* or *no* **sodium** content, and *richness* in **potassium.** This contributes to their diuretic effect since increased sodium intake results in fluid retention in the tissues (edema), and reduces urine volume.

Naturally, the diuretic action of these foods is much less intense than diuretic medications. However, they have the advantage that they can be used every day throughout life without risk of side effects.

Increase

- ARTICHOKE
- CELERY
- EGGPLANT
- BORAGE
- CAULIFLOWER
- ASPARAGUS
- RED MOMBIN
- GREEN BEAN
- APPLE
- PEACH
- MELON
- LOQUAT
- PEAR
- WATERMELON
- GRAPE

Celery

Celery's essential oil or essence is an effective diuretic. It also increases the elimination of waste products with the urine such as uric acid and urea.

RENAL LITHIASIS

Definition

Also called **nephrolithiasis, urolithiasis, urinary lithiasis,** or **kidney stones.** It consists of the formation of calculi or stones in the interior of the kidney. It may also occur in the urinary bladder, but less frequently.

Causes

The calculi or stones form because the substances normally dissolved in the urine precipitate and accumulate in a solid mass.

Most calculi are formed of **calcium oxalate, magnesium ammonium phosphate, calcium phosphate,** or **urates.** Once a calculus has been passed and been analyzed, a ***specialist*** can prescribe a *more specific* **diet** to help *avoid* the formation of ***new* calculi.**

Diet

The foods described here as either beneficial or detrimental are generally useful in most cases, and can contribute significantly to reduced risk of calculus formation.

Those who have suffered the excruciating pain of kidney stones normally wish to do everything possible to avoid a repeat of the experience. This includes certain modifications to dietary habits such as those described here.

Increase

WATER
DIURETIC FOODS (THE SAME AS FOR SCANTY URINE PRODUCTION)
LEMON
HAZELNUT
FIBER
MAGNESIUM

Reduce or eliminate

SALT
PROTEINS
DAIRY PRODUCTS
CHEESE
MEAT
ALCOHOLIC BEVERAGES
BEER
COFFEE
CHOCOLATE
CALCIUM
GREEN LEAFY VEGETABLES
VITAMIN C

Lemon has been successfully used in preventing, and even dissolving kidney stones. The lemon treatment is the most effective means of use.

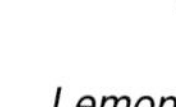

Lemon

KIDNEY FAILURE

Definition

This is the *loss of the kidneys' capacity to produce urine,* and expel the waste material produced within the body. There are two types of kidney failure:

- **Acute,** which requires hospitalization.
- **Chronic,** which is the type considered in this work. It typically evolves progressively throughout life. In serious cases, kidney **dialysis** becomes necessary to remove the toxins from the blood that the kidneys are no longer capable of eliminating through the urine.

Diet

A vegetarian diet has *many advantages* over the omnivorous diet in cases of kidney failure: generally, it contains less sodium and phosphorus, as well as *fewer* proteins and substances that overload the kidneys.

The foods whose consumption should be either increased or decreased, within the scope of a treatment plan established by a specialist, can contribute appreciably to improving the course of kidney failure.

Increase

DIURETIC FOODS (THE SAME AS FOR SCANTY URINE PRODUCTION)
ARTICHOKE
SQUASH
CHESTNUT
DATES
CORN
POTATO
FISH OIL

Reduce or eliminate

PROTEINS
SODIUM
SHELLFISH
MEAT
PHOSPHORUS
POTASSIUM
VITAMINS AND SUPPLEMENTS

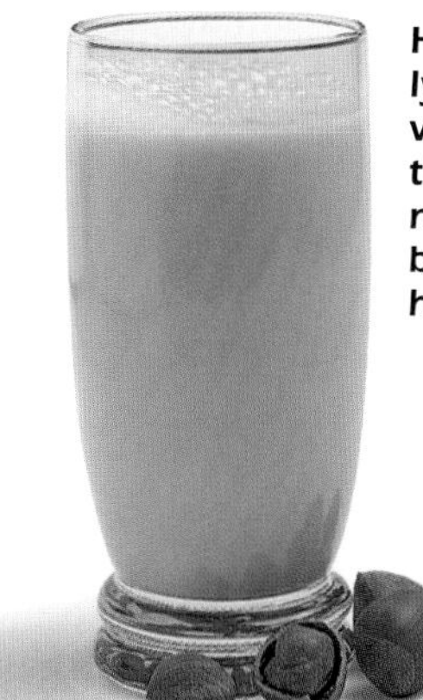

Hazelnut milk is a highly nutritious beverage, very well tolerated by the sick and the unnourished, which can be easily prepared at home.

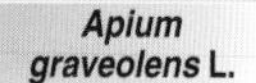

Celery

Cleanses the blood and reduces cholesterol

Celery is refreshing and invigorating.

CELERY composition
per 100 g of raw edible portion

Energy	16.0 kcal = 67.0 kj
Protein	0.750 g
Carbohydrates	1.95 g
Fiber	1.70 g
Vitamin A	13.0 µg RE
Vitamin B_1	0.046 mg
Vitamin B_2	0.045 mg
Niacin	0.490 mg NE
Vitamin B_6	0.087 mg
Folate	28.0 µg
Vitamin B_{12}	—
Vitamin C	7.00 mg
Vitamin E	0.360 mg α-TE
Calcium	40.0 mg
Phosphorus	25.0 mg
Magnesium	11.0 mg
Iron	0.400 mg
Potassium	287 mg
Zinc	0.130 mg
Total Fat	0.140 g
Saturated Fat	0.037 g
Cholesterol	—
Sodium	87.0 mg

1% 2% 4% 10% 20% 40% 100%

% Daily Value (based on a 2,000 calorie diet) provided by 100 g of this food

Synonyms: *Pascal celery, True celery.*

French: *Céleri;* ***Spanish:*** *Apio.*

Description: *The stalks and leaves of celery ('Apium graveolens' L.), a herbaceous plant of the botanical family Umbelliferae.*

THE TASTE of celery is unique. Its crunchy tender stalks do not go unnoticed in salads, no matter how many other ingredients it may contain. Moreover, it is precisely the essential oil responsible for its taste that also gives it most of its healthful properties.

PROPERTIES AND INDICATIONS: From a nutritional standpoint, celery does not stand out. It is quite poor in carbohydrates (1.9%) and proteins (0.75%) and has virtually no fat.

The active substances that it contains make it useful in the following cases:

• **Edema** (retention of liquids), **kidney stones, gout,** increase in **uric acid, arthritis** thanks to the *remarkable* **diuretic** *effect* of its ***essential oil.*** This oil causes a dilation of the renal arteries, with the consequent increase in urine volume and excretion of waste substances such as urea and uric acid.

• **Metabolic acidity:** Due to its richness in *alkalizing* ***mineral salts,*** celery acts as a *true* **alkalizer** capable of neutralizing excess acids in the body. A diet rich in meat and animal products produces excess acidity in the blood and internal organs, which has multiple negative health effects, such as increased calcium loss, the formation of renal calculi, and fluid retention, among others.

Celery, *particularly* if drunk as a broth **[❷]**, has an **alkalizing** and **remineralizing** effect similar to that of the onion (see p. 142). It neutralizes excess blood acid and facilitates the urinary elimination of metabolic acids.

• **Hypertension:** Celery contains considerable sodium (some 87 mg/100 g), thanks to which it is used to prepare ***celery salt.*** In spite of this, celery has a hypotensive effect since its essential oil contains an effective vasodilator called ***3-butylptalide.*** This, combined with its **diuretic** effect, makes it particularly beneficial to those suffering from hypertension.

Celery combines very well with onion both in broth and in salad. Both products act as alkalizers and to eliminate acidic metabolic residues.

• **Excess cholesterol:** An interesting experiment was conducted at the University of Singapore[4] to demonstrate celery's capacity to reduce blood cholesterol level. During eight weeks two groups of laboratory guinea pigs were fed a very high fat diet. Two tablespoons of celery juice were added to the daily diet of one of the groups. At the end of the eight weeks, these animals presented significantly lower cholesterol levels than those that had not been fed celery juice.

• **Diabetes:** Celery contains small amounts of ***glycoquin,*** a substance similar in action to insulin, which reduces blood sugar level. Thus, although celery contains a moderate amount of carbohydrates, it is indicated for diabetics.

• **Psoriasis:** Celery contains ***psoralens,*** substances that can produce hypersensitivity to sunlight in predisposed individuals.[5] These same substances provide a protective effect in cases of psoriasis, a disease that is difficult to treat, which is characterized by reddish eruptions and scales on the skin.

Preparation and use

❶ **Raw in salads:** Tender crunchy stalks are used.

❷ **Boiled:** This is used in preparing depurant broths, whether by itself or with onion, nettles, parsley, or cabbage.

❸ **Fresh juice:** This is made using stalks and leaves. One-half glass is drunk with each meal with lemon to taste.

Asparagus

Stimulates the kidneys

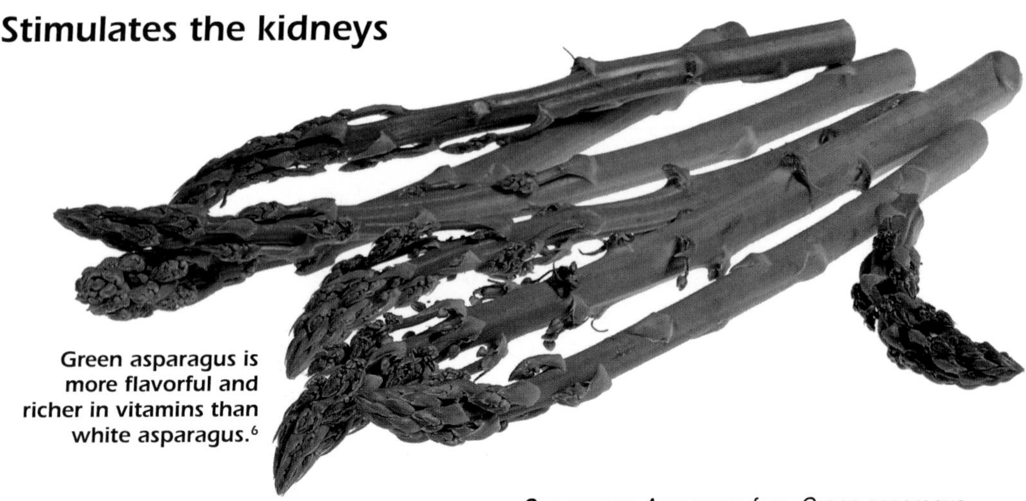

Green asparagus is more flavorful and richer in vitamins than white asparagus.[6]

Synonyms: *Asparagus fern, Green asparagus, White asparagus, Special bean.*

French: *Asperge;* ***Spanish:*** *Espárrago.*

Description: *Tender stalks and buds of the asparagus bed ('Asparagus officinalis' L.), aherbaceous plant of the botanical family Liliaceae that reaches a height of 1.5 m. The stalks are covered with tiny scalelike leaves'.*

ASPARAGUS composition
per 100 g of raw edible portion

Energy	23.0 kcal = 98.0 kj
Protein	2.28 g
Carbohydrates	2.44 g
Fiber	2.10 g
Vitamin A	58.0 µg RE
Vitamin B_1	0.140 mg
Vitamin B_2	0.128 mg
Niacin	1.54 mg NE
Vitamin B_6	0.131 mg
Folate	128 µg
Vitamin B_{12}	—
Vitamin C	13.2 mg
Vitamin E	2.00 mg α-TE
Calcium	21.0 mg
Phosphorus	56.0 mg
Magnesium	18.0 mg
Iron	0.870 mg
Potassium	273 mg
Zinc	0.460 mg
Total Fat	*0.200 g*
Saturated Fat	*0.046 g*
Cholesterol	—
Sodium	*2.00 mg*

1% 2% 4% 10% 20% 40% 100%

% Daily Value (based on a 2,000 calorie diet) provided by 100 g of this food

ANYONE who has ever eaten even a small amount of asparagus has noticed that after a few minutes the urine has a unique odor. This is due to asparagine, the active substance in asparagus that forms part of its volatile essential oil. It is eliminated with the urine, increasing its volume.

PROPERTIES AND INDICATIONS: From a nutritional standpoint, asparagus is one of the lowest calorie foods available: only 23 kcal /100 g. This is due to its virtual lack of fat and very low carbohydrate content. However, it is among the vegetables highest in proteins: 2.28%, an amount close to that of spinach (2.86%).

It contains considerable fiber (2.1%), B group vitamins, folates, and vitamins A (provitamin), C, and E. In terms of minerals, it provides sig-

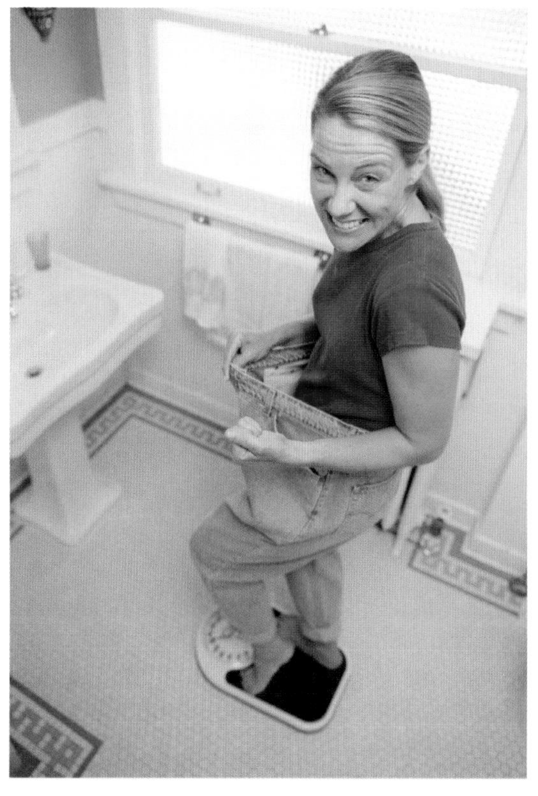

Asparagus provide few calories and quite a bit of fiber, so they contribute to producing a sensation of satiety in the stomach. Seasoned with a few drops of lemon juice, they are ideal in slimming diets.

These are its main applications:

- **Kidney disorders:** Asparagus is a good diuretic, which stimulates urine production in the kidneys. It aids in eliminating fluids retained in the tissues. Those suffering from nephritis (inflammation of the kidneys) should consume asparagus in moderation because of its significant stimulant effect on the kidneys.
- **Obesity,** because of its extremely low caloric content.
- **Eczema** of the skin, because of its depurant and detoxifying effect.
- **Constipation,** because of its dietary fiber content.

nificant amounts of potassium, phosphorous, iron, and magnesium, as well as various trace elements.[7] Taken together, this is a food that is quite rich in nutrients but low in calories.

Preparation and use

❶ **Cooked:** Asparagus is normally cooked for 5 to 10 minutes. It may also be fried or roasted. If the stalk is particularly tough, it should be peeled.

❷ **Canned:** Canned asparagus loses part of its vitamin content and fiber (hemicellulose),[6] but it retains its minerals and diuretic substances.

Watermelon

A gift to the kidneys

Scientific synonyms: *Cucurbia citrullus* L. = *Momordica lanata* Thunb.

Synonym: *Jubilee.*

French: *Melon d'eau, pastèque;*
Spanish: *Sandía, melón de agua.*

Description: *Fruit of the watermelon plant ('Citrullus lanatus' [Thumb.] Mansf.), a herbaceous creeping plant of the botanical family Cucurbitaceae, which produces from 3 to 5 fruits weighing from 3 to 10 kilos (about 6.6 to 22 lb; the "Florida Giant" may weigh up to 20 kilos, about 44 lb).*

WATERMELON composition
per 100 g of raw edible portion

Energy	32.0 kcal = 132 kj
Protein	0.620 g
Carbohydrates	6.68 g
Fiber	0.500 g
Vitamin A	37.0 µg RE
Vitamin B_1	0.080 mg
Vitamin B_2	0.020 mg
Niacin	0.317 mg NE
Vitamin B_6	0.144 mg
Folate	2.20 µg
Vitamin B_{12}	—
Vitamin C	9.60 mg
Vitamin E	0.150 mg α-TE
Calcium	8.00 mg
Phosphorus	9.00 mg
Magnesium	11.0 mg
Iron	0.170 mg
Potassium	116 mg
Zinc	0.070 mg
Total Fat	*0.430 g*
Saturated Fat	*0.048 g*
Cholesterol	—
Sodium	*2.00 mg*

1% 2% 4% 10% 20% 40% 100%

% Daily Value (based on a 2,000 calorie diet) provided by 100 g of this food

WATERMELON is a very refreshing fruit. Biting into its sweet-smelling pulp and feeling the mouth full of juice is a real hot-weather pleasure.

Watermelon, together with other melons, has quenched the thirst of humans for thousands of years. During their desert wanderings, the Israelites longed for the melons and watermelons that they had eaten in the land of the pyramids. Egypt and Mediterranean countries continue being the primary producers of this fruit.

Properties and indications: The watermelon's composition is similar to that of other melons, although it contains less vitamin C, folates, iron, and potassium, and somewhat more beta-carotene (provitamin A), vitamin B_1, and vitamin B_6.

Its properties are very similar to those of other melons (see p. 240): hydrating, remineraliz-

A good slice of watermelon is vastly superior as refreshment to bottled drinks. Children in particular take advantage of the refreshing and mineralizing effect of watermelon. It has been recently known that watermelons contain some amount of lycopene, the same carotenoid that is plentiful in tomatoes. Lycopene is the substance responsible for the red color in both the tomato and the watermelon. In the body it acts as a powerful antioxidant and as a protective factor against prostate cancer (see p. 266).

Preparation and use

❶ **Fresh:** This is usually how watermelon is eaten. It is not recommended as dessert, since it is somewhat indigestible because of its large water content.

❷ **Juice:** Watermelon juice is recommended for those with frail stomachs since it does not contain the pulp fiber, which may be indigestible.

ing, alkalizing, diuretic, and laxative. Watermelon may be even *more* **diuretic** *than* other **melons.**

Watermelon is indicated for **disorders involving the kidneys and the urinary tract** (kidney failure, lithiasis, infection), and whenever a **depurant treatment** is called for to remove toxins from the blood. Treatment with watermelon may be done by alternating the fresh fruit with its juice, which is better tolerated in the stomach.

Diabetics tolerate watermelon well because of its low sugar content. Since it only provides 32 kcal/100 g, and produces an immediate sensation of satiety, it is beneficial in **weight-loss treatments.**

Hazelnut

Preventer of kidney stones

HAZELNUT (FILBERT) composition
per 100 g of raw edible portion

Energy	632 kcal = 2,643 kj
Protein	13.0 g
Carbohydrates	9.20 g
Fiber	6.10 g
Vitamin A	7.00 µg RE
Vitamin B_1	0.500 mg
Vitamin B_2	0.110 mg
Niacin	4.74 mg NE
Vitamin B_6	0.612 mg
Folate	71.8 µg
Vitamin B_{12}	—
Vitamin C	1.00 mg
Vitamin E	23.9 mg α-TE
Calcium	188 mg
Phosphorus	312 mg
Magnesium	285 mg
Iron	3.27 mg
Potassium	445 mg
Zinc	2.40 mg
Total Fat	*62.6 g*
Saturated Fat	*4.60 g*
Cholesterol	—
Sodium	*3.00 mg*

1% 2% 4% 10% 20% 40% 100% 200% 500%
% Daily Value (based on a 2,000 calorie diet) provided by 100 g of this food

Synonyms: *Filbert, Turkish filbert, American hazelnut, European hazel, Cob, Cobnut, Chinese hazel.*

French: *Noisette;* ***Spanish:*** *Avellana.*

Description: *Seed of the fruit of the hazelnut tree ('Corylus avellana' L.), tree or bush of the botanical family Betulaceae that reaches 2 to 4 m in height. The seed is dicotyledonous and is enclosed in a hard, woody almost spherical pericarp measuring about 2 cm in diameter.*

Although the hazelnut is called an oil-bearing nut, the same as the almond or walnut (see pp. 58, 74), its edible portion is not the whole fruit, but rather the seed.

AT ONE TIME or another, every hiker, mountaineer, or cyclist has carried a handful of hazelnuts in the pocket because of the energy they provide. They go very well with raisins, dried figs, and dates (see pp. 91, 147, 148).

Properties and indications: In spite of being a highly concentrated food, hazelnuts are quite easily digested, easier even than almonds and walnuts. They provide so much energy that a small handful of hazelnuts (about 50 g) provides the necessary calories for an hour's worth of physical exercise (316 kcal).

The leaves of the hazelnut are beneficial in cases of varicose veins and hemorrhoids, both as an infusion and topical application.

The nutritional value of the hazelnut is similar to that of almonds. However, hazelnuts surpass almonds in calories, fats, vitamin B_1, and folates. On the other hand, almonds provide more proteins, calcium, phosphorous, iron, and niacin than hazelnuts.

Hazelnuts are a good source of ***fats*** (62%), ***proteins*** (13%), vitamins B_1 and B_6, and ***minerals*** (particularly calcium, phosphorous, magnesium, and manganese).

As with other nuts, hazelnuts contain virtually no provitamin A (beta-carotene) and vitamin C. They are relatively poor in carbohydrates. Because of this, it is of benefit for those involved in physical activity such as athletes, to combine them with dried fruits that are rich in carbohydrates such as raisins, dried figs, and dates.

The use of hazelnuts is particularly indicated in cases of:

- **Kidney stones:** Dr. ***Valnet,***[8] a distinguished French phytotherapist, underscores the benefits of hazelnuts in preventing the formation of kidney stones. Making them a regular part of the diet of those suffering from renal lithiasis, particularly in cases of **urate** calculi, gives positive results. A handful of hazelnuts every morning gives good results.
- **Diabetes:** Since they are low in carbohydrates and are a good source of energy, hazelnuts are a good complement to a diabetic diet.
- Whenever there is a need for higher energy levels: **athletes, youth,** and people **weakened** by debilitating disease. They are also beneficial as part of the diets of **pregnant** women.

Preparation and use

❶ **Raw:** When hazelnuts are eaten raw, they should be well chewed whether they are fresh from the tree or dried.

❷ **Roasted:** Roasted hazelnuts are tastier than raw, and are easier to digest for most individuals.

❸ **Oil:** Hazelnut oil is used very little because it becomes rancid very quickly.

❹ **Horchata:** After soaking hazelnuts for 8 hours, they are mashed to a homogenous paste. This is then mixed with water (one glass of water for each 30 g of hazelnuts) and left to soak for an additional two hours. After this, it is strained through a fine sieve. The liquid thus prepared is hazelnut horchata.

Melon

A source of living water

Synonyms: *Muskmelon, Sweet melon.*

French: *Melon;* ***Spanish:*** *Melón.*

Description: *Fruit of the melon plant ('Cucumis melo' L.), of the botanical family Cucurbitaceae.*

MELON composition
per 100 g of raw edible portion

Energy	26.0 kcal = 110 kj
Protein	0.900 g
Carbohydrates	5.40 g
Fiber	0.800 g
Vitamin A	3.00 µg RE
Vitamin B_1	0.060 mg
Vitamin B_2	0.020 mg
Niacin	0.400 mg NE
Vitamin B_6	0.120 mg
Folate	17.0 µg
Vitamin B_{12}	—
Vitamin C	16.0 mg
Vitamin E	0.150 mg α-TE
Calcium	5.00 mg
Phosphorus	7.00 mg
Magnesium	8.00 mg
Iron	0.400 mg
Potassium	210 mg
Zinc	0.160 mg
Total Fat	*0.100 g*
Saturated Fat	*0.025 g*
Cholesterol	—
Sodium	*12.0 mg*

1% 2% 4% 10% 20% 40% 100%

% Daily Value (based on a 2,000 calorie diet) provided by 100 g of this food

MODERN LIFE has not affected the picturesque melon stands in warm regions around the world. Farmers cut samples of melon so clients can test the sweet succulence of these delicious fruit for themselves. No ice cream or soft drink can quench the thirst of the hot months of summer as well as a juicy melon.

PROPERTIES AND INDICATIONS: Melons are, above all, ***water.*** The percentage of water content ranges from 90% to 95% depending on the variety. The water from melons, as with that from all juicy fruits, must not be confused with tap water or even pure spring water. It is ***not* passive, inert** water that is a simple vehicle for salts and solutions, but living water that has been in intimate contact with the protoplasm of vegetable cells. The water in melons is biological water that has been involved in the thousands, perhaps millions of chemical reactions that take place within living plant cells.

Those who complain that melon gives them indigestion should try eating it before or between meals.
It is better to eat melon before a meal than afterwards as a dessert. Eating it after a meal dilutes gastric juices and puddles the stomach, disturbing digestion.

This may be why nothing quenches summer thirst like a big slice of melon. Moreover, nothing is as helpful to the kidneys as the ***"plant serum"*** that is the water in melons.

Melons contain less ***sugar*** (5.4%) than other fruits, *virtually no* ***fat*** (0.1%), and a respectable amount of ***proteins*** (0.9%). However, above all, melons provide a *well-balanced* supply of ***vitamins*** and ***minerals.*** Most notable are vitamins C, B_6, B_1, and folates, but small amounts of the remaining vitamins, except B_{12}, are present, as well.

Melons contain all ***mineral*** nutrients, notably ***potassium, iron,*** and ***magnesium.*** One 2.5 kg melon contains the daily need for iron for an adult male (10 mg), and more than half of the magnesium requirement, which is 350 mg.

Melons are hydrating, remineralizing, alkalizing, diuretic, and laxative.

Their most important indications are:

• **Urinary conditions:** Melon consumption enriches the blood with mineral salts and vitamins and facilitates the filtering capacity of the kidneys. After eating melon, the kidneys are better able to effectively remove waste material and toxins produced through metabolic processes. Melons' ***"living water"*** and their dissolved minerals are major contributors to this.

Melons can benefit all who wish to improve **renal function** and particularly those suffering from:

– Early stage **kidney failure,** whose **primary symptoms** are fluid retention and scanty urine output.

– **Kidney stones** and **granules,** particularly those that are uric in composition. Thanks to their *remarkable* **alkalizing** *ability,* melons increase the solubility of the acidic salts that make up uric calculi, and facilitate their dissolution and elimination.

– **Urinary infections** (pyelonephritis, cystitis): Although melons are not urinary antiseptics, their **alkalizing** effect in the urine helps stop the proliferation of the coliform bacilli that cause urinary infections (Escherichia coli and others), which require an acidic medium to grow.

• Excess uric acid, manifested by **uratic** (gouty) **arthritis** and **gout.**

• Chronic **constipation** due to intestinal atony.

• **Dehydration** accompanied by mineral loss, as occurs in diarrhea, excessive perspiration, or fever crises. Although melons are laxative, they may be used without difficulty in case of diarrhea caused by gastroenteritis.

Preparation and use

❶ **Fresh:** This is the best way to eat melons. They are not recommended as dessert since the large amount of liquid they contain interferes with digestion.

❷ **Preserves:** Melons are used to make a variety of delicious confiture and jams.

Eggplant

Diuretic and digestive

EGGPLANT composition
per 100 g of raw edible portion

Energy	26.0 kcal = 107 kj
Protein	1.02 g
Carbohydrates	3.57 g
Fiber	2.50 g
Vitamin A	8.00 µg RE
Vitamin B_1	0.052 mg
Vitamin B_2	0.034 mg
Niacin	0.748 mg NE
Vitamin B_6	0.084 mg
Folate	19.0 µg
Vitamin B_{12}	—
Vitamin C	1.70 mg
Vitamin E	0.030 mg α-TE
Calcium	7.00 mg
Phosphorus	22.0 mg
Magnesium	14.0 mg
Iron	0.270 mg
Potassium	217 mg
Zinc	0.140 mg
Total Fat	*0.180 g*
Saturated Fat	*0.034 g*
Cholesterol	—
Sodium	*3.00 mg*

1% 2% 4% 10% 20% 40% 100%

% Daily Value (based on a 2,000 calorie diet)
provided by 100 g of this food

Synonyms: *Guinea squash, Aubergine, Brinjal.*

French: *Aubergine;* ***Spanish:*** *Berenjena.*

Description: *Fruit of eggplant ('Solanum melongena' L.), an annual herbaceous plant of the botanical family Solanaceae.*

FEW VEGETABLES come in such a wide variety of shapes, sizes, and colors. Eggplants are round, oval, elongated like bananas, small as eggs, or large as melons. Their skin may be purple, green, yellow, reddish, and even white. They have only one characteristic in common: the whitish color of its flesh and seeds.

PROPERTIES AND INDICATIONS: The flesh of the eggplant, which is botanically a fruit, contains a certain amount of carbohydrates, very little protein, and virtually no fat. Vitamins and minerals are present in small amounts, the most notable being potassium, calcium, sulfur, iron, and vitamins B and C.

Thanks to its diuretic action, roasted eggplants are very adequate for those who have suffered from kidney stones and wish to prevent their recurrence.

These are its properties:

- **Diuretic:** Eggplant increases urine output, stimulating the filtering capacity of the kidneys. Eating them is of benefit in cases of renal **lithiasis** (kidney stones), **edema** (fluid retention), **hypertension,** and **cardiovascular** disease.

- **Digestive tonic:** Eggplant *promotes* biliary function, gently stimulating **biliary** discharge as well as production of **pancreatic juice.** It is beneficial for those suffering from **slow digestion** and **biliary dyspepsia.**

- Gentle **laxative** because of its cellulose (vegetable ***fiber***) content.

- **Cancer prevention:** Recent investigations have shown that fruits from the family Solanaceae, such as the eggplant, as well as the tomato (see p. 264), are *very rich* in ***phytochemicals.*** These substances protect against the formation of cancers.

Preparation and use

❶ **Cooked** (*never raw*) in many culinary preparations. Fried eggplant is the least digestible. The *healthiest* form of preparation is **baked** and seasoned with oil and garlic. When served with peppers, it forms a typical Catalan dish, *escalivada.*

Caution

*Eggplants contain a certain amount of **solanine,** a substance that almost completely disappears when the fruit is completely ripe.*

*Solanine is a toxic alkaloid that produces **digestive disturbances,** but it **disappears with the heat** of cooking.*

*Because of this, eggplants must **always** be eaten **ripe and cooked.***

Blueberry

Prevents and treats cystitis

Related species: *See box p. 247.*

Synonyms: *Highbush blueberry, late sweet blueberry.*

French: *Airelle;* ***Spanish:*** *Arándano.*

Description: *The fruit of any of several plants of the genus 'Vaccinium'. They are small berries of dark blue color. The plants are deciduous small bushes of the family Ericaceae, reaching from 25 to 50 cm in height.*

BLUEBERRY composition
per 100 g of raw edible portion

Energy	56.0 kcal = 236 kj
Protein	0.670 g
Carbohydrates	11.4 g
Fiber	2.70 g
Vitamin A	10.0 µg RE
Vitamin B_1	0.048 mg
Vitamin B_2	0.050 mg
Niacin	0.409 mg NE
Vitamin B_6	0.036 mg
Folate	6.40 µg
Vitamin B_{12}	—
Vitamin C	13.0 mg
Vitamin E	1.00 mg α-TE
Calcium	6.00 mg
Phosphorus	10.0 mg
Magnesium	5.00 mg
Iron	0.170 mg
Potassium	89.0 mg
Zinc	0.110 mg
Total Fat	*0.380 g*
Saturated Fat	*0.032 g*
Cholesterol	—
Sodium	*6.00 mg*

1% 2% 4% 10% 20% 40% 100%

% Daily Value (based on a 2,000 calorie diet)
provided by 100 g of this food

BLUEBERRIES are small fruits rarely reaching more than a centimeter in diameter, and growing on a small, unobtrusive bush. Some may think they are insignificant.

Traditionally, these small wild fruits have been relegated to a role of garnish to other foods, or as confiture or filling for pies and pastries.

However, this small fruit of the woods contains great possibilities. Recent years have produced a proliferation of investigative works highlighting the remarkable dietary and therapeutic virtues of the blueberries.

PROPERTIES AND INDICATIONS: Blueberries contain an average of 11.4% carbohydrates, *most* of which are ***fructose*** and other sugars. They have *very little* ***fat*** and ***protein.*** Among its minerals the most significant is ***potassium,*** and among its ***vitamins,*** vitamin ***A.***

However, their **medicinal properties** are due to other non-nutritive components, such as **organic acids, tannin, myrtilin** (glucoside pigment), and **anthocyanins,** all of which give them antiseptic, vascular-protective, and astringent properties.

These are its indications:

- **Urinary infections:** blueberry and cranberry juices have *remarkable* **antiseptic** and **antibiotic** effects on the germs that cause urinary infections, particularly *Escherichia coli.* This has been proven in recent years and is the most important application of this fruits.

The most studied species regarding this antiseptic effect within the urinary system are two that are grown in North America:

- **Cranberry** *(Vaccinium oxycoccus),*
- **American cranberry** *(Vaccinium macrocarpon).*

All of these species are similar in composition and effects. Therefore, blueberries have similar antiseptic properties as the more studied cranberries.

Cranberries and blueberries have two significant advantages over most of the antibiotics used to treat repeated infections of the lower urinary tract (cystitis):

- They ***prevent*** the **adherence of bacteria** to the cells that line the interior of the urinary bladder.[9] This adherence is a persistent phenomenon in lower urinary tract infections such as cystitis, and partially explains the frequent reinfections that are common when treatment is based on regular antibiotics.
- They do ***not*** provoke bacterial **resistance** to this antibiotic effect, a phenomenon that is common with antibiotics.

Cranberry juice, in particular **[❸]** is a medicinal food recommended in cases of chronic or relapsing **cystitis.** Drinking 300 ml (a large glass) of cranberry juice a day, was sufficient to halve the incidence of bacteriuria and pyuria (presence of bacteria and pus in the urine, respectively) in a group of women with a propensity toward repeated cystitis.[9, 10] Naturally, it may be assumed that freshly collected juice will be even more effective.

To be effective in cases of repeated cystitis, it is necessary to drink cranberry juice daily from

Preparation and use

❶ **Fresh:** Blueberries and cranberries can be stored fresh for only a brief period. They are best when eaten at harvest and combine very well with milk or yogurt.

❷ **Juice:** This is obtained by squeezing the fresh, ripe fruit. A simple way to do this is to strain the fruit and filter the resulting liquid.

❸ **Preserves:** blueberries and cranberries are used to prepare compotes, juices, jams and jellies.

Cranberry treatment

*This treatment is based on **fresh** fruit that has either been **pureed** or cooked. For a period of **three to five** consecutive days, one eats from **half a kilo to one kilo** a day distributed into **four sittings,** as the **only food.***

Children** or **frail** individuals may also have **milk.

*This treatment eliminates **oxyurids,** tiny intestinal parasites that are fairly common in children.*

Common blueberries are dark blue in color, but there are other species, cranberries, that are red. All of these species have a juicy, bittersweet, and aromatic pulp. Cranberries tend to be somewhat more acidic.
Cranberries are ideal for women, since they are effective in cases of urinary infection and help improve venous circulation in the legs.

one to three months. In persistent cases, there is no adverse risk in continuing up to six months.

• **Kidney stones:** Cranberries and blueberries contain ***quinic acid,*** a substance eliminated through the urine.[11] This substance acidifies the urine and helps prevent the formation of calcium phosphate calculi (it does not affect other types of calculi). Cranberry juice can even help dissolve calcium phosphate calculi that are already present.

• **Infectious diarrhea:** The **antimicrobial action** of cranberries and blueberries is effective within the digestive tract, as well, together with the astringent effect of ***tannins.*** These normalize and rebalance the intestinal flora, preventing the excessive proliferation of *Escherichia coli,* the most common germ within the intestine. Blueberries and cranberries are particularly indicated in cases of **disbacteriosis** (disturbance of the intestinal bacterial flora), generally due to the use of antibiotics. They are very effective against **flatulence** (excess intestinal gas).

• **Circulatory disorders:** Blueberries act to protect the walls of the capillaries and veins because of their ***anthocyanin*** content. They reduce inflammation and swelling in the tissues. Their regular consumption is recommended in cases of swollen **lower extremities, varicose veins, phlebitis,** and **varicose ulcers,** as well as **hemorrhoids.**

• **Vision loss due to retinal deterioration:** The ***anthocyanins*** (substances responsible for the color in this group of fruits, more abundant in blue species) in blueberries improve retinal function and visual acuity.

Thus, blueberries and cranberries are highly recommended in cases of **diabetes, hypertension,** or **arteriosclerosis,** diseases that affect the retina, producing a loss of visual acuity.

Blueberries and Cranberries

All blueberries and cranberries belong to the genus *Vaccinium* and are similar in composition and properties, with some differences.

The primary difference in classification is by color:

Blueberries

These are dark blue or purple in color and have the following characteristics:

- They are sweeter than cranberries.
- They are richer in ***anthocyanins.***
- They are *recommended* for **circulatory disorders** (varicose veins, hemorrhoids) and those of the **retina,** although they are also effective against **cystitis** and **diarrhea.**

- **Bilberry** (*Vaccinium myrtillus* L.): Described in page 244, also known as huckleberry and whortleberry. It is a wild European relative of the blueberry. It also grows in California and the American Southwest. Wild bilberries are typically 0.5 to 1.0 cm in diameter and very rich in medicinal ingredients.
- **Highbush blueberry*** (*Vaccinium corymbosum* L.): Similar to the bilberry, but larger. Its juicy berries measure up to 2.5 cm in diameter. They are widely cultivated in North America.
- **Lowbush blueberry** (*Vaccinium angustifolium*): These are raised in the northeastern United States (the state of Maine) and Canada (the province of Quebec). The fruit measures from 1 to 1.5 cm.

Bilberry
('Vaccinium myrtillus')

Cranberry
('Vaccinium oxycoccus')

Cranberries

- These are bitterer than blueberries.
- They contain more **acidifying** substances that affect the urine.
- They are *more effective* for **infections** of the **urinary** and **digestive tracts.**

- **Cranberry**** (*Vaccinium oxycoccus* L.): Found in northern regions of Europe and North America. Their fruit is bright red and measures from 0.5 to 1.0 cm in diameter. These are the bitterest of the Vaccinium.
- **American cranberry***** (*Vaccinium macrocarpon*): It is similar to cranberry, but somewhat larger, and slightly oval.
- **Cowberry****** (*Vaccinium vitisidaea* L.): These grow in temperate and cold regions of the Northern Hemisphere. Their red aggregate fruits are somewhat acid.

* ***Synonyms:*** *Blueberry;* ***Fr.:*** *Myrtille;* ***Sp.:*** *Arándano americano.*

** ***Synonyms:*** *European cranberry;* ***Fr.:*** *Canneberge, airelle des marais;* ***Sp.:*** *Arándano agrio.*

*** ***Synonyms:*** *[large American] Cranberry;* ***Sp.:*** *Arándano trepador.*

**** ***Synonyms:*** *Foxberry;* ***Fr.:*** *Airelle rouge;* ***Sp.:*** *Arándano rojo.*

13

Foods for the Reproductive System

DIET HAS a significant impact on both male and female reproductive organs. A diet that provides the daily 25 g of fiber for an adult contributes significantly to preventing the pain and other variations of the menstrual cycle. Fiber is found *only* in **plant-based** foods such as **fruits, whole grains, vegetables** (including leafy greens), and **legumes.** This is confirmed by a study at the University of British Columbia in Vancouver (Canada), which found that vegetarian women had fewer ovulation problems than omnivorous women.[1]

Soy and its derivatives such as **tofu** or **soymilk,** contain ***phytoestrogens*** that regularize the menstrual cycle, prevent excessive prostate growth and reduce the risk of cancer. They have no feminizing effect, in contrast to estrogen hormones.[2]

FIBROCYSTIC MASTOPATHY

Definition

This is a *benign disease* of the breast characterized by the appearance of small, occasionally painful, **cysts** that vary in size throughout the menstrual cycle. It typically affects women between 30 and 50 years of age. It is referred to as benign since its course is not serious or life-threatening, as opposed to breast cancer.

In some cases, cysts are associated with **fibromas** or **fibroadenomas,** which are hard nodules of constant size and not typically painful.

Diet

It is a well-established fact that **diet** is a fundamental factor in the genesis of breast disease, both benign and cancerous.

Increase

FIBER
VITAMIN A
VITAMIN E

Reduce or eliminate

SATURATED FAT
MEAT
STIMULANT BEVERAGES

Red meat

Bacon

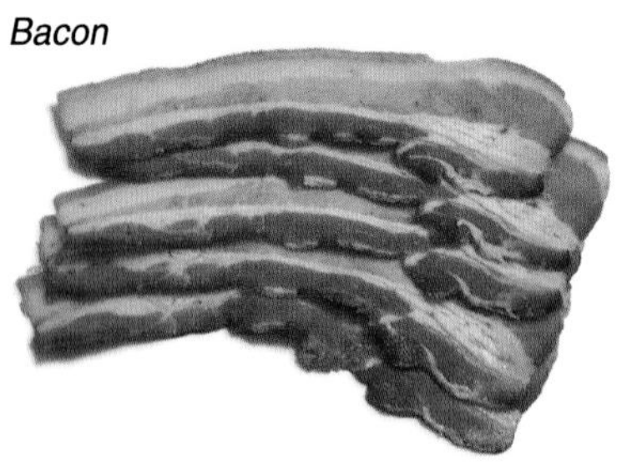

The relationship between saturated fats (primarily that of animal origin) and breast cancer is well known. It has also been demonstrated that the more fat is consumed, the greater risk of breast fibromas and cysts.[3]

DYSMENORRHEA

Definition

This is an *irregular* and *painful menstrual cycle* that affects general health. In some cases it is associated with **premenstrual syndrome** (PMS), a disorder experienced in days prior to menstruation. **Fluid retention** (particularly in the breasts) and **changes** in **mood** are characteristics of PMS.

Causes

Although dysmenorrhea may have organic or hormonal causes, a healthful diet can contribute a great deal of relief. Soy and its derivatives, as well as other legumes, contain substances that act as hormones called ***phytoestrogens,*** which can help regulate the menstrual cycle.

Diet

On the other hand, an **artificial diet** based on refined and processed products ***aggravates*** dysmenorrhea.

Increase

SOY
DIURETIC FOODS
FIBER
OILS
VITAMINS, SUPPLEMENTS
MAGNESIUM
FLAVONOIDS

Reduce or eliminate

SALT
STIMULANT BEVERAGES
SUGARS

In general, all vegetable oils rich in polyunsaturated fatty acids (corn, soy, grape seed, wheat germ, etc.) are beneficial. Primrose oil and fish oil, taken as dietary supplements, can reduce cramping and uterine pain.

SEXUAL IMPOTENCE

Definition

Sexual impotence is the condition that some men experience when they cannot obtain or maintain an erection that is sufficiently firm to permit coitus or copulation. Sexual impotence is not cured with products or substances that increase sexual desire since the issue is not desire but the capacity to perform.

Causes

Sexual **potency** is a *consequence* of **good health,** both physical and mental. All unhealthful foods reduce sexual potency and promote impotence.

Life Style

The use of **tobacco, alcoholic** beverages, and **coffee** is one of the *most common **causes*** of impotence. Arteriosclerosis and diabetes also cause this disorder since they reduce blood circulation in the arteries of the penis.

Increase

- ANTIOXIDANTS
- WHEAT GERM
- ZINC

Reduce or eliminate

- ALCOHOLIC BEVERAGES
- CHOLESTEROL
- SATURATED FAT
- STIMULANT BEVERAGES

Fruits and vegetables

Antioxidants prevent arteriosclerosis and improve blood flow to the arteries that supply the erectile tissue of the penis, which allow erection. Provitamin A and vitamins C and E are the natural substances with greatest antioxidant power, all of which are vegetable in origin. A diet rich in fruits, whole grains, and vegetables contribute to the maintenance of sexual potency better than any other food or product.

PROSTATIC ADENOMA

Definition

This is also known as benign prostatic hypertrophy, is an enlargement of the prostate that affects men over the age of 50.

When the size of this gland is larger than normal, it compresses the urethra (urinary duct) that passes through it, making urination difficult. This benign disease is not related to prostate cancer (see Chapter 18).

Diet

Although due to hormonal causes, certain foods can postpone or relieve hypertrophy of this gland, while others that irritate the urinary tract, aggravate it.

Increase

- TOMATO
- SOY
- NUTS
- ZINC
- SELENIUM
- FIBER

Reduce or eliminate

- SPICES
- COFFEE

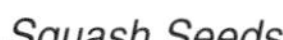

Squash Seeds

Zinc deficiency can promote excess prostate growth. Shellfish, particularly oysters, contain zinc, but they are not a healthful source of this mineral. Wheat germ, sesame, maple sugar, oil-bearing nuts, squash seeds, and legumes are also rich in zinc and present none of the risks of shellfish.

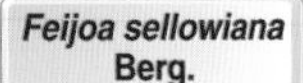

Feijoa

Ideal for pregnancy

FEIJOA composition
per 100 g of raw edible portion

Energy	49.0 kcal = 205 kj
Protein	1.24 g
Carbohydrates	6.13 g
Fiber	4.50 g
Vitamin A	—
Vitamin B_1	0.008 mg
Vitamin B_2	0.032 mg
Niacin	0.289 mg NE
Vitamin B_6	0.050 mg
Folate	38.0 µg
Vitamin B_{12}	—
Vitamin C	20.3 mg
Vitamin E	—
Calcium	17.0 mg
Phosphorus	20.0 mg
Magnesium	9.00 mg
Iron	0.080 mg
Potassium	155 mg
Zinc	0.040 mg
Total Fat	*0.780 g*
Saturated Fat	—
Cholesterol	—
Sodium	*3.00 mg*

1% 2% 4% 10% 20% 40% 100%

% Daily Value (based on a 2,000 calorie diet) provided by 100 g of this food

Scientific synonym: *Acca sellowiana* (Berg.) Burret.

Synonyms: *[Pineapple] guava, Guavasteen.*

French: *Goyave de Montevideo;*
Spanish: *Feijoa, guayaba-piña.*

Description: *Fruit of the feijoa tree ('Feijoa sellowiana' Berg.), of the botanical family Myrtaceae that reaches 7 m in height.*

THE FEIJOA is related to the guava (see p. 118) and both belong to the same botanical family. Its pulp, cream or salmon-colored, is soft and gelatinous, and its flavor is reminiscent of pineapple. Although the center of the fruit is filled with small seeds, they are soft and barely noticeable when eating the fruit.

Properties and indications: The feijoa contains small amounts of fat and protein, and, in greater percentage, carbohydrates. It is quite rich in ***vitamin C*** (about 20 mg/100 g), although much less than the guava (183 mg

The feijoa is beneficial to pregnant women because of its richness in folates, iodine, and vegetable fiber.

/100 g). It also contains small amounts of B group vitamins and minerals. Its composition is remarkable for these nutrients:

✓ ***Folates:*** The feijoa is among the *richest* of fresh fruits in these substances, which are essential for the formation of **blood** cells. *Lack* of folates during **pregnancy** *can lead* to **anemia,** as well as fetal birth **defects.**

✓ ***Iodine:*** This fruit's content of this trace element (50 to 100 µg/100 g) is greater than other fruits and approximates saltwater fish (150 to 350 µg/100 g).

The feijoa is particularly indicated in the following cases:

- **Pregnancy,** because of its rich supply of folates and iodine, which are very important during gestation.
- **Goiter** caused by **hypothyroidism** when this is the result of insufficient iodine in the diet.
- **Constipation,** because of its richness in vegetable fiber.

Preparation and use

❶ **Raw:** The fruit must be peeled. Some varieties are somewhat coarse, particularly when they are not completely ripe.

❷ **Culinary preparations:** The feijoa lends itself well to the preparation of juices, compotes, and jams.

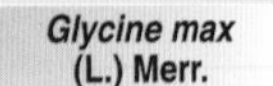

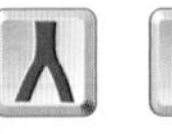

Soybean

The superlegume

Per equal weight, soybeans contain more proteins and iron than meat, more calcium than milk, and more vitamins B_1, B_2 and B_6 than eggs; and all of this with no cholesterol.

Scientific synonyms: *Dolichos soja,* L., *Phaseolus max* L., *Soy hispida* Moench.

Synonym: *Soy.*

French: *Soja;* ***Spanish:*** *Soja, soya.*

Description: *Soybeans are the seeds of the soy plant ('Glycine max' [L.] Merr.), a herbaceous plant of the botanical family Leguminosae that grows to a height from half a meter to one meter. The spheroid seeds, or soybeans, are 8 to 10 mm in diameter and grow within a pod similar to that of peas.*

SOYBEAN composition
per 100 g of raw edible portion

Energy	416 kcal = 1,742 kj
Protein	36.5 g
Carbohydrates	20.9 g
Fiber	9.30 g
Vitamin A	2.00 µg RE
Vitamin B_1	0.874 mg
Vitamin B_2	0.870 mg
Niacin	10.5 mg NE
Vitamin B_6	0.377 mg
Folate	375 µg
Vitamin B_{12}	—
Vitamin C	6.00 mg
Vitamin E	1.95 mg α-TE
Calcium	277 mg
Phosphorus	704 mg
Magnesium	280 mg
Iron	15.7 mg
Potassium	1,797 mg
Zinc	4.89 mg
Total Fat	*19.9 g*
Saturated Fat	*2.88 g*
Cholesterol	—
Sodium	*2.00 mg*

1% 2% 4% 10% 20% 40% 100% 200% 500%

% Daily Value (based on a 2,000 calorie diet)
provided by 100 g of this food

THOSE THAT have made a careful study of the Japanese language have discovered that, surprisingly, there is no word referring to a "hot flash," the vasomotor symptom characterized by sudden vasodilation with a sensation of heat commonly suffered by menopausal women. Obviously, this is not because Japanese women do not experience menopause, but simply because they pass this period of hormonal change without symptoms.

Soon, investigators found that Japanese and Chinese women, in addition to not experiencing menopausal problems, have a lower incidence of breast cancer. Besides, not only women, but also men in the Far East experienced better reproductive health and lower cholesterol.

The explanation for all of this is not found in genetic or racial factors, but rather in lifestyle, specifically, diet. As is well known, Far Eastern cultures derive the bulk of their protein not from meat, but from legumes such as soy, and, to a lesser degree, from fish.

Numerous studies confirm that soy specifically, which many Japanese, Chinese, and Koreans eat daily, is responsible for their better reproductive health and lower levels of breast and prostate cancer.

Soy is a staple food in China where it has been cultivated for more than three millennia. Its use spread to Japan in the seventh century of the Christian era. It did not arrive in Europe until a thousand years later, the 17th century. It was first cultivated in the United States in the 19th century.

It was not until well into the 20th century that soy was used as food for humans in North America and Europe. Fortunately, recent decades have brought new discoveries highlighting the healing properties of this food. Consequently, it is receiving the attention it deserves, although three thousand years late!

PROPERTIES AND INDICATIONS: The soybean is possibly the richest natural food that exists in proteins, vitamins, and minerals. It contains valuable phytochemicals, as well. Its extraordinary capacity to nourish and prevent disease is better understood by reviewing its composition:

✓ ***Protein:*** Soy is nature's richest source of proteins. It contains 36.5%; meat, with 20%, and eggs, with 12.5%, fall far behind.

However, quantity is only part of the story. Soy offers **quality.** Its proteins meet the amino acid needs of the body, both for adults and children.[4]

Generally, legume proteins are deficient in the essential sulfurated amino acid methionine. However, soy protein contains enough of this important amino acid to meet adult needs (but not those of nursing infants), and, thus be considered complete. The biological value of soy protein is comparable to that of meat.

Preparation and use

❶ **Cooked soybeans:** These beans must be soaked for several hours and then boiled for 60 to 90 minutes, preparing them as any other legume. Their flavor is rather unique, and not necessarily to everyone's taste. Mung beans or so-called **green soy,** and **adzuki** (see p. 256) are *more appropriate* than common soybeans for cooking.

❷ **Flour:** This is available in two types: defatted (50% protein) and whole (40% protein). Either type, when mixed with wheat flour, increases nutritional value and produces a dough that is very suitable for a variety of bakery applications, without the need for adding eggs (soy lecithin acts as an emulsifier, just as does the lecithin in eggs). Many delicious vegetarian dishes may be based on soy flour.

❸ **Soy protein:** This is available in a variety of forms (concentrated, isolated, or texturized). Its protein concentration ranges from 70% to 96%. It is particularly suited to preparing meatless dishes.

❹ **Soymilk:** Also referred to as soy beverage, this is a substitute for cow's milk, but with less calcium and no vitamin B_{12}.

❺ **'Tofu', 'miso', 'tempeh'** (see p. 258).

Green Soy and Adzuki

Green Soy

The so-called green soy or mung bean (*Vigna radiata* [L.] Wilczek) is originally from India and is gaining in popularity because of its pleasant taste and digestibility. It is eaten **boiled** after it has been soaked, as is the case with all legumes. (Cooking time: approximately 45 minutes). They may also be eaten as **sprouts.**

Adzuki

Adzuki (*Vigna angularis* [Willd.] Ohwi et Ohashi), is also appropriate cooked, although it requires a longer cooking time than green soy (50-60 minutes). It is also very nutritious and tasty.

Experiments carried out by the French National Institute of Agronomic Research, show that soy proteins are **digested** and **absorbed** as *easily* as those of cow's **milk.**[5]

✓ ***Fat:*** In contrast to other legumes such as beans or lentils that contain less than 1% fat, soy can reach 19.9%. Since soy's ***fatty acids*** are primarily ***unsaturated,*** soy fat *helps* ***reduce* cholesterol** level.

✓ ***Carbohydrates:*** These make up 20.9% of their weight, and are composed of a variety of oligosaccaharides, saccharose, and a small amount of starch. In contrast to other legumes such as lentils, beans, mung beans, or adzuki, which are rich in starch, soy contains very little. Thus, they are *well tolerated* by **diabetics.**

✓ ***Vitamins:*** One hundred grams of soy provide half of the daily requirements of vitamins B_1 and B_2, and 20% of the need for vitamins B_6 and E. This surpasses all other legumes. However, in common with all legumes (except sprouts), soy is poor in vitamin C and contains very little provitamin A.

✓ ***Minerals:*** Soy contains high amounts of minerals: One hundred grams provide 15.7 mg of iron, five times more than meat, an amount that more than meets the daily need of an adult male for this mineral. Even though it is ***non-heme iron,*** which is more difficult to absorb than the heme iron found in meat, the simultaneous presence of vitamin C in the intestine from fresh fruits and vegetables eaten in the same meal significantly increases absorption of iron from soy.

Soy is also very rich in ***phosphorus, magnesium,*** and ***potassium:*** One hundred grams provide for most of the daily requirement of these minerals. It is also quite rich in calcium. On the other hand, soy has the advantage of containing *virtually no* ***sodium,*** a mineral that causes fluid retention in the tissues. This makes it very suitable in cases of cardiovascular disease.

Soy is also a good source of the trace elements ***copper, zinc,*** and ***manganese.***

✓ ***Fiber:*** Soy contains 9.3% fiber, most of which is soluble. However, products derived from soy contain much less fiber (tofu, for example, contains 1.2%). Soy fiber contributes to regularity in the digestive tract and reduces cholesterol level.

✓ ***Non-nutritive substances:*** Soybeans contain an abundance of chemical substances that are not nutrients in the strict sense of the word, but they are remarkably active within the body. Some of these, such as isoflavones, are considered phytochemicals. The discovery of these substances constitutes one of the greatest advances in nutrition science in recent years. These are the most noteworthy:

- ***ISOFLAVONES:*** These constitute soy's most important non-nutritive component, which is responsible for most of its therapeutic properties. These are a type of ***phytoestrogen*** (vegetable-based female hormone), with a similar effect as estrogen, but without its undesirable side effects.

  The most important soy isoflavones are ***genistein*** (discovered in 1987) and ***daidzein.*** Some researchers assert that soy products supply between 100 and 200 mg of isoflavones per 100 g,[6] while others view the amounts as somewhat less. Soy oil and soy-based baby formulas do not contain them.

- ***PHYTOSTEROLS:*** These substances are similar to cholesterol, but are of vegetable origin. Their effect is to block absorption of the cholesterol contained in foods, thus reducing its level in the blood.

- ***PROTEASE INHIBITORS:*** These substances are present in soy, and, to a lesser degree, in other legumes. In large doses, such as in raw soy, they are toxic and are considered an antinutritive factor.[7] However, processing soy (cooking, soaking, fermentation, etc.) reduces their concentration a great deal.

  In low doses, such as that found in cooked soy or its derivatives, protease inhibitors have a valuable **anticarcinogenic** effect due to mechanisms that are not well understood.[8]

- ***PHYTIC ACID:*** This is found primarily in grain bran and in soy, as well. Although it interferes with the absorption of iron and other minerals, it is capable of neutralizing the action of carcinogens found in foods.[9]

As can be seen, soy is highly nutritious (it supplies 416 kcal/100 g) and very rich in active ingredients that explain its dietary and therapeutic indications:

• **Women's disorders:** Eating soy and its derivatives helps women maintain hormonal balance because of its isoflavones (vegetable estrogens). The benefits derived are the following:

- **Regulation of the menstrual cycle,** particularly in pre-menopausal women.[10]
- **Relief from the symptoms of menopause: *Regular consumption*** of soy or

Soy is the most widely cultivated legume in the world, possibly because it requires no fertilizer and It produces more higher quality protein in less time.

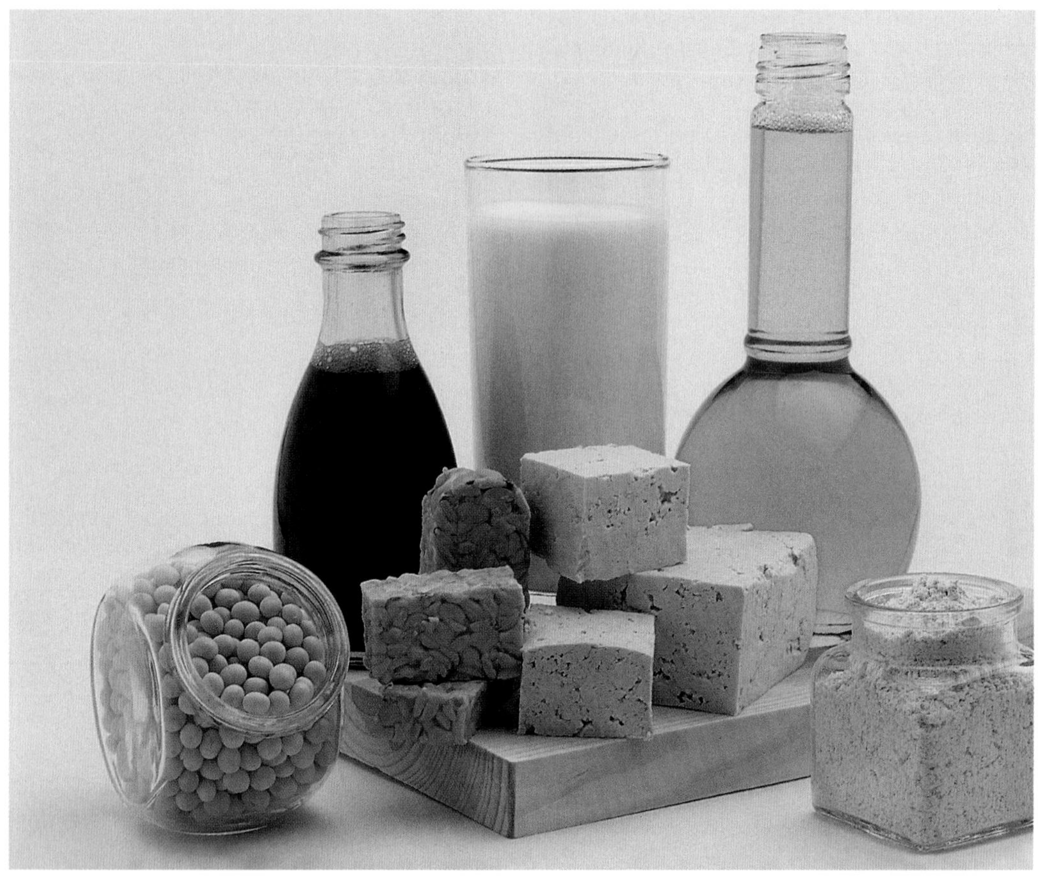

It can be said with full assurance that soy has become a true star among foods, not only for its nutritional value, which is greater than that of meat, but also for its great range of culinary and for dietetic possibilities.
It may be used as a **legume** in a variety of hot and cold dishes. It is an excellent substitute for cow's milk (**soymilk or beverage**) and cheese (**'tofu', 'tempeh', 'miso'**). Its sauces, such as tamari, are nutritious and provide flavor to a wide variety of dishes. The **oil** extracted from soy is excellent from both nutritional and therapeutic standpoints.
Texturized soy protein is used in the kitchen and the food industry the same as meat, but free from meat's drawbacks.

its derivatives that are richest in isoflavones (*tofu*, soymilk or beverage, soy flour, protein extract) helps alleviate the disorders associated with menopause.

Of course, hormone replacement therapy based on estrogen eliminates the symptoms of menopause. It also helps avoid osteoporosis and lowers heart attack risk. It does, however, increase breast and uterine cancer risk by hormonal overstimulation caused by the estrogen used.

A diet based on soy and its derivatives represents a valid and effective estrogen hormone-replacement therapy. It has the same beneficial effects on the bones and heart,[11] with the great advantage that it protects against breast and uterine cancers.

– **Reduced breast cancer risk:** Studies conducted at the University of Southern California (USA) clearly show that the more *tofu* a woman eats, the lower her risk of breast cancer.[12] The protective effect of tofu is noted in both pre and postmenopausal women.

'Tofu' is the soy product that is *richest* in ***isoflavone-type phytoestrogens,*** followed by **soymilk** (beverage).[13] These substances, which include ***genistein,*** act as **cytostatics,** in other words, they stop the *in vitro* development of cancerous breast cells.[14, 15]

• **Men's disorders:** It is curious that soy's phytoestrogens induce the beneficial effects of natural estrogen, but without the side effects. This is the case for men as well as for women. Men who regularly eat soy enjoy:

– ***Lowered risk*** of **prostate cancer.**[9, 16] Japanese men have a lower mortality rate due to prostate cancer because of the consumption of soy products, particularly *tofu.*[17]

– ***Lowered risk*** of **heart attack:** Phytoestrogens, as well as those produced within the body, prevent arteriosclerosis and improve the health of the heart and arteries.[18]

Experiments carried out on male monkeys show that regular consumption of phytoestrogen-rich soy products has no undesirable effects on the male reproductive system.[19]

• **Elevated cholesterol:** That regular consumption of soy and its derivatives reduces total blood cholesterol level is an established fact.

• **Arteriosclerosis:** Until now, it was though that the process of hardening of the arteries was irreversible. However, it has been found that because of soy's effect, the arteries become less rigid and narrow. This is good news for those with arteriosclerosis and its consequent reduction in blood flow to the coronary (heart attack, angina), cerebral, iliac, and other arteries.

• **Thrombosis:** It has been demonstrated experimentally that soy ***genistein*** prevents the formation of thromboses (clots) in the arteries, inhibiting the formation of thrombin (the substance that initiates the coagulation process), and platelet stickiness.[20] The formation of a thrombus or clot within an artery is the most serious consequence of arteriosclerosis. Thrombosis of the coronary arteries leads to **heart attack.** Thrombosis in the cerebral arteries results in **stroke.**

In contrast to the West, Far Eastern peoples get most of their protein from soy, rather than meat. Consequently, they enjoy better health in their reproductive organs (prostate, uterus, breast). It may also explain their remarkable vitality and fertility.

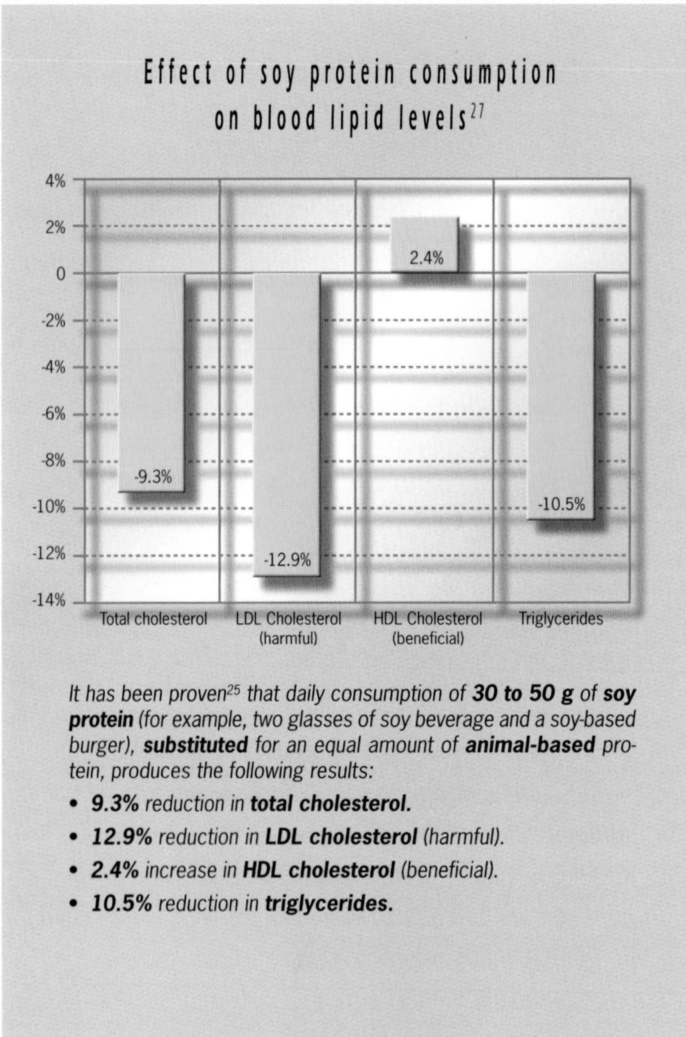

• **Kidney failure:** Soy proteins do not interfere with kidney function, in contrast to the effect of animal proteins.[24] Substituting soy products for meat benefits kidney function, both in the case of failure and nephrosis (degeneration of kidney tissue causing protein loss through the urine).[25]

• **Infant diet:** Soy provides high quality protein for children that can adequately meet their nutritional and developmental needs. In cases where soy-based infant formulas are used exclusively (because of intolerance to milk), the amino acid methionine is usually added as a supplement.

Soymilk (beverage), *tofu*, soy flour, and soy protein are quite suitable for children because of their ease of digestion and their nutritional value. Additionally, there are three specific indications for the use of soy products for infant diets:

– Persistent **diarrhea** accompanied by malabsorption and malnutrition.

– **Lactose intolerance.**

– **Childhood allergies:** A soy-based diet cures many cases of skin eruptions, atopic dermatitis, asthma and other childhood allergic reactions.

• **Cancer prevention:** The National Cancer Institute of the United States is dedicating a great deal of attention to the anticarcinogenic effects of soy and its derivatives.[26]

Daily consumption of soy products reduces the risk of breast, colon, rectal, stomach, prostate, and lung cancers.

• **Osteoporosis:** Heavy ***use of animal-based proteins*** provokes a loss of calcium through the urine, and is considered one of the *primary contributing* factors to osteoporosis in developed countries.[21, 22]

On the other hand, **soy *proteins*** reduce the urinary ***loss*** of ***calcium*** and ***increase* mineralization** and bone **density.**[23] This effect is particularly pronounced in menopausal women. The estrogenic effect of soy's isoflavones also contributes to this.

Soy: negative aspects

Although soy is highly nutritious and possesses extraordinary healing properties, it does have some drawbacks that must not be ignored. None of these are insoluble and should in no way discourage consumption of this superlegume that may rightly be considered a true dietary medicine.

Uric acid

All legumes produce uric acid, with soy producing the most (380 mg/100 g). Beef produces 130 mg/100 g (variety meat more), and milk produces none.

Soy's uric acid poses no risk to health, particularly if the diet is rich in vegetables that alkalize the urine and facilitate excretion.

Very low content of provitamin A and vitamin C

Consequently, soy and its products must always be accompanied by fresh fruits and vegetables that are rich in provitamin A (carotene) and vitamin C. This vitamin facilitates the absorption of the iron in soy, among other functions.

Antinutritive factors

All raw legumes contain toxic substances. Soy is no exception. They are known as antinutritive factors since they interfere with the absorption of other nutrients.[28]

Fortunately, soy's antinutritive factors ***disappear*** partially or completely when it is processed in any of these ways:

- Soaking in water and cooking
- Fermentation
- Sprouting
- Industrial processing

Allergies

Eating soy seldom produces allergies. However, the **dust** from soybeans provokes serious respiratory allergies in sensitive individuals.

Flatulence

Soybeans, as all legumes, contain an ***oligosaccharide*** type of hydrocarbon in their skin that provokes digestive flatulence. Soaking and cooking eliminates most of this.

Lack of vitamin B_{12}

Soy lacks this vitamin, as is the case with all vegetable foods. Fortunately, some soy products are supplemented with this vitamin.

Genetically engineered soy

Although there are no known health problems, their cultivation may present a threat to the environment.

Soy

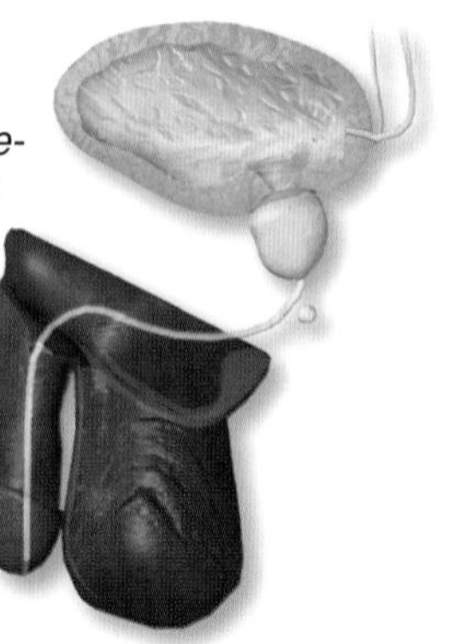

Cancer

Soy consumption *reduces* the **risk** of various types of cancer,[9] particularly

- Breast,
- Prostate, and
- Colon.

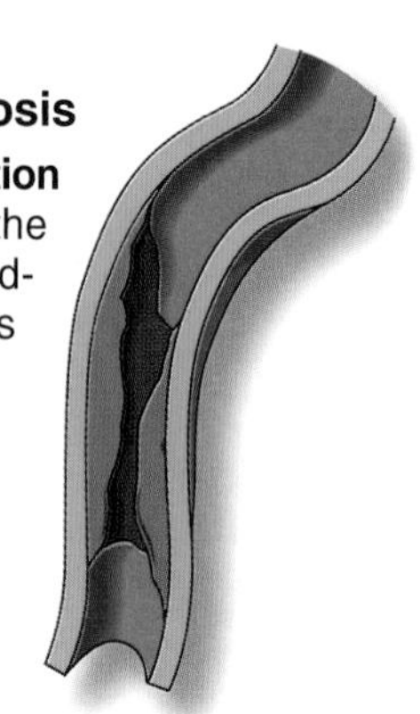

Arteriosclerosis

***Regular* consumption** of soy prevents the narrowing and hardening of the arteries known as arteriosclerosis.

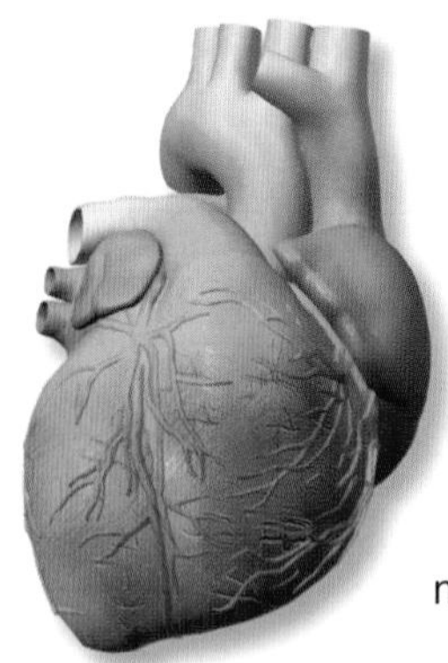

Heart

Soy *reduces* the **risk** of coronary **thrombosis** and **heart attack.**

Regular soy **consumption** *prevents* **arteriosclerosis** and makes the blood more fluid, which improves blood circulation through the coronary arteries.

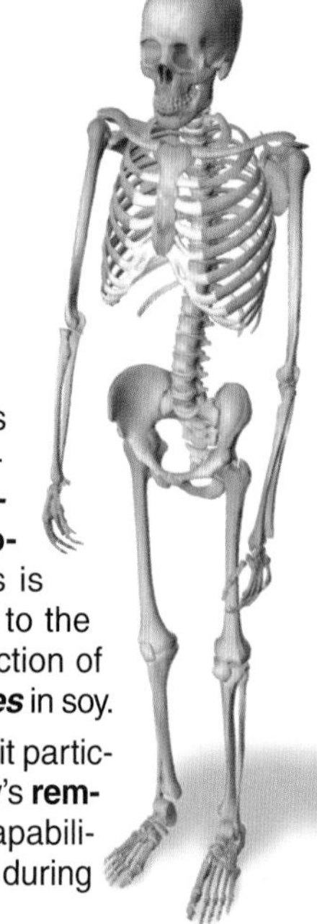

Bones

Soy increases calcium density and ***prevents*** **osteoporosis.** This is due *primarily* to the **estrogenic** action of the ***isoflavones*** in soy.

Women benefit particularly from soy's **remineralizing** capability, particularly during menopause.

Eating a daily serving of soy for a few months is enough to produce beneficial effects.

A serving consists of:

- A dish of cooked soy
- Two glasses of soymilk (beverage)
- 30 to 50 g of 'tofu'
- A soy-based burger

'ositive aspects

Provides proteins:

- ***Major* amounts** (***more*** than any other **plant-based** food)
- ***Excellent*** biological **quality** (excellent substitute for animal proteins)
- *Useful* in ***supplementing*** the quality of **other proteins** such as thcse from corn or wheat
- ***Easily* digested** and **absorbed**

Cholesterol

Soy and its derivatives ***contain no*** cholesterol, as is the case with all plant-based foods. It is also *rich* in ***unsaturated fatty acids*** that *help* ***reduce*** cholesterol production within the body.

Menopause

Soy *relieves* unpleasant **symptoms** because of its ***isoflavones,*** a type of vegetable hormone that partially replaces the natural hormones produced by the ovaries.

Reduced estrogen production during menopause is one of the causes of the discomfort that many women experience during this life stage.

Infant diet

Soymilk (beverage) can be used as a substitute for cow's milk in infant formulas.

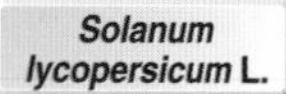

Tomato

Protector of the prostate

TOMATO composition
per 100 g of raw edible portion

Energy	21.0 kcal = 90.0 kj
Protein	0.850 g
Carbohydrates	3.54 g
Fiber	1.10 g
Vitamin A	62.0 µg RE
Vitamin B_1	0.059 mg
Vitamin B_2	0.048 mg
Niacin	0.728 mg NE
Vitamin B_6	0.080 mg
Folate	15.0 µg
Vitamin B_{12}	—
Vitamin C	19.1 mg
Vitamin E	0.380 mg α-TE
Calcium	5.00 mg
Phosphorus	24.0 mg
Magnesium	11.0 mg
Iron	0.450 mg
Potassium	222 mg
Zinc	0.090 mg
Total Fat	*0.330 g*
Saturated Fat	*0.045 g*
Cholesterol	—
Sodium	*9.00 mg*

1% 2% 4% 10% 20% 40% 100%

% Daily Value (based on a 2,000 calorie diet) provided by 100 g of this food

Scientific synonym: *Lycopersicon esculentum* Mill.

French: *Tomate;* ***Spanish:*** *Tomate.*

Description: *Aggregate fruit of the tomato ('Solanum lycopersicum' L.), a herbaceous plant of the botanical family Solanaceae. They may be red, green, or yellow.*

AFTER THE POTATO (see p. 190), the tomato is the most widespread plant of the botanical family Solanaceae. It is cultivated throughout the world. It was introduced to Europe by Spaniards who brought it from Peru and Mexico in the 16th century. However, it was more than two hundred years before the tomato achieved any degree of acceptance in France, Germany, and Northern Europe.

The tomato's similarity to the red fruit of the belladonna, a toxic plant of the same botanical family, led to the belief that it was poisonous. In fact, this vegetable was not completely accepted in German and North American cuisine until well into the 20th century.

The tomato was much better received in Southern Europe. From its arrival in the 16th century it held an exalted place in Spanish and Italian cuisine to such a degree that today it is an essential part of the Mediterranean diet.

Nutrition experts have rediscovered the tomato. They see it as much more than an ingredient in salads or sauces. The healing power that the tomato exercises on a variety of disorders, as well as its preventive effect on certain types of cancer, particularly that of the prostate, make this vegetable a universally recognized **medicinal food.**

PROPERTIES AND INDICATIONS: Fresh tomatoes contain a great deal of water (almost 94% of their weight). They contain small amounts of carbohydrates (3.54%), proteins (0.85%), and fats (0.33%). Its carbohydrates are formed primarily of glucose and fructose. Together, these nutrients provide 21 kcal/100 g, one of the lowest amounts of any plant-based foods, lower even than asparagus (23 kcal/100 g).

However, the tomato's nutritional and therapeutic value is in its rich vitamin and mineral content, as well as its non-nutritive substances.

In terms of ***vitamins,*** the most abundant is vitamin **C** (19.1 mg/100 g), an amount that is less than the orange (53.2 mg/100 g), but enough to make the tomato effective against scurvy. A 100 g tomato supplies a third of the adult daily need for this vitamin.

Vitamins B_1, B_2, B_6, niacin, and folates are all present in significant amounts. Provitamin A is present (62 µg RE/100 g), although much less than in carrots (2,813 µg RE/100 g) or mango (389 µg RE/100 g).

Most notable among its ***minerals*** are potassium (222 mg/100 g), followed by iron (0.45 mg/100 g), magnesium, and phosphorus. Tomatoes are a good source of ***iron,*** since they contain about nine times as much as milk (0.45 mg/100 g) per equal weight, although tree time less than eggs (1.44 mg/100 g). However, surprising though it may seem, an average-size tomato weighing 180 g contains the same amount of iron as an average egg (about 60 g).

Non-nutritive components are substances present in foods, which, although not considered nutrients in the traditional sense, play important roles within the body. The most noteworthy of these in the tomato are:

✓ ***Vegetable fiber:*** Tomatoes contain a small amount (1.1%) of ***soluble*** fiber in their pulp and

Preparation and use

➊ **Raw:** This is the most healthful way to eat tomatoes.

➋ **Fried:** Fried tomatoes are tasty but somewhat difficult to digest for those with frail stomachs.

➌ **Juice and tomato** sauce: These are rich in vitamin C and mineral salts. However, industrially prepared products typically contain a great deal of salt and other additives that may provoke allergic reactions.

Tomato and oxalic acid

*For many years, tomatoes were eliminated from the diets of those with **kidney stones** because of their oxalic acid content. This substance, together with calcium, forms insoluble salts (calcium oxalate) which precipitate in the form of calculi or stones.*

*However, there is **no** reason for **removing** tomatoes from the diets of kidney patients. Their **oxalic acid** content is **extremely low** (5.3 mg/100 g), similar to many other foods and lower than lettuce (17 mg/100 g), tea (83 mg/100 g), or spinach (779 mg/100 g).[29]*

*Tomatoes increase **urine output** and **purify** the blood, which aids kidney function.*

Tomatoes stewed or fried with a little oil are a better source of lycopene than raw tomatoes. Lycopene, which gives tomatoes their red color, prevents prostate degeneration. According to studies carried out at the University of Düsseldorf (Germany),[30] lycopene from stewed or fried tomatoes is much better absorbed than that from raw tomatoes. Although they may be somewhat difficult to digest for those with frail stomachs, stewed tomatoes and tomato sauce are more effective sources of lycopene than raw tomatoes.

particularly in the mucilage surrounding the seeds. This fiber contributes to the tomato's cholesterol-reducing and laxative effects.

✓ ***Organic acids,*** particularly malic and oxalic, which contribute to the tomato's unique flavor. As the tomato ripens, the concentration of these acids diminishes and its sugar content increases.

In spite of the acidic taste, which results from the presence of these acid substances, the tomato has the same effect as the lemon: It has an **alkalizing** effect on the blood, organic tissues, and the urine. This is because it contains many more alkalizing substances (mineral salts) than acids.

✓ ***Lycopene:*** This vegetable pigment belongs to the group of ***carotenoids*** that gives tomatoes their typical red color. In contrast to beta-carotene, lycopene does not transform to vitamin A. Because of this, lycopene was thought to be of no physiological importance. However, new evidence is coming to light that emphasizes its importance within the body.

At Heinrich-Heine University in Düsseldorf (Germany), a center of tomato ***LYCOPENE*** research, the following conclusions have been reached:[31]

- Lycopene is normally present in human blood (0.5 µmol per liter of plasma). *Together* with ***beta-carotene,*** it is the most abundant ***carotenoid*** in the human body.
- Lycopene is also found in the **testicles,** the **prostate,** and the **suprarenal** glands.
- Lycopene is an *extremely potent* **antioxidant,** preventing the deterioration that free radicals produce in the DNA of the cells.
- Lycopene intervenes in the mechanisms that control cellular growth. Without its presence, cells reproduce in a more disorderly manner.

Because of its composition, tomatoes are particularly indicated in the following cases:

• **Prostate conditions:** A variety of studies conducted at Harvard University (USA)[32, 33] show that men who regularly eat fresh tomato, as well as tomato sauce or juice, are at *much lower risk* of **prostate cancer.**

This fact is easily explained bearing in mind that the tomato is the *richest* food source of ***lycopene,*** the carotenoid that protects the cells of the prostate from oxidation and abnormal growth. Regular tomato consumption in any form has been shown to be an *important* factor in the **prevention** of prostate cancer, one of the most frequent cancers among males.

Bearing in mind what is known about the effect of lycopene on prostatic tissue,[30, 31] it may be deduced that regular tomato consumption promotes proper prostate function overall. In addition to preventing cancerous degeneration of its cells, tomato can also reduce excessive growth (benign adenoma or **hypertrophy**) of the prostate, which is so common in men beyond age 50.

• **Depurant:** Tomatoes are *remarkable* blood **alkalizers,** which neutralize and help eliminate metabolic waste products, most of which are acidic. They are also **diuretic,** thus facilitating the work of the kidneys. Their regular consumption is *highly recommended* to "cleanse" the blood in case of **gout** (excess uric acid), kidney failure with an increase in blood **urea,** or **chronic presence of toxins** in the body because of a diet rich in meats and animal proteins.

• **Depressed immune system:** Because of their richness in vitamins and minerals, and above all antioxidant carotenoids (lycopene and beta-carotene), tomatoes *naturally stimulate* the immune functions of the body. They *increase* the infection-fighting **capabilities** of the body, which are the ones that finally eliminate infectious agents (contrary to common belief, antibiotics are not responsible for this).

• **Arteriosclerosis:** Because of their antioxidant effect, tomatoes prevent the oxidation of the **cholesterol** transported by low-density lipoproteins (LDL), which cause the narrowing and hardening of the arteries associated with arteriosclerosis. Tomatoes are *very useful* as a **prophylactic** for all who experience circulatory system disorders, including angina and heart attack.

• **Cancerous disorders:** It has been noted that tomato consumption protects against prostate cancer. Studies performed in Italy[32] show that regular tomato consumption also has a protective effect from cancers of the mouth, esophagus, stomach, colon, and rectum. Investigators describe this typical Mediterranean food as *highly protective* against all types of **cancers** of the **digestive tract.**

Red tomatoes are richer in lycopene (an antioxidant carotenoid that protects against arteriosclerosis and cancer) than green varieties.

14

Foods for Metabolism

METABOLISM is the entire complex of ***biochemical reactions*** that are constantly occurring within the body to produce **energy** and **maintain life.**

In the broadest sense, all foods are metabolized, since, when they are eaten, they are all involved in the chemical processes of the body.

However, the foods described in this chapter are *more* involved than others in metabolic processes, or they are involved *more directly*.

For example, mushrooms and loquats reduce blood sugar levels in diabetics, cherries and leeks facilitate the elimination of waste products, and whole wheat provides a balanced proportion of nutrients required to produce energy within the body.

Eating to avoid

Reduce total caloric intake

For a diet to be effective for losing weight, it must supply ***fewer* calories** than those the **body burns.**

Choose low-energy-producing foods

Increase consumption of foods supplying few calories in proportion to their weight such as **vegetables** and **fruits.**

Maintain a balanced proportion of the sources of calories

The calories consumed in a weight-loss diet should ***not*** be concentrated *only* on ***proteins*** or ***fats*** as some propose.

Ideally, the caloric intake in a healthy weight-loss diet should be balanced *among* the **three food energy** sources as illustrated in the graph below.

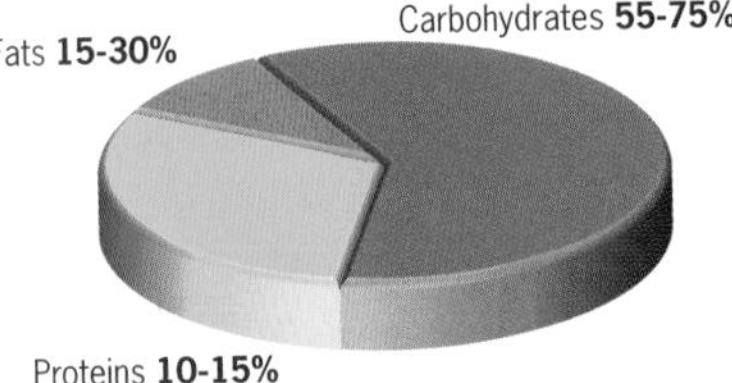

Learn healthful dietary habits

- **Eat slowly,** chewing all foods carefully. It is a proven fact that eating in this way reduces the amount of food consumed, thus fewer calories.
- ***Do not* eat** between meals.
- ***Avoid* anxiety** and **worry** at mealtime, since this unconsciously leads to greater consumption.
- Make **breakfast** and **lunch** the ***primary* meals** of the day, ***eliminating* supper** or ***reducing*** it to a salad or a little fruit.

Choose satiating foods

These tend to be ***fiber-rich.*** As it retains water, fiber increases in volume in the stomach and produces a sense of satiety.

Foods that produce this sensation are **vegetables** in general, **seaweed, sweet potato,** and some **fruits,** such as cherries.

A solid breakfast prevents obesity, while a light one fosters it.

weight gain

Cherries or pastry?

Calories are not the only important thing

One-half kilo of **cherries** (about 1 pound) supplies ***360 kcal,*** approximately the same as ***100 g*** (about 3.5 ounces) of chocolate **pastry.**

Eating the same number of calories, the pastry fosters obesity, while the cherries prevent it.

In a weight-loss diet, not only is the ***number*** of calories important, but their ***source,*** as well. Equal amounts of calories from grains, vegetables, legumes, and fruits are less fattening than sweets, refined baked goods, sausages, and patés.

1/2 Kilo of cherries

- Is eaten **slowly** (about 10 minutes).
- Produces a feeling of **satiety.**
- Supplies rapidly absorbed simple *sugars,* but since they are combined with ***fiber,*** they are absorbed more **slowly** than if they were part of a pastry.
- Contains ***B*** group ***vitamins,*** which facilitate the metabolism of sugars.

One hundred grams of pastry

- Are eaten **rapidly** (a minute or less).
- Are ***not filling,*** so one continues eating.
- Contain ***saturated fats*** and ***refined carbohydrates,*** which become **fatty deposits** in the body unless intense physical exercise is done to burn them.

Whole grain cereals and breads, legumes, and fruits supply carbohydrates that can be safely eaten in controlled amounts in a healthful weight loss diet.

Diabetics, like the obese, must become accustomed to eating controlled and weighed portions of each food, with the objective of not exceeding the total daily allowance and maintaining the balance among nutrients.

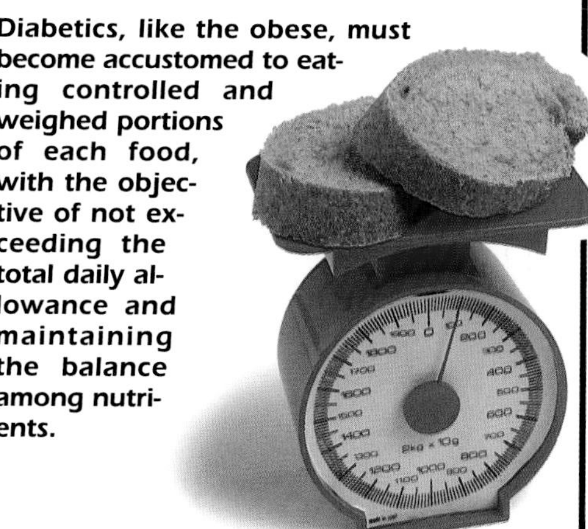

Foods and the

As foods are metabolized within the body, they are assimilated and utilized for vital functions and they tend to *increase* or *reduce* the **acidity** of **blood** and other body **fluids.**

It is important to note the fact that a more or less acidic **taste** of a food is ***not an indicator*** of **the reaction** the food will produce when metabolized.

For example, lemons, oranges, and other fruits have an acidic taste because of their content of citric and other organic acids. However, when these acids and other components of these fruits are metabolized within the body, they leave ***alkaline mineral* residues,** resulting in their alkalizing effect instead of being acidic as might be expected.

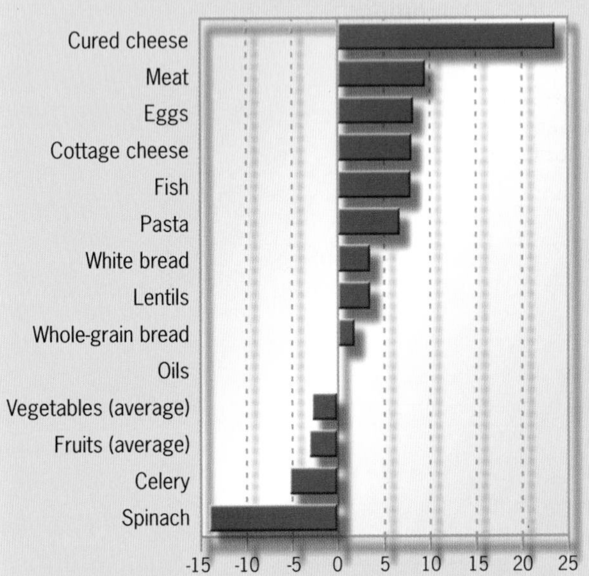

These figures measure the mEq (milliequivalent) of acid anions (chlorides, sulfates, phosphates, and organic acids) or alkaline cations (potassium, sodium, calcium, and magnesium) that are excreted in the urine after eating 100 g of each of these types of foods, according to a study conducted at the Research Institute on Childhood Nutrition in Dortmund (Germany).[1]

- ***Positive values:*** *Indicate that the food in question induces the elimination of acid anions, thus it is* ***acidifying.***
- ***Negative values:*** *Indicate that the food induces the elimination of alkaline cations, thus it is* ***alkalizing.***

Meats and their derivatives, as well as fish, eggs, and cured cheese, acidify the body. If the body, in turn, is not able to compensate for or eliminate these excess acids, a number of disorders may result.

Vegetables and most fruits are alkalizers and help compensate for excess acids produced normally within the body.

cid/alkaline balance

Narrow limits

The ***pH,*** or level of **acidity** in the **blood** and extracellular fluid, must be maintained within ***very precise*** **limits** in order to carry out vital functions properly: between ***7.35*** and ***7.45.***

Bearing in mind that a ***pH*** level of ***7*** is **neutral** (neither acid nor alkaline), **blood,** with an ***average*** of ***7.4,*** is **slightly alkaline** or basic.

The body's constant tendency is toward acidity. Consequently, there is an equally constant struggle to eliminate excess acids.

Consequences of acidification

Many disorders result from the acidification of the blood and body:

- The *tendency* to **osteoporosis** and **decalcification.**
- The *tendency* to **arteriosclerosis** and **coronary disease.**
- *Greater probability* of **arthritis.**
- The *tendency* to retain fluid in the tissues (**edema**).
- *Greater risk* of urate or cystine **calculi** in the kidneys.
- *Higher* **cancer** *risk:* Cancer cells seem to develop faster in an acidic environment.

Avoiding acidity

- ***Increase*** consumption of **alkalizing foods** that reduce the formation of acids in the body, such as vegetables and most fruits.
- ***Restrict*** the use of **acidifying foods,** particularly cured cheeses, meat, shellfish, fish, and eggs. Grains, walnuts, peanuts, lentils, and soy are also acidifying but not to the same extent as animal-based products.
- ***Improve*** **kidney function** by drinking plenty of **water** and eating diuretic **fruits** and **vegetables** (see p. 230, table ***"Scanty urine"***).

Acidifying and alkalizing foods

*Most **plant-based** foods are **alkalizing,** except grains and some legumes. **Animal-based** foods are all **acidifying,** except milk and yogurt.*

	pH↓ Acidifying	pH↑ Alkalizing
Fruits	Plums, blueberries, and cranberries	All other fruits
Nuts	Walnuts, peanuts, cashews	Almonds, chestnuts
Grains	All grains, whole and refined, and their derivatives (bread, pasta, etc.)	
Legumes	Soy, lentils	Chickpeas, common beans
Vegetables		All
Dairy products	Cheese	Milk, yogurt
Eggs, fish, shellfish, and meat	All of these and their derivatives	

UNDERWEIGHT

Caution

When one loses weight for no apparent reason, a complete medical review is necessary to determine the cause and eliminate any malignant process.

Causes

The *most common* **causes** of weight loss are: digestive disorders, febrile disease, intestinal parasites, excess physical activity or out of proportion to the amount of food taken in, and hormonal disorders such as hyperthyroidism.

Diet

To **regain weight,** the diet must meet three requisites:

1. It must provide *sufficient* **calories** in the form of ***carbohydrates.*** This way the body can utilize dietary proteins to synthesize new proteins. If there are not enough calories in the diet, the body uses proteins for energy, and not for body tissue.
2. It must provide an adequate supply of ***B*** group ***vitamins,*** which are essential to the metabolism of ***carbohydrates,*** converting them to energy.
3. It must maintain the *correct* **proportion** of **calories** from the three energy nutrients: carbohydrates (60%), fats (30%), and proteins (10%).

With the goal of taking in as many calories as possible, concentrated foods that are also rich in B vitamins are recommended.

Increase

ALFALFA
WHOLE GRAINS
OATS
WHEAT
LEGUMES
CHESTNUT
POTATO
SUNFLOWER SEEDS
FENUGREEK
FIG
BREADFRUIT

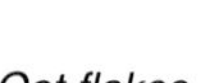

Oat flakes

This is the grain that yields the highest-energy output, and one of the easiest to digest and assimilate because of its mucilage content, which soothes the digestive tract.

PHYSICAL FATIGUE

Definition

This is a state of physical weakness produced by *normal physical activity that should not produce exhaustion.* This represents one of the most frequent medical complaints. It is also referred to as **tiredness, exhaustion lack of energy,** or **asthenia.**

Cause

Hormonal, cardiac, or respiratory disturbances cause physical fatigue. Infections cause fatigue, as well, whether acute such as influenza, or chronic such as tuberculosis.

Diet

An ***inadequate*** **diet** can also cause physical fatigue. When the diet consists of a great deal of refined or processed foods (typical "junk food"), the reserves of certain nutrients that can only be found in fresh fruits and vegetables, such as vitamin C, are exhausted. On the other hand, a diet that is predominantly plant-based and is simply prepared provides the body with a strength and resistance that is unavailable with more sophisticated foods.

In addition to correcting the cause of fatigue, surmounting it is necessary. A healthful diet including the foods and products recommended in this table will be useful to attain that goal.

Increase

WHEAT GERM
SESAME
ROYAL JELLY
POLLEN
GRAPE
WATERCRESS
APRICOT
BARBERRY
HONEY

Reduce or eliminate

STIMULANT BEVERAGES
CHOCOLATE
GUARANA

Coffee

Although they produce momentary relief, coffee, tea, and mate do not solve the problems that cause exhaustion. Their overuse aggravates fatigue.

ELEVATED TRIGLYCERIDES

Definition

Triglycerides are a *type of fat that circulates within the blood and forms part of the* **lipoproteins,** *together* with ***cholesterol*** and **phospholipids.** An *increased* triglyceride level contributes to **arteriosclerosis,** and, as a consequence, heart attack and stroke.

Triglycerides are formed chemically of glycerin and fatty acids and are found in *all* **fats. Oils** are made up primarily of triglycerides.

Causes

Diabetes, hypothyroidism, and liver disorders can increase triglyceride levels, although in most cases the cause is hereditary.

Food or nutrient diet

It has been proven that certain foods, such as those described in this table, may reduce triglyceride levels and, consequently, the risk of arteriosclerosis and heart disease.

 **Increase**

SOY
COMMON BEAN
AVOCADO
ONION
GUAVA
WHEAT GERM
FISH OIL

Reduce or eliminate

TOTAL FAT
FRUCTOSE
SUGARS

It has been found that eating 120 g of cooked beans a day for three weeks, reduces the levels of cholesterol and triglycerides in the blood by 10%.[1]

GOUT

Symptoms

Gout is manifested by inflammation and sharp joint pain because of *crystallized deposits* of **uric acid.** The joint most affected tends to be the metatarsal-phalangeal (the base of the great toe). Men and postmenopausal women tend to suffer the most from gout, because of a hormonal effect.

Causes

Uric acid forms in the body through two mechanisms:

- From foods, as a waste product of the metabolism of certain proteins called **nucleo-proteins.**
- From the body's own cells: When uric acid is produced faster than the kidneys can eliminate, its level in the blood increases and it is deposited in various tissues, such as those surrounding the joints. There it causes inflammation and pain. This is known as gout.

Diet

Foods recommended for those suffering from gout must meet two conditions:

1. They must contain ***little*** **purine** that results in uric acid.
2. They must *aid* in the *elimination* of **uric acid. Alkalizing** foods *increase* elimination of uric acid in the urine, while **acidifying** foods have the *opposite* effect.

Fruits and most **vegetables** meet these two conditions.

 **Increase**

THE SAME AS FOR METABOLIC ACIDOSIS (see chart p. 273)
LEMON
FRUIT
NUTS
VEGETABLES
DAIRY PRODUCTS
CHERRIES
STRAWBERRY
GRAPE
APPLE
CELERY
TOMATO

 **Reduce or eliminate**

VARIETY MEATS
MEAT
SHELLFISH
FATTY FISH
ALCOHOLIC BEVERAGES
STIMULANT BEVERAGES
BREWER'S YEAST
LEGUMES
SPINACH
FRUCTOSE
MUSHROOMS
ASPARAGUS

DIABETES

Definition

The so-called **diabetes 'mellitus'** is a disorder of the metabolism of glucose. It is quite common in Western countries. In reality, this term includes two diseases whose common characteristic is an elevated level of sugar in the blood:

- **Type I diabetes,** also known as **juvenile diabetes** or **insulin-dependent** diabetes. Due to a viral infection, a toxin, or an autoimmune reaction, all reinforced by a hereditary predisposition, the insulin-producing cells of the pancreas are destroyed. These diabetics tend to be thin and must receive insulin from infancy.
- **Type II diabetes,** also called **adult onset diabetes** or **non-insulin dependent** diabetes. Its causes are unknown, but it is ***exacerbated*** by a diet rich in sweets and refined products and poor in whole grains.[2]

Diet

Foods that are recommended and advised against: Those foods recommended in this table contribute significantly to the control of diabetes and the avoidance of its complications. They should therefore be included in any **dietetic plan** established by a ***specialist.***

Those foods whose use should be reduced or eliminated have been shown to initiate or exacerbate diabetes. The diabetic that bears these simple recommendations in mind will have accomplished a great deal toward control of the disease.

Increase

LEGUMES
VEGETABLES
WHOLE GRAINS
FRUIT
NUTS
ARTICHOKE
CELERY
AVOCADO
ONION
MUSHROOM
NOPAL
POTATO
WHEAT GERM

Reduce or eliminate

SUGARS
REFINED BAKED GOODS
HONEY
SATURATED FAT
CHOCOLATE
SHELLFISH
MEAT
MILK
ALCOHOLIC BEVERAGES
SALT

Meat

Eating a great deal of meat is associated with higher risk of diabetes.[3] This disease occurs less frequently among vegetarians.

HYPOGLYCEMIA

Definition

This is a metabolic disorder caused by a *drop in blood glucose level* to a point below the minimum necessary for proper brain function (about 80 mg/100 ml). It is manifested by weakness, a feeling of hunger, and nervousness. When this drop is serious, it may produce cold sweat, dizziness, palpitations, fainting, and even coma.

Causes

The *most common* **cause** of hypoglycemia is *excess* **insulin** due to:

- An elevated dose injected as an anti-diabetic treatment,
- An extreme increase in insulin secretion by the pancreas itself as it responds to a sudden increase in glycemia caused by sugar consumption.

Diet

A balanced diet with regular meal times and few sweets can help prevent hypoglycemia, although in acute situations it may be necessary to administer a certain amount of sweets or sugar to raise the blood glucose level.

Increase

WHOLE GRAINS
LEGUMES
NUTS

Reduce or eliminate

SUGARS
REFINED BAKED GOODS
ALCOHOLIC BEVERAGES
STIMULANT BEVERAGES

Milk

Several studies have shown that infants fed with cow's milk show a greater tendency to type I diabetes (insulin-dependent). Diabetics should reduce milk consumption as a simple precaution.

Update for diabetics

Classic diet for diabetics

Until recently, diabetics were prescribed a diet:

- Low in all types of carbohydrates
- Rich in proteins and fats

The use of whole grains, legumes, and fruits was discouraged because of their complex hydrocarbon (starch) and sugar content, which were transformed into glucose during digestion.

This carbohydrate-poor diet seemed the most logical for diabetics, and apparently allowed good blood-glucose level control. Nevertheless, it has been shown that diabetics eating this type of diet have a higher incidence of arteriosclerosis and cardiovascular disease, including heart attack.

Excess ***fat*** and ***protein,*** which *promotes* ***arteriosclerosis,*** combined with a lack of grains, legumes, and antioxidant fruits explain the *long-term* ***harm done*** by this type of diet.

Today's diabetic diet

Dietetic treatment of diabetics is constantly overcoming the old taboos concerning the drawbacks of carbohydrates. Today's dietary recommendation is:

1. *Rich* in ***complex carbohydrates*** (***starch***).
2. *Rich* in ***fiber.***
3. *Low* in ***fat,*** particularly saturated animal fat.[4]
4. *Low* in ***sugar.***

This approach provides *better results* in ***controlling*** **glycemia,** ***preventing*** **complications,** and improving **longevity** of diabetics.

The complete list of foods that are recommended and of those that should be avoided appears on page 276.

Green leafy vegetables and nuts are also appropriate for diabetic diets.

Starchy vegetables such as the sweet potato, and fresh fruits may be eaten in controlled amounts.

Whole grains and legumes fulfill the four dietary objectives for diabetics since they contribute to the control of glucose better than any other type of food. Additionally, their liberal use prevents diabetes.[2]

Mushrooms

Reduce insulin need

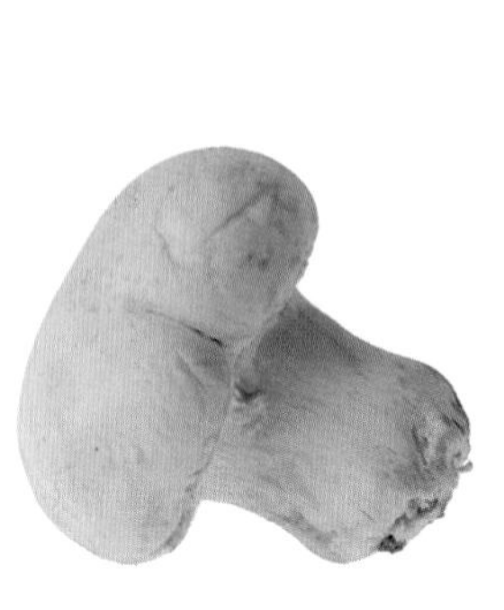

Related species:
Agaricus campestris L. (wild mushroom).

Synonyms: *Morel, Field mushroom, Forest mushroom, Pink-bottom, Portabello, Vegetable meat.*

French: *Champignon;* ***Spanish:*** *Champiñón, champiñón cultivado, seta de París.*

Description: *The mushroom is the fruiting body of the fungus 'Agaricus bisporus' L., which belongs to the family Agaricaceae of the class Basidiomycota. They are formed of three distinct parts: the* ***pileus,*** *which is the white, fleshier portion that measures between 5 and 10 cm in diameter. The* ***stipe*** *is cylindrical with the annulus. The* ***Lamellae*** *are located under the pileus and are where the spores are formed.*

MUSHROOM composition
per 100 g of raw edible portion

Energy	25.0 kcal = 106 kj
Protein	2.09 g
Carbohydrates	3.45 g
Fiber	1.20 g
Vitamin A	—
Vitamin B_1	0.102 mg
Vitamin B_2	0.449 mg
Niacin	4.90 mg NE
Vitamin B_6	0.097 mg
Folate	21.1 µg
Vitamin B_{12}	—
Vitamin C	3.50 mg
Vitamin E	0.120 mg α-TE
Calcium	5.00 mg
Phosphorus	104 mg
Magnesium	10.0 mg
Iron	1.24 mg
Potassium	370 mg
Zinc	0.730 mg
Total Fat	0.420 g
Saturated Fat	0.056 g
Cholesterol	—
Sodium	4.00 mg

1% 2% 4% 10% 20% 40% 100%

% Daily Value (based on a 2,000 calorie diet)
provided by 100 g of this food

MUSHROOMS are very much appreciated for their pleasant flavor and whitish appearance. Their culinary use dates to the beginning of the 20th century, when it came into common use in the French capital.

PROPERTIES AND INDICATIONS: Mushrooms contain 2.1% quite complete proteins, approximately the same as the potato, but with less than a third of the calories (25 kcal/100 g). However, frying mushrooms increases their caloric content a great deal.

Studies carried out with laboratory animals at the University of Surrey (UK) show that mushrooms produce significant improvement in the course of diabetes.[5] They also supply proteins, B group vitamins, and very few carbohydrates.

Preparation and use

❶ **Raw:** Fresh mushrooms may be thinly sliced and eaten raw. They must be cleaned very well. Some studies suggest that raw mushrooms *may* have some **carcinogenic effect** because of their agaritine content,[6,7] although others deny it.[8,9] As a preventive measure it is probably best not to eat them raw.

❷ **Cooked Roasted:** fried or in a variety of culinary preparations. They require very little cooking time (a few minutes).

❸ **Preserves:** Mushrooms retain their flavor and aroma quite well when they are canned, frozen, and particularly, dried.

They are quite rich in ***vitamins B₁, B₂, niacin,*** and ***folates,*** as well as the minerals ***potassium, phosphorus,*** and ***iron,*** and ***trace elements.*** However, they are poor in vitamin C and calcium, and contain virtually no provitamin A or vitamin E.

They are **digested slowly,** and sometimes with **difficulty** because of the chitin they contain and the nature of their proteins, which are rich in nucleic acids. They are not recommended in cases of gout (see p. 275).

Mushrooms are particularly useful in diet therapy because of their **anti-diabetic** action. Their very low carbohydrate content (3.45%) and richness in proteins and B group vitamins contributes to this effect. Experiments with diabetic laboratory animals have shown that eating mushrooms reduces the need for insulin to regulate blood glucose.[5]

The obese may eat mushrooms as well as diabetics because of their satiating effect and their low caloric content, as long as they are not fried or cooked with oil.

Breadfruit

Nutritious and energy-producing

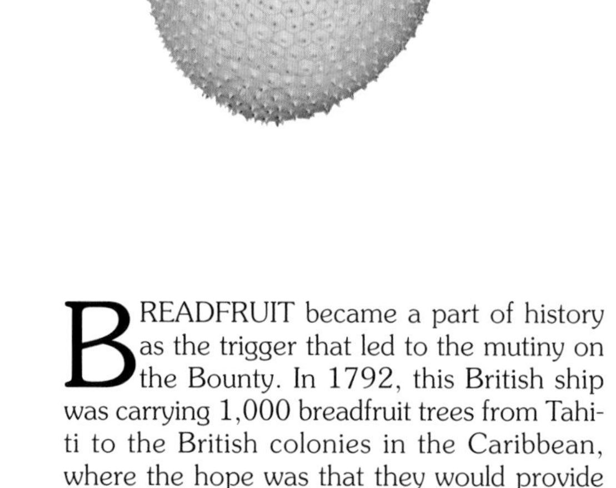

Related species: *Arctocarpus heterophylla* Lam. (Jackfruit).

Synonyms: *Breadnut, Sukun.*

French: *Fruit de l'arbre à pain;*
Spanish: *Fruto del pan, frutapán.*

Description: The fruit of the breadfruit tree ('Arctocarpus communis' Forst.), a tree of the botanical family Moraceae, which reaches a height of 20 meters.

BREADFRUIT composition
per 100 g of raw edible portion

Energy	103 kcal = 432 kj
Protein	1.07 g
Carbohydrates	22.2 g
Fiber	4.90 g
Vitamin A	4.00 µg RE
Vitamin B_1	0.110 mg
Vitamin B_2	0.030 mg
Niacin	0.900 mg NE
Vitamin B_6	0.100 mg
Folate	14.0 µg
Vitamin B_{12}	—
Vitamin C	29.0 mg
Vitamin E	1.12 mg α-TE
Calcium	17.0 mg
Phosphorus	30.0 mg
Magnesium	25.0 mg
Iron	0.540 mg
Potassium	490 mg
Zinc	0.120 mg
Total Fat	*0.230 g*
Saturated Fat	*0.048 g*
Cholesterol	—
Sodium	*2.00 mg*

1% 2% 4% 10% 20% 40% 100%

% Daily Value (based on a 2,000 calorie diet) provided by 100 g of this food

BREADFRUIT became a part of history as the trigger that led to the mutiny on the Bounty. In 1792, this British ship was carrying 1,000 breadfruit trees from Tahiti to the British colonies in the Caribbean, where the hope was that they would provide abundant fruit to feed the slaves.

Blight, the captain of the Bounty, found it necessary to ration the crew's water in order to provide for the fresh water needs of the trees. This fact provoked the famous mutiny that ended in the South Pacific on the solitary island of Pitcairn.

PROPERTIES AND INDICATIONS: The fresh breadfruit's pulp is approximately 70% water, but once dried its composition is similar to

In the 18th century many ships transported breadfruit trees from the Polynesian islands to those of the Caribbean, where they were planted to provide the nourishing breadfruit to the hardworking men that were harvesting sugar cane, cocoa, and other crops.

wheat flour. Wheat flour contains more protein, but less fat, minerals, and vitamins than breadfruit.

The case then, is that this fruit may be used as a substitute for wheat flour in tropical regions where there is a lack of bread-producing grains. It ***cannot*** be said that breadfruit is a complete food, but it is **nutritious** and **healthful.** When combined with other protein-rich foods such as beans or other legumes, breadfruit is an important component in the diets of tropical countries.

Breadfruit's most ample nutrient is ***STARCH,*** which makes up most of its carbohydrates, as is the case with wheat flour. During the digestion process, starch is slowly transformed into **glucose,** the most important energy source for the body's cells.

Preparation and use

❶ **Pulp:** Breadfruit pulp is juicy and filled with fine threads. Its taste is mild and quite neutral. It may be eaten raw, or cooked, roasted, or fried.

❷ **Seeds:** The fruit of certain varieties of breadfruit contains numerous seeds that are eaten roasted as if they were chestnuts.

❸ **Flour:** This is prepared from dried breadfruit. It is mixed with grain flours and used to make bread.

Peach palm

A storehouse of energy

PEACH PALM composition
per 100 g of raw edible portion

Energy	196 kcal = 816 kj
Protein	2.60 g
Carbohydrates	37.1 g
Fiber	4.60 g
Vitamin A	201 µg ER
Vitamin B_1	0.050 mg
Vitamin B_2	0.160 mg
Niacin	1.40 mg NE
Vitamin B_6	0.300 mg
Folate	28.0 µg
Vitamin B_{12}	—
Vitamin C	35.0 mg
Vitamin E	2.40 mg α-TE
Calcium	14.0 mg
Phosphorus	46.0 mg
Magnesium	163 mg
Iron	1.00 mg
Potassium	264 mg
Cinc	1.40 mg
Total Fat	*4.40 g*
Saturated Fat	*0.700 g*
Cholesterol	—
Sodium	*3.00 mg*

1% 2% 4% 10% 20% 40% 100%

% Daily Value (based on a 2,000 calorie diet)
provided by 100 g of this food

Scientific synonym:
Guilelma gasipaes (H.B.K.) Bailey.

Synonym: *Pejebaye.*

Spanish: *Pejibaye, pijibay.*

Description: *Fruit of the peach palm ('Bactris gasipaes' L.), a tree of the botanical family Palmae.*

THIS FRUIT was eaten in Central and South America before the arrival of European colonizers. Today it forms part of the traditional diet of countries such as Colombia and Venezuela.

PROPERTIES AND INDICATIONS: ***Carbohydrates*** *predominate* in the composition of the peach palm representing more than 40% of their weight. The bulk of this is ***starch,*** although there are also simple carbohydrates or ***sugars.*** They also contain fats and proteins, although in lower proportions than carbohydrates. They contain a signi-

The peach palm is a type of palm tree that grows in tropical areas of the American continent. Like the dates from other palm trees, it constitutes a good energy source. Those who practice a sport or do physical exercise, whether young or old, will benefit from its energizing effect.

Dates

ficant amount of ***vitamin A*** in the form of carotenoids,[10] which are quite heat-resistant, and, in lower proportion, vitamins B_1, B_2, C, and niacin. As for minerals, they contain small amounts of calcium, phosphorus, and iron.

Because of their high starch content, the peach palm is a very ***high-energy*** fruit. Each gram of starch provides the body with 4 calories when it is metabolized.

Peach palm fruit is indicated in the following cases:

- **Growth** periods (childhood, adolescence).
- **Athletes,** persons involved in **physical labor,** and whenever there is a greater energy demand.
- **Malnutrition, undesired weight loss, convalescence** from debilitating disease.

Preparation and use

❶ **Raw:** The pulp of the peach palm is starchy with a pleasant flavor.

❷ **Boiled:** This is how this fruit is typically prepared. It is boiled for 30 to 45 minutes in salted water. After they have been peeled, they are served with a variety of sauces or with cottage cheese.

❸ **Roasted:** Roasted peach palm has a very pleasant taste.

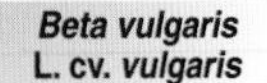

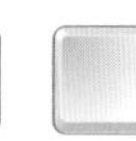

Chard

Light and Flavorful

Scientific synonym: *Beta cycla* L.

Synonyms: *Swiss chard, Seakale-beet, Leaf beet, Sea kale chard.*

French: *Bette;* ***Spanish:*** *Acelga.*

Description: *Brilliant green leaves and white stalks of 'Beta vulgaris' L. ssp. 'vulgaris' cv. 'Vulgaris', a herbaceous plant of the botanical family Chenopodiaceae.*

CHARD composition
per 100 g of raw edible portion

Energy	19.0 kcal = 80.0 kj
Protein	1.82 g
Carbohydrates	0.270 g
Fiber	3.70 g
Vitamin A	610 µg ER
Vitamin B_1	0.100 mg
Vitamin B_2	0.220 mg
Niacin	0.883 mg NE
Vitamin B_6	0.106 mg
Folate	14.8 µg
Vitamin B_{12}	—
Vitamin C	30.0 mg
Vitamin E	1.50 mg α-TE
Calcium	119 mg
Phosphorus	40.0 mg
Magnesium	72.0 mg
Iron	3.30 mg
Potassium	547 mg
Cinc	0.380 mg
Total Fat	*0.060 g*
Saturated Fat	*0.009 g*
Cholesterol	—
Sodium	*201 mg*

1% 2% 4% 10% 20% 40% 100%

% Daily Value (based on a 2,000 calorie diet) provided by 100 g of this food

ALTHOUGH chard is one of the oldest green leafy vegetables known, praised by the Greeks more than 2,500 years ago, there are those who view it as an ordinary vegetable of little value.

But the chard remains, with its showy thick white stalks and brilliant green leaves, waiting for humans to recognize its dietary benefits.

PROPERTIES AND INDICATIONS: Chard is noteworthy because of its ***provitamin A*** and ***iron*** content.

Broth made of chard or other vegetables has a remarkable alkalizing effect on the blood and the body tissues, thanks to its abundance of mineral salts of alkaline reaction. That is why it fosters the disposal of metabolic toxic waste which has an acidic nature, like uric acid.

Preparation and use

❶ **Leaves:** Boiled in water or steamed, cooked in oil, or served with oil and lemon, they constitute a healthful and light dish.

❷ **Fresh leaves:** These may be eaten raw in salad.

❸ **Stalks:** According to some, this is the tastiest part of the plant and may be substituted for cardoon. They are prepared boiled, battered, roasted, or as part of a vegetable soup.

These are its most important indications:

- **Obesity:** Chard is capable of satisfying the appetite with very few calories (about 20 kcal /100 g). Regardless how it is prepared [❶,❷,❸], chard constitutes an ideal dish, particularly for supper, for those wishing to lose weight.
- **Blood depurant (purifier) and alkalizer,** because of its richness in ***mineral*** salts.
- **Digestive and laxative:** Recommended in cases of **gastritis, constipation,** and **hemorrhoids.**
- **Anemia,** because of its high iron content.

Chard contains considerable ***oxalic acid,*** although not as much as spinach (see p. 36). Because of this, it should be used in moderation in case of kidney stones.

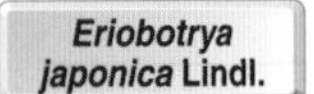

Loquat

An effective anti-diabetic

Synonyms: *Japanese medlar, Japanese plum, Tanaka.*

French: *Nèfle;* ***Spanish:*** *Níspero, níspera.*

Description: *Fruit of 'Eriobotrya japonica' Lindl., an evergreen tree of the botanical family Rosaceae that reaches a height of 5 meters. Trees are also used as ornamental.*

LOQUAT composition
per 100 g of raw edible portion

Energy	47.0 kcal = 196 kj
Protein	0.430 g
Carbohydrates	10.4 g
Fiber	1.70 g
Vitamin A	153 µg ER
Vitamin B_1	0.019 mg
Vitamin B_2	0.024 mg
Niacin	0.263 mg NE
Vitamin B_6	0.100 mg
Folate	14.0 µg
Vitamin B_{12}	—
Vitamin C	1.00 mg
Vitamin E	0.890 mg α-TE
Calcium	16.0 mg
Phosphorus	27.0 mg
Magnesium	13.0 mg
Iron	0.280 mg
Potassium	266 mg
Cinc	0.050 mg
Total Fat	*0.200 g*
Saturated Fat	*0.040 g*
Cholesterol	—
Sodium	*1.00 mg*

1% 2% 4% 10% 20% 40% 100%

% Daily Value (based on a 2,000 calorie diet)
provided by 100 g of this food

PROPERTIES AND INDICATIONS: Some are a little disappointed when they open a loquat and find that half of its volume is seeds. However, that opinion quickly changes when they taste the succulent fruit, even when it is only a portion of the whole.

The ***sugars*** fructose and levulose make 10.4% of its edible portion. Their fat and protein content is negligible (0.2% and 0.4%, respectively).

Vitamin A (in the form of provitamin) is the most abundant, with 153 µg RE/100 g. B complex vitamins, C, and E are present, although in small amounts.

In terms of ***minerals,*** loquats contain significant amounts of iron, calcium, and magnesium, although the most abundant is ***potassium.***

Loquats supply few calories (47 kcal /100 g), but abundant water (86.7%) and mineral salts, which bolster their **diuretic** action.

They are rich in astringent ***tannins*** (2.5%), as well as numerous ***triterpenic*** aromatic substances, which give them their anti-diabetic properties.

These are its indications:

- **Diabetes:** Investigations conducted at the Federico II University in Naples[11] (Italy) have found that loquat extracts reduce the level of sugar in the urine of diabetic rats. Sesquiterpenic glucosides and triterpenoids, non-nutritive substances present in loquats, have been identified as those responsible for this anti-diabetic action.

The loquat's anti-diabetic effect has also been demonstrated in humans according to studies carried out at the Autonomous University of Mexico.[12]

It makes sense, then, to recommend liberal use of loquats in cases of diabetes. As is the case with other fruits, the fact that they contain sugar does not affect their appropriateness for those suffering from this disease.

Preparation and use

❶ **Fresh:** This is the best way to eat loquats. They must be ripe. If they are not, they are very acidic.

❷ **Compotes and jams:** The use of these products is not common, although it is the only way to eat loquats other than during spring months. Unfortunately, they lose most of their properties when prepared in this way.

❸ **Loquat treatment:** This in done in spring and consists of eating from 1 to 2 kilos of loquats a day as the primary food for 2-3 days. They may be accompanied by small amounts of toasted bread or crackers.

- **Liver disorders:** A loquat treatment in the springtime [❸] gives good results in cases of chronic liver disease: hepatitis, fatty degeneration of the liver, and cirrhosis. It may be repeated every two or three weeks.

A **loquat treatment** decongests the liver and reduces its volume in case of hepatomegalia (enlargement of the liver). It also reduces ascites (accumulation of fluid in the abdominal cavity), which often accompanies liver degeneration.

- **Infectious diarrhea** (gastroenteritis, enterocolitis, and colitis). Loquats have a mild **astringent** and **normalizing** effect on the digestive tract. They also **provide water** and restore mineral salts. They are highly recommended as a *first* **solid food** after periods of fasting or liquid diet that are necessary in cases of infectious diarrhea. One may eat up to a kilo of well-ripened loquats a day, bearing in mind that they are only available in the spring.

- **Kidney disorders:** the loquat is an *effective* **diuretic,** which increases urine production and facilitates elimination of uric sediments through the kidneys. Loquats are recommended in cases of **gout,** excess **uric acid, kidney stones** (particularly urate stones), as well as **kidney failure** because of their low protein and significant mineral content.

- **Common cold:** It has been demonstrated that one of the types of substances contained in loquats, ***triterpenic esters,*** have a significant **antiviral effect,** particularly against the rhinoviruses that cause the common cold.[13] Eating loquats in the spring to prevent and cure colds is highly recommended. It is unfortunate that the antiviral effects of loquats do not act on the AIDS virus.

Diabetics benefit from loquats.

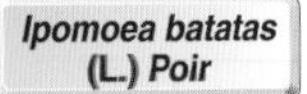

Sweet potato

A feeling of satisfaction

SWEET POTATO composition
per 100 g of raw edible portion

Energy	105 kcal = 439 kj
Protein	1.65 g
Carbohydrates	21.3 g
Fiber	3.00 g
Vitamin A	2,006 µg ER
Vitamin B_1	0.066 mg
Vitamin B_2	0.147 mg
Niacin	1.01 mg NE
Vitamin B_6	0.257 mg
Folate	13.8 µg
Vitamin B_{12}	—
Vitamin C	22.7 mg
Vitamin E	0.280 mg α-TE
Calcium	22.0 mg
Phosphorus	28.0 mg
Magnesium	10.0 mg
Iron	0.590 mg
Potassium	204 mg
Cinc	0.280 mg
Total Fat	*0.300 g*
Saturated Fat	*0.064 g*
Cholesterol	—
Sodium	*13.0 mg*

1% 2% 4% 10% 20% 40% 100% 200% 500%

% Daily Value (based on a 2,000 calorie diet)
provided by 100 g of this food

Synonyms: *Batata [dulce], Camore, Kumara.*

French: *Batate [douce];* ***Spanish:*** *Batata, boniato, papa dulce.*

Description: *Tuber of the sweet potato, 'Ipomoea batatas' Poir., a perennial herbaceous plant of the botanical family Convolvulaceae, with trailing vines reaching a height of 30 cm to 1 m.*

GREAT AMOUNTS of sweet potato are eaten in Central America, particular Haiti, its point of origin. The Spaniards introduced it to Europe, from where it has spread throughout the world.

PROPERTIES AND INDICATIONS: ***Carbohydrates*** *predominate* in the sweet potato's composition, constituting approximately 21.3% of its weight. These carbohydrates are in the form of ***starch*** and ***sugars*** (primarily ***saccharose***) in different proportions, depending on the variety. The more saccharose, the sweeter the tuber.

Their ***fat*** and ***protein*** content is minimal, less than the potato. It is *very rich*, however, in ***beta-carotene*** (provitamin A), particularly in the more yellow varieties.

The sweet potato is quite digestible, although it must be well chewed to mix it with saliva.

The sweet potato contains an appreciable amount of cellulose-type ***fiber.*** This makes the sweet potato highly digestible and gives it a soothing effect on the intestinal walls.

The sweet potato has three dietetic and therapeutic applications:

- **Obesity:** Contradictory though it may seem, consumption of sweet potatoes protects against obesity. It is certainly a starch-rich food, with a good deal of calories (a little more than potato). However, they have a property that makes them very useful in case of obesity: they produce a **sensation of satiety.**

The sweet potato aids the obese in reducing caloric intake by producing a full sensation in the stomach and reducing appetite. Of course, it is necessary to eat sweet potatoes in *controlled amounts* so as no to exceed the recommended daily caloric intake.

Although sweet potatoes are rich in starch, and, therefore, calories, they have the unique feature of producing a sensation of satiety, thus calming the appetite.
Although 100 grams of sweet potatoes have only 105 calories, they can relieve feelings of hunger for several hours.

Of course, sweet potatoes should not be the staple of the diet because of their lack of fats and proteins. However, when combined with milk, legumes, or oil-bearing nuts, they are nutritious and still satiating.

- **Arteriosclerosis** and circulatory disorders: Sweet potatoes' richness in ***beta-carotene*** (provitamin A) makes them very appropriate in cases of arteriosclerosis.

Sweet potatoes are almost totally lacking in ***saturated fats*** and **sodium,** as well. These are the two most pernicious enemies of the circulatory system. Regular sweet potato consumption is recommended in cases of **arteriosclerosis, lack** of adequate **blood flow,** and **hypertension.**

- **Increased need for energy:** The abundant use of sweet potatoes is very beneficial to those individuals involved in intense physical activity, **athletes,** and those **convalescing** from debilitating diseases. In these cases, sweet potatoes may be eaten as the primary dish at dinner two or three times a week.

Preparation and use

❶ **Oven-roasted:** This is the most common preparation technique for sweet potatoes. They may also be roasted over coals. They must be roasted whole, without removing the peel.

❷ **Puree with milk:** Once sweet potatoes are roasted or cooked, they are well mixed with milk to a consistent paste. Because they are generally sweet enough, especially if they are yellow, there is no need to add sugar. Their nutritional value can be increased by adding an egg yolk.

❸ **Pastry:** Sweet potatoes are used to make a variety of delicious products such as jams and candies.

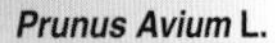

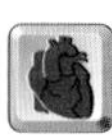

Cherry

Satisfies the hunger and purifies the blood

A treatment with cherries one or two days a week allows weight loss while purifying the body and cleansing the blood. The slowness with which cherries must be eaten partially explains their satiating effect.

Related species: *Prunus cerasus* L. (sour cherry).

French: *Cerise;* ***Spanish:*** *Cereza, guinda.*

Description: *Fruit of the cherry tree ('Prunus avium' L.), of the botanical family Rosaceae that reaches a height of 20 meters. The fruit is a drupe about 2 cm in diameter whose color varies from light red to deep purple.*

CHERRY composition

per 100 g of raw edible portion

Energy	72.0 kcal = 300 kj
Protein	1.20 g
Carbohydrates	14.3 g
Fiber	2.30 g
Vitamin A	21.0 µg ER
Vitamin B_1	0.050 mg
Vitamin B_2	0.060 mg
Niacin	0.400 mg NE
Vitamin B_6	0.036 mg
Folate	4.20 µg
Vitamin B_{12}	—
Vitamin C	7.00 mg
Vitamin E	0.130 mg α-TE
Calcium	15.0 mg
Phosphorus	19.0 mg
Magnesium	11.0 mg
Iron	0.390 mg
Potassium	224 mg
Cinc	0.060 mg
Total Fat	*0.960 g*
Saturated Fat	*0.216 g*
Cholesterol	—
Sodium	*2.00 mg*

1% 2% 4% 10% 20% 40% 100%

% Daily Value (based on a 2,000 calorie diet) provided by 100 g of this food

Properties and indications: Traditionally cherries have been considered a sweet, pleasant fruit, but one of little nutritional or dietetic importance.

However, it is now known that, while none of its nutrients is particularly outstanding, it contains all of them in small amounts (except for vitamin B_{12}). Of its 14% ***sugars,*** the most important is ***fructose,*** which makes cherries appropriate for diabetics. ***Fats*** and ***proteins*** represent about 1% each.

Cherries contain small amounts of vitamins A, B, C, and E, as well as all minerals and trace elements: calcium, phosphorus, magnesium, iron, sodium, ***potassium*** (the most abundant), zinc, copper, and manganese.

However, cherries also contain small amounts of non-nutritive components:

✓ ***Organic acids:*** Malic, succinic, and citric, which act as **stimulants** to the digestive glands and as blood **purifiers.**

✓ ***Soluble vegetable fiber,*** which is formed primarily of ***pectin.*** One hundred grams of cherries provide 10% of RDA (Recommended Daily Allowance) of vegetable fiber. This explains their gentle **laxative** and **hypolipedemic** (cholesterol lowering) effects.

✓ ***Flavonoids*** that give them **diuretic, antioxidant,** and **anticarcinogenic** properties.

✓ ***Salicylic acid,*** the natural precursor to aspirin, acts as an **anti-inflammatory** and **antirheumatic.** It is present in very small amounts, around 2 mg per kg of cherries, but sufficient to have an effect.

Cherries are a pleasant, easy-to-eat fruit. They are particularly beneficial in the following cases:

• **Obesity:** The fact that cherries must be eaten one by one makes them effective in cases of obesity. Eating 360 calories of pastry only requires a few bites. On the other hand, eating the same amount of calories in the form of cherries means one-half kilo (about one pound). This may take 15 minutes and result in a much greater feeling of satiety than after eating the sweet, eliminating the desire to continue eating.

Cherries' **diuretic** and **depurant** (purifying) effect, coupled with their *virtual lack* of ***sodium*** and ***fats,*** potentiate their **weight loss effect.**

• **Diabetes:** Diabetics tolerate controlled amounts of cherries very well since half of their ***sugars*** are ***fructose.*** As in the case of all fruit treatments, that associated with cherries **[❷]** is not recommended for diabetics except under professional supervision.

• **Depurant (purifying) treatments [❷]:** According to Dr. ***Valnet,*** a distinguished French phytotherapist, one or two days of treatment with cherries represents an excellent depurant (purifier) for the body in general, which facilitates the elimination of wastes and toxins.

• **Chronic disorders: *Ample* use** of cherries, particularly as a **weekly treatment [❷]**, is recommended for all types of chronic conditions such as arthritis, gout, chronic rheumatism, arteriosclerosis, chronic constipation, autointoxication due to improper diet, chronic hepatopathy, cardiac failure, convalescence from infectious disease, and cancer.

Preparation and use

❶ **Fresh:** Cherries must be eaten one by one, chewing them well.

❷ **Cherry treatment:** This is done by eating one-half kg of ripe cherries as the only food three or four times a day for two or three days. Those with **delicate stomachs** may **boil** them before eating. For a *stronger effect,* one may drink several cups of a tea made by **boiling** 50 g of **cherry stems** in a liter of water for 5 minutes.

❸ **Culinary recipes:** Cherries fit perfectly into a variety of fruit pies, jams, and compotes.

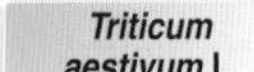

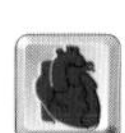

Wheat

The king of grains

Description:** The fruit of wheat ('Triticum aestivum' L.), a herbaceous plant of the botanical family Gramineae. It is formed of the **pericarp** or bran, the **endosperm** or nucleus, and the **germ.

WHEAT composition
per 100 g of raw edi,ble portion

Energy	331 kcal = 1,385 kj
Protein	10.4 g
Carbohydrates	61.7 g
Fiber	12.5 g
Vitamin A	—
Vitamin B_1	0.394 mg
Vitamin B_2	0.096 mg
Niacin	4.80 mg NE
Vitamin B_6	0.272 mg
Folate	41.0 µg
Vitamin B_{12}	—
Vitamin C	—
Vitamin E	1.44 mg α-TE
Calcium	27.0 mg
Phosphorus	493 mg
Magnesium	126 mg
Iron	3.21 mg
Potassium	397 mg
Cinc	2.63 mg
Total Fat	*1.56 g*
Saturated Fat	*0.289 g*
Cholesterol	—
Sodium	*2.00 mg*

1% 2% 4% 10% 20% 40% 100%

% Daily Value (based on a 2,000 calorie diet) provided by 100 g of this food

EACH YEAR planet Earth produces about 600 million metric tons of wheat that feeds billions of persons. No other grain is as widespread as wheat.

Almost four thousand years after Joseph, the son of Jacob, fed the people of Egypt with reserves of grain, wheat continues to provide more food to more people than any other product in the world. In Europe, almost all of America, most of Africa and Asia, and in Australia, wheat is essential to human nutrition.

PROPERTIES AND INDICATIONS: A grain of wheat, formed of the bran or pericarp, the endosperm, and the germ, is an ***almost* whole food,** which contains all of the nutrients that the body needs, with the following exceptions:

- Provitamin A (beta-carotene),
- Vitamin C, and
- Vitamin B_{12}, as is the case with all plant-based foods.

The remaining nutrients are all contained in a grain of whole wheat, including ***fiber.*** *All* are present in ***appropriate*** **proportions,** except ***fats*** and ***calcium,*** which are limited.

✓ ***Carbohydrates:*** These are the most abundant nutrients in wheat, constituting 76%. Most are in the form of ***starch.*** Only a small portion (1% to 2%) is sugars.

The *more* ***fiber*** accompanies this starch, the *slower* the ***glucose*** is released. Because of this, **whole wheat** and its flour are *better tolerated* by **diabetics** than white flour that has been stripped of its fiber since whole wheat does not produce sudden changes in blood glucose level.

✓ ***Protein:*** 90% of wheat's proteins are ***glutein*** and ***gliadin,*** two proteins which, when isolated from the remaining grain components and mixed with water, form a spongy mass called ***gluten.*** Summing up, gluten is the protein content of the endosperm, in other words, the white flour (without the germ or bran).

Because of the ***GLUTEN***, dough "rises," expands with carbon dioxide gas during fermentation. As the gluten expands, it forms the typical "bubbles" in the dough because of its elasticity.

However, gluten presents two drawbacks:

- It can produce **intolerance** in certain individuals. This results in celiac disease in children and sprue in adults.
- It is an ***incomplete protein*** since, although it contains all essential amino acids, its proportion of ***lysine*** is *insufficient* to meet the body's needs.
  The quality of gluten's proteins increases significantly when wheat and its derivatives are combined with legumes or dairy products, which provide extra lysine.

It is interesting that the ***protein*** of the **wheat germ,** which is different from gluten, also contains excess ***lysine.*** This compensates in part for gluten's deficiency. This is only partial because the germ is very small, making up only 2.5% of the grain. It contains little protein, but

Preparation and use

❶ **Whole grain:** Nothing, except possible pesticide contamination, prevents eating wheat just as it comes from the stalk (this was common in antiquity as described in the account of Jesus' disciples in Palestine[14]). It must be very well chewed, spitting out the toughest portions of the bran. The grain can also be toasted, making it easier to chew and digest.

❷ **Flakes:** These are prepared by cooking and rolling the **whole grain.** These flakes provide the value of all parts of the grain and only suffer a slight nutritional loss from heating. They may be eaten after soaking or cooking in milk or vegetable broth. They form part of the famous muesli breakfast food.

❸ **Flour:** This fine powder results from grinding or milling the grain. **Whole-wheat** flour contains *all* parts of the grain, and **refined** flour contains only the endosperm (see p. 295). Flour is used to make bread and a wide variety of baked goods (see p. 72).

❹ **Sprouts:** Wheat sprouts are very tender and healthful. In contrast to the dry grain, they contain ***provitamin A*** and ***vitamin C.***

❺ **Bulgur wheat:** Cracked and vaporized hard wheat grains. They are quite whole and require less cooking than whole grain wheat. Bulgur wheat is used as a substitute for rice.

of excellent quality. In spite of this, whole wheat or its flour provides more nourishing proteins than those of simple white flour.

✓ ***Fats:*** Wheat contains about 1.56%, of which more than ***half*** is found in the **germ** and **bran.** These are primarily polyunsaturated fatty acids, among which ***linoleic*** acid predominates.

✓ ***Fiber:*** Whole wheat contains 12.5% fiber, most of which is ***insoluble*** (lignified) and can be found primarily in the **bran.** This fiber gives wheat its significant **laxative** effect.

✓ ***Vitamins:*** Wheat is a good source of vitamins ***B_1, B_2, B_6, niacin, folates,*** and vitamin ***E.*** The **germ** and **bran** are *richer* in vitamins than the endosperm. Wheat does not contain vitamin C, B_{12}, or provitamin A.

✓ ***Minerals:*** Wheat provides good amounts of phosphorus, magnesium, iron, and potassium, as well as trace elements, among which zinc, copper, and manganese stand out. The rarest mineral is ***calcium.***

Whole wheat and whole-wheat flour are staple foods throughout the world and (except in cases of gluten intolerance) may be eaten daily. Whole wheat is particularly recommended in the following cases:

- **Increased nutritional need:** Periods of rapid growth (childhood and adolescence), athletes, pregnancy, lactating mothers, convalescence from debilitating disease, etcetera. Wheat is an excellent energy source (331 kcal/100 g). Because of its richness in B vitamins, the glucose released by its starch is very easily metabolized.

- **Digestive disorders:** Wheat is very easily digested, requiring minimal effort on the part of the digestive system to provide a wide variety of nutrients.

Wheat's effect as a laxative and regulator of bowel movement requires special mention. All who suffer from constipation should eat whole wheat in whatever form every day. Regular consumption of this whole grain helps prevent intestinal diverticulosis, hemorrhoids, colon cancer, as well as eczema and headache caused by the autointoxication resulting from chronic constipation.

- **Chronic disorders:** Regular consumption of whole wheat or flour helps prevent the so-called diseases of civilization, which are initiated in many cases by excess refined foods: arteriosclerosis, diabetes, rheumatism, and even cancer.[15]

Why is white flour used more than whole wheat?

Why, if it has been amply proven that whole-wheat flour is more nutritious and healthful, is white flour used much more widely in human nutrition?

- ***Demands of the population:*** *White flour has always been more valued than brown or whole grain.*
- ***White flour is easier to store:*** *Whole-wheat flour can be stored only a few weeks before it becomes rancid.*
- *The* ***presence of antinutritive factors*** *in bran, such as phytates, that theoretically can interfere with the absorption of iron and zinc in the intestine. This has caused some specialists to downplay the importance of whole grains from a nutritional standpoint. However, there is no reason for this.*

Anatomy of a grain of wheat

Three well differentiated parts with nutritive properties that are mutually complementary.

The wheat grain has been called the **"whole egg,"** because its three parts (**bran, endosperm,** and **germ**) form a balanced nutritional unit.

Because of this someone, referring to wheat, has said, "what God has joined, let no man tear asunder."

Bran or Pericarp

(see p. 297)

(14,5% of the grain)

This is the outer covering of the grain after removing the straw or shell. It is formed of six layers, all of which are rich in ***cellulose fiber.***

Aleurone layer [4]
The cells of this layer are *very rich* ***in proteins, fats, vitamins,*** and ***minerals.*** However, because of its thick cellulose walls, these nutrients are trapped inside, and are only released when it is finely **ground.**

Hyaline membrane [5]
This, together with the aleurone layer, represents 62% of the weight of the bran.

Tubular layer
Transverse layer
Longitudinal layer
These three layers are very thin and together constitute 11% of the weight. They are formed primarily of cellulose.

Epidermis
This represents 27% of the weight of the bran. The presence of ***lignin,*** together with ***cellulose,*** gives it its typical woody consistency.

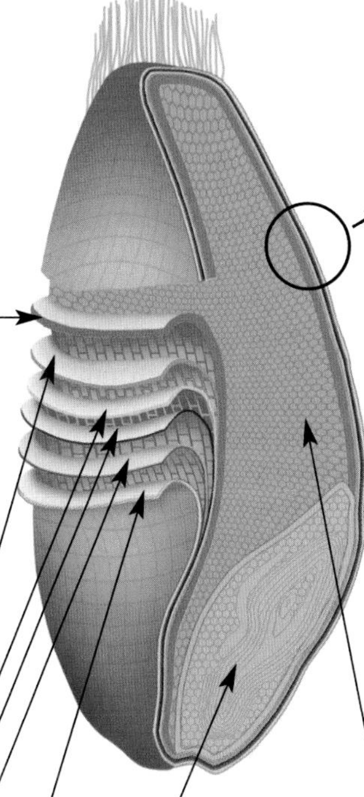

Microscopic detail of a grain of wheat

[1] Internal cellulose membrane of the endosperm
[2] Starch granules
[3] Gluten
[4] Aleurone layer
[5] Hyaline membrane
[6] External bran layers

Germ (see p. 296)

(2,5% of the grain)

This is the grain **embryo,** from which a new wheat plant will sprout.

The germ contains *three-fourths* of all of the ***vitamins B*** and ***E*** in the grain.

Endosperm or Nucleus

(83% of the grain)

The white flour from the endosperm contains a *considerable amount* of ***proteins*** (**gluten**), although they are incomplete. Their **quality** *increases* when they are ***combined*** with lysine-rich proteins such as those contained in:

- **wheat germ,** just as it occurs naturally in whole-grain products;
- **milk** and dairy products;
- **legumes.**

Wheat germ

A treasure-trove of vitamins and healing properties

The germ is the portion of the grain richest in nutrients and active substances, particularly:

- ***Proteins*** (23,2%), *more complete* than those of the gluten from the endosperm since they are not lysine-deficient.
- ***Essential fatty acids*** (9,72%), such as linoleic acid and alpha-linolenic acid (omega-3).
- ***Vitamins*** B_1, B_2, B_6, niacin, and folates.
- ***Vitamin E***, a powerful antioxidant.
- ***Minerals,*** particularly phosphorus, magnesium, iron, and trace elements.
- ***Enzymes*** such as the antioxidant superoxide-dismutase.
- ***Octacosanol:*** This substance is found in wheat germ and its oil and in lower proportions in other seed oils. Its chemical formula is $C_{28}H_{58}O$. It has been shown to naturally improve fatigue resistance and performance in athletes.[16]

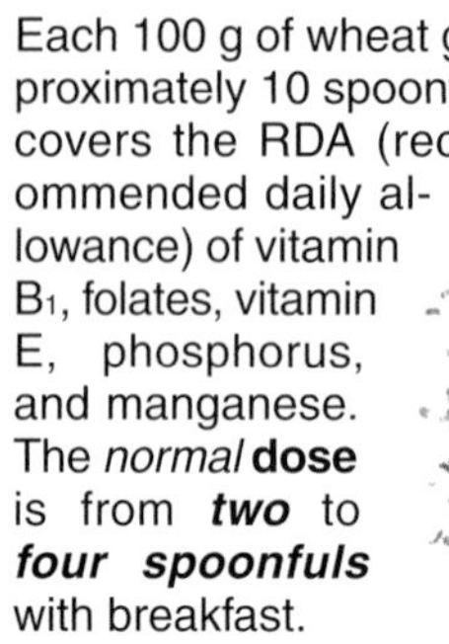

Each 100 g of wheat germ (approximately 10 spoonfuls) covers the RDA (recommended daily allowance) of vitamin B_1, folates, vitamin E, phosphorus, and manganese. The *normal* **dose** is from ***two*** to ***four spoonfuls*** with breakfast.

Its use is specifically recommended in the following cases:

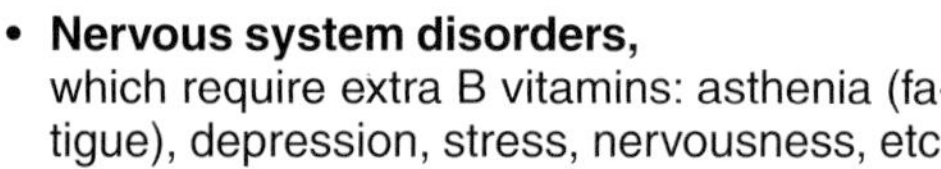

- **Nervous system disorders,** which require extra B vitamins: asthenia (fatigue), depression, stress, nervousness, etc.
- Male and female **sterility** from gonadal causes since ***vitamin E*** promotes sperm production and ovulation.
- **Hyperlipidemia** (increased fats in the blood), particularly types IIa and IIb.
- **Cancer, cardiac** disease (heart attack and angina): Because of its **antioxidant** effect, it halts degenerative cellular processes, aging, and arteriosclerosis.
- **Diabetes:** The anti-diabetic effect is attributed to the combined action of vitamins B_1 and E, which are abundant in wheat germ.
- Whenever there is an **increased need for nutrition:** Athletes, students under particular intellectual stress, pregnant or lactating women.

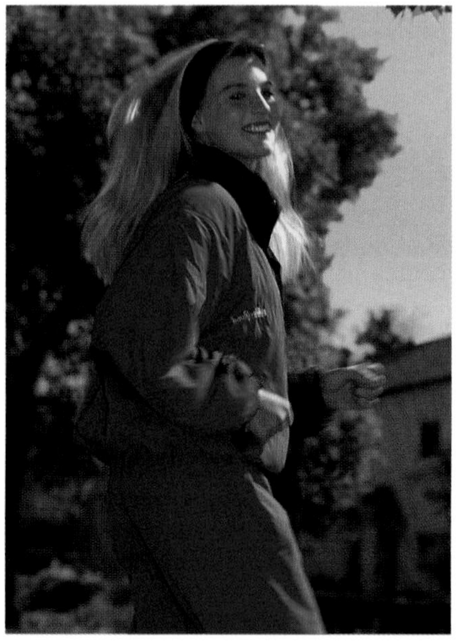

Wheat germ and its oil improve physical condition and resistance to fatigue.

Wheat bran

Its action could be compared to a sponge or broom acting on the interior of the intestine.

Composition

Wheat bran contains abundant proteins, fats, vitamins, and minerals, although these are poorly utilized by humans since they are encapsulated in undigestible cellulose fiber. However, *interest* in bran has less to do with what it provides than with its ***fiber richness,*** which reaches ***42.8%.***

Bran fiber is made up of ***cellulose, hemicellulose,*** and ***lignin*** (which gives it a hard, woody consistency).

Physiological activity

Bran produces three primary effects in the intestine:

- It retains water, *increasing* the **volume** and **weight** of the feces. Each ***gram*** of bran increases fecal weight by ***2-3 grams.***
- It *increases* the **speed** of fecal movement through the intestine.
- It *adsorbs* —in other words, retains and eliminates through the feces— **irritants, toxic substances, cholesterol, biliary salts,** and **carcinogens** that are in the intestine.

Benefits of bran

- It ***compensates*** for the **lack of fiber** in the diets based on refined foods, although eating whole grains is preferable to eating refined grains and adding bran to compensate.
- It ***prevents*** **constipation:**[18] It is necessary to take from 20 to 30 g a day for at least a week to achieve the desired effect.
- It ***reduces*** **cholesterol levels,** although **oat** bran is much *more effective.*
- It reduces the risk of diverticulitis, colon cancer, coronary disease, and breast cancer.[19]

Drawbacks to bran

- **Intestinal irritation:** Bran can irritate the intestinal mucosa because of the toughness of the lignin it contains. Its use is discouraged in cases of colitis and irritable bowel[19] (see pp. 199, 200).
- **Its phytate content:** Phytates form insoluble compounds of iron, zinc, and calcium, which impedes the absorption of these minerals in the intestine.
  - However, when *cooked, sprouted,* or *fermented* **whole grains** are consumed (bread, pastries), **phytates** have ***no*** *negative effects* on the absorption of iron, zinc, or calcium.[20]
- **Pollution:** Bran is in contact with the outside, and can be contaminated by:
  - Pesticides.
  - Heavy metals.

Correct usage of bran

- It is ***preferable*** to consume bran in its **natural state,** that is, with the rest of the kernel, as a part of the whole-grain wheat or its derivatives.
- In case bran is eaten on *its own,* we insist that ***30 g*** (about one ounce) ***a day not*** be **exceeded.** If possible, it should come from biological plantations.

It is preferable to consume bread and whole grains in which bran is present to eating bran on its own. In this case, 30 g (two spoonfuls, about one ounce) a day should not be exceeded.

15

Foods for the Musculoskeletal System

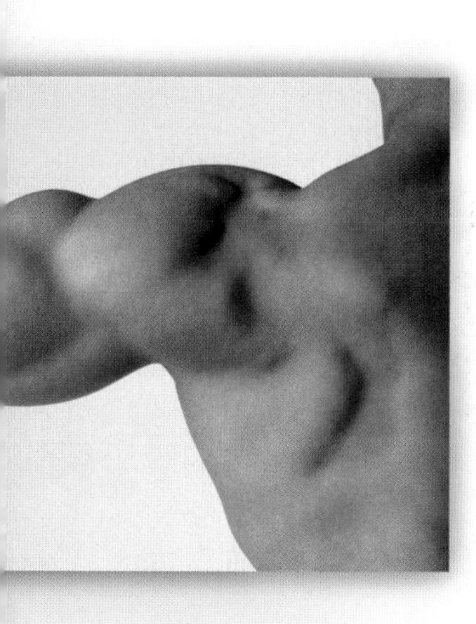

DIET PLAYS a decisive role in the proper condition of the musculoskeletal system, which includes the **bones** and the **structures** surrounding them, which makes bodily movement possible: **muscles, joints, tendons,** and **fasciae** or aponeurosis.

Foods *can* ***contribute*** to the health of the musculoskeletal system in the following ways:

- By ***providing carbohydrates, vitamins,*** and ***minerals*** necessary to maintain correct muscle **tone** and strength.
- By ***preventing*** **uric acid** deposits in the joints, thus avoiding their inflammation and deterioration (see p. 275).
- By ***reducing*** **arthritis** or inflammation of the joints (see p. 302).
- By ***preventing*** **osteoporosis** by providing the ***calcium, phosphorus,*** and ***magnesium*** necessary to maintain proper skeletal mineralization (see p. 300).

OSTEOPOROSIS

Definition

This is the ***reduction*** of bone ***mass*** and ***density*** to the point that it can result in *bone* deformation or fracture. In reality loss of bone mass is a natural process beginning around the ages of 40 or 50. However, it is only referred to as osteoporosis when it reaches a pathological level.

Prevention

Several factors can play a role in preventing or halting this loss of bone mass, thus *reducing* the **risk** of osteoporosis:

- Taking in ***enough*** **calcium** during childhood, when the skeleton is **developing.** Children and adolescents whose calcium intake is insufficient risk suffering osteoporosis as adults. Adults, as well, must take in a certain amount of calcium since bone is being formed and destroyed continually during the entire life. The RDA (Recommended Dietary Allowance) of calcium for adults is between 500 and 800 mg in order to replace losses of this mineral and to form new bone tissue.
- ***Reduction*** in the **elimination of calcium:** *Excess* **proteins** and **salt,** as well as **caffeine,** *increase* **urinary** calcium **loss.** Additionally, a diet based on meat, fish, and shellfish **acidifies** the blood. The body tries to compensate for this excess acidity by releasing alkalizing minerals such as calcium from the bones. In this way, bones are deprived of calcium, fostering osteoporosis. Fruits and vegetables are **alkalizers,** and, although they contain little calcium, they halt the urinary loss of this mineral from the bones.

  The reduction in hormone production that accompanies **menopause** also encourages calcium loss. This is more pronounced in some women than in others. **Soy** and its derivatives contain ***phytoestrogens*** (vegetable hormones) that can partially compensate for this reduced ovarian production, reducing the risk of osteoporosis.
- ***Sufficient*** **sun exposure:** Sunlight is necessary for vitamin D synthesis in the skin. This vitamin is essential in transferring calcium from the intestine to the bloodstream. Fair-skinned individuals produce sufficient vitamin D with an exposure to the sun of 5 to 10 minutes a day. Darker-skinned individuals require twice as much or more.
- ***Sufficient*** **physical exercise:** Those with a sedentary lifestyle experience more bone destruction than formation. Physical exercise halts the loss of bone mass and helps prevent osteoporosis.

An ***adequate*** **diet** is the ***most influential*** factor in osteoporosis prevention, but not only during adulthood, but also in infancy and childhood. The more calcium retained within the skeleton during development, the greater the reserve for the adult, and the later the onset of osteoporosis.

 **Increase**

CALCIUM
SOY
ALMOND
TOFU
CABBAGE
SPROUTS
MOLASSES
COCONUT
ALFALFA
ORANGE
LEAFY GREEN VEGETABLES
TURNIP
VITAMIN D
VITAMIN SUPPLEMENTS
SESAME SEED

 **Reduce or Eliminate**

MEAT
FISH
AGED CHEESE
SALT
TOTAL FAT
WHITE SUGAR
CHOCOLATE
STIMULANT BEVERAGES
ALCOHOLIC BEVERAGES
SOFT DRINKS
PHOSPHORUS
WHEAT BRAN

Milk

Milk is a very good source of calcium (around 120 mg/100 g). The bioavailability (the portion that is absorbed) of this calcium is quite high (20% to 40%) since lactose (milk sugar) and vitamin D facilitate its absorption. Although milk and dairy products are not the only sources of calcium, their consumption during childhood and adolescence helps prevent osteoporosis in adulthood.[1]
Conversely, it has been proven that milk or dairy foods taken by adults do not contribute to the prevention of osteoporosis.
Therefore, in spite of being high in calcium, milk and dairy products are not sufficient neither necessary to have healthy bones.

OSTEOARTHRITIS

Definition

Osteoarthritis is characterized by a ***progressive painful erosion of articular*** (joint) cartilage. It is also known as degenerative joint disease. Overloading the joints with excess weight or labor is one of the primary causal factors in this disease. It particularly affects the **hip** and the **knee.**

Diet

The **primary objective** in dietetic treatment of osteoarthritis is **weight loss**. Consuming appropriate amounts of bone-building ***minerals*** and ***sulfur,*** which is necessary in maintaining cartilage, also contributes to the prevention or halt the development of osteoarthritis.

Avoiding obesity is the first rule of arthritis treatment.

Increase

- CALCIUM
- LEGUMES
- WHOLE GRAINS
- MOLASSES
- ALFALFA
- COCONUT

Tender alfalfa

Soy has been shown effective in halting the loss of bone mass resulting after menopause.
This loss is a consequence of reduced ovarian hormone production. Soy and soy derivatives, particularly tofu, provide plant-based hormones (phytoestrogens such as isoflavones) that replace those produced by the ovaries and enhance the mineralization of the skeleton.[2] Soy also provides calcium.

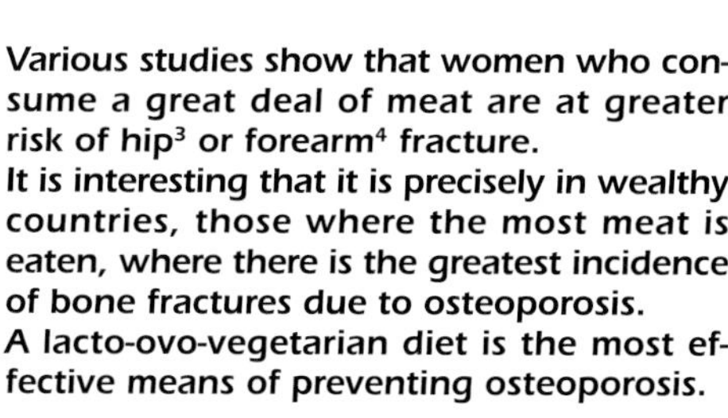

Various studies show that women who consume a great deal of meat are at greater risk of hip[3] or forearm[4] fracture.
It is interesting that it is precisely in wealthy countries, those where the most meat is eaten, where there is the greatest incidence of bone fractures due to osteoporosis.
A lacto-ovo-vegetarian diet is the most effective means of preventing osteoporosis.

RHEUMATOID ARTHRITIS

Definition

This is an **inflammation of the joints** of unknown cause. It is most frequent in middle-aged women. It affects the small joints of the hands and feet, and produces inflammation, pain, functional disability, and joint deformation.

Diet

Those with rheumatoid arthritis also tend to suffer from anemia, stomach ulcers, protein loss, and a certain level of malnutrition. Because of this, and because certain foods worsen the disease, an adequate diet is important. These are the potential results of three types of **diet:**

- **Omnivorous:** based on meat and animal products: ***Worsens*** the disease and aggravates the inflammation of the joints.
- **Ovolactovegetarian:** This diet produces a degree of **improvement** when it *replaces* an omnivorous diet. Yogurt is the best-tolerated dairy product.
- **Strict vegetarian** (vegan): This diet produces the **best results,** particularly if it emphasizes raw fruits and vegetables.

Rheumatoid arthritis patients present an increased index of antibodies to two types of intestinal bacteria: *Escherichia coli* and *Proteus mirabilis.* Both of these species proliferate under an omnivorous diet and decrease when the diet is vegetarian or with the consumption of "biotic" yogurt.[5, 6] This helps explain the fact that rheumatoid arthritis improves with a vegetarian diet.

Increase

FRUIT
LEGUMES
SOY
VEGETABLES
NUTS
WHOLE GRAINS
OILS
FISH OIL
SAUERKRAUT
WALNUT
WHEAT GERM
YOGURT

Reduce or Eliminate

MEAT
PORK
ALCOHOLIC BEVERAGES
MILK
EGG
ADDITIVES

Broccoli

A diet based on raw fruits and vegetables provides substantial improvement in the process of rheumatoid arthritis, reducing inflammation, pain, and joint deformation.

A wide range of experiences prove that a vegetarian diet reduces the inflammation of rheumatoid arthritis, while an omnivorous diet aggravates it.[7, 8, 9]
One of the reasons for this is meat's high levels of arachidonic acid, a fatty acid that the body uses to produce eicosanoids. These substances initiate inflammatory processes.[10]

RICKETS AND OSTEOMALACIA

Definition

Both of these diseases consist of the **softening** and **deformation** of the **bones** caused by insufficient mineralization, particularly lack of calcium. The minerals in question are those that give bones their characteristic hardness.

Rickets is associated with ***childhood***, while **osteomalacia** is found in ***adults.***

In osteoporosis there is a loss of bone mass and the bones become spongy and less dense, lending themselves to fracture. In rickets and osteomalacia there is sufficient bone mass, also called bone matrix, formed of proteins; however, this matrix lacks sufficient minerals.

Cause

The *most common* cause of both diseases is ***vitamin D deficiency*** due to lack of exposure to the sun or of insufficient dietary consumption.

Diet

In both cases, in addition to vitamin D and calcium, other minerals (phosphorus and magnesium) and trace elements (such as boron and fluorine) are necessary for bone mineralization.

Increase

VITAMIN D
CALCIUM
CABBAGE
ORANGE
ALFALFA
MOLASSES
ALMOND
COCONUT

Reduce or Eliminate

WHEAT BRAN
SPINACH

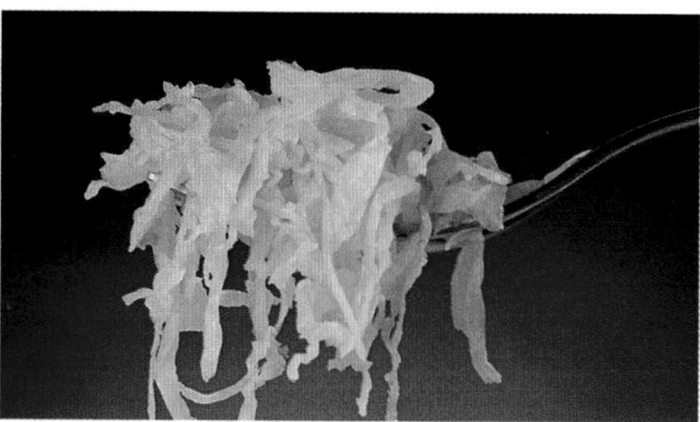

All varieties of cabbage, including cauliflower and broccoli, supply easily absorbed calcium. Sauerkraut (fermented cabbage) provides this as well.

CARPAL TUNNEL SYNDROME

Causes

This is produced by the compression of the median nerve as it passes through the carpal tunnel in the wrist. It is caused by the entrapment of the median nerve at the wrist, within the carpal tunnel.

Symptoms

It is characterized by nocturnal hand paresthesia (tingling sensation and pain), and sometimes sensory loss and wasting in the median hand distribution.

Treatment

This condition *often* requires **surgical intervention** to release the nerve. However, certain foods provide some relief.

Increase

VITAMIN B6
WHEAT GERM

Reduce or Eliminate

ALCOHOLIC BEVERAGES
STIMULANT BEVERAGES (COFFEE, TEA, MATÉ, ETC.)

MUSCLE CRAMPS

Definition

These *involuntary, painful* ***muscle contractions*** *often occur in the leg muscles at night.*

Causes

Certain factors ***foster*** cramping: **dehydration,** *loss* of **minerals** due to diarrhea, vomiting, polyuria (excess urination), or perspiration; *intense* **physical exercise;** and *disorders* of **venous circulation** in the legs related to varicose veins.

Increase

WATER
MAGNESIUM
POTASSIUM
VITAMIN B
PURIFYING BROTH
FRUIT
ISOTONIC BEVERAGES

Purifying broth

A cup of purifying broth at bedtime helps prevent muscle cramps. It is mainly made with onion and celery.

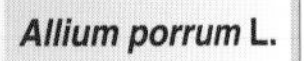

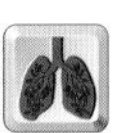

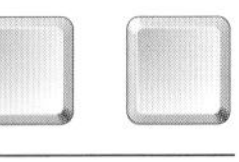

Leek

Eliminates uric acid

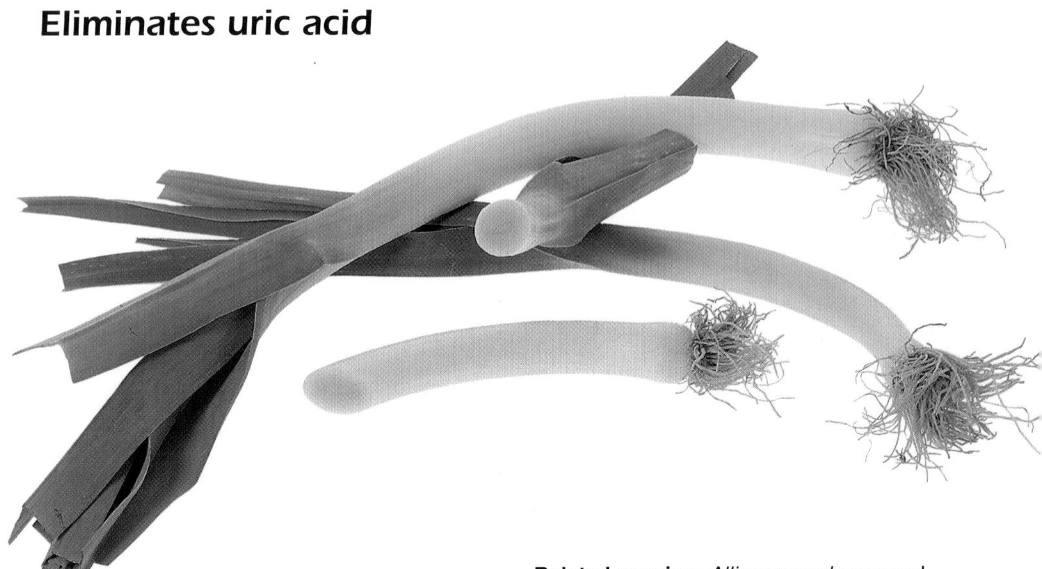

Related species: *Allium ampeloprasum* L.

Synonym: *Poor-man's-asparagus.*

French: *Poireau;* ***Spanish:*** *Puerro, ajo puerro.*

Description: *Stalks of the leek ('Allium porrum' L.), a herbaceous plant of the botanical family Liliaceae.*

LEEK composition

per 100 g of raw edible portion

Energy	61.0 kcal = 255 kj
Protein	1.50 g
Carbohydrates	12.4 g
Fiber	1.80 g
Vitamin A	10.0 µg RE
Vitamin B_1	0.060 mg
Vitamin B_2	0.030 mg
Niacin	0.600 mg NE
Vitamin B_6	0.233 mg
Folate	64.1 µg
Vitamin B_{12}	—
Vitamin C	12.0 mg
Vitamin E	0.920 mg α-TE
Calcium	59.0 mg
Phosphorus	35.0 mg
Magnesium	28.0 mg
Iron	2.10 mg
Potassium	180 mg
Zinc	0.120 mg
Total Fat	*0.300 g*
Saturated Fat	*0.040 g*
Cholesterol	—
Sodium	*20.0 mg*

1% 2% 4% 10% 20% 40% 100%

% Daily Value (based on a 2,000 calorie diet) provided by 100 g of this food

LEEKS DIFFER from **onions** in that they have virtually no bulb, but do develop much more stalk. These, together with **garlic,** belong to the same botanical family and share many properties.

PROPERTIES AND INDICATIONS: The composition of the leek is similar to that of the onion (see p. 142), although it contains *more* ***carbohydrates*** (12.3%), *more* ***folic acid*** (64.1 µg/100 g), and *more* ***minerals.*** Among these, the most notable are ***calcium*** (59 mg/100 g), ***magnesium*** (28 mg/100 g), and ***iron*** (2.1 mg/100 g). One-half kilo of leeks provides the 10 mg of iron that an adult needs in a day, and one-third of the daily need for calcium. Their vitamin content is negligible.

Leeks, strawberries or raspberries, and apples are very appropriate to ease the elimination of uric acid from the blood, thereby preventing gout crises.

Leeks also contain an ***essential oil*** similar to that found in onions, although in lower concentration. Its indications are as follows:

- **Uratic arthritis:** The body produces uric acid daily as a residue of the metabolism of proteins, which is excreted through the urine. When excess uric acid is produced, it tends to deposit in joints, causing inflammation and pain (arthritis). Leeks' **alkalizing** and **diuretic** effects increase urinary elimination of uric acid. They are particularly beneficial for those suffering from arthritis, gout and kidney disorders.
- **Bronchitis and sinusitis,** due to their mucolytic (fluidization of mucus) effect and the antiseptic properties of their essence.
- **Constipation,** because of the laxative effect of their fiber. Leeks can produce intestinal flatulence.

Preparation and use

❶ **Raw:** When they are young and tender, they may be eaten raw in salads, as are onions.

❷ **Boiled** or steamed: Prepared with oil and lemon or mayonnaise, this is an exquisite dish.

❸ **Cooked:** As part of a variety of dishes. Leeks combine well with potatoes and eggs.

Turnip

Calcium-rich leaves

TURNIP composition
per 100 g of raw edible portion

Energy	27.0 kcal = 114 kj
Protein	0.900 g
Carbohydrates	4.43 g
Fiber	1.80 g
Vitamin A	—
Vitamin B_1	0.040 mg
Vitamin B_2	0.030 mg
Niacin	0.550 mg NE
Vitamin B_6	0.090 mg
Folate	14.5 µg
Vitamin B_{12}	—
Vitamin C	21.0 mg
Vitamin E	0.030 mg α-TE
Calcium	30.0 mg
Phosphorus	27.0 mg
Magnesium	11.0 mg
Iron	0.300 mg
Potassium	191 mg
Zinc	0.270 mg
Total Fat	*0.100 g*
Saturated Fat	*0.011 g*
Cholesterol	—
Sodium	*67.0 mg*

1% 2% 4% 10% 20% 40% 100%

% Daily Value (based on a 2,000 calorie diet) provided by 100 g of this food

French: *Navet, chou-rave;*
Spanish: *Nabo, colinabo.*

Description: *Roots and leaves of turnip plant ('Brassica rapa' L.), of the botanical family Cruciferae. Because it is a tuberous (enlarged) root and not a tuber, the turnip does not have sprouts or eyes, as does the potato. Turnips may be round, cylindrical, and conical. Their external color is white or reddish; internally, they are always white or yellowish.*

THE PEOPLES of Central Europe owe much to the lowly turnip. Although today this vegetable is rather neglected from a culinary and nutritional point of view, these roots have served dietary needs from antiquity, both for humans and for livestock.

PROPERTIES AND INDICATIONS: The turnip contains considerably more water than the potato (92% as compared to 79%). This reduces its energy-producing potential: carbohydrates, 4.43%; proteins, 0.9%; fats, 0.1%.

It contains small amounts of ***B complex vitamins*** (B_1, B_2, B_6, niacin, and folates). It also contains a good supply of ***vitamin C*** (100 g of turnips supplies 21 mg of this vitamin, more than one-third of the daily requirement for an adult male). Turnips lack provitamin A (beta-carotene), vitamins E, and B_{12}.

The turnip's most abundant ***mineral*** is potassium (191 mg/100 g), followed by sodium (67 mg/100 g). It also contains small amounts of calcium, phosphorus, and iron, as well as trace elements. It is quite high in ***fiber*** (1.8%).

Taken as a whole, the turnip provides little energy (27 kcal/100 g), virtually no fat, and considerable fiber. Because of its non-nutritive compounds, which are similar to those in cabbages (see p. 182), but not well understood yet, the turnip is **alkalizing, blood-purifying** (depurant), and **diuretic.**

These are its therapeutic indications:

• **Gout** (uratic arthritis): Eating turnips facilitates urinary elimination of the **uric acid,** normally produced as the body metabolizes proteins. When there is an excess of this substance, it creates a toxic state in the body (gout) in which uric acid crystals are deposited particularly in the joints, causing inflammation and rheumatic pain.

Eating turnips "cleanses" the blood of uric acid, as well as other metabolic residues. Thus, they provide relief for those with gout or others suffering from **rheumatic** pain caused by uric acid.

• **Obesity:** Turnips provide a considerable sensation of satiety with few calories (27 kcal /100 g). They are a nourishing component effective in weight loss diets, easily digested and lacking fat.

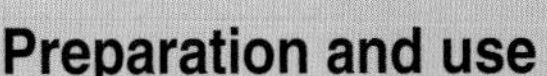

Preparation and use

❶ **Root:** This is eaten cooked accompanying rice dishes and legumes. Rice with beans and turnips is a typical dish of the Valencian Levant in eastern Spain.

❷ **Fresh leaves** (greens): May be eaten raw in salad or cooked like spinach.

Turnip greens

This is the most calcium-rich of the leafy green vegetables and much more nutritious than the turnip itself.

Generally, the tops of turnips, or turnip greens have been discarded or fed to animals. Today it is known that turnip greens are much more nutritious than the turnip itself. Many are learning to enjoy the pleasant flavor and vitamin and mineral richness of this leafy green.

They may be eaten raw in salad (when they are fresh) or cooked in the same manner as spinach.

Turnip greens provide almost twice the proteins and fiber as the root, although fewer carbohydrates. However, their most outstanding nutritional feature is their *concentration* of ***vitamins*** and ***minerals,*** which is several times that of the root. Most notable among these are calcium, provitamin A (beta-carotene), vitamin C, folates, and iron.

Chestnut

Invigorates the muscles

CHESTNUT composition
per 100 g of raw edible portion

Energy	213 kcal = 890 kj
Protein	2.42 g
Carbohydrates	37.4 g
Fiber	8.10 g
Vitamin A	3.00 µg RE
Vitamin B_1	0.238 mg
Vitamin B_2	0.168 mg
Niacin	1.63 mg NE
Vitamin B_6	0.376 mg
Folate	62.0 µg
Vitamin B_{12}	—
Vitamin C	43.0 mg
Vitamin E	—
Calcium	27.0 mg
Phosphorus	93.0 mg
Magnesium	32.0 mg
Iron	1.01 mg
Potassium	518 mg
Zinc	0.520 mg
Total Fat	*2.26 g*
Saturated Fat	*0.425 g*
Cholesterol	—
Sodium	*3.00 mg*

1% 2% 4% 10% 20% 40% 100%

% **Daily Value** (based on a 2,000 calorie diet) provided by 100 g of this food

French: *Châtaigne;* ***Spanish:*** *Castaña.*

Description: *Seed of the fruit of the chestnut tree ('Castanea sativa' Mill.), a robust tree of the botanical family Fagaceae.*

THE GERMAN physician and nutritionist W. Heupke, considered one of the founders of the modern German school of nutrition, called chestnuts "the small loaves of bread that nature provides."[11]

PROPERTIES AND INDICATIONS: The chestnut is one of nature's *richest* ***carbohydrate*** sources (37.4%), *comparable only* to **legumes** and **grains.** These carbohydrates are formed primarily of ***starch*** (85%), and ***saccharose*** (15%). There is virtually no glucose or fructose.

Chestnuts also contain proteins (2.42%) and fats (2.26%), most of which are mono and polyunsaturated.

Even though they contain no vitamin E and little vitamin A, they are quite rich in vitamin C and, above all, in B complex vitamins: B_1, B_2, B_6, and niacin. This ***B vitamin*** concentration is *similar* to that of **whole wheat** (including the germ).

The chestnut's mineral content is noteworthy for its *richness* in ***potassium*** (518 mg /100 g) and its *low* ***sodium*** content (3 mg/100 g), which makes it *very beneficial* for those with **hypertension** or **cardiovascular disorders.** It also contains a significant amount of iron (1 mg/100 g), as well as magnesium, calcium, phosphorus, and the trace elements zinc, copper, and manganese.

Chestnuts act as a muscle tonic, **alkalizer,** astringent, and galactagogue (promotes milk flow).

Chestnuts are indicated in the following cases:

- **Physical fatigue due** to intense muscular exercise (athletes, manual laborers) or malnutrition. They have a tonic effect on the muscles, providing a sensation of energy and well-being.
- **Growth periods:** Chestnuts are a good source of the calories, vitamins, and minerals needed for musculoskeletal development of adolescents.
- **Arteriosclerosis** and cardiovascular conditions: Chestnuts provide energy but *very little* ***fat*** and ***sodium.*** Their *high* ***potassium*** *content* helps prevent hypertension.
- **Diarrhea:** Chestnut puree **[❹]**, in particular, is an excellent food in cases of diarrhea because of its mild astringent and regulating effects.
- **Kidney failure:** Chestnuts are a recommended food for those suffering from kidney failure because their **alkalizing** effect partially compensates for excess acid in the blood.
- **Lactating mothers:** Chestnuts are galactagogues (they promote milk flow). They also provide a great deal of nutrition to the lactating mother.

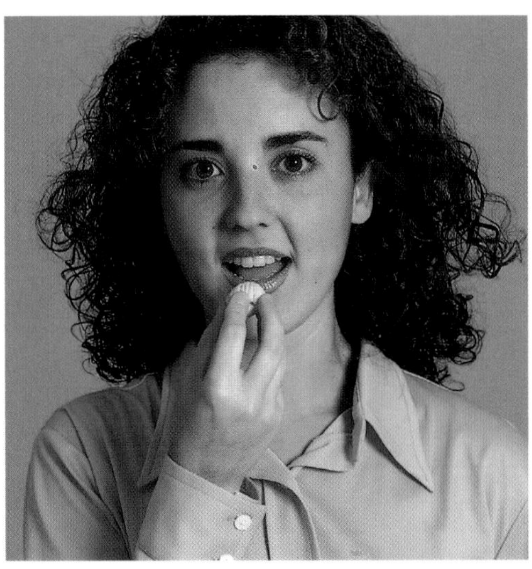

Chestnuts are not just a sweet or a snack, but a very nutritious and invigorating food.

Preparation and use

❶ **Raw:** Chestnuts should only be eaten raw when they are ***very tender,*** and even then they must be very well chewed to begin digestion in the mouth.

❷ **Cooked:** Once shelled, they are boiled for 20-30 min. Aromatic herbs such as cumin, fennel, or thyme may be added to the water.

❸ **Roasted** either in the oven or over coals. They may be roasted with the shell, which must be cut to relieve pressure. Roasted chestnuts are delicious.

❹ **Chestnut puree:** After boiling, the chestnuts are mashed to a consistent paste. Brown sugar or honey may be added. The paste may also be mixed with milk.

❺ **'Marron glacé':** is a classic exquisite French sweet made from the best quality chestnuts and egg white.

Coconut

Mineral-rich

COCONUT composition
per 100 g of raw edible portion

Energy	354 kcal = 1,480 kj
Protein	3.33 g
Carbohydrates	6.23 g
Fiber	9.00 g
Vitamin A	—
Vitamin B_1	0.066 mg
Vitamin B_2	0.020 mg
Niacin	1.19 mg NE
Vitamin B_6	0.054 mg
Folate	26.4 µg
Vitamin B_{12}	—
Vitamin C	3.30 mg
Vitamin E	0.730 mg α-TE
Calcium	14.0 mg
Phosphorus	113 mg
Magnesium	32.0 mg
Iron	2.43 mg
Potassium	356 mg
Zinc	1.10 mg
Total Fat	33.5 g
Saturated Fat	29.7 g
Cholesterol	—
Sodium	20.0 mg

1% 2% 4% 10% 20% 40% 100% 200% 500%

% Daily Value (based on a 2,000 calorie diet)
provided by 100 g of this food

Synonym: *Cokernut.*

French: *Noix de coco;* ***Spanish:*** *Coco.*

Description: *Seed of the coconut palm ('Cocos nucifera' L.), a tree of the botanical family Palmae that reaches 20 meters in height. In spite of its name, the fruit is botanically not a nut, but a drupe that weighs up to 2.5 kilos (about 5 pounds).*

The coconut is formed of a rough yellow or orange exterior husk (exocarp); a fibrous intermediate layer equivalent to the fleshy part of common fruits (mesocarp); and the central core (endocarp), which contains the seed, formed of the white pulp that is the edible portion.

THE COCONUT palm is a survivor. It resists the worst of nature like no other. It bows before the power of tropical cyclones without losing its hold on the earth. And when the storm has passed, these elegant trees stand tall on the tropical beaches as if nothing had happened.

Amazingly, their fruit, the coconut, is capable of riding the ocean waves for hundreds, even thousands of miles without losing its ability to germinate. How vitally indomitable these seemingly fragile trees are!

In Sanskrit, the language of ancient India, the coconut palm is called *kalpa vriksha,* which means, "the tree that provides everything necessary for life." And this is not an exaggeration. It is well known that the inhabitants of the islands of Polynesia have survived, sometimes for generations, based on the coconut. The coconut provides liquid for drinking and solid food; its fiber is used for everything from ropes to toothbrushes. Palm trunks and fronds are used for sandals, textiles, and even houses.

The vital strength and resistance of the coconut, as well as the flexibility of the palm, seem to proclaim the medicinal properties of this unique fruit.

PROPERTIES AND INDICATIONS: The composition of coconut pulp varies with its degree of ripeness. When the fruit is green (6 to 7 months) the pulp is gelatinous, contains a great deal of water, and its ***nutritional*** *content* is *less.*

As the coconut *matures,* the pulp becomes firmer, with less water and its ***nutrients*** are *more concentrated.* At this point it contains a fair proportion of ***carbohydrates*** (6.23%), proteins (3.33%), and mineral salts, particularly ***magnesium, calcium,*** and ***phosphorus.***

Composition of coconut oil (Fat)

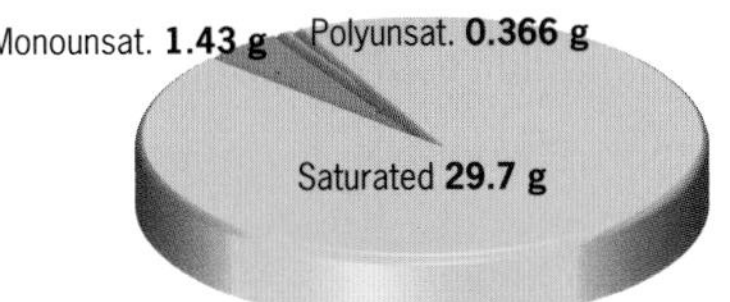

COCONUT
Percentage distribution of
fatty acids

*Most of the coconut's **fatty acids** are **saturated,** which led many nutrition specialists to believe that they promoted cholesterol formation, as is the case with the saturated fatty acids found in animal-based fats.*
*However, most of the coconut's fatty acids have a unique property that differentiates them from those of animal origin: their molecule contains from 6 to 14 carbon atoms. Today it is known that these **short and medium chain fatty acids** found in coconuts do **not increase cholesterol** levels, in spite of being saturated. Animal fats are predominantly long chain saturated fatty acids such as stearic acid (18 carbon atoms) that do increase the levels of cholesterol in the body.*

Preparation and use

❶ **Ripe pulp:** This may be eaten raw, whole or grated; or roasted, forming part of a variety of dishes.

❷ **Gelatinous pulp**: This is obtained from green coconuts. It is eaten with a spoon once the nut has been opened. It contains the same nutrients as ripe coconut, but in lower concentrations.

❸ **Coconut water**: This is the liquid found inside the coconut. The greener the fruit, the more water there is. Coconut water is an excellent thirst quencher.

❹ **Coconut milk:** Refreshing and nutritious. Its preparation is described in p. 312. It may be made adding water or cow's milk.

❺ **Copra:** This is sun-dried coconut pulp.

❻ **Coconut oil:** This is prepared industrially by processing copra under high pressure.

Coconut milk

This is obtained by squeezing grated ripe coconut pulp.

1. **Finely grate** the coconut **pulp** or put it in a blender.
2. **Add one-half liter of boiling water** and let stand for one-half hour. Cow's milk may be used in place of water.
3. **Prepare a cotton cloth** and fill it with the coconut paste.
4. **Twist the cloth containing the paste** until all of the liquid has been removed.
5. To take full advantage of the coconut, the **hot water** process may be **repeated** with the remaining pulp repeating steps 3 and 4.
6. Coconut milk is used as a **soft drink** or **added** to fruit shakes or other dishes.

However, the *most abundant* nutrient in the coconut is ***fat,*** which makes up more than a *third* of its mature weight.

The dietary and therapeutic properties of the coconut depend on its mineral content, particularly ***magnesium.*** Ripe coconut pulp contains 32 mg/100 g, and coconut water contains 25 mg/100 g. Although these are not large quantities, they surpass that of all **animal-based foods,** including meat, fish, milk, and eggs.

Most of the body's ***MAGNESIUM*** is found in the bones (60%) and the muscles (26%). It contributes to bone hardness and healthy cartilage in the joints. *Lack* of magnesium in the muscles produces **cramps** and nervous **excitability.**

In addition to a certain amount of magnesium, coconuts contain other minerals of great importance to the musculoskeletal system such as ***calcium*** and ***phosphorus.***

A food such as the coconut that provides these ***minerals*** in *proper proportion* contributes to healthy **bones, joints,** and **muscles,** all of which make up the musculoskeletal system.

Coconut consumption (pulp or water **[❶,❷,❸]**) has a beneficial impact on the musculoskeletal system in the following cases:

- Bone **decalcification** (loss of calcium).
- **Osteoporosis** (demineralization and loss of bone mass).
- **Musculoskeletal** pain due to excess tension or lack of muscular relaxation, particularly back pain.

Because of their **remineralizing** effect, coconuts are also recommended:

- During **infant teething** to promote healthy enamel formation.
- In cases of **brittle hair** or **nails.**

It is interesting that coconut **WATER** or **MILK** **[❸,❹]** are *almost as rich* in ***minerals*** as the pulp itself, but with the advantage that they *contain no* ***fat.*** A liter of coconut water contains about 300 mg of magnesium, which is the RDA (Recommended Dietary Allowance) of this mineral for an adult.

Coconuts from other palms

Various types of tropical palms also produce fruits similar to the coconut:

Sea coconut or Seychelles coconut (*Lodoicea maldivica*): This enormous coconut may weigh 25 kilos. It is similar in composition to the common coconut. It is grown in the islands of the Indian Ocean and in Madagascar.
Spanish: *Coco de mar.*

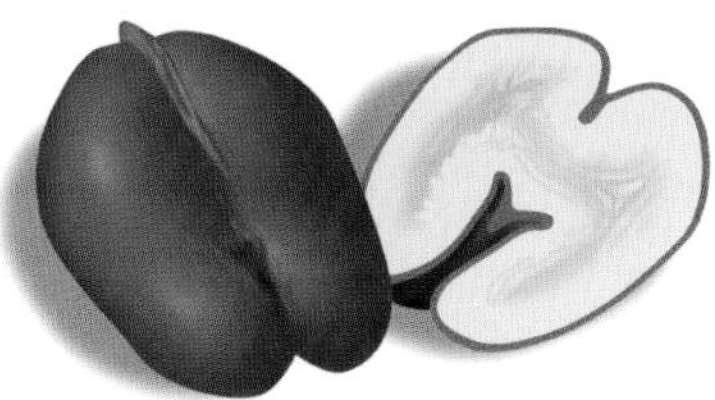

King coconut (*Cocos nucifera* var. *aurantiaca*): This yellow or orange variety of the common coconut contains less pulp but *much more* ***water*** (up to one-half liter). The water of this coconut is more aromatic and refreshing than the common coconut.
French: *Noix de coco;*
Spanish: *Coco de beber.*

Beach palm (*Bactris major* Jacq.): This is the fruit of a palm that reaches 30 meters in height that grows wild. They are also cultivated in Panama, Colombia, and Venezuela. The fruits are yellow and grow in enormous bunches of up to 4,000 pieces. The pulp has a bittersweet taste. It is used to extract a very pleasant juice used to make soft drinks, gelatins and jams.
French: *Corossol;* ***Spanish:*** *Corozo.*

Palmyra palm (*Borassus flabellifer* L.): This is the fruit of a palm cultivated in southern India, Sri Lanka, and Malaysia. They grow in bunches like coconuts, but are considerably smaller (10-12 cm). Its pulp is grated and strained to make a delicious **beverage.**
French: *Palmier à vin;*
Spanish: *Palmira.*

Salak *(Salacca edulis* Reinw.): This palm, which reaches 5 meters and has large fronds, is cultivated in Indonesia and Thailand. The ***pulp,*** which is divided into three sections, is white, of firm consistency, and bittersweet taste. It acts as an **astringent.**
French: *Zalacca;*
Spanish: *Salaca.*

16

Foods for the Skin

DIET PLAYS a prominent role in the condition of the **skin** and its related structures such as the **nails** and **hair.** Skin possesses three physical characteristics:

1. It is ***sensitive*** to **nutritional deficiencies:** The skin's **cells** are being ***replaced*** constantly. Therefore, they need a constant supply of nutrients for the production of new cells.
   This makes the skin particularly sensitive to nutritional deficiencies, especially ***proteins, essential fatty acids, vitamins A*** and ***C, iron,*** and ***zinc.***
2. **Eliminatory organ:** The skin is referred to as ***"the third kidney"*** since it is actively involved in the body's purifying processes. Certain amounts of the toxins that circulate within the blood are eliminated through the skin. However, the eliminatory capability of

the skin can be overtaxed when there is an increased concentration of toxins because of:

- **Kidney** or **liver** *failure.*
- **Constipation.**
- A **diet** *based* on **meat** products, particularly sausages, shellfish, and variety meats.

Under these conditions the skin suffers ***internal*** **poisoning,** and reacts with various pathological manifestations, such as eczema, dermatoses, and a variety of eruptions.

3. **Source of allergic reactions:** Many food-based allergic reactions are manifested through the skin.

A healthful diet does more for the health and beauty of the skin than any external applications or cosmetic treatments.

ACNE

Definition

This is the *hypertrophy and infection of the skin's sebaceous glands.* These glands produce **sebum,** an *oil that protects the skin.* When the follicles of these glands are obstructed, which may result from a variety of causes, the sebum accumulates within and the glands swell. Since the sebum cannot flow properly, the glands become infected and inflamed, producing pustular eruptions typical of acne.

Causes

This disease manifests itself most frequently during adolescence. These are its causal factors:

- **Genetics.**
- **Hormones,** particularly the **androgens** responsible for masculinization.
- Emotional **stress.**
- A **diet** that is poor in fruit, nuts, grains, legumes, vegetables, and rich in refined products, animal fats, and additives. A typical diet based on hamburgers, French-fries, and ice-cream or sweets is an example of a diet that promotes acne.

 **Increase**

FRUIT
VEGETABLES
WHOLE GRAINS
SOY
VITAMIN E

 **Reduce or Eliminate**

SUGARS
REFINED BAKED GOODS
SATURATED FATS
MILK
CHOCOLATE
SALT

Chocolat
Biscuits

A diet that is rich in sugars and products made with them (candy, etc.) fosters acne development.

Dry skin

Definition and causes

Because of age, excess fat insulation, and harsh chemical substances, **skin cells** *tend* to **dehydrate** (lose moisture). This makes the skin rough, cracked, and unattractive.

Diet

Certain foods such as those described here ***protect*** skin cells and ***prevent* dehydration** and ***premature aging.***

Increase

Beans
Carrot
Peanut
Mango
Cucumber
Sunflower seeds

Sunflower seeds

Cellulitis

Definition

The term cellulitis is used to describe two distinct disorders:

- ***Infection of the subcutaneous tissue*** just below the dermis. This infection tends to be quite ***serious*** and is generally the result of wounds or other trauma to the skin. Dental infections cause cellulitis of the face and neck.
- ***Inflammation or variation of the subcutaneous tissue*** that is not infected, which is noted particularly in obese women. The skin loses its smoothness and takes on an irregular "orange peel" appearance.

This second type of cellulitis is ***not*** itself **serious.** It is primarily an **esthetic** issue. It is important, however, because it is evidence of poor health.

Causes

Obesity and hormonal imbalances, excess skin insulation (results in dry, less elastic skin), and fluid and toxin retention contribute to the development of cellulitis.

Diet

A healthful diet acts ***from within*** and tends to provide better results than external cosmetic skin treatments.

Hair fragility

Causes and treatment

Healthy hair requires good nutrition. Vitamin and mineral deficiencies can prematurely affect the beauty and strength of the hair.

Hair **loss** is normally due to **hormonal** factors. However, a healthful diet that provides all of the vitamins, minerals, and trace elements necessary can contribute to the health of remaining hair.

Increase

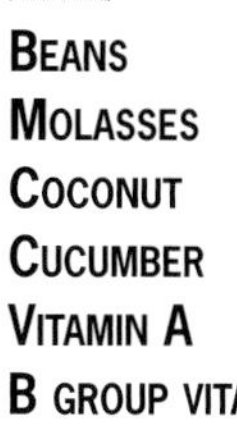

Beans
Molasses
Coconut
Cucumber
Vitamin A
B group vitamins

Beans

Increase

Diuretic foods
(see p. 230)
Fruit
Whole grains
Legumes
Fiber
Vitamin A

Reduce or Eliminate

Saturated fat
Salt
Alcoholic beverages
Sugars

Whole bread

A fiber-rich diet reduces cellulitis, possibly because fiber retains and removes toxic substances in the intestine.

ALLERGIES

Definition

An allergy is the *body's* ***rejection*** *of a chemical substance known as an* ***allergen*** *or antigen.* This reaction is disproportionately intense related to the minute amount of the allergen or its seeming innocuousness.

Causes

Any chemical substance whether ingested with food, inhaled, or introduced into the body by any other means can cause an allergic reaction.

Foods as a cause of allergy

The following foods *frequently* cause allergic reactions. Their consumption can also contribute to allergic reactions to other foods or substances. For instance, in sensitized individuals milk may precipitate an allergic reaction to other foods or substances and potentiate other allergic reactions.[1]

Antiallergenic diet

In any instance of allergy where the cause is not absolutely clear, an antiallergenic diet is recommended that **eliminates foods** that often cause allergies, such as those in this table. Afterwards, slowly and in a carefully controlled manner, foods may be added back until the symptoms reappear.

Abstinence from the foods listed here can improve any type of food allergy.

Symptoms

Allergic symptoms tend to appear most frequently on the skin, the respiratory system, and the digestive system, independently of the port of entry of the allergen. Many cases of eczema, rhinitis, asthma, migraine, and colitis are allergic reactions, and may be initiated or exacerbated by one or more of the foods listed here.

Mussel

Shellfish is the most frequent cause of allergies.

 **Reduce or Eliminate**

- MILK
- FISH
- SHELLFISH
- EGG
- MEAT
- CURED CHEESES
- ADDITIVES
- ALCOHOLIC BEVERAGES
- SPICES
- CHOCOLATE
- HONEY
- GLUTEN
- NUTS
- VEGETABLES
- FRUIT

PSORIASIS

Definition

This is a hereditary skin disease characterized by redness and scaling of the skin on various parts of the body (elbows, knees, scalp, thorax, etc.).

Heath counsels

Sunbathing is of benefit, while stress and infections aggravate it.

 **Increase**

- VEGETABLES
- FISH OIL
- MOLASSES
- VITAMIN A

 **Reduce or Eliminate**

- SATURATED FAT
- MILK
- MEAT
- ALCOHOLIC BEVERAGES

Cow's milk is one of the most frequent causes of allergy in infants and adolescents. Allergy to milk is produced by the rejection of milk proteins and is manifested in cutaneous (eczema, atopic dermatitis, urticaria), digestive (flatulence, diarrhea), and respiratory (asthma) symptoms.[2, 3]

Dermatitis and Eczema

Definition

These terms are practically synonymous. Both refer to a skin condition characterized by *irritation and inflammation, redness, itching, blistering, and scaling.*

Causes

These are the ***most influential* factors** in the appearance of dermatitis.

- **Food allergy,** particularly to one or more of the foods listed in ***"Allergies"***. Their consumption initiates or exacerbates dermatitis.
- **Contact** with allergens.
- **Deficiency** in one or more of these nutrients: niacin, vitamin B_6, vitamin A, essential or polyunsaturated fatty acids, and trace elements.

Diet

Atopic dermatitis, atopy, or atopic eczema is a type of dermatitis seen in **infants** and **children** with a *family history* of allergies. It is usually accompanied by **asthma** or other allergic manifestations. **Dietetic treatment** is *most effective* and consists primarily of ***eliminating* cow's milk** and **other** allergenic **foods.**

The best result is gained in **adults** through an **antiallergenic diet** based on raw vegetables that excludes those foods described in the ***"Allergies"*** table.

Urticaria is a type of *dermatitis typified by itching and redness of the skin.* It is caused by the release of **histamine,** a substance that produces a variety of allergic reactions.

Increase

Niacin
Soymilk (beverage)
Vegetables
Artichoke
Sunflower seeds
Oil supplements
Molasses
Acidified whey
Vitamin B_6
Vitamin A

Reduce or Eliminate

The same as for allergies
Milk
Salt

Artichoke

Artichokes stimulate the liver and the kidneys' detoxifying and purifying (depurant) function. This contributes to the healing of many cases of dermatitis caused or aggravated by toxins in the blood.

A Raw-foods Diet Benefits the Skin

Many skin conditions, particularly those that are allergy-related, disappear by eating a diet based on raw fruits and vegetables for several days. Fruits and vegetables are best eaten in their natural state without any culinary or industrial processing. Salads may be dressed with oil and lemon.

Slowly other foods such as bread, grains, legumes, dairy products, etcetera, are added back into the diet until the food or foods are identified that are causing the skin allergy. In many cases, the causal agents are **additives** or **spices.** In addition to avoiding the food that causes the skin conditions, those with sensitive skin will improve with a diet rich in unprocessed, raw plant-based foods.

Peanut

Nourishes and fortifies the skin

PEANUT composition
per 100 g of raw edible portion

Energy	567 kcal = 2,374 kj
Protein	25.8 g
Carbohydrates	7.64 g
Fiber	8.50 g
Vitamin A	—
Vitamin B_1	0.640 mg
Vitamin B_2	0.135 mg
Niacin	16.2 mg NE
Vitamin B_6	0.348 mg
Folate	240 µg
Vitamin B_{12}	—
Vitamin C	—
Vitamin E	9.13 mg α-TE
Calcium	92.0 mg
Phosphorus	376 mg
Magnesium	168 mg
Iron	4.58 mg
Potassium	705 mg
Zinc	3.27 mg
Total Fat	*49.2 g*
Saturated Fat	*6.83 g*
Cholesterol	—
Sodium	*18.0 mg*

1% 2% 4% 10% 20% 40% 100% 200% 500%

% Daily Value (based on a 2,000 calorie diet) provided by 100 g of this food

Synonyms: *Groundnut, Earthnut, Goober [pea], Runner peanut, Spanish peanut, Mani.*

French: *Cacahuète;* ***Spanish:*** *Cacahuete, cacahuate, maní.*

Description: *Seeds of the subterranean fruit of the peanut plant ('Arachis hypogea' L.), an annual herbaceous plant of the botanical family Leguminosae measuring 30 to 40 cm in height.*

IT IS VERY uncommon, even in the great variety that is the vegetable kingdom, that a plant's **fruit** develops ***underground***. However, this is the case with the peanut. When the ovary of the flower is fertilized, it goes underground where it develops to maturity.

Because of this, some believe that the peanut is a root or a tuber; however, it is a **subterranean fruit.** The peanut is a legume, and as happens with all of this botanical family, the fruit is a pod within which seeds, the edible portion, grow.

Peanuts were staples in the diet of native peoples of Central America before the arrival of the Europeans. Although some historians place their origin in Brazil, and others in East Asia, it is certain that Caribbean natives cultivated peanuts in the remote past.

Today peanuts are one of the most popular oil-bearing nuts because of their taste and nutritive properties.

PROPERTIES AND INDICATIONS: Peanuts are a highly nutritious food whose nutrient concentration surpasses any animal-based food, including meat. Within the vegetable kingdom only the walnut (see p. 74) and the almond (see p. 58) can compare with it in nutritional richness.

Peanuts *conspicuously exceed* **meat** and **eggs** in carbohydrates, fats, proteins, vitamins B_1, C, E, and niacin. They are also superior in terms of minerals such as calcium, magnesium, and potassium. And all this *without* ***cholesterol*** *or excess* ***saturated fatty acids.***

Preparation and use

❶ **Roasted:** It is usually enough to roast peanuts 5 to 10 minutes if they have been shelled; 14 to 20 minutes if not. Ideally, salt should not be added.

❷ **Fried in oil:** Fried peanuts are very tasty, if somewhat indigestible.

❸ **Raw:** Raw peanuts are difficult to digest, and some varieties have an unpleasant flavor.

❹ **Peanut butter:** This is made lightly roasting and grinding peanuts to a homogenous paste. This highly concentrated and nutritious product may be profitably substituted for dairy butter.

❺ **Peanut flour:** This is rich in protein, and in some countries is mixed with wheat flour to produce highly nutritious bread and other baked goods.

It is certain that peanuts are one of the most concentrated foods available. It is true that there are some foods such as honey or oil that surpass peanuts in some particular nutrient (carbohydrates and fats, respectively). However, only oil-bearing nuts, particularly peanuts, contain all the ***basic nutrients*** in such *high concentrations.*

This demonstrates just how appropriate they are from a nutritional standpoint. They are not a simple snack or a complement for other foods. If peanuts' caloric content (567 kcal /100 g) is ignored and they are simply added to the regular diet, one runs the risk of the consequences of obesity. Stomach discomfort and indigestion result from quickly eating quantities of peanuts and not chewing and salivating them properly.

Persons who eat peanuts without regard for the fact that they are such a concentrated and nutritious food tend to complain that they are indigestible. If they are eaten in moderation, using them to replace other foods, rather than to complement them, they are well tolerated and easily assimilated.

This is a detailed review of the peanut's nutrient properties:

✓ ***Proteins:*** Peanut proteins, which can reach 26% of their weight in some varieties (meat never surpasses 20%), are rather poor in the amino acids ***methionine, lysine,*** and ***threonine.*** As a result, in order to supply *all* necessary ***amino acids*** required to produce complete proteins, peanuts should be eaten *with* other foods such as:

- **Whole grains** (*very rich* in ***methionine***),
- **legumes** (*rich* in ***lysine*** and ***threonine***), or with
- **Brewer's yeast** (*rich* in ***methionine*** and ***threonine***).

✓ ***Fats:*** Fats constitute almost half the peanut's weight, and can be extracted as oil. They are formed of a *balanced combination* of polyunsaturated, monounsaturated, and saturated ***fatty acids,*** saturated being the least abundant. Peanuts contain a *significant share* of the essential ***unsaturated linoleic and linolenic fatty acids*** that the body cannot

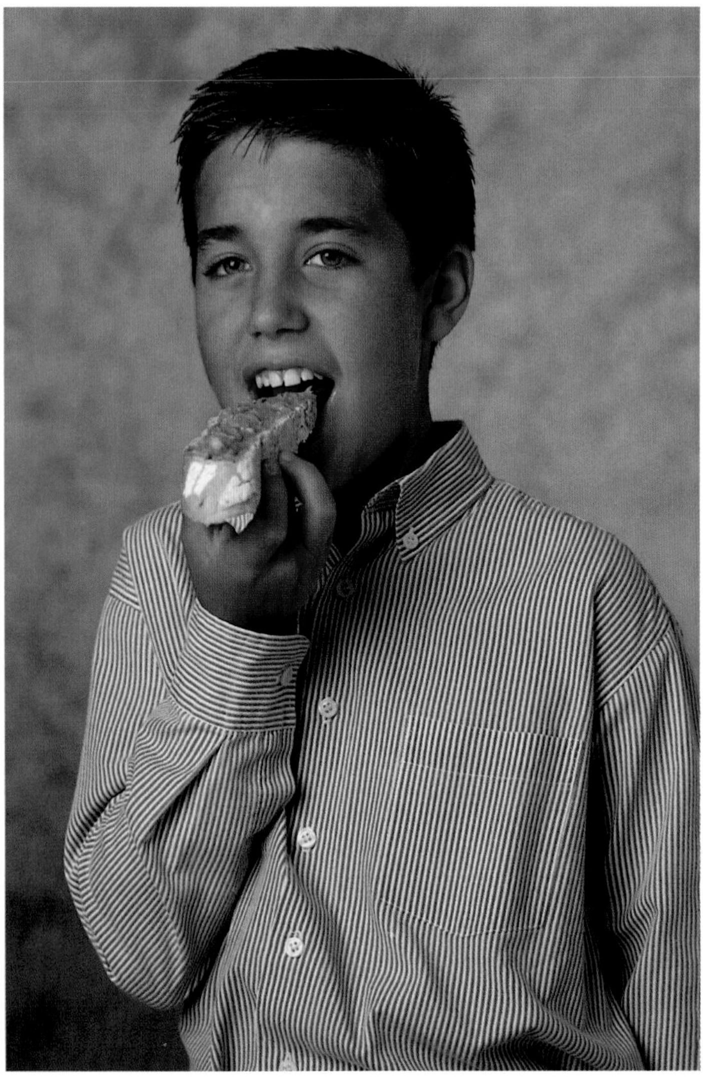

Peanut butter, made from ground peanuts, is very popular in North America. It can be profitably used as a substitute for dairy butter since it contains more nutrients (particularly vitamin B_3 of niacin) and reduces cholesterol levels.

synthesize and that must be supplied in the diet. ***FATTY ACIDS*** play a vital role in the formation and restoration of the skin, as well as brain tissue. They are also involved in the immune system and in the heart metabolism, since they are the primary energy source for the **heart muscle.** In the same way that the brain needs above all glucose to maintain its activity, the heart "burns" fatty acids to obtain the energy necessary for its beats.

✓ ***Carbohydrates:*** Peanuts contain a considerable amount of carbohydrates (up to 10%), particularly ***starch*** and ***maltose.*** This is one of the reasons why it is important to chew and salivate them well so the ptyalin in the saliva can initiate their digestion. If they arrive in the colon without having been properly digested, in other words, not having been completely transformed into glucose, they produce fermentation and intestinal gas.

✓ ***Vitamins:*** Peanuts contain a certain amount of B complex vitamins (B_1, B_2, and B_6), with a very small amount of vitamins A and C.

Their vitamin E content is noteworthy (about 9.13 mg/100 g), less than sunflower seeds (see p. 110), walnuts (see p. 74), or almonds (see p. 58), but much greater than that of butter (1.58 mg/100 g) or eggs (1.05 mg /100 g), which are the richest animal-based sources of this vitamin.

However, peanuts reach a true record among foods in their ***niacin*** content. Niacin, also known as vitamin B_3, acts as a coenzyme within the body that facilitates the numerous chemical reactions essential to carbohydrate and fat metabolism, allowing these nutrients to provide energy to the cells. Lack of niacin manifests itself by dry, cracked, red skin, as well as muscular weakness and dyspepsia (indigestion). Serious niacin deficiency produces a disease known as **pellagra,** characterized by the so-called three **"D's": d**ermatitis (red, cracked skin), **di**arrhea, and **d**ementia.

✓ ***Minerals:*** Peanuts are *particularly rich* in ***potassium*** (670 mg/100 g), and *low* in ***sodium,*** assuming that no salt has been added. They also contain significant amounts of phosphorus, calcium, magnesium, and iron. They are an excellent source of ***trace elements*** such as zinc, copper, and manganese, containing even more than **fish** or **meat.**

✓ ***Vegetable fiber:*** Peanuts are relatively poor in cellulose carbohydrates (vegetable fiber), and as a result, they can cause **constipation** if a large amount is eaten at once, and without being accompanied with fruit or whole grains.

This rich nutrient composition explains the following applications for the peanut:

- **Skin conditions:** *Regular* peanut *consumption* promotes good health for both the skin and the mucosa because of its *high levels* of ***niacin*** and ***unsaturated fatty acids.*** Both substances are essential for skin cell regeneration and health.

- **Cardiac conditions:** Given peanuts' *rich* ***essential fatty acid*** content, it is highly recommended for heart patients. These fatty acids are the *essential* energy source for the cells of the **heart.** They also *help* ***lower*** **cholesterol** levels, thus improving blood circulation of the coronary arteries.

Peanuts are *low* in ***sodium,*** and *high* in ***potassium,*** which protects against **hypertension** and **fluid retention** in the tissues. Again, these benefits assume that the peanuts are **unsalted.**

Peanut oil

Cold-pressed peanut oil (first and second extraction) is clear, fluid, and has a delicate flavor. Peanut oils that are not fluid should be rejected since this indicates that the unsaturated fatty acids have become saturated (hydrogenated), thus losing their dietetic interest.

As a kitchen oil it is used extensively for frying since it does not smoke until the temperature is very high. This allows frying at very high temperatures without decomposition of the oil.

Peanut oil is very rich in unsaturated fatty acids, and is highly recommended both taken orally or as a lotion on the skin in cases of eczema, dry skin, or dermatitis in general.

The peanut is the highest protein of any oil-bearing nut, and one of the most concentrated foods that nature offers. Because of this, it should not be considered a mere between-meal snack.

Cucumber

Cleanses and beautifies the skin

French: *Concombre;* ***Spanish:*** *Pepino.*

Description: *Fruit of the 'Cucumis sativus' L., a herbaceous vine of the botanical family Cucurbitaceae that reaches approximately one meter in height. Cucumbers are eaten unripe since ripe specimens lose their crispness and become spongy and yellow. They measure from 15 to 25 cm in length and about 5 cm in diameter.*

CUCUMBER composition
per 100 g of raw edible portion

Energy	**13.0 kcal = 53.0 kj**
Protein	**0.690 g**
Carbohydrates	**1.96 g**
Fiber	**0.800 g**
Vitamin A	**21.0 µg RE**
Vitamin B_1	**0.024 mg**
Vitamin B_2	**0.022 mg**
Niacin	**0.304 mg NE**
Vitamin B_6	**0.042 mg**
Folate	**13.0 µg**
Vitamin B_{12}	—
Vitamin C	**5.30 mg**
Vitamin E	**0.079 mg α-TE**
Calcium	**14.0 mg**
Phosphorus	**20.0 mg**
Magnesium	**11.0 mg**
Iron	**0.260 mg**
Potassium	**144 mg**
Zinc	**0.200 mg**
Total Fat	***0.130 g***
Saturated Fat	***0.034 g***
Cholesterol	—
Sodium	***2.00 mg***

1% 2% 4% 10% 20% 40% 100%

% Daily Value (based on a 2,000 calorie diet) provided by 100 g of this food

EATING a cucumber is like drinking a glass of water. Bearing in mind that 96% of its weight is water, a 250-g cucumber contains 240 g of water. However, this does not mean that it is of little nutritional value! Those 10 grams of solid material in a 250-g cucumber are of *great* **biological** *value* and **healing power.**

PROPERTIES AND INDICATIONS: Cucumbers are among the *most* ***water-rich*** foods, and as a result only contain 13 kcal/100 g. Their protein (0.69%), carbohydrate (1.96%), and fat (0.13%) content is very low. They also contain small amounts of provitamin A, and vitamins B, C, and E.

Their *high* dietary and therapeutic *value* resides in their ***minerals,*** which are ***highly* alkaline.** They contain potassium, calcium, phosphorus, magnesium, and iron, as well as various trace elements, most notably **sulfur.**

Cucumbers have the following medicinal properties:

- **Alkalizer:** They neutralize excess acidic waste produced in the body as a consequence of the consumption of animal-based foods.
- **Depurant:** They facilitate the elimination of waste substances from the bloodstream through either the urine or the skin.
- **Diuretic:** They increase urine output.
- **Laxative:** Given their high water content (96%) and soluble fiber content (0.8%), they facilitate the movement of the feces through the intestine.

These are cucumbers' primary applications:

• **Skin conditions:** Cucumbers hydrate the skin and provide the ***sulfur*** needed for healthy skin cells, **nails,** and **hair.** At the same time, they **"cleanse" the bloodstream** of toxic wastes. They are recommended for all who are suffering from eczema, dermatosis, and psoriasis. Applied locally directly on the skin, cucumbers are an effective **beauty** treatment.

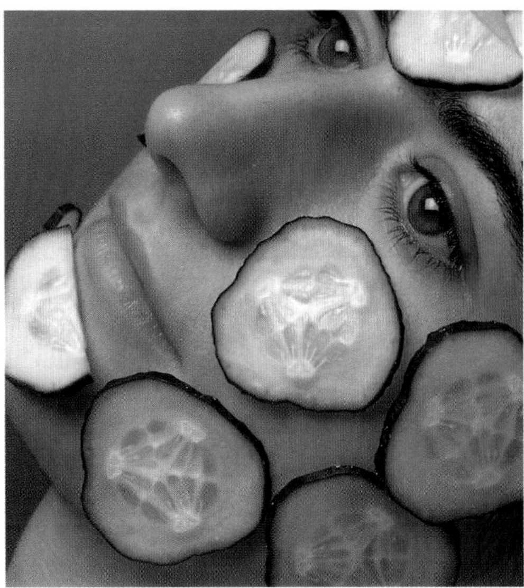

The health and beauty of the skin depend more of the purity of the blood than on the topical application of cosmetic products. True beauty comes from the inside.

The best results are obtained by combining cucumbers' internal properties and their external effect on the skin. This is done by:

- Rubbing it directly on the skin.
- Preparing thin slices and placing them on affected skin areas.

• **Constipation** due to intestinal atony.

• **Excess uric acid** and a diet rich in animal-based foods, since it facilitates the elimination of uric acid and other waste substances.

• **Obesity,** because they contain very few calories and produce a certain feeling of satiety.

• **Diabetes,** because of their low carbohydrate content while providing a certain amount of vitamins and minerals.

Preparation and use

❶ **Raw:** Cucumbers are usually eaten this way. Since they are harvested unripe, they must be well chewed to prevent indigestion. They may be eaten in salad with oil and lemon or blended with tomato and other vegetables to make gazpacho. They should be **peeled** to avoid pesticide residue if they have not been organically grown.

❷ **Cooked:** They may be baked with cheese, used in soups, or cooked with other vegetables.

❸ **Pickled:** A particular type of smaller cucumber is prepared in salt and vinegar to preserve them. Because of these two products, pickles are rather unhealthful.

Mango

Nourishes the skin and protects the arteries

Synonyms: *Man-gay, Mangga, man-kay.*

French: *Mangue;* ***Spanish:*** *Mango.*

Description: Fruit of the mango ('Mangifera indica' L.), an evergreen tree of the botanical family Anacardiaceae, which grows to a height of 25 m. The fruit is ovoid with a thin yellow, orange, or greenish skin, and a hard flat pit.

MANGO composition

per 100 g of raw edible portion

Energy	65.0 kcal = 273 kj
Protein	0.510 g
Carbohydrates	15.2 g
Fiber	1.80 g
Vitamin A	389 µg RE
Vitamin B_1	0.058 mg
Vitamin B_2	0.057 mg
Niacin	0.717 mg NE
Vitamin B_6	0.134 mg
Folate	14.0 µg
Vitamin B_{12}	—
Vitamin C	27.7 mg
Vitamin E	1.12 mg α-TE
Calcium	10.0 mg
Phosphorus	11.0 mg
Magnesium	9.00 mg
Iron	0.130 mg
Potassium	156 mg
Zinc	0.040 mg
Total Fat	*0.270 g*
Saturated Fat	*0.066 g*
Cholesterol	—
Sodium	*2.00 mg*

1% 2% 4% 10% 20% 40% 100%

% Daily Value (based on a 2,000 calorie diet) provided by 100 g of this food

THE MANGO tree is an example of tropical nature's exuberance. An average tree, about 20 m in height, produces about 4 million blossoms a year! Of these, "only" 25,000 will develop into fruit. This enormous production of fruit has led natives in many tropical regions to consider the mango a natural pantry.

If one considers that a mango tree lives for more than one hundred years, it is reasonable that it will produce more than 2 million pieces of fruit! Moreover, bear in mind that this quantity is not at the expense of quality. Each mango is a masterwork of nature for its aroma, its delicate flavor, and its dietary and therapeutic properties.

PROPERTIES AND INDICATIONS: Mango pulp is 81.7% water, somewhat less than the peach (87.7%) or the plum (85.2%). Of its 15.2 g of carbohydrates per 100 g of edible portion, most consists of ***sugars*** (glucose, fructose, and saccharose). Unripe mangos contain a certain amount of starch, which converts to sugar as the fruit ripens. Their proportion of proteins (0.51%) and fats (0.27%) is very low.

The most notable nutrients in the mango's composition are:

✓ ***Provitamin A:*** 100 g of mango contains 389 µg RE (retinol equivalents), which represents 1,295 IU of vitamin A. Bearing in mind that the daily requirement of this vitamin is 1,000 µg RE, a 300-g mango alone provides the RDA (Recommended Dietary Allowance) of this important vitamin.

The mango is the fresh fruit with the greatest ***vitamin A*** content,[4] followed by the cantaloupe (322 µg RE/100 g, although both are much below the carrot (2,813 µg RE/100 g).

Sixteen types of carotenoids have been identified in the mango that are responsible for its vitamin A action. The *most abundant* of these is ***beta-carotene.***

CAROTENOIDS are vegetable pigments, generally yellow or orange, that convert to vitamin A within the body. ***Vitamin A*** is essential to the maintenance of epithelial tissues, such as the skin and the mucosae that line the body's internal systems. Carotenoids are *potent* **antioxidants** that neutralize oxidizing **free radicals,** which are molecules *responsible* for cellular **aging.**

✓ ***Vitamin C:*** With 27.7 mg/100 g, the mango is a good source of vitamin C. A medium-sized mango (300 g) provides 138% of the adult daily requirement of this vitamin.

✓ ***Vitamin E:*** A 300 g mango provides 33% of the daily requirement for this vitamin for an adult male. This is one of the richest fresh fruits in this vitamin.

Mangos also contain significant amounts of ***vitamins B1, B2, B6,*** and ***niacin.*** In terms of ***minerals, potassium*** is most notable, with smaller amounts of magnesium and iron.

Mangos contain a variety of non-nutritive components such as ***soluble fiber*** (pectin), ***organic acids*** (citric and malic), and ***tannins.***

To have an idea of the complexity of the complexity of the mango's composition, it should suffice to say that 41 ***aromatic substances***[5] have been identified that combine to give this fruit its unique fragrance.

These are the primary therapeutic applications of mangos:

• **Skin conditions:** Eating mangos helps maintain healthy skin. It has been proven that vitamin A deficiency produces skin dryness and scaling. Mangos contribute to proper skin hydration and tone.

Eating abundant amounts of mangos is recommended in cases of eczema, dermatosis (skin degeneration), skin dryness, and as a preventive of premature skin aging.

• **Retinal conditions:** Vitamin A, whose action is potentiated by the simultaneous presence of vitamins C and E, is necessary to good vision. Mango consumption is recommended whenever there is vision loss due to retinal conditions such as night blindness, optic nerve atrophy, or thrombosis in the central retinal artery.

• **Arteriosclerosis:** Mangos are *rich* in the ***three*** *most* powerful *antioxidant* ***vitamins:***

Preparation and use

❶ **Fresh:** This is the *best way* to eat mangos. Poor quality mangos are very fibrous and have a very strong turpentine flavor. The best have little fiber and a smooth, aromatic pulp, reminiscent of a peach. Mangos are harvested green and store well from one to two weeks in the refrigerator.

❷ **Preserves:** Mangos are used to make jellies and jams, and can also be canned in syrup.

The variety of mango called 'Manila', shown here, is one of the best. Its intense yellow color indicates its richness in beta-carotene (provitamin A).

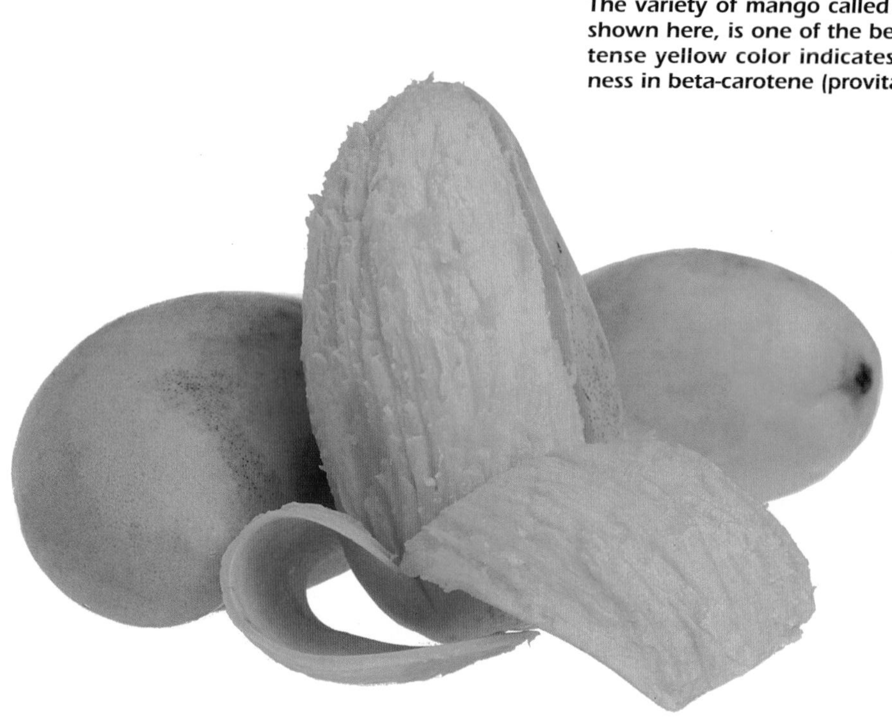

A, C, and ***E.*** Each of these is potent in its own right, but much more so as a *combined unit.* They prevent the oxidation of the cholesterol-bearing lipoproteins that circulate in the bloodstream. The oxidation of these substances initiates the depositing of cholesterol on the arterial walls, leading to their deterioration.

Mangos are of great benefit to the circulatory system and should be included in the diet of all who experience poor blood circulation to the extremities or in the coronary arteries (angina or heart attack).

• **Hypertension:** Mangos are diuretic (increase urine production). They are *quite rich* in ***potassium*** and *low* in ***sodium.*** This makes them highly recommended in cases of high blood pressure since they aid in its control.

• **Diabetes:** Diabetics can benefit from eating mangos because this fruit's positive effect on the arteries helps prevent the circulatory complications associated with diabetes.

Mangos are well tolerated by these patients. It has been shown that after eating mangos, the blood glucose level of non-insulin-dependent diabetics is lower than might be expected.[6]

Mango is the richest in provitamin A among all fresh fruits. Because of that and its abundance in other antioxidant vitamins like C and E, it contributes to keeping a beautiful complexion and preventing a premature old age.

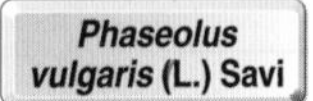

Bean

Nourishing even the skin

French: *Haricot;* **Spanish:** *Judía, alubia, alubia seca, judía seca, fríjol.*

Description: The seed of 'Phaseolus vulgaris' [L.] Savi, of the botanical family Leguminosae. The fruit of the plant is a green pod that contains various dicotyledonous seeds (beans). The pods are eaten as a vegetable before they have ripened. These are called green beans.

BEAN, WHITE composition

per 100 g of raw edible portion

Energy	333 kcal = 1,395 kj
Protein	23.4 g
Carbohydrates	45.1 g
Fiber	15.2 g
Vitamin A	—
Vitamin B_1	0.437 mg
Vitamin B_2	0.146 mg
Niacin	5.10 mg NE
Vitamin B_6	0.318 mg
Folate	388 µg
Vitamin B_{12}	—
Vitamin C	—
Vitamin E	0.530 mg α-TE
Calcium	240 mg
Phosphorus	301 mg
Magnesium	190 mg
Iron	10.4 mg
Potassium	1,795 mg
Zinc	3.67 mg
Total Fat	*0.850 g*
Saturated Fat	*0.219 g*
Cholesterol	—
Sodium	*16.0 mg*

1% 2% 4% 10% 20% 40% 100% 200% 500%

% Daily Value (based on a 2,000 calorie diet) provided by 100 g of this food

WHETHER BEANS were brought from America or were known in Europe before Columbus returned from his journeys has long been the subject of lively debate among naturalists and historians.

It seems sure that beans were known and eaten in the Old World from antiquity. The Arabs established themselves in Spain in the eighth century. They made what is now known as Andalusia one of the most highly developed regions of the known world during the Middle Ages, where the arts, sciences, and agriculture flourished.

A prominent Hispano-Arabic physician known as "the excellent doctor Abu Zacaria Ihaia," who lived in Seville between the twelfth and thirteenth centuries, describes a dozen or so varieties of beans.[7] He states that they "benefit the stomach and are of delicate flavor."

On the other hand, Columbus notes in his journal that beans, larger than the ones he knew in Spain, formed the base of the diet of Native Americans, together with corn and chilies (hot peppers).

These New World beans were introduced in Spain where they were immediately successful because of their excellent quality. In contrast to other foods from the Americas, such as potatoes and tomatoes, which took centuries before they were accepted, these beans quickly made their way to tables throughout Europe. Most of the beans grown throughout the world today are from American varieties.

PROPERTIES AND INDICATIONS: No one who has eaten a dish of beans can say that they have left the table hungry. In addition to being filling, beans are truly nutritious.

Proteins are beans' most notable nutrient, a fact that has earned them the appellative ***"poor man's meat."***

Preparation and use

❶ **Cooked beans** are used in a wide variety of dishes. They cannot be eaten raw. They cook better in soft water (low calcium content). It is best to soak beans in cold water for several hours before cooking.

❷ **Boiled and pureed** to eliminate the skin. This is the least digestible portion of the bean and may cause flatulence.

The following is a detailed review of the characteristics of the ***PROTEINS*** in beans:

- ***Protein content:*** The protein percentage in beans varies according to variety between 21% and 24%, which is ***equal*** to or *even* ***greater*** than *animal-based* foods such as fresh tuna, beef, or chicken. The protein in these foods varies from 18% to 21% by weight.
- ***Biological value:*** The biological value of a protein is an index that measures the suitability of its amino acid composition. The closer to the ideal for the human body, the higher a protein's biological value. With 100 as the index of a perfect protein, those in beans have a quality of 85%. This is a relative low number compared with eggs (94%). However, it is comparable to milk (85%) and superior to meat (75%).

  The relatively low biological value of bean proteins is due to their lack of ***methionine,*** an essential amino acid that acts as a limiting factor. However, thanks to the process of ***supplementation,*** when bean proteins are combined with those of other plant-based foods rich in methionine such as **grains, sesame** or **sunflower seeds,** or **yeast,** the body receives all necessary amino acids in the proper proportion. In other words, ***combining*** two partially incomplete proteins results in a complete protein.
- The ***digestibility*** of bean proteins is 83%, considerably less than that of eggs (99%), milk (98%), and meat (97%). This means that the body utilizes somewhat less of the proteins from beans than those of animal origin. It has been shown[8] that the proteins in black beans are the easiest to digest, followed by kidney beans and white beans.

In addition to proteins, beans also contain noteworthy proportions of the following nutrients:

✓ Vegetable ***fiber:*** Beans are very rich in vegetable fiber, as is the case with all legumes. One hundred grams of dried beans provide 15.2 g of fiber, more than half the RDA (Recommended Dietary Allowance) for an adult (25 g). The fiber in beans *helps* ***prevent* constipation** and ***lower*** blood **cholesterol** levels.

Essential amino acids in various foods

Amino acid	Beans		Eggs		Beef	
	mg/100 g	%	mg/100 g	%	mg/100 g	%
ISOLEUCINE	927	12	778	14	915	12
LEUCINE	1,685	22	1,091	20	1,542	20
LYSINE	1,593	21	863	16	1,690	22
METHIONINE	234	3	416	8	514	7
PHENYLALANINE	1,154	15	709	13	836	11
THREONINE	878	11	634	11	873	12
TRYPTOPHAN	223	3	184	3	213	3
VALINE	1,016	13	847	15	952	13
Total	7,710	100	5,522	100	7,535	100

Complete proteins with beans

*As the accompanying table shows, bean proteins contain **all essential amino acids,** as do eggs and meat.*

*However, beans, like all legumes, are **poor** in the amino acid **methionine.***

*To make up for this small deficit and obtain a complete protein it is **enough to combine** beans with some other food that is rich in methionine such as:*

- ***Grains** (wheat, rice, corn, oats, etc.),*
- ***Sesame** or **sunflower seeds,***
- ***Brewer's yeast.***

✓ ***Folates:*** A serving of cooked beans (one bowl), supplies approximately the RDA for folates for an adult (200 µg). The need for folates *increases* during **pregnancy** to 400 µg. Persons at high risk for coronary disease should increase folates intake, as well. In either case, beans are an excellent source.

✓ ***Iron:*** 100 g of beans provides more than 10 mg of iron, which is the RDA for an adult male. This makes beans one of the best sources of this mineral. Since this is ***nonheme iron,*** it requires ***vitamin C*** for improved absorption. Thus, adding a few drops of lemon is advantageous.

✓ ***Niacin*** and ***pantothenic acid,*** two vitamin factors that are very important for healthy skin.

Beans are poor in provitamin A, vitamin C, fats, and lack vitamin B_{12} as do most plant-based foods.

Dried beans are a nutritious and energy-producing food with complete proteins if they are combined with grains or other protein sources. But in addition to these undeniable nutritive properties, beans are therapeutic for the following conditions:

- **Skin diseases:** Beans act to protect the skin and mucosa because they are a good source of

It is a tradition in Mediterranean countries that the main dish for the dinner is based on legumes: beans, lentils, or chickpeas. This is one of the reasons for the low incidence of heart attack in Southern Europe.

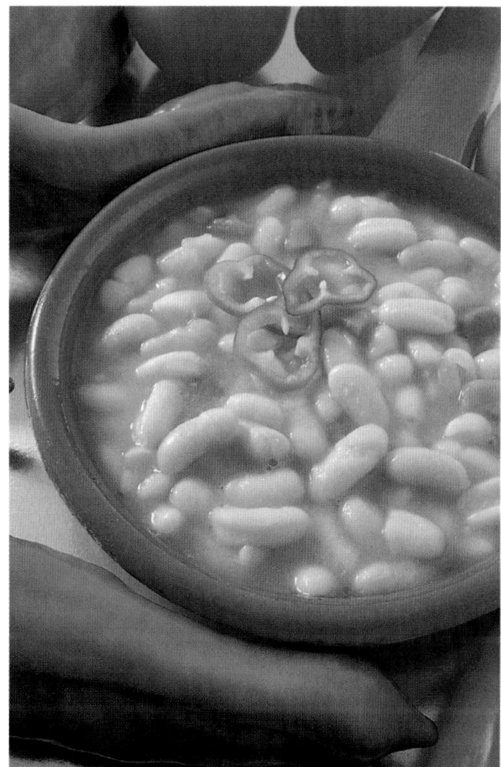

two vitamin factors that are very important to the health of integumentary tissue: niacin and pantothenic acid.

✓ ***NIACIN,*** also called ***PP factor*** or ***vitamin B3,*** is actively involved in many cellular chemical reactions. Serious niacin deficiency causes the disease called **pellagra,** characterized by the **three "D's": d**ermatitis, **d**iarrhea, and **d**ementia. Although this disease is not common today, less serious deficiency leads to a variety of skin conditions such as cracking and scaling.

Beans are a good source of niacin because they provide:

- ***Preformed niacin*** (0.479 mg/100 g), which is shown in the composition graph.
- ***Tryptophan,*** an essential amino acid that the body converts to ***niacin.*** Dried beans are one of the richest foods sources of tryptophan (277 mg/100 g), more than meat (199 mg/100 g), or eggs (152 mg/100 g). These 277 mg of tryptophan are converted to 4.62 mg of additional niacin, which, when added to the 0.479 mg of preformed niacin, provide 5.1 mg/ 100 g of niacin (26.8% of RDA)

✓ ***PANTOTHENIC ACID*** is also involved in cellular metabolism. Its lack produces skin conditions and hair fragility, as well. Beans contain 0.732 mg/100 g, more than double that of meat.

Because of all these factors, beans are recommended in cases of eczema, itching skin, dry skin, cutaneous allergies, and general dermatosis.

Beans have also been proven to benefit the hair follicles and are recommended for **hair loss** and **fragility, seborrhea,** and **dandruff.**

• **Cholesterol:** Eating beans regularly is a good method for keeping cholesterol levels within acceptable limits. An experiment carried out in the United States[9] demonstrated that eating 120 g of beans a day for three weeks lowered cholesterol and triglyceride levels by 10%.

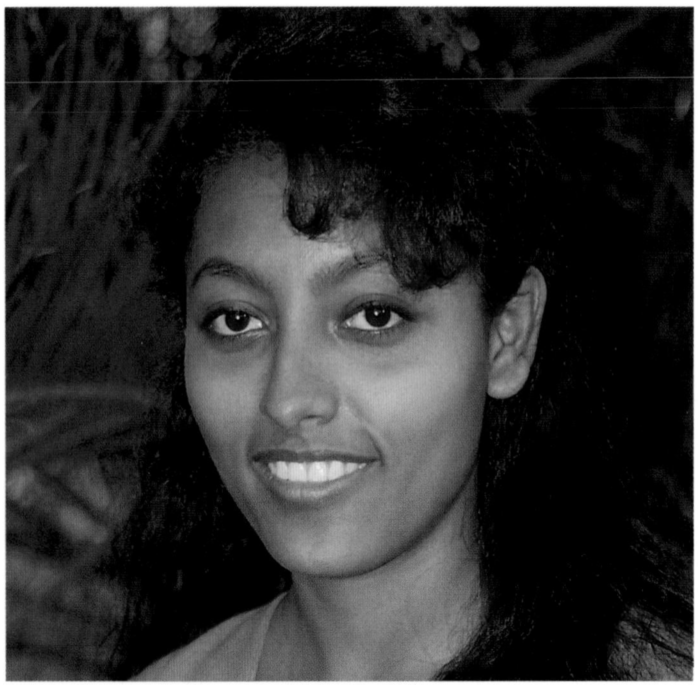

The darker the bean's skin, the stronger its flavor, and the more digestible its proteins. Beans are a good source of niacin and pantothenic acid. These vitamin factors are essential for healthy, beautiful skin.

This may be due to their ***fiber*** content (15.2%), which scours cholesterol and its precursors (biliary salts) from the intestine and prepares their excretion with the feces.

• **Constipation and colon conditions:** Beans' *high* ***cellulose fiber*** *content* (20% by weight) makes them of benefit against constipation and in the *prevention* of **diverticulosis** and colon and rectal **cancer.**

• **Hypertension:** Beans are ideal for those with high blood pressure (hypertension) because they are *low* in ***sodium*** and *high* in ***potassium.***

• **Anemia and convalescents:** This legume contains more than 10.4 mg/100 g of iron, an amount greater than that of meat or spinach (both contain approximately 3 mg/100 g). This, combined with their nutritive properties, makes beans a highly suitable food for anemics and the undernourished.

Beans are in reality seeds found in the fruit or pods of plants belonging to the botanical family Leguminosae.

Bean Varieties

White bean

This small ovoid bean is used for a variety of dishes. Its soft texture makes it ideal for puree.

Cooking time: ***1½ to 2** hours.*

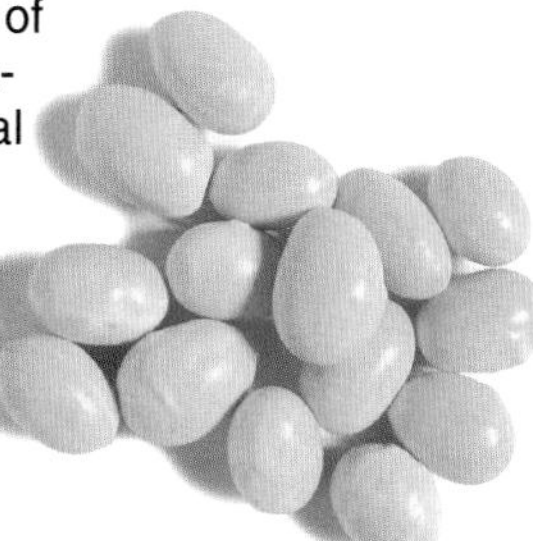

Brown haricot

These have an intense flavor, but not as much as kidney beans.

Cooking time: ***1** hour.*

Black beans

Oval shaped and dark in color. Their flavor is somewhat sweet, reminiscent of mushroom. They are used in stews and mixed with rice.

Cooking time: ***1½** hour.*

Pinto bean

Medium-sized, ovoid shaped. This bean is used extensively in Italian cuisine.

Cooking time: ***1½ to 2** hours.*

Black-eyed pea

These are characterized by their black spot. Their skin is among the thinnest of all beans.

Cooking time: ***½ to 1** hour.*

Kidney bean

This bean has a very soft texture and intense flavor. It combines well with chilies (peppers), salads, and rice. *Cooking time:* ***1½** hours.*

Lima

This flat bean has a creamy texture and mild flavor.

Cooking time: ***1 to 1½** hours.*

17

Foods for Infections

THROUGHOUT life, the body is in a constant struggle against pathogenic microorganisms and foreign substances that attack it, which are called **antigens.** The combination of tissues and cells responsible for defending the body from these antigens is referred to as **immune system.**

There are foods particularly beneficial in cases of infection because they:

• ***Improve*** the function of the **immune system.** The healthy functioning of this complex defense system against infectious agents and foreign substances requires specific nutrients:

– ***Proteins,***

– ***Antioxidant vitamins*** (A, C, and E),

– ***Trace elements*** such as iron, selenium, zinc, and copper.

These nutrients must be included in the diet of those suffering from any infection, as described in ***"Immune System, Weak"*** (see p. 339).

• **Contain antibiotic substances:** These foods help the immune system combat infectious agents, as described in ***"Infections"*** (see p. 339).

- **Promote the depuration** (purification) of the body: They are foods that increase the elimination of waste products through the kidneys, the liver, and the skin. The best foods for promoting this cleansing in cases of infection are listed in ***"Fever"***.

Citrus fruits such as oranges, tangerines, and lemons are particularly beneficial in case of infection since they supply antioxidant vitamins such as C and beta-carotene or provitamin A, which promote a healthy immune system. Vitamin C, together with the flavonoids in citrus fruits, strengthens resistance to viruses.

FEVER

Diet

Fever is generally an *indication that the body is **combating** some **infection.*** Although the foods recommended here do not reduce fever, nor do they directly fight infection, they play an important role in healing. In case of fever, the **diet** must be:

- **Easily digested and nutritious.**
- **Abundant in liquids** to replace the water lost through high temperature and avoid dehydration.
- **Rich in vitamins** that strengthen such as provitamin A (beta-carotene), and vitamin C.
- **Rich in alkalizing mineral salts** that neutralize excess free radicals and acidic waste products formed as a result of the infection.

Fruits and **vegetables** meet these requirements very well and should form the ***basis*** of the diet, *particularly* during the **acute phase.**

Increase

WATER
FRUIT JUICES
CITRUS FRUITS
BARLEY WATER
DEPURANT BROTH
BORAGE
MELON
RASPBERRY

Fruit juice

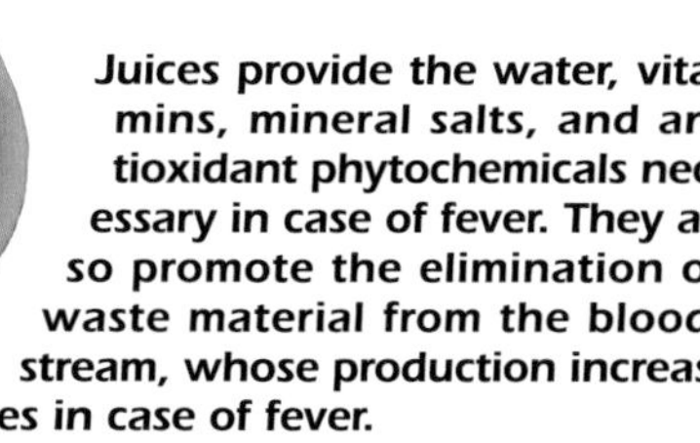

Juices provide the water, vitamins, mineral salts, and antioxidant phytochemicals necessary in case of fever. They also promote the elimination of waste material from the bloodstream, whose production increases in case of fever.

IMMUNE SYSTEM, WEAK

Definition

This is a weakening of the immune system, commonly referred to as lowered resistance.

Functions of the immune system

Fundamentally there are two, which are vital to the survival of any living organism:

- **Identification** of all types of microorganisms and foreign substances that are potentially dangerous.
- **Destruction** of these microorganisms, substances, or foreign cells.

Contributors to a weakened immune system:

These vary widely, and in some cases are unknown. These are some of the most common:

- **Under or malnourishment.** Lack of any essential nutrient, particularly the vitamins and trace elements noted here, can reduce the body's immune response.
- **Stress,** either physical or psychological.
- **Chemotherapy** (anti-cancer medication).
- **Infectious diseases.**
- **AIDS:** Immune system deficiency caused by a viral attack on the body's defense mechanisms.

Diet

The foods described in this table contribute in special ways to the proper function of this complex defense system.

Increase

ANTIOXIDANTS
PROTEINS
TRACE ELEMENTS
CITRUS FRUITS
OILS
PROPOLIS
ROYAL JELLY
GARLIC
YOGURT
ACEROLA
KIWI
TOMATO
ALFALFA

Reduce or eliminate

ALCOHOLIC BEVERAGES
WHITE SUGAR
SHELLFISH
TOTAL FAT
COFFEE

INFECTIONS

Diet

The ***natural* antibiotics** found in some foods and plants are ***less* potent** than pharmaceutical antibiotics. However, they have the ***advantage*** of ***not*** producing **resistant** germs and ***not* altering** the body's normal **bacterial flora**.

In case of infection, it is important to bear in mind, as well, those foods that are recommended and discouraged for ***weakened immune system*** and ***fever*** (see the previous section, see p. 338).

Increase

THE SAME AS FOR IMMUNE SYSTEM, WEAK
GARLIC
ONION
LEMON
CABBAGE
RADISH
EUROPEAN CRANBERRY

Reduce or eliminate

THE SAME AS IN CASES OF IMMUNE SYSTEM, WEAK

Norway lobster

Shellfish often contain toxins, bacteria, and viruses that threaten the immune system.

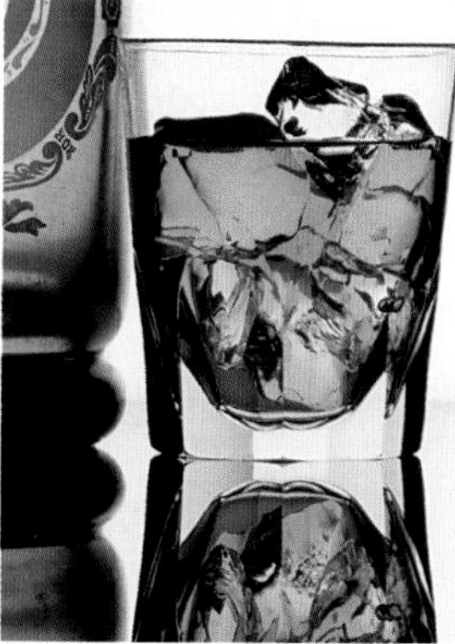

Alcohol depresses many body functions, including the immune function. Regular consumption of alcoholic beverages diminishes the body's ability to resist disease.

COLDS AND FLU

Causes

Colds and flu are caused by related **viral infections.** A cold may be the beginning or first manifestation of the flu.

Symptoms

Cold symptoms include increased mucus production and inflammation of the upper respiratory system (nose and throat). **Flu** produces more generalized symptoms that include headache and musculoskeletal pain.

Diet

The diet should be similar in either case, both to prevent infection and to promote a cure. ***No* food *cures*** colds or flu, ***nor*** does any **antibiotic** or other medication. The body's own defenses must combat viral infections. Because of this, a proper diet is essential to strengthen the **immune system.**

Complications

When there is a **bronchial condition** with thick yellow mucus and cough, the recommendations for ***"Bronchitis"*** (see. 140) must also be considered.

Increase

THE SAME AS FOR IMMUNE SYSTEM, WEAK
FRUIT
VEGETABLES
GARLIC
PROPOLIS
VITAMIN C
SELENIUM
ZINC

Reduce or eliminate

SALT
SUGARS
MILK

Sweets

Sugars reduce the immune response to infections. Excessive consumption of candies, chocolate, pastries, and other refined products made with white sugar fosters the development of colds and flu.

AIDS

Definition

AIDS (**acquired immune deficiency syndrome**) produces a reduction in immune response to infections and cancer.

Causes

It is caused by the retrovirus **HIV,** which attacks and destroys the body's lymphocytes (defensive cells).

An artificial diet poor in fruits, vegetables, grains, and nuts tends to be deficient in antioxidant vitamins (A, C, and E) and promotes the development of the disease.[1]

Diet

AIDS patients tend to be malnourished, which, in turn aggravates weaknesses in the immune system. Weight loss in case of AIDS is sign of a poor prognosis. Various factors ***lead*** to **malnourishment:**

- ***Frequent* infections** that result from reduced resistance.
- The ***inability* to assimilate fats,** which are eliminated through the feces. These feces appear foamy and greasy (steatorrhea). This digestive disorder, which is present in about one-fourth of AIDS patients, also prevents assimilation of fat-soluble vitamins (A, D, and E).[2]
- **Anti AIDS medication:** These usually produce digestive side effects such as nausea and vomiting, which aggravate malnutrition.

Nutrition is of vital importance because it can help improve resistance and slows the progression of AIDS.

Increase

THE SAME AS IN CASES OF IMMUNE SYSTEM, WEAK
FRUIT
WHOLE GRAINS
NUTS
LEGUMES
VEGETABLES
YOGURT
ANTIOXIDANTS
VITAMIN A
B VITAMINS
VITAMIN C
SELENIUM

Reduce or eliminate

THE SAME AS IN CASES OF IMMUNE SYSTEM, WEAK

Eggplant

CANDIDIASIS

Definition

This is a mycosis or infection caused by *'Candida albicans'*, a microscopic fungus or yeast normally found in the mouth, the intestine, and on the skin.

Causes

When the **immune system is compromised** (lowered resistance) due to diabetes, intense antibiotic treatment, cancer, or other causes, **candida** fungi *proliferate* and produce the infection known as candidiasis or **moniliasis.**

Symptoms

It affects the vagina, the anus, the mouth, or areas of skin affected by moisture or friction (for example, the groin, the axillae, or under the breasts).

Diet

Diet contributes to boost the immune system and the balance of the intestinal bacterial flora, which favors the cure of candidiasis.

Increase

- THE SAME AS IN CASES OF IMMUNE SYSTEM, WEAK
- YOGURT
- GARLIC
- FOLATES
- IRON

Reduce or eliminate

- SUGARS
- ALCOHOLIC BEVERAGES
- CHOCOLATE
- BREWER'S YEAST
- CURED CHEESES
- BREAD

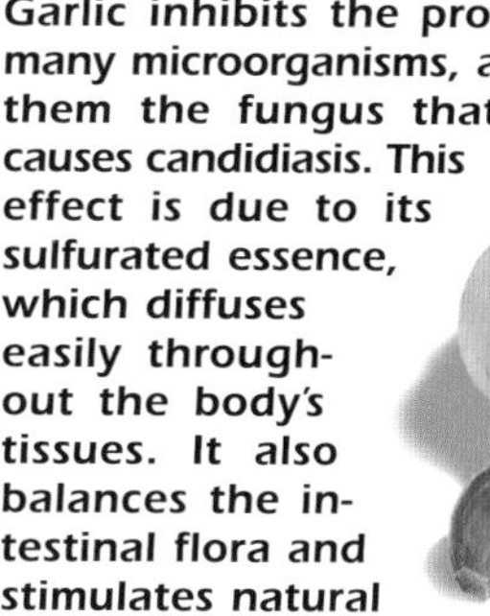

Garlic inhibits the proliferation of many microorganisms, among them the fungus that causes candidiasis. This effect is due to its sulfurated essence, which diffuses easily throughout the body's tissues. It also balances the intestinal flora and stimulates natural immunity.

PHARYNGITIS

Definition

This is the ***infection or inflammation*** *of the mucosa of the pharynx or throat. In many cases,* it is ***connected*** with a **tonsil** infection. These are lymph glands located in the throat. When this is the primary infection, it is called **tonsillitis.**

Diet

Cases of pharyngitis respond to foods that combine a topical soothing and disinfecting action with their general effect on the body.

Increase

- VITAMIN A
- CITRUS FRUITS
- PROPOLIS
- HONEY
- OKRA
- BORAGE

Borage

Borage soothes the mucosa of the throat and helps fight infection. It is most effective cooked and eaten with its broth, or as fresh juice.

CYSTITIS

Definition

This is an **inflammation of the urinary bladder,** usually because of infection. It affects women more frequently for anatomical reasons.

Diet

These dietetic guidelines can help cure cystitis and prevent its return. They are also of benefit in any other type of urinary infection.

Increase

- THE SAME AS FOR SCANTY URINE
- WATER
- BLUEBERRY AND CRANBERRY
- SQUASH SEEDS
- CITRUS FRUITS
- ONION

Reduce or eliminate

- SPICES
- CHILIES
- COFFEE
- SOFT DRINKS
- SUGARS

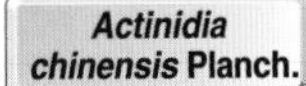

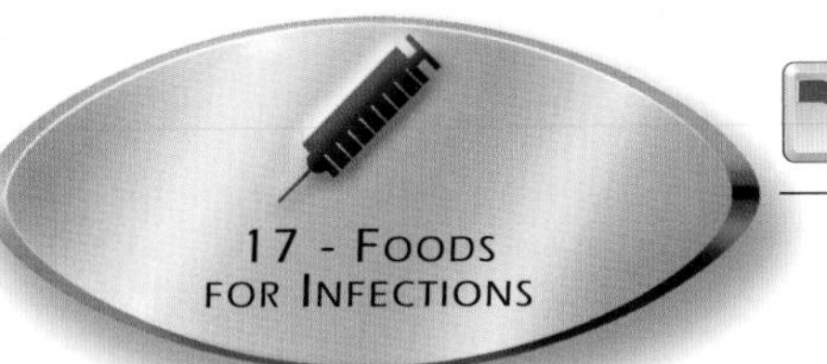

Kiwi

Increases resistance and prevents anemia

KIWI

Composition

per 100 g of raw edible portion

Energy	61.0 kcal = 254 kj
Protein	0.990 g
Carbohydrates	11.5 g
Fiber	3.40 g
Vitamin A	18.0 µg RE
Vitamin B_1	0.020 mg
Vitamin B_2	0.050 mg
Niacin	0.500 mg NE
Vitamin B_6	0.090 mg
Folate	38.0 µg
Vitamin B_{12}	—
Vitamin C	98.0 mg
Vitamin E	1.12 mg α-TE
Calcium	26.0 mg
Phosphorus	40.0 mg
Magnesium	30.0 mg
Iron	0.410 mg
Potassium	332 mg
Zinc	0.170 mg
Total Fat	0.440 g
Saturated Fat	0.029 g
Cholesterol	—
Sodium	5.00 mg

1% 2% 4% 10% 20% 40% 100% 200% 500%

% Daily Value (based on a 2,000 calorie diet) provided by 100 g of this food

Synonyms: *Chinese gooseberry, Kiwifruit, Yang tao.*

French: *Kiwi;* ***Spanish:*** *Kiwi.*

Description: *The kiwi is the fruit of the actinidia ('Actinidia chinensis' Planch.), a tree of the botanical family Actinidiaceae. Its size and shape is similar to an egg, but more cylindrical. Its brown peel covers a green, juicy pulp that is very pleasantly tart.*

THE KIWI is an exotic fruit from the foothills of the Himalayas, and today, from New Zealand, that holds pleasant surprises. The first is, that its rather unattractive, fuzzy skin hides spectacular green pulp. The more than two hundred tiny edible black seeds that each fruit contains form a unique radial pattern. But the greatest of the kiwi's surprises is its richness in vitamin C, which far surpasses citrus.

PROPERTIES AND INDICATIONS: The kiwi contains a moderate amount of carbohydrates in the form of sugars (11.5%), 1% proteins, and less than 0.5% fat. Its most noteworthy components are:

✓ ***Vitamin C:*** The kiwi's content of this vitamin is almost double that of **oranges** and **lemons** (see pp. 346, 128). Only guavas (183 mg/100 g), and acerolas, with more than one gram per 100 g (1,000 mg/100 g) of edible portion surpass kiwi in this vitamin. One kiwi covers the RDA (Recommended Dietary Allowance) of this vitamin.

✓ ***Other vitamins:*** Kiwis are also *very rich* in ***vitamin E,*** and contain considerable amounts of vitamins B_6, B_2, niacin, B_1 and A.

✓ ***Folates:*** Kiwis are noteworthy for their 38 µg/100 g, an amount close to that of eggs (47 µg/100 g), and greater than meat (6-13 µg /100 g) or milk (5 µg/100 g). Kiwis are among the *richest* fresh fruits in folates, together with the feijoa (see p. 252).

✓ ***Minerals:*** Kiwis are among the *most mineral-rich* fruits, particularly potassium, magnesium, and iron. They contain significant amounts of ***copper,*** a trace element that, together with ***vitamin C,*** aids ***iron*** absorption in the intestine.

✓ ***Fiber:*** Kiwis contain 3.4 g/100 g, most of which is ***soluble*** (pectin and mucilage). Kiwis *surpass* most fresh fruits such as apples (2.7 g /100 g), and plums (1.5 g/100 g) in fiber content.

To give a clearer idea of a kiwi's nutritional richness, note that it contains 17 times more vitamin C, 6 times more magnesium, 5 times more proteins, and double the iron than an ***apple*** (see p. 216).

Preparation and use

❶ **Fresh:** kiwis are normally eaten in their natural state. This fruit is very hardy and easily transported. They are usually harvested somewhat green since they ripen well off the tree.

Kiwis provide these nutritional benefits:

• **Stimulates the immune system** because of its ***vitamin C*** content, potentiated by the presence of many other vitamins and minerals that make it much *more effective* than ***pharmaceutical preparations.***

Eating kiwis regularly (one a day, at least) is beneficial for anyone suffering from any type of infectious disease, whether in the acute phase or in convalescence.

• Enriches the blood thus reducing **anemia:** Kiwis can be very beneficial in cases of anemia because of their ***iron, vitamin C,*** and ***copper*** content (the latter two facilitate the absorption and assimilation of iron), as well as ***folates.*** This is particularly true when this condition is due to iron deficiency.

• Benefits mother and fetus during **pregnancy:** Because they stimulate the immune system and promote blood production, kiwis are *highly recommended* during pregnancy. But there is another reason: they are rich in ***folates,*** which helps ***prevent* spinal column birth defects** such as spina bifida.

• Reduces **excess cholesterol and arteriosclerosis:** The ***soluble*** vegetable ***fiber*** in kiwis reduces the absorption of cholesterol and its precursors in the intestine, which reduces its level in the blood. This eliminates one of the causes of arteriosclerosis: excess cholesterol in the bloodstream.

Kiwis are also *very rich* in ***antioxidant vitamins*** such as ***C*** and ***E*** that prevent cholesterol from adhering to arterial walls and forming atheroma plaque. Their *high* ***potassium*** content and *low* amount of **sodium** *contributes* to ***prevention*** of **hypertension.**

• Relieves **constipation:** Because of their richness in ***soluble fiber,*** kiwis are a mild laxative that facilitates fecal movement through the intestine.

• Increases stamina in **athletes:** An experiment[3] conducted at the University of Beijing (China) demonstrated that athletes who eat kiwis show a 24% *increase* in **stamina** over the control group. The Chinese investigators attribute this result to the kiwi's richness in vitamin C and minerals.

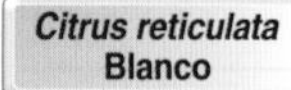

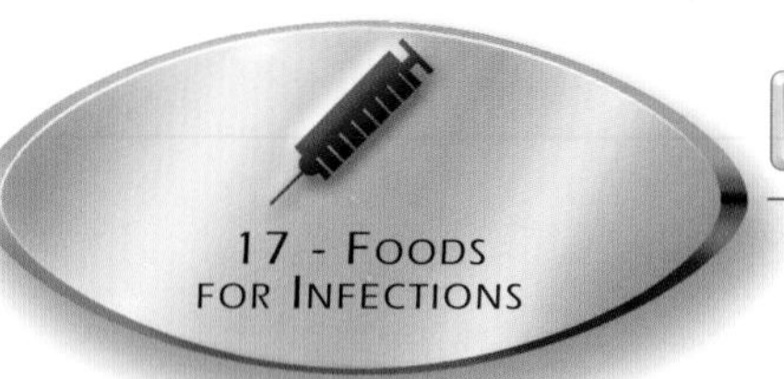

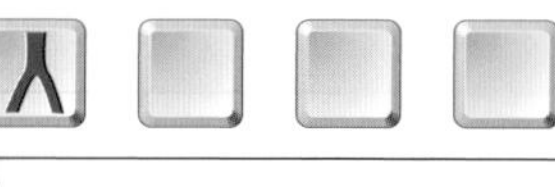

Tangerine

Difficult to eat just one

Synonyms: *Mandarin orange.*

French: *Mandarine;* ***Spanish:*** *Mandarina.*

Description: *Fruit of the tangerine tree ('Citrus reticulata' Blanco), a tree of the botanical family Rutaceae that is very similar to the orange tree, although somewhat smaller and more fragile. The two best-known varieties are the satsuma, which is light orange or greenish in color, and the clementine, which is smaller, sweeter, and deep orange in color.*

TANGERINE
Composition
per 100 g of raw edible portion

Energy	44.0 kcal = 184 kj
Protein	0.630 g
Carbohydrates	8.89 g
Fiber	2.30 g
Vitamin A	92.0 µg RE
Vitamin B_1	0.105 mg
Vitamin B_2	0.022 mg
Niacin	0.260 mg NE
Vitamin B_6	0.067 mg
Folate	20.4 µg
Vitamin B_{12}	—
Vitamin C	30.8 mg
Vitamin E	0.240 mg α-TE
Calcium	14.0 mg
Phosphorus	10.0 mg
Magnesium	12.0 mg
Iron	0.100 mg
Potassium	157 mg
Zinc	0.240 mg
Total Fat	*0.190 g*
Saturated Fat	*0.022 g*
Cholesterol	—
Sodium	*1.00 mg*

1% 2% 4% 10% 20% 40% 100%

% Daily Value (based on a 2,000 calorie diet)
provided by 100 g of this food

PEELING and eating tangerines is so simple that it is a favorite fruit of children. Its pleasant sweetness, and low acidity combined with its tender pulp make this citrus one of the most popular in the world.

Tangerines have been raised in Southern Europe, North Africa, and North America since the nineteenth century when they arrived from China. This is the latest species of citrus to arrive in the West from China (oranges were introduced in Europe in the 16th century).

PROPERTIES AND INDICATIONS: The tangerine's composition is *very similar* to that of the **orange** (see p. 346), although vitamin C, minerals, organic acids, and most other ***nutrients*** are found in *lower* proportions.

The tangerine's properties are also the *same* as the **orange** although less intense. Consequently, tangerines fight infections, make the blood more fluid, are hypotensive, laxative, antiallergenic, remineralizing, depurant (purifying), and anticarcinogenic. Because they are so easy to eat and digest, they are *particularly* beneficial for **children** and the **elderly.**

Tangerines have two notable applications:

- Childhood **fevers,** because of their ability to fight infection, reinvigorate the body, and replace lost minerals. They are highly recommended in cases of **colds, flu,** and **throat infections.**
- **Hypertension:** Tangerine treatment **[❷]** provides excellent results in cases of hypertension and arteriosclerosis.

Citrus prevents cancer

All fruits possess anticarcinogenic properties and eating fruit regularly contributes to preventing cancer. However, citrus fruits are remarkable for their balanced combination of anticarcinogenic substances: vitamin C, flavonoids, limonoids, and pectin.

All of these substances potentiate one another to achieve a striking prophylactic effect. This means that each one taken in isolation and purified is not as effective as when it is consumed as part of an orange or a lemon, for example.

The anticarcinogenic effect of these components of citrus has been confirmed using laboratory animals, reaffirming the validity of numerous statistical studies that relate citrus consumption to lowered cancer risk.

It is highly likely that it has a similar effect in human beings, not only on prostate cancer, but on other types of cancer, as well.

Preparation and use

❶ **Fresh:** Peeling and eating tangerines while enjoying their aroma is a true delight. To gain the full benefit of their therapeutic value, one should eat 6 to 8 a day.

❷ **Tangerine treatment:** As is the case with an orange treatment, this is done by eating 1.5 to 2 kilos (about 3 to 4 pounds) of tangerines as the only food for one or two days a week for a month. Additional liquids should be unnecessary with this amount of fruit since this treatment is usually done in fall or winter.

Orange

Much more than vitamin C

Related species: *Citrus aurantium* L. (Bitter orange).

French: *Orange;* ***Spanish:*** *Naranja.*

Description: *Aggregate fruit of the orange tree ('Citrus sinensis' Osbeck), an evergreen tree of the botanical family Rutaceae. The orange, like all citrus, is composed of various fruits joined to form an apparently simple fruit.*

ORANGE
Composition
per 100 g of raw edible portion

Energy	**47.0 kcal = 197 kj**
Protein	**0.940 g**
Carbohydrates	**9.35 g**
Fiber	**2.40 g**
Vitamin A	**21.0 µg RE**
Vitamin B_1	**0.087 mg**
Vitamin B_2	**0.040 mg**
Niacin	**0.432 mg NE**
Vitamin B_6	**0.060 mg**
Folate	**30.3 µg**
Vitamin B_{12}	—
Vitamin C	**53.2 mg**
Vitamin E	**0.240 mg α-TE**
Calcium	**40.0 mg**
Phosphorus	**14.0 mg**
Magnesium	**10.0 mg**
Iron	**0.100 mg**
Potassium	**181 mg**
Zinc	**0.070 mg**
Total Fat	***0.120 g***
Saturated Fat	***0.015 g***
Cholesterol	—
Sodium	—

1% 2% 4% 10% 20% 40% 100%

% Daily Value (based on a 2,000 calorie diet) provided by 100 g of this food

"IT IS COMPLETELY absurd that in this region vitamin C supplements should be recommended by physicians," declared Professor Stepp in his seminal lecture at the School of Medicine at Valencia (Spain).

It was during the 1940's and the pharmaceutical industry was filled with pride at its ability to synthesize most vitamins. Professor ***Stepp,*** a distinguished German scientist who was world-known for his studies on vitamins, was attending a scientific conference in Mediterranean city of Valencia. Some local colleagues took him to visit the beautiful orange groves in the Valencian countryside, where he had the privilege of eating some of the world's best tree-ripened fruit. It was then that this German man of science and advocate of synthetic vitamins forgot his science and exclaimed:

"How much more healthful it is to enjoy a good Valencian orange than to take the best vitamin C supplement that our industry has to offer!"

Professor Stepp was absolutely correct: A ***natural* orange** is ***superior*** to any pharmaceutical preparation as a ***source*** of ***vitamin C***. Today it is known that in addition to vitamin C, oranges contain about 170 ***phytochemicals*** that *potentiate* and *complement* the action of this vitamin in the body. All of these, together with the sense of well-being, even pleasure, that one gains from eating an orange – pleasure is also a health factor,– cause its health effects to be much greater than would be expected from its 50 mg/100 g of vitamin C. In spite of what promoters of pharmaceutical chemistry may claim, the 50 mg/100 g of vitamin C in oranges provides much more to the body than 50 mg or 500, of any pill or medication.

Preparation and use

❶ **Fresh:** When eating an orange, the white inner peel (mesocarp) should be included, as well as the pulp fiber as long as it is not tough.

❷ **Juice:** Ideally orange juice should be drunk fresh-squeezed since vitamin C loses its potency over time and exposure to light. Canned orange juice loses some of its natural vitamin C, although some bottlers enrich it with synthetic vitamin C.

❸ **Orange treatment:** This treatment should be followed for one or two days per week for three or four weeks. It consists of eating only oranges each day, and drinking only fresh juice. Ten to twelve oranges may be eaten and 2 to 4 glasses of juice may be drunk each day. If the oranges are very bitter, two teaspoons of honey may be added to each glass of juice.

PROPERTIES AND INDICATIONS: The following components are noteworthy:

✓ ***Sugars*** in moderate amounts (about 9.35 g /100 g), easily assimilated by the body and tolerated by diabetics in controlled amounts; they are ***saccharose, dextrose,*** and ***levulose.***

✓ ***Minerals,*** among which ***potassium*** and ***calcium*** *stand out.* Oranges also contain smaller but significant amounts of ***iron*** and ***magnesium.***

✓ ***Vitamins:*** In addition to vitamin C (45-60 mg/100 g), oranges contain ***carotenoids*** that are responsible for their typical color (provitamin A), ***vitamin B_1*** and ***vitamin B_2.***

✓ ***Folic acid,*** in an amount of 30-40 mg /100 g. ***FOLIC ACID*** is an *essential* nutrient for proper development of the **fetal nervous system.** It also acts as an **antioxidant** whose presence in the blood is necessary to the proper function of the defensive cells (leukocytes or **white blood cells**).

✓ Vegetable ***fiber*** in the form of ***pectin,*** which fights **cholesterol.** Fiber is the only component of the orange that is not present in orange juice.

✓ ***Organic acids,*** *particularly* ***citric*** acid, which potentiates the activity of ***vitamin C*** and *facilitates* the *elimination* of toxic residues such as **uric acid** from the body.

✓ ***Carotenoids,*** substances similar to beta-carotene, which also transform into vitamin A in the body. They act as powerful **antioxidants.** Of the 20 carotenoids found in the orange, the most prominent are beta-cryptoxanthin, lutein, and zeaxanthin.[4, 5]

✓ ***PHYTOCHEMICALS,*** are substances found in very small amounts in foods but they play very important roles within the body. It is calculated that there are about 170 different phytochemicals in the orange,[5] and more may yet be discovered.

From a chemical standpoint, there are two main groups of phytochemicals in the orange:

- ***Flavonoids:*** These are powerful antioxidant, anti-inflammatory, and anticarcinogenic glucosides. They also have a positive effect on the circulatory system.[6] The best known (there are many others) are rutin, tangeretin, nobiletin, naringin, hesperidin, and quercetin.
- ***Limonoids:*** These substances are responsible for the orange's aroma, which forms part of its essence. Chemically these are terpenes, the most abundant of which is ***d-limonene.*** This substance found in oranges prevents the formation of tumors in experimental animals after they have been given known carcinogens.[7]

Thanks to its extraordinary chemical composition, the orange increases resistance to disease, protects the arteries, is antiallergenic, alkalizing, remineralizing, and anticarcinogenic.

Its dietetic and therapeutic applications are:

• **Infectious diseases:** Oranges should always be part of the diet of anyone with an infectious disease, or those who wish to avoid them. Studies show that at least four oranges a day (about 250 mg of vitamin C) are needed to achieve results. It is important to note that vitamin C or eating oranges *cannot prevent* **colds** or **flu.** However, they have been proven to *shorten* the length of the disease and reduce the *severity* of symptoms.

Oranges have the following **effects on infections,** thanks to the combination of ***vitamin C*** and the other natural chemical substances they contain:

- They *increase* the disease-fighting ***capabilities*** of the **white blood cells.**
- They *increase* the **number** and **longevity** of **white blood cells.** This is attributed to the combined effect of ***folic acid*** and ***vitamin C.***
- They *slow,* but do not completely halt the ***development*** of **viruses** within human cells. The orange's ***flavonoids,*** together with ***vitamin C,*** are responsible for this action.
- They *increase* the ***production*** of **interferon,** an antiviral protein produced within the body itself.

Thus, **eating** oranges ***daily*** is indicated for not only colds and flu, but for any type of infectious disease, including those associated with childhood, and even AIDS.

• **Thrombosis, arteriosclerosis, and cardiovascular disease:** The ***flavonoids*** found in oranges, *potentiated* by ***vitamin C,*** *inhibit* the buildup of **clot-forming platelets** in the blood. Thus, oranges help make the blood more fluid and improve circulation, particularly in the two organs requiring the most consistent blood supply: the **brain** and the **heart.**

Green oranges may be ripe

*To develop their **typical orange color,** oranges require **several consecutive cold nights** while they are still **on the tree.** This is common in **temperate countries.***

*However, in **tropical countries** it is very **common** to find **ripe** oranges that are **green,** because they have not been exposed to the cold.*

*The **point of ripeness** of an orange is not judged by its **external color,** but by the **proportion** of **sugar** and **acid** in its juice. In mature fruits this proportion is approximately **6:1,** in other words, six times more sugar than acid.*

Orange juice has become very popular as a breakfast drink and natural refreshment. Its composition is similar to that of orange, but with less calcium and fiber. Both of these nutrients are found primarily in the pulp.

Bottled juices made from reconstituted juice are a good alternative to natural juice. The vitamin C lost in processing is calculated at about 10%. The remaining vitamins, folic acid, and minerals are quite well maintained in bottled juice. In any case, in the absence of fresh juice, bottled or frozen juice is better than nothing.

Four oranges a day is the recommended dose for those wishing to increase resistance to infections.

Oranges also contain four *highly effective* **antioxidants** that mutually *potentiate* themselves: ***vitamin C, quercetin*** (a flavonoid-type phytochemical), ***provitamin A,*** and ***folic acid.*** The result is a *powerful* **antioxidant** effect on all of the body's cells. Today it is known that arteriosclerosis and the aging process itself have their biochemical origin in oxidizing phenomena. High doses of vitamin C (1 g daily for 6 weeks) reduces blood pressure.[8]

The **PULP** of the orange, *including* the white **inner peel** or mesocarp, is *rich* in ***pectin,*** a type of soluble ***fiber*** that lowers cholesterol levels.

Regular orange **consumption,** including the pulp, and even the mesocarp (the white inner peel), is associated with *reduced* blood **cholesterol,** *lowered* **blood pressure,** and *lower risk* of **arteriosclerosis**, **arterial thrombosis,** and **heart disease.**

• **Constipation:** oranges help cure constipation and intestinal atony through two mechanisms:

– They stimulate the emptying of the gallbladder (**cholagogic effect**), with the subsequent laxative effect of bile in the intestine.

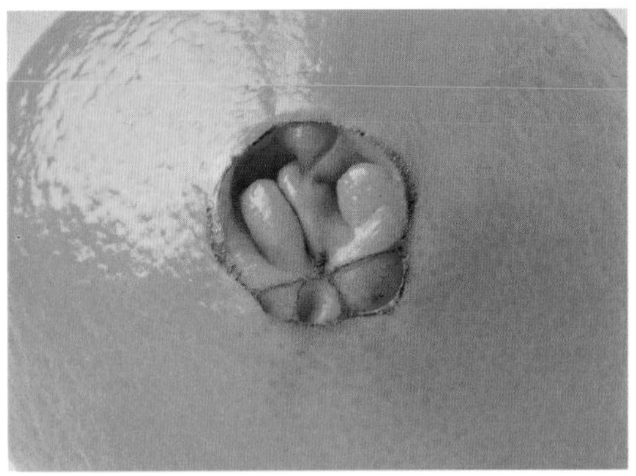

The domestic navel orange is one of the most highly prized. Its name reflects the unique form of its calyx.

– Their soft vegetable fiber *stimulates* **peristaltic** action in the intestine.

In addition to relieving constipation, oranges alleviate the **hemorrhoids** that often accompany it. To achieve the best results in both cases, an orange treatment should be followed **[❸]**.

• **Allergies:** Persons with high levels of vitamin C in the blood suffer less from allergies. This is probably because vitamin C is partially agonistic to the effects of histamine, the substance that initiates allergic episodes. Eating four or five oranges a day (or their equal in juice), contributes to the prevention of the appearance of allergic reactions such as **rhinitis** or **bronchial asthma.**

• **Demineralization:** With their 30-40 mg /100 g of calcium, oranges are the richest citrus fruit in this invaluable mineral (milk contains 119 mg). Additionally, oranges' ***citric acid*** *improves* calcium *absorption* in the intestine. Oranges also contain ***magnesium*** and ***phosphorus.***

Vitamin C is an *essential* factor in the growth and maintenance of the **bones, teeth,** and **cartilage.** Oranges are recommended in cases of **osteoporosis,** rickets, and whenever an increased supply of mineral salts is required.

• **Excess uric acid (gout):** A treatment with oranges **[❸]** (as with lemons, see p. 129) is *very effective* in dissolving and eliminating the uric acid deposits within the joints that cause uratic **arthritis. Kidney stones** may also be at least partially dissolved with an orange treatment.

All of this is because of the alkalizing effect of oranges and all citrus fruits in general. Although it seems a paradox, oranges are an ***excellent*** blood **alkalizer** in spite of their acid taste (see p. 272).

• **Eye conditions:** Because of their *richness* in ***carotenoids,***[4] as well as other ***antioxidants,*** oranges are useful in *preventing* **macular degeneration** of the retina, the principal cause of blindness in individuals over the age of 65 in Western countries.

• **Cancer prevention:** ***Vitamin C*** has an anticarcinogenic effect, as do the ***phytochemicals*** contained in oranges and other citrus fruits. Numerous studies have proven that *eating at least* one orange or other citrus fruit a day *prevents* various types of cancer. Patients that have already been diagnosed with this disease can also benefit from *abundant* orange consumption.

Citrus to eat and drink

Lime [1]

Citrus aurantiifolia (Christm.-Panz.) Sw. = *Limonia aurantiifolia* Christm.-Panz.

French: *Lime, limette;* ***Spanish:*** *Lima.*

The lime is similar in color, size, and shape to the lemon, but its flavor is less sour and much sweeter. It is grown primarily in Central America, Florida, and California.

Its ***vitamin C*** and ***B*** content is *somewhat inferior.* It is used for beverages because of its pleasant aroma.

Lemon (see p. 128) [2]

Citrus limon (L.) Burm.

Possibly the citrus with the *most* scientifically *proved* **medicinal applications.**

Tangerine (see p. 344) [3]

Citrus reticulata Blanco

This is the sweetest and mildest-flavored citrus.

Bitter orange (EMP p. 153) [4]

Citrus aurantium L. = *Citrus vulgaris* Risso.

Synonyms: *Seville orange.*

French: *Orange amère;* ***Spanish:*** *Naranja amarga, naranja agria.*

These are not edible raw because of their strong flavor. They are only used in confectionery and jellies.

The bitter orange is the one *most used* for **phytotherapeutic** purposes since its **leaves, blossoms,** and **peel** contain *high* concentrations of ***essences*** and other ***active substances.***

Orange [5]

Citrus sinensis Osbeck.

This is the most widely cultivated and valued citrus. It is described in detail on these pages.

Kumquat [6]

Fortunella margarita (Lour.) Sw.

Related species: *Fortunella japonica* [Thunb.] Sw. (round kumquat)

Synonyms: *Oval kumquat.*

Spanish: *Naranjita china, kumquat* [oval].

These are grown especially in Indonesia, Australia, and Florida. Their size varies between 2 and 3 cm in diameter.

Kumquats are eaten with the skin, which is soft and slightly acid. It is an aromatic and pleasant fruit.

Grapefruit (see p. 103) [7]

Citrus paradisi MacFad. = *Citrus maxima* (Burm.) Merr. = *Citrus decumanus* L.

Grapefruits are effective against **arteriosclerosis.** They are used in **weight loss diets** because of their **detoxifying** properties.

Calamondin

Citrus mitis Blanco

Spanish: *Calamondín, lima filipina.*

This citrus is grown in tropical countries. It is orange in color and measures about 2.5 cm in diameter. It is very juicy with a slightly bitter taste. It is used to make beverages and jellies.

Citron

Citrus medica L.

Spanish: *Cidra, toronja.*

Its fruits are large, weighing as much as two kilos. The peel is typically yellow, very thick and wrinkled.

Although it contains *less* ***vitamin C*** than other citrus, its ***calcium*** content is *higher.*

Litchi

Reduces inflammation and prevents infections

LITCHI
Composition
per 100 g of raw edible portion

Energy	66.0 kcal = 276 kj
Protein	0.830 g
Carbohydrates	15.2 g
Fiber	1.30 g
Vitamin A	—
Vitamin B_1	0.011 mg
Vitamin B_2	0.065 mg
Niacin	0.720 mg NE
Vitamin B_6	0.100 mg
Folate	14.0 µg
Vitamin B_{12}	—
Vitamin C	71.5 mg
Vitamin E	0.700 mg α-TE
Calcium	5.00 mg
Phosphorus	31.0 mg
Magnesium	10.0 mg
Iron	0.310 mg
Potassium	171 mg
Zinc	0.070 mg
Total Fat	*0.440 g*
Saturated Fat	*0.099 g*
Cholesterol	—
Sodium	*1.00 mg*

1% 2% 4% 10% 20% 40% 100% 200% 500%

% Daily Value (based on a 2,000 calorie diet) provided by 100 g of this food

Synonyms: *Lychee, Lychi, Litchi nut.*

Spanish: *Litchi, mamoncillo chino.*

Description: *Fruit of the litchi ('Litchi chinensis' Sonn.), an evergreen tree of the botanical family Sapindaceae that reaches a height of 12 m. The fruit, which hangs in bunches is oval-shaped, and measures 3 to 4 cm in diameter. It encloses a single brown pit.*

THE LITCHI is one of the symbols of the great nation of China, where it has been cultivated for more than four thousand years. Its red, pink, or green rind encloses a shiny, sweet, somewhat tart pulp that smells faintly of roses.

PROPERTIES AND INDICATIONS: Litchis contain a significant proportion of ***carbohydrates*** in the form of sugars (15.2%), although very few proteins (0.83%), and fats (0.44%). They contain less water than most

Vitamin C found in kiwi, citrus fruits and other fruits and vegetables has the following functions:

- **Antioxidant: It neutralizes free radicals, which are substances causing cellular aging, DNA deterioration, and cancer.**
- **Antitoxin: Neutralizes the action of a variety of toxic substances, such as nitrosamines found in cured meats.**
- **Strengthens the immune system against infections.**
- **Contributes to the formation of collagen, fibrous tissue necessary for wound healing.**
- **Improves the consistency of bones and teeth.**
- **Strengthens capillary and arterial walls.**
- **Facilitates the absorption of nonheme iron (that contained in plant-based foods, dairy products, and eggs).**

fresh fruits (81.8%), which makes them quite concentrated and energy producing (66 kcal/100 g).

Litchis contain all vitamins except provitamin A and vitamin B_{12}, but they are noted for their ***vitamin C*** content (71.5 mg/100 g), which is superior to oranges or lemons. One hundred grams of litchis supply more than the daily vitamin C requirement of an adult male (60 mg).

Investigators in Calcutta (India) have found that litchi **LEAVES** have **anti-inflammatory, analgesic** and **antipyretic** (fever-reducing) effects.[9] The fruit contains the same active substances as the leaves, but in lower proportions.

Because of their analgesic and antipyretic effects, as well as their vitamin C richness that increases disease resistance, litchis are *highly recommended* in cases of **infectious diseases,** as a ***complement*** to specific treatment. Additionally, **eating** litchis ***regularly*** **stimulates the immune system** and helps **prevent** disease.

Preparation and use

❶ **Fresh:** Their white pulp, whose consistency is reminiscent of the grape, combines well with other fruits, and even rice.

❷ **Dried:** They store very well dried, and their nutrient concentration is multiplied three times. However, they lose 20 to 50% of their vitamin C.

❸ **Frozen:** Litchis store well frozen for periods of up to a year, which facilitates their long-range transport. They lose 10% to 15% of their vitamin C.

❹ **Canned:** These are usually prepared in syrup.

Acerola

The richest fresh fruit source of vitamin C

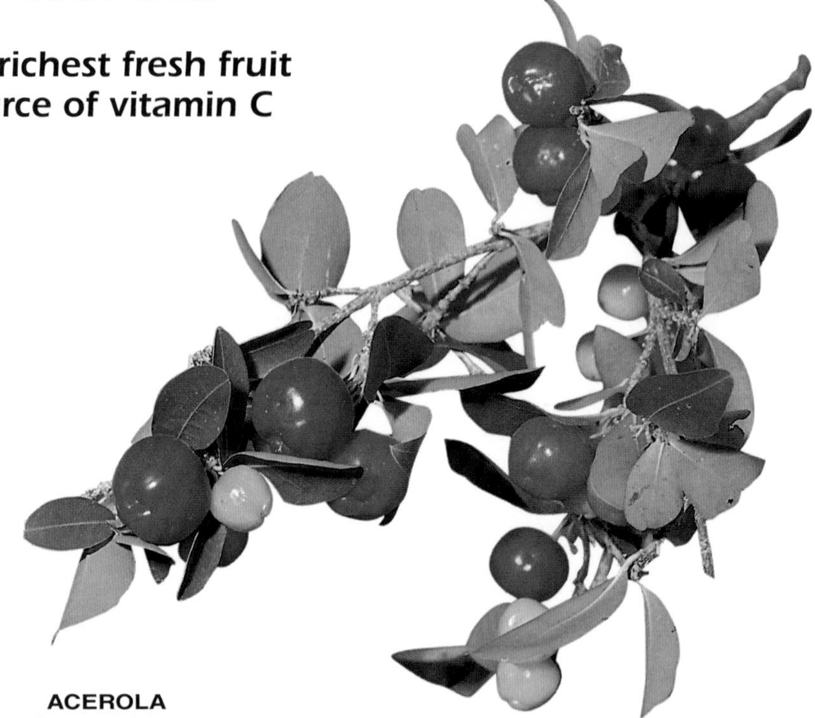

ACEROLA Composition
per 100 g of raw edible portion

Energy	32.0 kcal = 132 kj
Protein	0.400 g
Carbohydrates	6.59 g
Fiber	1.10 g
Vitamin A	77.0 µg RE
Vitamin B_1	0.020 mg
Vitamin B_2	0.060 mg
Niacin	0.400 mg NE
Vitamin B_6	0.009 mg
Folate	14.0 µg
Vitamin B_{12}	—
Vitamin C	1,678 mg
Vitamin E	0.130 mg α-TE
Calcium	12.0 mg
Phosphorus	11.0 mg
Magnesium	18.0 mg
Iron	0.200 mg
Potassium	146 mg
Zinc	0.100 mg
Total Fat	*0.300 g*
Saturated Fat	*0.068 g*
Cholesterol	—
Sodium	*7.00 mg*

1% 2% 4% 10% 20% 40% 100% 200% 500%
% Daily Value (based on a 2,000 calorie diet) provided by 100 g of this food

Related species: *Malpighia punicifolia* L.

Synonyms: *Spanish pine, Neapolitan medlar.*

French: *Angerolle, angerolier;* ***Spanish:*** *Acerola.*

Description: *Fruit of 'Malpighia glabra' L., a tree of the botanical family Malpighiaceae.*

WHEN THE SPANIARDS first arrived in the Caribbean islands in the sixteenth century, they found a tree with fruit similar to those of the azarole cultivated in Europe, and they named it acerola. Those explorers had no idea then that the Caribbean acerola is much richer in vitamin C than the European fruit.

PROPERTIES AND INDICATIONS: The acerola was a little appreciated fruit until 1946 when some investigators at the University of Puerto Rico analyzed its ***vitamin C*** content. They declared that they had discovered nature's ***rich-***

When the body needs more vitamin C

*An adult needs a minimum of **60 mg** a day of vitamin C. It must be borne in mind that this vitamin **is not stored** in the cells, and **must be taken in every day.** Fresh **fruits** and **vegetables** are the **only sure source** of vitamin C.*

***Serious vitamin C deficiency** results in the disease of **scurvy,** but fortunately, today, it is very rare, at least in developed countries. However, **slight deficiencies** of vitamin C are **common.** These produce **lowered resistance** to **infections, listlessness,** and **joint pain**. In the developed world, it is possible for individuals to be suffering from lack of vitamin C and not being aware of it.*

*In many cases, this lack is relative since it is due to **increased need.** This occurs in the following situations:*

- *Any type of **infection***
- ***Pregnancy** and **lactation***
- *Surgical **operations***
- ***Tobacco** use*
- ***Extreme physical effort***

To meet the vitamin C requirement occasioned by these situations, which are double or triple the normal need, one should eat at least two oranges, or four tangerines, or two kiwis, or 200 g (about half a pound) of litchis, or a handful of acerolas.

est source of this vitamin (up to 2,520 mg /100 g, according to the variety, in other words, more than 50 times that of lemons.[10]

In addition to vitamin C, acerolas also contain a whole series of natural substances that accompany it and potentiate its action: ***organic acids*** such as malic acid, and ***flavonoids*** such as rutin and hesperidin.

According to Schneider,[11] elevated doses of ***VITAMIN C*** increase the production of ***interferon***, a protein that inhibits the proliferation of viruses, and stimulates the immune system and halts the growth of tumoral cells.

Because of these properties, the acerola is highly recommended for all types of **infectious** disease, particularly those of viral origin (flu, colds, etc.) and as a *complement* to the prevention and treatment of **cancer** (see p. 360).

Preparation and use

❶ **Raw:** This fruit must be completely ripe before it can be eaten, and even then, it is quite sour.

❷ **Juice:** Acerola juice is usually blended with other sweeter fruit juices.

❸ **Commercial use:** Acerola pulp is used to make jellies and gelatin deserts. It is also dried and powdered. All of these industrial applications are rich in vitamin C.

Azarole

This is the fruit of a bush or tree of the botanical family Rosaceae (*Crataegus azarolus* L.).

It is similar to the cherry, and, as the acerola described here, it is very rich in ***vitamin C*** (275 mg/100 g).

18

Foods and Cancer

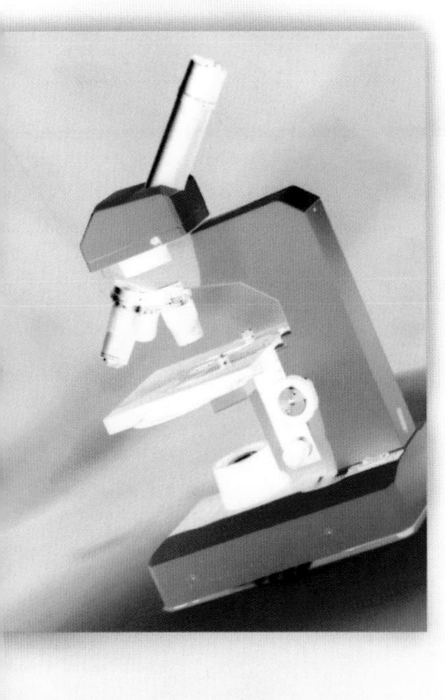

CANCER is possibly the ***most* feared and fearful** disease of all that affect humanity. Enormous efforts are being made throughout the world in order to discover its causal factors.

The ***most important*** of these factors, ***improper* diet,** was noted by Ellen G. White and other leaders of the health reform movement that developed in the second half of the nineteenth century in the United States.[1]

Unfortunately, the medical establishment paid scant attention to the proposals of proponents of natural medicine. Consequently, until only recently anyone who might suggest that certain foods might help prevent or treat cancer was considered a charlatan.

However, in recent decades there has been a rapid increase in scientific evidence that eating certain foods has a great deal to do with cancer.[2]

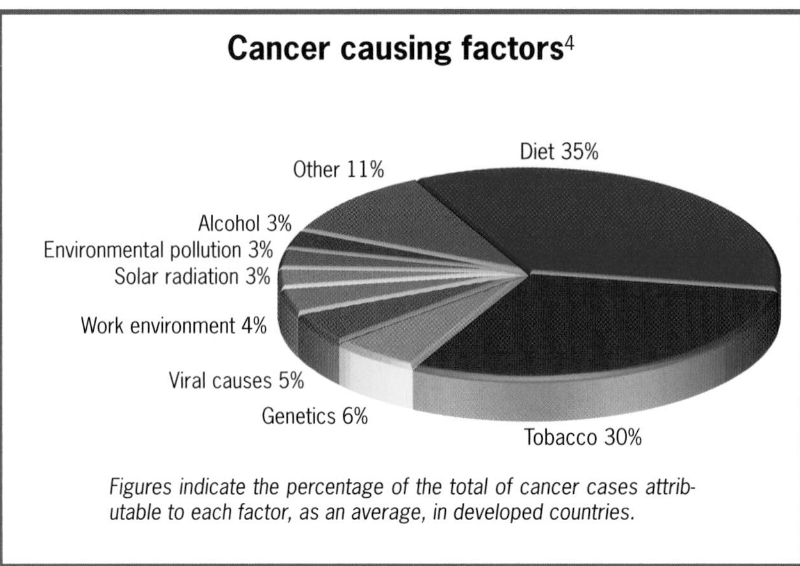

Figures indicate the percentage of the total of cancer cases attributable to each factor, as an average, in developed countries.

The foods that are customarily eaten in developed countries are the most important source of carcinogens.[3]

Foods as a cause of cancer

As illustrated in the graph above, diet is today's ***primary*** *cancer-causing* **factor.** It is truly ironic that foods, which should provide health and life, should become the principal cause of cancer and death.[3]

Something must be wrong with the dietary habits of the bulk of the developed world's population: they are eating ***too many*** **animal-based foods,** which *foster* cancer, in proportion to plant-based foods, which help protect against it.

To reduce cancer risk, avoid:

- **Cured meats** (sausages, cured ham, bacon, etc.), **grilled** meats, and **very well done** or **fried** meats.
- ***Excess*** **calories** from **protein** or **fat** sources, *particularly* from **animal** sources such as meat, fish, eggs, or milk.
- **Smoked, pickled, salted,** or ***highly*** **spiced** foods.
- Consuming ***very*** **hot** foods and beverages.
- **Alcoholic beverages, coffee,** and **tobacco:** When these are combined, they *potentiate* their carcinogenic effect.

Foods in the prevention of cancer

Foods that are suitable for humans, as described in the first chapter of this work, protect against cancer, instead of fostering it. This is precisely the effect of fruits, nuts, grains, legumes, and vegetables.

Cancer prevention requires an increase in

- ***Provitamin A*** and ***vitamins C*** and ***E***
- ***Fiber***
- ***Phytochemical elements***

All of these food components have been experimentally and epidemiologically shown to be anticarcinogens. They are found almost ***exclusively*** in **plant-based** foods.

Foods in the treatment of cancer

Above all, foods play a vital role in cancer ***prevention.*** However, even when cancer has been diagnosed, diet continues to be vitally important.

Cancer, Carcinogens, and Anticarcinogens

- ***Cancer:*** *An uncontrolled proliferation of cells producing a malignant tumor. It invades surrounding tissues and may entail* ***metastasis*** *(other tumors of the same type appearing far from the original site). Its natural evolution leads to death.*
- ***Carcinogen:*** *Food, substance, or other agent that fosters the development of cancer. The most common* ***carcinogens*** *are* ***tobacco*** *smoke, certain food* ***additives*** *such as* ***nitrites,*** *the* ***substances*** *that form during the* ***cooking of meat, chemical contaminants*** *such as* ***pesticides,*** *some* ***viruses*** *and* ***molds,*** *and* ***radiation.***
- ***Mutagens:*** *Substances that produce mutations or changes in the genetic code of the cells. Many of these mutations cause cells to become cancerous. Thus, mutagens are also carcinogens. Mutagens are formed when foods, particularly meat products, are* ***fried*** *or* ***roasted.***
- ***Anticarcinogens*** *or* ***cancer protection:*** *Food or substance that* ***neutralizes*** *the action of carcinogens and slows or* ***prevents the development*** *of cancer. Virtually* ***all*** *anticarcinogens are* ***plant-based.***

All the anticarcinogenic foods described on the following two pages, particularly fruit treatments, salads, and fresh juices, are additional treatment resources that should not be ignored. There is experimental evidence documenting their effectiveness in slowing the development of malignant cells, demonstrating that their use as a therapeutic tool is well founded.

There is an intimate relationship between cancer and the diet: Some cause it while others help prevent it.
For those wishing to reduce the risk of cancer, this is the most concise dietary counsel: adopt a vegetarian diet.

Foods that

Fruit

Fruit, together with vegetables, is the ***most* effective** anticarcinogenic food. Certain rigorously conducted scientific studies conducted throughout the world have shown that ***abundant*** fruit **consumption** prevents most of the cancers that affect humans.

Grapefruits

Plums

- **Citrus,** such as **lemons** (see p. 128), **oranges** (see p. 346) and **grapefruit** (see p. 102): Their anticarcinogenic capacity is due to the combined effect of ***vitamin C, flavonoids, limonoids,*** and ***pectin*** (see p. 345).
- **Plums** (see p. 220) and **apples** (see p. 216): These protect against colon cancer.
- **Pineapples** (see p. 180): Prevent stomach cancer.
- **Grapes:** The ***resveratrol*** they contain, particularly in the skin, is anticarcinogenic.
- **Blackberries** and other aggregate fruits such as **strawberries, blueberries**, and **currants** are rich in ***anthocynanins,*** *powerful* **antioxidants** that *neutralize* the carcinogenic effect of **free radicals.**
- **Acerolas** (see p. 354), **guavas** (see p. 118) and **kiwis** (see p. 342), because of their high ***vitamin C*** content.

Strawberry

Olive oil

Studies conducted in Spain and the United States reveal that when it is ***substituted*** for other dietary **fats** olive oil consumption reduces breast cancer risk.

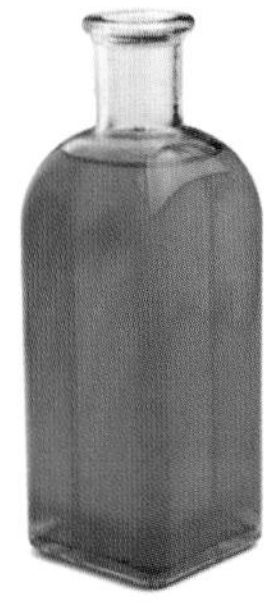

Whole grains

The ***fiber*** in whole grains accelerates movement through the bowel. It also retains and removes carcinogenic substances that may be in the digestive tract, excreting them with the feces.

Rye bread

Grains also contain ***phytates,*** which act as anticarcinogens, although they also reduce iron and zinc absorption.

help prevent cancer

Vegetables

All vegetables protect against cancer to a greater or lesser degree. Their richness in ***provitamin A, vitamin C,*** and **antioxidant *phytochemicals*** explain this anticarcinogenic effect. Here are the most effective:

- **Red beets**

  These contain anticarcinogenic ***phytochemicals*** (see p. 126).

- **Carrots**

  Their high concentration of ***beta-carotene*** (provitamin A), other ***carotenoids,*** and ***fiber*** (see p. 32), explains carrots' proven anticarcinogenic effect.

- **Botanical family Solanaceae**

  The vegetables of this family protect against cancer, particularly **tomatoes** (see p. 264), **sweet peppers** (see p. 188) and **eggplants** (see p. 242). This is attributed to their richness in ***beta-carotene*** (provitamin A), ***carotenoids,*** and ***vitamin C,*** all of which are potent **antioxidants.**

- **Botanical family Liliaceae**

  All of the vegetables of this family, particularly **onions** (see p. 142) and **garlic,** contain ***flavonoids*** and ***sulfurated essences*** that protect against cancer.

- **Crucifers**

  The plants of this botanical family contain a variety of ***sulfurated phytochemicals*** whose anticarcinogenic effect has been demonstrated in laboratory animals (see p. 183). This effect persists even after cooking.

  Cabbage (see p. 182), **cauliflower** (see p. 154), **broccoli** (see p. 72) and **radishes** (see p. 174) are the crucifers best known for their cancer prevention properties.

Tomato

Broccoli

Yogurt

In contrast to milk, whose consumption is related with a variety of cancers, yogurt protects against this disease, particularly **breast cancer.**

Its content of ***active* bacterial** cultures (in **"bio"** biotic yogurt) and ***lactic acid*** partially explains this protective effect.

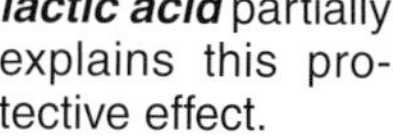

Natural yogurt

Legumes

Legumes in general protect against cancer because of their richness in ***fiber*** and anticarcinogenic ***phytochemicals*** such as ***phytic acid*** and ***phytates.***

Soy and its derivatives

Soy (see p. 254) and its derivatives, particularly **tofu** and **soymil**, provide a variety of anticarcinogenic ***phytochemicals.*** The most effective are the isoflavones ***genistein*** and ***daidzein.*** They are particulary effective against **breast and prostate cancer.**

Chickpeas

Foods that

Meat

Numerous scientific studies, both experimental and statistical, have revealed that meat consumption is a *significant* **risk factor** in most types of cancer (brain, lung, stomach, kidney, urinary bladder, uterus, ovarian, and prostate, among others).

Meats *particularly* **detrimental** are:

- The so-called **red meats** (beef, lamb, and pork),
- Meat cooked **well-done** or grilled on a **barbecue,**
- **Fried** meat,
- **Salted** and/or **cured** meats such as ham, bacon, and sausages.

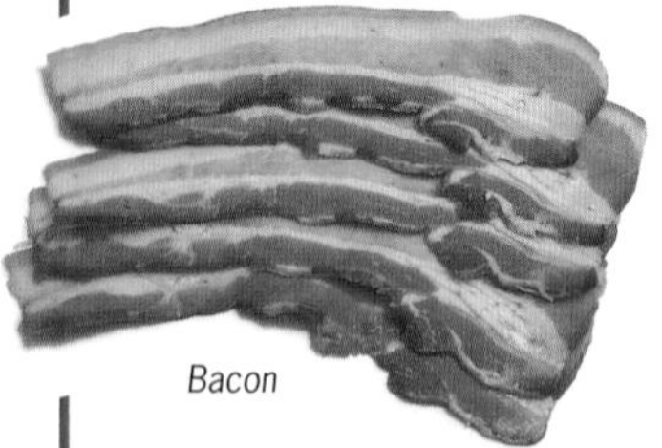
Bacon

Alcoholic beverages

All alcoholic beverages *promote* cancer, even those considered to have medicinal value such as wine or beer. These do not require large doses to induce cancer. This effect is present even with moderate consumption.

One glass of wine a day increases the risk of breast cancer in women by 250%.[5]

Whiskey

Milk

According to various studies, ***excessive*** whole milk (not nonfat) **consumption** is associated with the appearance of some types of cancer: breast, lung, ovarian, prostate, and urinary bladder.

Whole milk

Shellfish

Prawn

These tend to be ***contaminated*** with carcinogenic **chemical substances** that have been dumped into the sea.

Eggs

There is statistical evidence that excess egg consumption (*more* than ***three*** per *week*) is associated with cancers of breast, stomach, lung, pancreas, colon, endometrium, and ovaries.

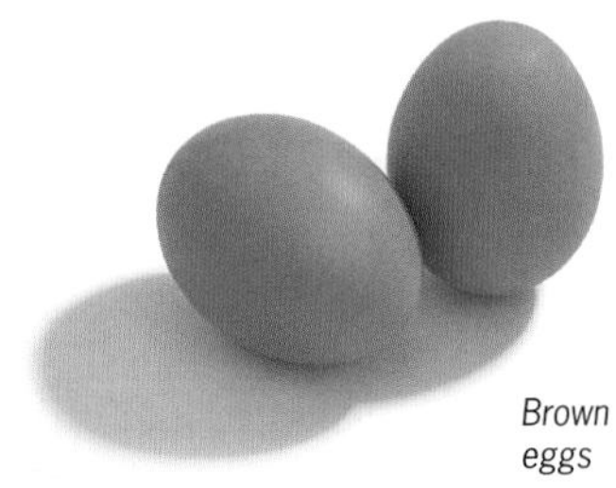
Brown eggs

promote cancer

Fish

There is less experimental and statistical evidence concerning cancer and fish than there is concerning meat. However, there is a relationship between regular fish consumption (particularly salted or cured fish) and cancers of the larynx, nasopharynx, endometrium, and pancreas.

Spices

A diet that is rich in hot spices can be a risk factor for certain types of cancer such as cancer of the mouth and esophagus.

Nutmeg

Coffee

Coffee consumption has been associated with cancer of the urinary bladder and with fibrocystic mastopathy or fibrocystic disease of the breast, which can be precancerous.

This effect is not due to the caffeine in coffee, but rather to some of the components in its essence. Consequently, **decaffeinated** coffee *also* increases the risk of urinary bladder cancer.[6]

Refined products

When white bread, rolls, and other refined products are used *in place* of **whole grains** in the diet, there is a corresponding relation to the formation of cancer. At least three characteristics of their composition explain this relationship:

- *Lack* of ***fiber.***
- *Excess* **sugar** content.
- **Trans fatty acids:** This type of fatty acids is commonly found in refined industrial baked goods. Fried foods and margarine also contain *trans* fatty acids. In addition to raising cholesterol levels and promoting arteriosclerosis and heart attack, these fatty acids are related to cancer of the breast and the endometrium.

White bread

Sugar

Various epidemiological studies have related ***excess*** white sugar (saccharose) **consumption** with the following types of cancer:

- Colon cancer,
- Stomach cancer,
- Cervical cancer.

White sugar

Diet for preventing

The tables on these pages (364-367) have been prepared based on the most recent studies published in the world's most prestigious scientific and medical journals. They reflect the most current understanding on the relationship between diet and cancer.

Prevention of cancer of the larynx

Increase

- Fruit
- Green leafy vegetables
- Vegetable oils
- Antioxidant vitamins (A, C, and E)

Reduce or eliminate

- Alcoholic beverages
- Cured meta
- Maté

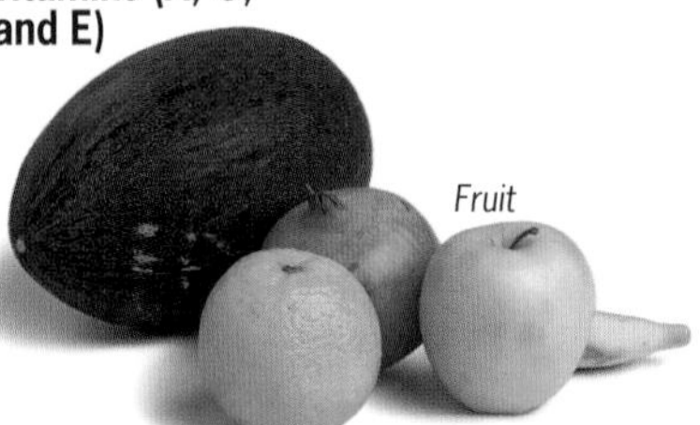

Fruit

Prevention of nasopharyngeal cancer

Increase

- Vegetables
- Carotene (provitamin A)

Reduce or eliminate

- Salted fish (particularly for infants)
- Very hot tea or infusions
- Smoked products
- Salted products

Spinach

Prevention of brain cancer

Increase

- Vitamins, particularly C and E

Reduce or eliminate

- Hot dogs. Their consumption by pregnant women increases the risk of cancer in their children
- Hamburgers
- Cured and roasted meat
- Processed pork products such as boiled ham (York ham) and bacon
- Fried foods

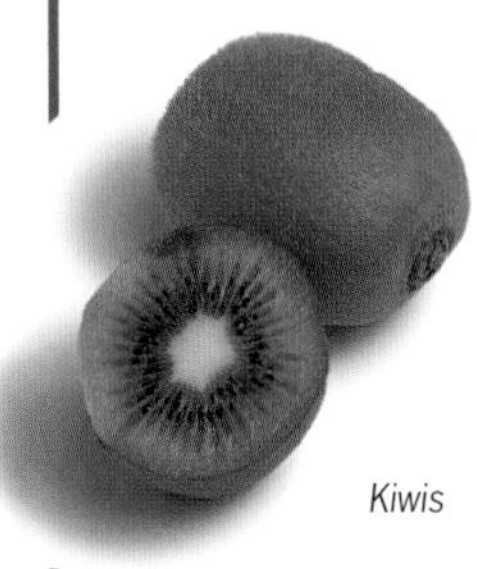

Kiwis

Prevention of cancer of the mouth

Increase

- Fruit particularly citrus
- Vegetables, particularly those rich in carotenes

Reduce or eliminate

- Alcoholic beverages, particularly wine and liquors
- Meat, especially roasted or barbecued
- Chilies (hot peppers)
- Maté

Citrus

...each type of cancer (1)

Prevention of esophageal cancer

Increase

- Fruits, especially citrus fruits
- Vegetables
- Beta-carotene (provitamin A) and carotenoids
- Fiber

Reduce or eliminate

- Alcoholic beverages
- Very hot beverages, especially mate
- Red meats, particularly barbecue
- Pickles

Whole grain rice

Prevention of lung cancer

Increase

- Fruits and vegetables

Reduce or eliminate

- Cured meats (sausages, bacon)
- Beer
- Whole milk and dairy products
- Eggs
- Refined baked goods

Vegetables

Prevention of stomach cancer

Increase

- Fruits, particularly citrus and pineapple
- Vegetables, independent of their nitrate content
- Garlic and onion
- Whole grain bread
- Vegetable oil
- Pasta and rice

Reduce or eliminate

- Red meta, especially well-done
- Cured meats and sausages, especially homemade
- Beer
- Salt-cured foods
- Eggs
- Rolls and pastries
- Sugar
- Saturated fat

Garlic

Prevention of liver cancer

Increase

- Vegetales
- Beta-carotene (provitamin A)

Reduce or eliminate

- Pork
- Wine and other alcoholic beverages
- Moldy foods or those with aflatoxin residue

Mango

Diet for preventing

Prevention of Breast Cancer

 **Increase**

- Soy, tofu, soymilk
- Fruit
- Vegetables especially carrots and spinach
- Olive oil
- Garlic
- Yogurt
- Fiber
- Vitamin C
- Beta-carotene (provitamin A)
- Vitamin E

 **Reduce or eliminate**

- Red meat (fish and skinless chicken are not detrimental)
- Processed pork (sausages, ham, etc.)
- Eggs
- Milk (according to one study it is protective)
- High-fat cheese
- Fat
- Trans fatty acids (margarine and commercial baked goods)
- Alcoholic beverages, even in low doses
- Chocolate and pastries

Soy

Prevention of Colon Cancer

 **Increase**

- Fiber
- Fruit
- Vegetables particularly carrots and spinach
- Whole-grain bread and pasta
- Fermented dairy products (yogurt) and calcium

 **Reduce or eliminate**

- Red meats (beef, pork, lamb)
- Well-done meat
- Processed or cured meats
- Liver and other variety meats
- Eggs, particularly for women
- Fats and high-calorie foods[61], especially animal based
- Cured high-fat cheese
- Sugar, such as that added to coffee
- Alcoholic beverages, specifically wine

Whole-grain pasta

Prevention of Kidney Cancer

 **Increase**

- Fruit, particularly citrus and apples
- Salads
- Vitamin C
- Vitamin E

 **Reduce or eliminate**

- Red meats, meat products
- Chicken
- Fat
- Proteins

Apples

Prevention of Pancreatic Cancer

  **Increase**

- Fruit
- Vegetables, especially cabbages and tomatoes
- Grains
- Legumes
- Fiber
- Yogurt

 **Reduce or eliminate**

- Meat
- Fish
- Eggs
- Proteins
- Cholesterol
- Saturated animal fat
- Calories
- Alcoholic beverages

ach type of cancer (and 2)

Prevention of prostate cancer

Increase

- Fruit
- Tomatoes
- Dried fruits (dates, raisins)
- Legumes
- Soy, tofu, soymilk (beverage)
- Citrus pectin
- Garlic
- Fructose
- Vitamin E
- Carotenoids (lycopene)

Reduce or eliminate

- Red meats
- Milk
- Animal fat
- Calcium from foods or suplements

Tofu

Prevention of ovarian cancer

Increase

- Vegetables, particularly carrots
- Whole-grain bread and pasta
- Fish

Reduce or eliminate

- Meat
- Whole milk
- Saturated fat
- Eggs
- Butter

Whole-grain bread

Prevention of endometrial cancer

Increase

- Fruit
- Vegetables
- Whole grain cereals, breads, and pasta
- Legumes
- Garlic and onion
- Beta-carotene

Reduce or eliminate

- Red meat and cured meats
- Cured or salted fish
- Eggs
- Animal fat
- Margarine
- Cholesterol

Onion

Prevention of cancer of the urinary bladder

Increase

- Fruit
- Vegetables, particularly spinach and carrots
- Beta-carotene (provitamin A)
- Vitamin C
- Vitamin E

Reduce or eliminate

- Pork and lamb
- Coffee
- Milk
- Pickles
- Fat, particularly animal fat
- Fried foods
- Excess calories
- Sodium (salt)
- Wine, beer, and other alcoholic beverages

Carrots

Bibliography

Chap. 1: Foods for Humans

1. Genesis 1: 29.
2. Genesis 3: 18.
3. Nobmann, E.D.; Byers, T.; Lanier, A.P. et al. The diet of Alaska Native adults: 1987-1988 [see comments]. *Am. J. Clin. Nutr.*, **55:** 1024-1032 (1992).
4. Heber, D. The stinking rose: organosulfur compounds and cancer. *Am. J. Clin. Nutr.*, **66:** 425-426 (1997).
5. Bergman, J. Diet, Health and Evolution. *Creation Research Society Quarterly,* **34:** 209-217 (1998).
6. Martins, Y.; Pelchat, M.L.; Pliner, P. "Try it; it´s good and it's good for you" effects of taste and nutrition information on willingness to try novel foods. *Appetite,* **28:** 89-102 (1997).

Chap. 2: Foods for the Eyes

1. Strasburger et al. *Strasburger, Lehrbuch der Botanik,* Suttgart, Gustav Fischer Verlag, 33rd ed., 1991.
2. Seddon, J.M.; Ajani, U.A.; Sperduto, R.D. et al. Dietary carotenoids, vitamins A, C and E, and advanced age-related macular degeneration. *JAMA,* **272:** 1413-1420 (1994).
3. Tavani, A.; Negri, E.; La Vecchia, C. Food and nutrient intake and risk of cataract. *Ann. Epidemiol.*, **6:** 41-46 (1996).
4. Seddon, J.M.; Ajani, U.A.; Sperduto, R.D. et al. Dietary carotenoids, vitamins A, C and E, and advanced age-related macular degeneration. *JAMA,* **272:** 1413-1420 (1994).
5. Reddy, N.S.; Malewar, V.G. Bio-availability of iron from spinach cultivated in soil fortified with graded levels of iron. *Plant Foods Human Nutrition,* **42:** 313-318 (1992).
6. Satoh, T.; Goto, M.; Igarashi, K. Effects of protein isolates from radish and spinach leaves on serum lipids levels in rats. *Journal of Nutrition Science and Vitaminology of Tokyo,* **39:** 627-633 (1993).

Chap. 3: Foods for the Nervous System

1. Breakey, J. The role of diet and behaviour in childhood. *J. Paediatr. Child Health,* **33:** 190-194 (1997).
2. Lechky, O. If children are developing poorly, ask what they had for breakfast. *CMAJ,* **143:** 210-213 (1990).
3. Needleman, H.L.; Riess, J.A.; Tobin, M.J. et al. Bone lead levels and delinquent behavior. *JAMA,* **275:** 363-369 (1996).
4. Pollock, I.; Warner, J.O. Effect of artificial food colours on childhood behaviour. *Arch. Dis. Child.*, **65:** 74-77 (1990).
5. Tuormaa, T. E. The adverse effects of food additives on health: a review of the literature with special emphasis on childhood hyperactivity. *Journal of Orthomolecular Medicine,* **9:** 225-243 (1994).
6. Leira, R.; Rodriguez, R. Diet and migraine. *Rev. Neurol.*, May 24 **(129):** 534-538 (1996).
7. Pamplona-Roger G. D. *Encyclopedia of Medicinal Plants.* Editorial Safeliz, Madrid, 1998, p. 151.
8. Esko, K. et al: A comparison of diets with and without oats in adults with celiac disease. *The New England Journal of Medicine,* **333**: 1033-1037 (1995).
9. Hallfrish, J.; Scholfield, D.J.; Behall, K.M. et al.: Diets containing oat extracts improve glucose and insulin responses of mederately hypercholesterolemic men and women. *Am. J. Clin. Nutr.*, **61**: 379-84 (1995).
10. Marlett, J.; Hosig, K.B.; Vollendorf, N.W. et al.: Mechanism of serum reduction by oat bran. *Hepatology,* **20**: 1450-1457 (1994).
11. Dubois, C.; Armand, M.; Senft, M. et al.: Chronic oat bran intake alters postprandial lipemia and lipoproteins in healthy adults. *Am. J. Clin. Nutr.*, **61**: 325-333 (1995).
12. Braaten, J.: Oat beta-glucan reduces blood cholesterol concentration in hypercholesterolemic subjects. *Eur. J. Clin. Nutr.*, **48**: 465-474 (1994).
13. Beer, M.; Wood, P.J.; Scott, F.W. et al. Effects of oat gum on blood cholesterol levels in healthy young men. *Eur. J. Clin. Nutr.*, **49**: 517-522 (1995).
14. Pamplona-Roger G. D. *Encyclopedia of Medicinal Plants.* Editorial Safeliz, Madrid, 1998, p. 160.
15. Wolff R.L.; Bayard C.C. Fatty acid composition of some pine seed oils. *Journal of the American Oil Chemists Society,* **72**: 1043-1046 (1995).
16. *Present Knowdledge in Nutrition.* International Life Sciences Institute, ILSI-North America, 1990, 6th ed., p. 252.
17. WHO, Technical Report Series, 797. *Diet, Nutrition, and the Prevention of Chronic Diseases.* Report of a WHO Study Group. Geneva, 1990, p. 90.

Chap. 4: Foods for the Heart

1. Ness, A.R.; Powles, J.W. Fruit and vegetables, and cardiovascular disease: a review. *Int. J. Epidemiol.*, **26:** 1-13 (1997).
2. Ducimetiere, P.; Guize, L.; Marciniak, A. Arteriographically documented coronary artery disease and alcohol consumption in French men. *The CORALI Study. Eur. Heart. J.*, **14:** 727-733 (1993).
3. Constant, J. Alcohol, ischemic heart disease, and the French paradox. *Clin. Cardiol.*, **20:** 420-424 (1997).
4. Yuan, J.M.; Ross, R.K.; Gao, Y.T. et al. Follow up study of moderate alcohol intake and mortality among middle aged men in Shanghai, China. *British Medical Journal,* **314:** 18-23 (1997).
5. Camargo, C.A; Hennekens, C,H.; Gaziano, J.M. et al. Prospective study of moderate alcohol consumption and mortality in United States male physicians. *Arch. Intern. Med.*, **157:** 79-85 (1997).
6. Frankel, E.N.; Kanner, J.; German, J.B. et al. Inhibition of oxidation of human low-density lipoprotein by phenolic substances in red wine. *Lancet,* **341:** 454-457 (1993).
7. Singh, R.B.; Niaz, M.A.; Agarwal, P. et al. Effect of antioxidant-rich foods on plasma ascorbic acid, cardiac enzyme, and lipid peroxide levels in patients hospitalized with acute myocardial infarction. *J. Am. Diet. Assoc.*, **95:** 775-780 (1995).
8. Ornish, D.; Brown, S.E.; Scherwitz, L.W. et al. Can lifestyle changes reverse coronary heart disease? The Lifestyle Heart Trial [see comments]. *Lancet,* 336: 129-133 (1990).
9. Stoewsad, G. Bioactive organosulfur phytochemicals in Brassica oleracea vegetables (a review). *Food Chem. Toxicol.*, **33**: 537-543 (1995).
10. Preobrazhenskaya, M.; Bukhman, V.M.; Korolev, A.M. et al. Ascorbigen and other indole-derived compounds from brassica vegetables and their analogs as anticarcinogenic and inmunomodulating agents. *Pharmacol., Ther.*, **60**: 301-313 (1993).
11. Mehta, R.; Liu, J.; Constantinou, A. et al. Cancer chemopreventive activity of brassinin, a phytoalexin from cabagge. *Carcinogenesis,* **16**: 399-404 (1995).
12. Chen, M.; Chen, L.T.; Boyce, H.W. Cruciferous vegetables and glutathione: their effects on colon mucosal glutathione level and colon tumor development in rats induced by DMH. *Nutr. Cancer,* **23**: 77-83 (1995).
13. Fraser, G.; Sabate, J.; Beeson, L. et al. A possible protective effect of nut consumption on risk of coronary heart disease. *Archives of Internal Medecine,* **152:** 1416-1424 (1992).

14. Nagy, S.; Shaw, P.E. *Tropical and subtropical fruits.* Westport (Connecticut), 1980, The AVI Publishing Company, Inc., p. 548.

15. Quinn, L.A.; Tang, H.H. *Journal of the Amarican Oil Chemists Society,* **73:** 1585-1588 (1996).

16. Ako, H. et al. Healthful new oil from macadamia nuts. *Nutrition,* **11**: 286-288 (1995).

17. Segal I. et al. Fermentation of the carbohydrate of banana in the human large intestine. *American Journal of Gastroenterology,* **88:** 420-423 (1993).

18. Horigome T.; Sakaguchi E.; Kishimoto C. Hypocholesterolaemic effect of banana pulp in the rat fed on a cholesterol-containing diet. *British Journal of Nutrition,* **68:** 231-244 (1992).

19. Krishna G.C. Role of potassium in the pathogenesis of hypertension. *American Journal of Clinical Science,* **307:** S21-S25 (1994).

20. Gillman M.W. et al. Protective effect of fruits and vegetables on development of stroke in men. *JAMA,* **273:** 1113-1117 (1995).

21. Jansson, B. Dietary, total body, and intracellular potassium-to-sodium ratios and their influence on cancer. *Cancer Detect. Prev.* **14:** 563-565 (1990).

Chap. 5: Foods for the Arteries

1. Willett, W.C.; Ascherio, A. Trans fatty acids: are the effects only marginal? *Am. J. Public Health,* **84:** 722-724 (1994).

2. Kris-Etherton, P.M.; Shaomei, Y. Individual fatty acid effects on plasma lipids and lipoproteins: human studies. *Am. J. Clin. Nutr.,* **65** (suppl): 1628S-1644S (1997).

3. ASCN/AIN Task Force on Trans Fatty Acids. Position paper on trans fatty acids. *Am. J. Clin. Nutr.,* **63:** 663-670 (1996).

4. Gilani, A.H.; Asif, M.; Nagra, S.A. Energy utilization of supplemented cereal diets in human volunteers. *Arch. Latinoam. Nutr.,* **36:** 373-378 (1986).

5. Muir, J.G.; O'Dea, K. Measurement of resistant starch: factors affecting the amount of starch escaping digestion in vitro. *American Journal of Clinical Nutrition,* **56:** 123-127 (1992).

6. Mahan, L.K.; Arlin, M.T. *Krause's Food, Nutrition and Diet Therapy.* Philadelphia, W.B. Saunders Company, 8th ed.,1992.

7. *Present Knowdledge in Nutrition.* International Life Sciences Institute, ILSI-North America, 1990, 6th ed., p. 275.

8. Gaitan, E. et al. Antithyroid effects in vivo and in vitro of babassu and mandioca: a staple food in goiter areas of Brazil. *Eur. J. Endocrinol.,* **131:** 138-144 (1994).

9. Awoyinka, A.F.; Abegunde, V.O.; Adewusi, S.R. Nutrient content of young cassava leaves and assessment of their acceptance as a green vegetable in Nigeria. *Plant Foods Hum. Nutr.,* **47:** 21-28 (1995).

10. Araghiniknam, M. et al. Antioxidant activity of dioscrea and dehydroepiandrosterone (DHEA) in older humans. *Life Sciences,* **59:** PL147-157 (1996).

11. Hong-Wang; Guohua-Cao; Prior, R.L. Total antioxidant capacity of fruits. *Journal of Agricultural and Food Chemistry,* **44:** 701-705 (1996).

12. Meydani, M. Vitamin E. *The Lancet,* **345:** 170-175 (1995).

13. Bellice, M.C. et al. Vitamin E and coronary heart disease: the European paradox. *Eu. J. of Clinical Nutrition,* **48**: 822-831 (1994).

14. Perez-Jimenez, F. et al. Lipoprotein concentrations in normolipidemic males consuming oleic acid-rich diets from two different sources: olive oil and oleic acid-rich sunflower oil. *Am. J. Clinical Nutrition,* **62:** 769-775 (1995).

15. Rainey, C.; Affleck, M.; Bretschger, K. et al. The California avocado. *Nutr. Today,* **29:** 23-27 (1994).

16. Nagy, S.; Shaw, P.E. *Tropical and subtropical fruits.* Westport (Connecticut), 1980, The AVI Publishing Company, Inc., p. 143.

17. Grant, W.C. Influence of avocados on serum cholesterol. *Proc. Soc. Exp. Biol. Med.,* **104**: 45-47 (1960).

18. Alvizouri Muñoz, M. et al. Effects of avocado as a source of monounsaturated fatty acids on plasma lipid levels. *Arch. Med. Res.,* **23**: 163-167 (1992).

19. Simon, E. et al. The blockade of insulin secretion by mannoheptulose. *J. Israel Med. Sci.,* **2**: 785-799 (1966).

20. Lerman Garber, I. et al. Effect of a high-monounsaturated fat diet enriched with avocado in NIDDM [Non Insulin Dependent Diabetes Mellitus]. *Diabetes Care,* **17**: 311-315.

21. Martín-Canrejas, M.A. et al. Dietary fiber content of pear and kiwi pomaces. *Journal of Agricultural and Food Chemistry,* **43:** 662-666 (1995).

22. Krishna G.C. Role of potassium in the pathogenesis of hypertension. *American Journal of Clinical Science,* **307:** S21-S25 (1994).

23. Singh R.B.; Rastogi, S.S.; Singh, R. et al. Effects if guava intake on serum total and high-density lipoprotein cholesterol levels and on systemic blood pressure. *Am. J. Cardiol.,* **70:** 1287-1291 (1992).

24. Korpela, J.T.; Korpela, R.; Adlercreutz, H. Fecal bile acid metabolic pattern after administration of different types of bread. *Gastroenterology,* **103:** 1246-1253 (1992).

Chap. 6: Foods for the Blood

1. Tuntawiroon, M.; Sritongkul, N.; Brune, M. et al. Dose-dependant inhibitory effect of phenolic compounds in foods on nonheme-iron absorption in men. *Am. J. Clin. Nutr.,* **53:** 554-557 (1991).

2. Siegenberg, D. et al. Ascorbic acid prevents the dose-dependent inhibitory effects of polyphenols and phytates on nonheme-iron absorption. *Am. J. Clin. Nutr.,* **53:** 537-541 (1991).

3. Mahan, L.K.; Arlin, M.T. *Krause's Food, Nutrition and Diet Therapy.* Philadelphia, W.B. Saunders Company, 8th ed., 1992.

4. Siegenberg D. et al. Ascorbic acid prevents the dose-dependent inhibitory effects of polyphenols and phytates on nonheme-iron absorption. *Am. J. Clin. Nutr.* **53:** 537-541 (1991).

5. Schneider, Ernst. *La salud por la nutrición [Health through Nutrition].* Madrid, Editorial Safeliz, 1986, p. 520.

6. Wattenberg, L.W.; Coccia J.B. Inhibition of 4-(methylnitrosamino)-1-(3-pyridyl)-1-butanone caecinogenesis in mice by D-limonene and citrus fruit oils. *Carcinogenesis,* **12:** 115-117 (1991).

7. Panlasigui, L.N.; Panlilio, L.M.; Madrid, J.C. Glycaemic response in normal subjects to five different legumes commonly used in the Philippines. *Int. J. Food Sci. Nutr.,* **46:** 155-160 (1995).

8. Murray, I.E. et al. Volatile constituents of passion fruit, Passiflora edulis. *Aust. J. Chem.* **25:** 1920-1933 (1972).

9. Pamplona-Roger G. D. *Encyclopedia of Medicinal Plants.* Editorial Safeliz, Madrid, 1998, p. 167.

10. Genesis 43:11.

11. *Present Knowledge in Nutrition.* International Life Sciences Institute, Washington, 6th ed., 1990, p. 304.

Chap. 7: Foods for the Respiratory System

1. Cook, D.G.; Carey, I.M.; Whincup, P.H. et al. Effect of fresh fruit consumption on lung function and wheeze in children. *Thorax,* **52:** 628-633 (1997).
2. Numbers 11: 5.
3. Leclerc, H. *Précis de phytothèrapie.* Paris, Masson, 1983, p.69.
4. Hollman, P. et al. Absorption of dietary quercitin glycosides and quercitin in healthy ileostomy volunteers. *American Journal of Clinical Nutrition,* **62:** 1276-1282 (1995).
5. Schneider, Ernst. *La salud por la nutrición [Health through Nutrition].* Madrid, Editorial Safeliz, 1986, p. 498.
6. Dankert, J.; Tromp, T.F.; de Vries, H. et al. Antimicrobial activity of crude juices of Allium ascalonicum, Allium cepa and Allium sativum. *Zentralbl. Bakteriol* [Orig. A], **245:** 229-239 (1979).
7. Elnima, E.; Ahmed, S.A.; Mekkawi, A.G. et al. The antimicrobial activity of garlic and onion extracts. *Pharmazie,* **38:** 747-748 (1983).
8. Dorsch, W.; Scharff, J.; Bayer, T. et al. Antiasthmatic effects of onions. Prevention of platelet-activating factor induced bronchial hyperreactivity to hismine in guinea pigs by diphenylthiosulfinate. *Int. Arch. Allergy Appl. Immunol.,* **88:** 228-230 (1989).
9. Wagner, H. Search for new plant constituents with potential antiphlogistic and antiallergic activity. *Planta Med.,* **55:** 235-241 (1989).
10. Vertes, C.; Debreczeni, L.A. Effect of intracerebrally injected aminophylline, vinpocetinum, vasoactive intestinal peptide and onion extract on breathing pattern of rats. *Z. Erkr. Atmungsorgane,* **173:** 134-137 (1989).
11. Kleijnen, J.; Knipschild, P.; Riet, G. Garlic, onions and cardiovascular risk factors. *British Journal of Clinical Pharmacology,* **28:** 535-544 (1989).
12. Muldoon, M.; Kritchevsky, S.B. Flavonoids and heart disease. *British Medical Journal,* **312:** 458-459 (1996).
13. Knekt, P. et al. Flavonoid intake and coronary mortality in Finland: a cohort study. *British Medical Journal,* **312:** 478-481 (1996).
14. Sebastian, K.L. et al. The hypolipidemic effect of onion (Allium cepa) in sucrose fed rabbits. *Indian Journal of Physiology and Pharmacology,* **23:** 27-30 (1979).
15. You, W.C.; Blot, W.J.; Chang, Y.S. et al. Allium vegetables and reduced risk of stomach cancer. *Journal of the National Cancer Institute,* **81:** 162-164 (1989).
16. Dorant, E.; van den Brandt, P.A.; Goldbohm, R.A. et al. Consumption of onions and a reduced risk of stomach carcinoma. *Gastroenterology,* **110:** 12-20 (1996).
17. Davis, D.L. Natural anticarcinogens, carcinogens, and changing patterns in cancer: some speculation. Environ. *Res.,* **50:** 322-340 (1989).
18. Dorant, E.; van den Brandt, P.A.; Goldbohm, R.A. Allium vegetable consumption, garlic supplement intake, and female breast carcinoma incidence. *Breast Cancer Research and Treatment,* **33:** 163-170 (1995).
19. Dorant, E.; van den Brandt, P.A.; Goldbohm, R.A. A prospective cohort study on Allium vegetable consumption, garlic supplement use, and the risk of lung carcinoma in The Netherlands. *Cancer Research,* **54:** 6148-6153 (1994).
20. Mousa, O. Bioactivity of certain Egyptian Ficus species. *Journal Ethnopharmacology,* **41:** 71-76 (1994).

Chap. 8: Foods for the Digestive System

1. Stoewsad, G. Bioactive organosulfur phytochemicals in Brassica oleracea vegetables (a review). *Food Chem. Toxicol.,* **33** (6): 537-543 (1995).
2. Preobrazhenskaya, M. et al. Ascorbigen and other indole-derived compounds from brassica vegetables and their analogs as anticarcinogenic and inmunomodulating agents. *Pharmacol., Ther.,* **60** (2): 301-313 (1993).
3. Marks, H. Effect of S-methyl cysteine sulphoxide ands its metabolite methyl methane thiosulphinate, both occurring naturally in Brassica vegetables, on mouse genotoxicity. *Food Chem. Toxicol,* **31** (7): 491-495 (1993).
4. Osato, J.A.; Santiago, L.A.; Remo, G.M. et al. Antimicrobial and antioxidant activities of unripe papaya. *Life Sciences,* **53:** 1383-1389 (1993).
5. Satrija, F.; Nansen, P.; Bjorn, H. et al. Effect of papaya latex against Ascaris suum in naturally infected pigs. *Journal of Helminthology,* **68:** 343-346 (1994).
6. Livesey, G.; Wilkinson, J.A.; Roe, M. et al. Influence of the physical form of barley grain on the digestion of its starch in the human small intestine and implications for health. *Am. J. Clin. Nutr.,* **61:** 75-81 (1995).
7. Naismith, D.J.; Mahdi, G.S.; Shakir, N.N. Therapeutic value of barley in the management of diabetes. *Ann. Nutr. Metab.,* **35:** 61-64 (1991).
8. McIntosh, G.H. Colon cancer: dietary modifications required for a balanced protective diet. *Prev. Med.,* **22:** 767-774 (1993).

Chap. 9: Foods for the Liver

1. Englisch W, Beckers C, Unkauf M, Ruepp M. et al. Efficacy of Artichoke dry extract in patients with hyperlipoproteinemia. *Arzneimittelforschung* 2000 Mar; 50(3):260-5
2. Teubner, C.; Levin, H.G.; Lange, E. *Das Grosse Buch der Gemüse,* Teubner Edition, 1991, p. 64.
3. Rojanapo, W.; Tepsuwan, A. Antimutagenic and mutagenic potential of Chinese radish. *Environ. Health Perspect.,* **101** (suppl. 3): 247-252 (1993).

Chap. 10: Foods for the Stomach

1. Marotta, R.B.; Floch, M.H. Diet and nutrition in ulcer disease. *Med. Clin. North. Am.,* **75:** 967-979 (1991).
2. Helser, M.A.; Hotchkiss, J.H.; Roe, D.A. Influence of fruit and vegetable juices on the endogenous formation of N-nitrosoproline and N-nitrosothiazolidine-4-carboxylic acid in humans on controled diets. *Carcinogenesis,* **13:** 2277-2280 (1992).
3. Mehta, R. et al. Cancer chemopreventive activity of brassinin, a phytoalexin from cabagge. *Carcinogenesis,* **16** (2): 399-404 (1995).
4. Chen, M. Cruciferous vegetables and glutathione: their effects on colon mucosal glutathione level and colon tumor development in rats induced by DMH. *Nutr. Cancer,* **23** (1): 77-83 (1995).
5. Guo, Z. et al. Effects of phenethyl isothiocyanate, a carcinogenesis inhibitor, on xenobiotic-metabolizing enzymes and nitrosamine metabolism in rats, *Carcinogenesis,* **13** (12): 2205-2210 (1992)
6. Marks, H. et al. Effects of S-methyl cysteine sulphoxide and its metabolite mrthyl methane thiosulphinate, both occurring naturally in *Brassica* vegetables, on mouse genotoxicity. *Food Chem. Toxicol.,* **31** (7): 491-495 (1993).
7. Kim, D. et al. Biphasic modifying effect of indole-3-carbinol on diethylnitrosamine-induced preneoplasic glutathione

S-transferase placental form-positive liver cell foci in Sprague-Dawley rats. *Japon Journal Cancer Research,* **85** (6): 578-583 (1994).

8. PAMPLONA-ROGER G. D. *Encyclopedia of Medicinal Plants.* Editorial Safeliz, Madrid, 1998, p. 434.
9. SCHNEIDER, ERNST. *La salud por la nutrición [Health through Nutrition].* Madrid, Editorial Safeliz, 1986, p. 424.
10. ESPINOSA-AGUIRRE, J.J. ET AL. Mutagenic activity of urban air samples and its modulation by chili extracts. *Mutation Research,* **303:** 55-61 (1993).
11. ENSMINGER, A.H. ET AL. *The Concise Encyclopedia of Foods and Nutrition.* Boca Raton (Florida), CRC Press, 1995, p. 869.
12. WILDMANN, J. ET AL. Occurence of pharmacologically active benzodiazepines in trace amounts in wheat and potato. *Biochem. Pharmacol.,* **37:** 3549-3559 (1988).
13. WILDMANN, J. Increase of natural benzodiazepines in wheat and potato during germination. *Biochem. Biophys. Res. Commun,* **157:** 1436-1443 (1988).

CHAP. 11: FOODS FOR THE INTESTINE

1. BROSSARD J.; MACKINNEY G. The carotenoid of Diospyros kaki. *J. Agric. Food Chem.* **11:** 501-503 (1963).
2. MULDOON, M.F.; KRITCHEVSKY, SB: Flavonoids and heart disease. *British Medical Journal,* **312:** 458-459 (1996).
3. KNEKT, P. ET AL. Flavonoid intake and coronary mortality in Finland: a cohort study. *British Medical Journal,* **312:** 478-481 (1996).
4. SABLE, R.; SICART, R.; BERRY, E. Steroid pattern of bile and feces in response to fruit-enriched diet in hypercholesterolemic hamsters. *Annals of Nutrition and Metabolism,* **34:** 303-310 (1990).
5. OHKAMI, H. ET AL. Effects of apple pectin on fecal bacterial enzymes in azoxymethane-induced rat colon carcinogenesis. *Japan Journal of Cancer Research,* **86:** 523-529 (1995).
6. MAHAN, L.K.; ARLIN, M.T. *Krause's Food, Nutrition and Diet Therapy.* Philadelphia, W.B. Saunders Company, 1992, 8th ed.
7. TINKER L.F. ET AL. Prune fiber or pectin compared with cellulose lowers plasma and liver lipids in rats with diet-induced hyperlipidemia. *Journal of Nutrition,* **124:** 31-40 (1994).
8. SHANE, J.M.; WALKER, P.M. Corn bran supplementation of a low-fat controlled diet lowers serum lipids in men with hypercholesterolemia. *Journal of the American Dietetic Association,* **95:** 40-45 (1995).

CHAP. 12: FOODS FOR THE URINARY TRACT

1. HESSE, A.; SIENER, R.; HEYNCK, H. ET AL. The influence of dietary factors on the risk of urinary stone formation. *Scanning Microsc.,* **7:** 1119-1127 (1993).
2. SIENER, R.; HESSE, A. Einfluss verschiedener Kostformen auf die Harnzusammensetzung und das Kalziumoxalat-Steinbildungsrisiko [The effect of different food forms on the urine composition and the risk of calcium oxalate stone formation]. *Z. Ernahrungswiss.,* **32:** 46-55 (1993).
3. MASSEY, L.K.; ROMAN-SMITH, H.; SUTTON, R.A. Effect of dietary oxalate and calcium on urinary oxalate and risk of formation of calcium oxalate kidney stones. *J. Am. Diet. Assoc.,* **93:** 901-906 (1993).
4. TSI D. ET AL: Effects of aqueous celery *(Apium graveolens)* extract on lipid parameters of rats fed a high fat diet. *Planta. Med.,* **61** (1): 18-21, (1995).
5. GRAL N. ET AL: Étude des taux plasmatiques de psoralènes aprés ingestion de céléri. *Annal. Dermatol. Venereol.,* **120** (9): 599-603, (1993).
6. GUILLEN, R. ET AL. Dietary fibre in white asparagus before and after processing. *Z. Lebensm. Unters. Forsch.,* **200:** 225-228 (1995).
7. AMARO LOPEZ, M.A. ET AL. Influence of vegetative cycle of asparagus on copper, iron, zinc and manganese content. *Plants Foods in Human Nutrition,* **47:** 349-355 (1995).
8. VALNET, J. *Traitement des maladies par les légumes, les fruits et les céréals.* Paris, Librairie Maloine S.A. éditeur, p. 151.
9. FLEET, J.C.: New support for a folk remedy: cranberry juice reduces bacteriuria and pyuria in elderly women. *Nutr. Rev.* **52** (5): 168-170, (1994).
10. AVORN J. ET AL.: Reduction of bacteriuria and pyuria after ingestion of cranberry juice. *JAMA,* **271** (10): 751-754, (1994).
11. ENSMINGER, A.H. ET AL. *The concise encyclopedia of foods and nutrition.* Boca Raton (Florida), CRC Press, 1995, p. 342.

CHAP. 13: FOODS FOR THE REPRODUCTIVE SYSTEM

1. BARR, S.I.; JANELLE, K.C.; PRIOR, J.C. Vegetarian vs nonvegetarian diets, dietary restraint, and subclinical ovulatory disturbances: prospective 6-mo study. *Am. J. Clin. Nutr.,* **60:** 887-894 (1994).
2. ANTHONY, M.S. ET AL. Soybean isoflavones improve cardiovascular risk factors without affecting the reproductive system of peripubertal rhesus monkeys. *J. Nutr.,* **126:** 43-50 (1996).
3. MISHRA, S.K.; SHARMA, A.K.; SALILA, M. ET AL. Efficacy of low fat diet in the treatment of benign breast disease. *Natl. Med. J. India,* **7:** 60-62 (1994).
4. ENSMINGER, A.H. ET AL. *The concise encyclopedia of foods and nutrition.* Boca Raton (Florida), CRC Press, 1995, p. 971.
5. BAGLIERI, A. ET AL. Gastro-jejunal digestion of soya-bean-milk protein in humans. *British Journal of Nutrition* **72:** 519-532 (1994).
6. BARNES, S. Rationale for the use of genistein-containing soy matrices in chemoprevention trials for breast and prostate cancer. *J. Cell. Biochem. Suppl.,* **22:** 181-187 (995).
7. LIENER, I.E. Possible adverse effects of soybean anticarcinogens. *J. Nutr.,* **125** (3 Suppl): 744S-750S (1995).
8. CLAWSON, G.A. Protease inhibitors and carcinogenesis: a review. *Cancer Invest.,* **14:** 597-608 (1996).
9. KENNEDY, A.R. The evidence for soybean products as cancer preventive agents. *J. Nutr.,* **125** (3 Suppl): 733S-743S (1995).
10. CASSIDY, A. Biological effects of a diet of soy protein rich in isoflavones on the menstrual cycle of premenopausal women. *Am. J. Clin. Nutr.,* **60:** 333-340 (1994).
11. HONORÉ, E.K. ET AL. Soy isoflavones enhance coronary vascular reactivity in atherosclerotic female macaques. *Fertility and Sterility,* **67:** 148-154 (1997).
12. WU, A.H. Tofu and risk of breast cancer in Asian-Americans. *Cancer Epidemiol. Biomarkers Prev.,* **5:** 901-906 (1996).
13. PERSKY, V.; VAN-HORN, L. Epidemiology of soy and cancer: perspectives and directions. *J. Nutr.,***125** (3 Suppl): 709S-712S (1995).
14. DWYER, J.T. ET AL. Tofu and soy drinks contain phytoestrogens. *J. Am. Diet. Assoc.,* **94:** 739-743 (1994).
15. STOLL, B.A. Eating to beat breast cancer: potential role for soy supplements. *Ann. Oncol.,* **8:** 223-225 (1997).

16. MESSINA, M.J. ET AL. Soy intake and cancer risk: a review of the in vitro and in vivo data. *Nutr. Cancer*, **21:** 113-131 (1994).
17. ADLERCREUTZ, H. ET AL. Plasma concentration of phytoestrogens in Japanese men. *Lancet*, **342:** 1209-1210 (1993).
18. BARRET-CONNER, E. Estrogen and coronary heart disease. *JAMA*, **265:** 1861 (1991).
19. ANTHONY, M.S. ET AL. Soybean isoflavones improve cardiovascular risk factors without affecting the reproductive system of peripubertal rhesus monkeys. *J. Nutr.*, **126:** 43-50 (1996).
20. WILCOX, J.N.; BLUMENTHAL, B.F. Thrombotic mechanisms in atherosclerosis: potential impact of soy proteins. *J. Nutr.*, **125** (3 Suppl): 631S-638S (1995).
21. ABELOW, B.J.; HOLFORD, T.R.; INSOGNA, K.L. Cross-cultural association between dietary animal protein and hip fracture: a hypothesis. *Calcif. Tissue Int.*, **50:** 14-18 (1992).
22. BRESLAU, N.A.; BRINKLEY, L.; HILL, K.D. ET AL. Relationship of animal protein-rich diet to kidney stone formation and calcium metabolism. *J. Clin. Endocrinol. Metabol.* **66:** 140-146 (1988).
23. ARJMANDI, B.H. ET AL. Dietary soybean protein prevents bone loss in an ovariectomized rat model of osteoporosis. *J. Nutr.*, **126:** 161-167 (1996).
24. KONTESSIS. P. ET AL. Renal, metabolic and hormonal responses to ingestion of animal and vegetable proteins. *Kidney Int.*, **38:** 136-144 (1990).
25. GENTILE, M.G. ET AL. Treatment of proteinuric patients with a vegetarian soy diet and fish oil. *Clin. Nephrol.*, **40:** 315-320 (1993).
26. MESSINA, M.J.; BARNES, S. The role of soy products in reducing risk of cancer. *J. Natl. Cancer Inst.*, **83:** 541-546 (1991).
27. ANDERSON, J.W. ET AL. Meta-analysis of the effects of soy protein intake on serum lipids. *N. Eng. J. Med.*, **333:** 276-282 (1995).
28. LIENER, I.E. Implications of antinutritional components in soybean foods. *Crit. Rev. Food Sci. Nutr.*, **34:** 31-67 (1994).
29. MATAIX, J. ET AL. *Tabla de composición de alimentos españoles [Composition table of Spanish foods].* Universidad de Granada, 1995, 2nd ed., p. 316.
30. STAHL, W.; SIES, H. Uptake of lycopene and its geometrical isomers is greater from heat-processed than from unprocessed tomato juice in humans. *Journal of Nutrition*, **122:** 2161-2166 (1992).
31. STAHL, W.; SIES, H. Lycopene: a biologically important carotenoid for humans? *Arch. Biochem. Biophys*, **336:** 1-9 (1996).
32. FRANCESCHI, S. ET AL. Tomatoes and risk of digestive-tract cancers. International *Journal of Cancer*, **59:** 181-184 (1994).

CHAP. 14: FOODS FOR METABOLISM

1. ANDERSON J.W. ET AL. Serum lipid response of hypercholesterolemic men to single and divided doses of canned beans. *Am. J. Clin. Nutr.* **51:** 1013-1019 (1990).
2. SALMERON, J.; MANSON, J.E.; STAMPFER, M.J. ET AL. Dietary fiber, glycemic load, and risk of non-insulin-dependent diabetes mellitus in women. *JAMA,* **277:** 472-477 (1997).
3. SNOWDON, D.A.; PHILLIPS, R.L. Does a vegetarian diet reduce the occurrence of diabetes? *Am. J. Public. Health.*, **75:** 507-512 (1985).
4. FESKENS, E.J.; VIRTANEN, S.M.; RÄSÄNEN, L. ET AL. Dietary factors determining diabetes and impaired glucose tolerance. A 20-year follow-up of the Finnish and Dutch cohorts of the Seven Countries Study. *Diabetes Care,* **18:** 1104-1112 (1995).
5. SWANSTON-FLATT, S.K.; DAY, C.; FLATT, P.R. ET AL. Glycaemic effects of traditional European plant treatments for diabetes. Studies in normal and streptozotocin diabetic mice. *Diabetes Res.,* **10:** 69-73 (1989).
6. TOTH, B.; ERICKSON, J. Cancer induction in mice by feeding of the uncooked cultivated mushroom of commerce Agaricus bisporus. *Cancer Res.,* **46:** 4007-4011 (1986).
7. SHEPHARD, S.E.; GUNZ, D.; SCHLATTER, C. Genotoxicity of agaritine in the lacl transgenic mouse mutation assay: evaluation of the health risk of mushroom consumption. *Food Chem. Toxicol.,* **33:** 257-264 (1995).
8. MATSUMOTO, K. ET AL. Carcinogenicity examination of Agaricus bisporus, edible mushroom, in rats. *Cancer Lett.,* **58:** 87-90 (1991).
9. PAPAPARASKEVA, C.; IOANNIDES, C.; WALKER, R. Agaritine does not mediate the mutagenicity of the edible mushroom Agaricus bisporus. *Mutagenesis,* **6:** 213-217 (1991).
10. BLANCO, A; MUÑOZ, L. Contenido y disponibilidad biológica de los carotenoides de pejibaye (Bactris gasipaes) como fuente de vitamina A. *Archivos Latinoamericanos de Nutrición,* **42** (2): 146-154 (1992).
11. DE TOMMASI, N. ET AL. Hypoglycemic effects of sesquiterpene glycosides and polyhydroxylated triterpenoids of Eriobotrya japonica. *Planta Med.,* **57:** 414-416 (1991).
12. ROMAN-RAMOS, R. ET AL. Experimental study of the hypoglycemic effect of some antidiabetic plants. *Arch. Invest. Med. (Mexico),* **22:** 87-93 (1991).
13. DE TOMMASI, N. ET AL. Constituents of Eriobotrya japonica. A study of their antiviral properties. *Journal of Natural Products,* **55:** 1067-1073 (1992).
14. Luke, 6: 1.
15. JACOBS JR, D.R.; SLAVIN, J.; MARQUART, L. Whole grain intake and cancer: a review of the literature. *Nutr. Cancer,* **24:** 221-229 (1995).
16. ENSMINGER, A.H. ET AL. *The concise encyclopedia of foods and nutrition.* Boca Raton (Florida), CRC Press, 1995, p. 793.
17. BADIALI, D. Effect of wheat bran in treatment of chronic nonorganic constipation. A double-blind controlled trial. *Dig. Dis. Sci.,* **40:** 349-356 (1995).
18. ROSE, D.P.; LUBIN, M.; CONNOLLY, J.M. Effects of diet supplementation with wheat bran on serum estrogen levels in the follicular and luteal phases of the menstrual cycle. *Nutrition,* **13:** 535-539 (1997).
19. FRANCIS, C.Y.; WHORWELL, P.J. Bran and irritable bowel syndrome: time for reappraisal. *Lancet,* **344:** 39-40 (1994).
20. TORRE, M.; RODRIGUEZ, A.R.; SAURA-CALIXTO, F. Effects of dietary fiber and phytic acid on mineral availability. *Crit. Rev. Food Sci. Nutr.,* **30:** 1-22 (1991).

CHAP. 15: FOODS FOR THE MUSCULOSKELETAL SYSTEM

1. WELTEN, D.C.; KEMPER, H.C.; POST, G.B. ET AL. Longitudinal development and tracking of calcium and dairy intake from teenager to adult. *Eur. J. Clin. Nutr.,* **51:** 612-618 (1997).
2. ARJMANDI, B.H.; ALEKEL, L.; HOLLIS, B.W. ET AL. Dietary soybean protein prevents bone loss in an ovariectomized rat model of osteoporosis. *J. Nutr.,* **126:** 161-167 (1996).
3. ABELOW, B.J.; HOLFORD, T.R.; INSOGNA, K.L. Cross-cultural association between dietary animal protein and hip fracture: a hypothesis. *Calcif. Tissue Int.,* **50:** 14-18 (1992).

4. Feskanich, D.; Willett, W.C.; Stampfer, M.J. et al. Protein consumption and bone fractures inwomen. *Am. J. Epidemiol.,* **143:** 472-479 (1996).

5. Kjeldsen-Kragh, J.; Rashid, T.; Dybwad, A. et al. Decrease in anti-Proteus mirabilis but not anti-Escherichia coli antibody levels in rheumatoid arthritis patients treated with fasting and a one year vegetarian diet. *Ann. Rheum. Dis., Mar.,* **54:** 221-224 (1995).

6. Peltonen, R.; Nenonen, M.; Helve, T. et al. Faecal microbial flora and disease activity in rheumatoid arthritis during a vegan diet. *Br. J. Rheumatol.,* **36:** 64-68 (1997).

7. Peltonen, R.; Kjeldsen-Kragh, J.; Haugen, M. et al. Changes of faecal flora in rheumatoid arthritis during fasting and one-year vegetarian diet. *Br. J. Rheumatol.,* **33:** 638-643 (1994).

8. Kjeldsen-Kragh, J.; Mellbye, O.J.; Haugen, M. et al. Changes in laboratory variables in rheumatoid arthritis patients during a trial of fasting and one-year vegetarian diet. *Scand. J. Rheumatol.,* **24:** 85-93 (1995).

9. Kjeldsen-Kragh, J.; Haugen, M.; Borchgrevink, C.F. et al. Vegetarian diet for patients with rheumatoid arthritis–status: two years after introduction of the diet. *Clin. Rheumatol.,* **13:** 475-482 (1994).

10. Adam, O. Ernahrung als adjuvante Therapie bei chronischer Polyarthritis [Nutrition as adjuvant therapy in chronic polyarthritis]. *Z. Rheumatol.,* **52:** 275-280 (1993).

11. Heupke, W.; Weitzel, W. *Deutsches Obst und Gemüse in der Ernährung und Heilkunde* [Las frutas y hortalizas alemanas en la alimentación y en la terapéutica], Hippokrates Verlag, Stuttgart, 1950.

Chap. 16: Foods for the Skin

1. Hill, D.J.; Bannister, D.G.; Hosking, C.S. et al. Cow milk allergy within the spectrum of atopic disorders. *Clin. Exp. Allergy,* **24:** 1137-1143 (1994).

2. Norgaard, A.; Bindslev-Jensen, C. Egg and milk allergy in adults. Diagnosis and characterization. *Allergy,* **47:** 503-509 (1992).

3. Oehling, A.; Fernandez, M.; Cordoba, H. Skin manifestations and immunological parameters in childhood food. *J. Investig. Allergol. Clin. Immunol.,* **7:** 155-159 (1997).

4. Carlier, C. et al. Efficacy of massive oral doses of retinyl palmitate and mango (Mangifera indica L.) consumption to correct an existing vitamin A deficiency in Senegalese children. *British Journal of Nutrition,* **68:** 529-540 (1992).

5. Hunter, G.L.K.; Bucek, W.A.; Radford, T. Volatile components of canned Alphonso mango. *Journal of Food Science,* **39:** 900-903 (1974).

6. Roongpisuthipong, C. et al. Postprandial glucose and insulin responses to various tropical fruits of equivalent carbohydrate content in non-insulin-dependent diabetis mellitus. *Diabetes Research and Clinical Practice,* **14:** 123-131 (1991).

7. Ministerio de agricultura, pesca y alimentación de España. *Las legumbres* (colección Alimentos de España) *[The vegetables* (Collection Foods of Spain)]. Madrid, El País, 1992, p. 13.

8. Blanco, A. Bioavailability of aminoacids in beans.*Arch. Latinoam. Nutr.,* **41** (1): 38-52, (1991).

9. Anderson, J.W. et al. Serum lipid response of hypercholesterolemic men to single and divided doses of canned beans. *Am. J. Clin. Nutr.* **51** (6): 1013-1019 (1990).

Chap. 17: Foods for Infections

1. Liang, B.; Chung, S.; Araghiniknam, M. et al. Vitamins and immunomodulation in AIDS. *Nutrition,* **12:** 1-7 (1996).

2. Koch, J.; Garcia-Shelton, Y.L.; Neal, E.A. et al. Steatorrhea: a common manifestation in patients with HIV/AIDS. *Nutrition,* **12:** 507-510 (1996).

3. Chen, J.D. et al. The effects of actinidia sinensis Planc. (kiwi) drink supplementation on athletes training in hot environments. *Journal of Sports Medecine Physiology Fitness,* **30:** 181-184 (1990).

4. Chug-Ahuja, J.K. et al. The development and application of a carotenoid database for fruits, vegetables, and selected multicomponent foods. *J. Am. Diet. Assoc.,* **93:** 318-323 (1993).

5. Craig, W. Nutri-Fax vol. 5, n. 1. Departament of Nutrition, Andrews University, Michigan, USA.

6. Middleton, E; Kandaswami, C. Potential health-promoting properties of Citrus flavonoids. *Food Technology,* **48:** 115-119 (1994).

7. Wattenberg, L.; Coccia, J. Inhibition of 4-(methylnitrosamino)-1-(3-pyridyl)-1-butanone carcinogenesis in mice by D-limonene and citrus fruit oils. *Carcinogenesis,* **12:** 115-117 (1991).

8. Trout, D.L. Vitamin C and cardiovascular risk factors. *Am J Clin Nutr.,* **53:** 322-325S, (1991).

9. Besra, S.E. et al. Antiinflammatory effect of petroleum ether extract of leaves of Litchi chinensis Gaertn. *Journal of Ethnopharmacololy,* **54:** 1-6 (1996).

10. Nagy, S.; Shaw, P.E. *Tropical and subtropical fruits.* Westport (Connecticut), The AVI Publishing Company, Inc., 1980, p. 341.

11. Schneider, Ernst. *La salud por la nutrición [Health through Nutrition].* Madrid, Editorial Safeliz, 1986, p. 171.

Chap. 18: Foods and Cancer

1. White, E. *Counsels on Diet and Foods.* Review and Herald Publishing Association, 1976, p. 384, 385.

2. WHO, Technical Report Series, 797. *Diet, Nutrition, and the Prevention of Chronic Diseases.* Report of a WHO Study Group. Geneva, 1990.

3. Strickland, P.T.; Groopman, J.D. Biomarkers for assessing environmental exposure to carcinogens in the diet. *Am. J. Clin. Nutr.,* **61:** 710S-720S (1995).

4. Ensminger, A.H. et al. *The Concise Encyclopedia of Foods and Nutrition.* Boca Raton (Florida), CRC Press, 1995, p. 157 (graph adapted).

5. Willett, W.C.; Stampfer, M.J.; Colditz, G.A. et al. Moderate alcohol consumption and the risk of breast cancer. *N. Engl. J. Med.,* **316:** 1174-1180 (1987).

6. D'Avanzo, B.; La Vecchia, C.; Franceschi, S. et al. Coffee consumption and bladder cancer risk. *Eur. J. Cancer,* **28A:** 1480-1484 (1992).

The Encyclopedia of Medicinal Plants (EMP) refered in this work is published by Editorial Safeliz in two volumes and belongs to the Education and Health Library. It is from the same author of this work.

Abbreviations and Acronyms

ADI: Acceptable Daily Intake.

α-TE: Alpha-tocopherol equivalent.

°C: Centigrade (Celsius) degrees of temperature.

Carbohydr.: Carbohydrates.

Ch./Chap.: Chapter.

cl: Centiliter, one-hundredth of a liter.
1 cl = 0.01l; 1 l = 100 cl.

cm: Centímeter, one hundredth of a meter.
1 cm = 0.01 m; 1 m = 100 cm.

dl: Deciliter, one-tenth of a liter.
1 dl = 0.1 l;1 l = 10 dl.

DV: Daily value of a nutrient.

ed.: Edition

EMP: EMP = *Encyclopedia of Medicinal Plants*, Education and Health Library, Editorial Safeliz.

°F: Farenheit degrees of temperature.

g: Gram, one-thousandth of a kilogram.
1 g = 0.001 kg; 1 kg = 1,000 g.

HDL: High Density Lipoproteins.

IU.: International unit. It is the quantity of a biologically active substance, such as a hormone or vitamin, required to produce a specific response. It is used as a measure of the potency of a substance. Presently the microgram (µg) is prefered; for instance, 1 µg of vitamin A = 3.33 IU.

kcal: Kilocalorie or large calorie, usually refered as "calorie". It is defined as the amount of heat required to raise the temperature of 1 kilogram of water by 1°C at 1 atmosphere pressure. 1 kcal = 4,18 kj.

kg: Kilogram, the basic unit of mass in the International System.
1 kg = 1,000 g. 1 kg = 2.2046 pounds

kGy: KiloGray, a unit of measure of the amount of radiation absorbed by a body.
1 kGy = 1,000 Grays.

kj: Kilojoule. The "joule" is the International System unit of electrical, mechanical, and thermal energy.
1 kj = 1,000 joules.
1 kj = 0.24 kcal.

l: Liter, the metric unit of volume. One liter of water weights one kilogram.
1 l = 10 dl = 1,000 ml.
1 l = 0.2642 gallon.

L.: Abbreviation of Carolus Linnaeus, the great Swedish botanist of the XVIIIth century who named many of the plant species.

lb: Pound.

LDL: Low Density Lipoproteins).

m: Meter, the international standard unit of length:
1 m = 10 dm = 100 cm = 1,000 mm.
1 m = 39.37 inches.

Mb: Megabyte, unit of information equal to one million of bytes or characters.

mg: Miligram, a one-thousand of a gram.
1 mg = 0.001 g; 1 g = 1,000 mg.

Min.: Minerals.

ml: Mililiter, a one-thousand of a liter.
1 ml = 0.001 l; 1 l = 1,000 ml

mmol/l: Milimoles per liter, a way to measure the amount of a substance generaly used in blood tests.

MR: Mean requisite of a nutrient.

NE: Niacin equivalent.

oz: Ounze.

p.: Page.

pH: A measure of the acidity or alkalinity of a solution. The pH scale commonly in use ranges from 0 to 14. A pH of 7 is neutral, higher than 7 is alkaline, and lower than 7 is acidic.

ppm: Parts per million, a unit intented to measure the concentration of a substance.
1 ppm = 1 mg/kg = 0.1 mg/100 g.

Prot.: Proteins.

RDA: Recommended Dietary Allowance (see Vol.1, p. 384)

RE: Retinol equivalent (see Vol. 1, p. 389).

ssp.: Subspecies.

Syn.: Synonym.

USA: United States of America.

var.: Variety, related to botanical species.

Vol.: Volume.

µ: Micron, the one-millionth of a meter.
1 µ = 0.000001 m; 1 m = 1,000,000 µ.
1 mm = 1,000 µ.

µg: Microgram, the one-millionth of a gram.
1 µg = 0.000001 g; 1 g = 1,000,000 µg.
1 mg = 1,000 µg.

English Synonyms and Equivalents

Alkekengy = Winter cherry
Alligator pear = Avocado
American elderberry = Sweet elder, Eastern elderberry
Ananás = Pineapple
Anona = Cherimoya
Aubergine = Eggplant
Australian nut = Macadamia
Avocado = Alligator pear

Barley = Malt
Beechwheat = Buckwheat
Belgian endive = Witloof, French endive
Bilimbi = Carambola
Brazil nuts = Creamnuts, Paranuts
Breadfruit = Breadnut, Sukun
Broad bean = Fava bean

Calabaza = Squash
Carambola = Belimbing, Bilimbi, Star apple, Five-angled fruit, Star fruit
Cassava = Manioc, Yuca
Corn = Sweet corn, Maize
Courge = Squash
Courgette = Zucchini
Creamnuts = Brazil nuts
Custard apple = Cherimoya
Chard = Swiss chard, Seakale-beet, Leaf beet, Sea kale chard
Cherimoya = Custard apple, Anona
Chickpea = Ceci, Garbanzo [bean]
Chufa = Tiger nut

Earth almond = Tiger nut
Earthnut = Peanut
Eggplant = Aubergine, Brinjal
Elephant apple = Quince

Fava bean = Horse-bean, Field-bean, Tick-bean, Broad bean, Windsor bean
Feijoa = Pineapple guava, Guavasteen
Filbert = Hazelnut

See also the General Alphabetic Index

Five-angled fruit = Carambola

Garbanzo bean = Chick pea
Globe artichoke = Artichoke
Gourd = Squash
Granadilla = Passion fruit
Grapefruit = Shaddock
Green bean = String bean, Fresh bean, Snap bean, Peas
Grenade = Pomegranate
Guavasteen = Feijoa
Guayaba = Guava
Guinea squash = Eggplant

Hazelnut = Filbert,

Irish potato = Potato
Italian squash = Zucchini

Kaki fruit = Persimmon

Lucerne = Alfalfa

Macadamia = Australian nut,
Maize = Corn
Malt = Barley**Mani** = Peanut
Manioc = Cassava

Papaya = Pawpaw, Melon fruit
Papayuela = Wild papaya
Passion fruit = Granadilla
Pawpaw = Papaya
Peanut = Mani, Groundnut, Earthnut
Pepper = Sweet pepper, Bell pepper, Green pepper, Paprika
Persimmon = Kaki fruit, Sharon fruit, Chinese fig, Common persimmon, Kaki fruit
Pineapple guava = Feijoa
Prune = Plum
Pumpkin = Squash

Queensland nut = Macadamia
Sativa = Alfalfa

Shaddock = Grapefruit
Snap bean = Green bean
Squash = Pumpkin, Courge, Gourd
Star fruit = Carambola
String bean = Green bean
Sudan grass = Sorghum
Sugarcane = Noblecane, White sugar
Sukun = Breadfruit
Sunchoke = Jerusalem artichoke
Surinam cherry = Pitanga
Swamp cabbage = Heart of palm
Sweet anise = Fennel
Sweet bell pepper = Pepper
Sweet corn = Corn
Sweet elder = American **elderberry**
Sweet fennel = Fennel
Sweet melon = Melon
Sweet potato = Batata, Camore, Kumara
Sweet yam = Cush-cush yam, Indian yam
Swiss chard = Chard

Tangerine = Mandarin orange
Tiger nut = Chufa, Earth almond,

White asparagus = Asparagus
Wild guava = Costa Rican guava
Windsor bean = Fava bean
Witloof = Belgian endive

Yang tao = Kiwi
Yard-long bean = Asparagus bean, Asparagus cowpea
Yuca = Cassava

Zapote = White sapote
Zucchini = Courgette, Vegetable marrow, Golden zucchini, Italian squash
Zuttano = Avocado

Source of Illustrations

Lozano, Pablo
Chicharro, Ángel
Corel Stock Photo Library
Gazelle Technologies
Klenk, Gunther
Life Art
Photo Disc
Werner, Ludwig
Editorial Safeliz

General Alphabetic Index